OXFORD MONOGRAPHS IN PRIVATE INTERNATIONAL LAW

GENERAL EDITOR: P.B. CARTER QC
Emeritus Fellow of
Wadham College, Oxford

CORPORATIONS IN PRIVATE INTERNATIONAL LAW

A EUROPEAN PERSPECTIVE

OXFORD MONOGRAPHS IN
PRIVATE INTERNATIONAL LAW

General Editor: P.B. Carter QC
Emeritus Fellow of Wadham College, Oxford

The aim of the series is to publish works of quality and
originality in a number of important areas of private international law. The series is intended for both scholarly and
practitioner readers.

ALSO IN THIS SERIES

The Enforcement of Judgments in Europe
WENDY KENNETT

Claims for Contribution and Reimbursement in an
International Context
KOJI TAKAHASHI

The Hague Convention on International Child Abduction
PAUL BEAUMONT and PETER McELEAVY

Insolvency in Private International Law
IAN FLETCHER

Autonomy in International Contracts
PETER NYGH

Intellectual Property and Private International Law
JAMES J. FAWCETT and PAUL TORREMANS

Foreign Law in English Courts
RICHARD FENTIMAN

Declining Jurisdiction in Private International Law
JAMES J. FAWCETT

CORPORATIONS IN PRIVATE INTERNATIONAL LAW

A European Perspective

STEPHAN RAMMELOO
Lecturer in Law
University of Maastricht, Netherlands

OXFORD
UNIVERSITY PRESS

OXFORD
UNIVERSITY PRESS

Great Clarendon Street, Oxford OX2 6DP

Oxford University Press is a department of the University of Oxford.
It furthers the University's objective of excellence in research, scholarship,
and education by publishing worldwide in

Oxford New York

Athens Auckland Bangkok Bogotá Buenos Aires Cape Town
Chennai Dar es Salaam Delhi Florence Hong Kong Istanbul Karachi
Kolkata Kuala Lumpur Madrid Melbourne Mexico City Mumbai Nairobi
Paris São Paulo Shanghai Singapore Taipei Tokyo Toronto Warsaw

and associated companies in Berlin Ibadan

Oxford is a registered trade mark of Oxford University Press
in the UK and in certain other countries

Published in the United States
by Oxford University Press Inc., New York

© Oxford University Press 2001

British Library Cataloguing in Publication Data
Data available

Library of Congress Cataloging in Publication Data
Data available

ISBN 0–19–829925–7

1 3 5 7 9 10 8 6 4 2

Typeset by Hope Services (Abingdon) Ltd.
Printed in Great Britain
on acid-free paper by
Biddles Ltd.,
Guildford and King's Lynn

To Evelyn

General Editor's Preface

The treatment accorded to corporations in private international law has been marked by diversity and uncertainty. Moreover the subject has despite its importance been largely neglected in England. However, in the light of the current and ever increasing growth in transnational commercial activity the need for investigation, clarification and reform has become acute. Superimposed upon this is a requirement that provision be made to cater for the interaction of private international law and the relevant rules of European Union law. The whole subject is important and complex. Dr Rammeloo's comprehensive treatment of it contains a scholarly analysis of a mass of comparative information.

The subject matter of his book is private international law governing corporations, but the author also deals fully with European Union law in so far as it does, might or should interact with it.

The author's conclusions are illuminating and thought provoking. He advocates an integrated approach to private international law and European Union law. His elaboration of this proposal certainly merits the attention of law makers. Indeed the whole book should be of great interest and value to all lawyers who are concerned with the law governing corporations operating in a transnational context, be they law makers, practitioners or academics.

Wadham College, Oxford   P.B. Carter
22 November 2000

Preface

As a result of the steadily increasing globalization of the economy, companies increasingly operate beyond the national borders of the country in which they are established. However, cross-border company mobility presupposes freedom of establishment (including a right of migration) for legal persons.

In the first part of this book, private international law recognition theories are explored. Subsequently, a survey is given of EC law as it now stands with regard to the freedom of establishment of legal persons. Current EC law does not provide ready-made solutions to the problem of mutual recognition of foreign companies among EC member states. The controversy between the 'incorporation' theory and the 'real seat' theory still exists. This is due to the fact that cross-border company relationships have a highly complicated, multi-party character: company officials, creditors, employees, national tax and social security authorities, and so on are all involved.

Part 2 is devoted to current conflict of law developments in Europe, having regard to the recognition of foreign companies and the applicable proper law of the company. From a comparative perspective, the law of three 'incorporation' countries and three 'real seat' countries—five EC countries and Switzerland—is explored. Special attention is paid to recent changes in national legislation on private international law. Some of these legislative reforms have already had a considerable impact on cross-border company mobility in Europe.

More and more, awareness that cross-border company mobility is no longer the exclusive domain of either EC law or conflict of laws is growing. This feeling is further enhanced after the entry into force of the Treaty of Amsterdam on 1 May 1999. Accordingly, in Part 3 of the book, an integrated approach to EC law and private international law is advocated. First, an attempt is made to define the legal premises for a proper dialogue between the two disciplines of EC law and private international law. Thereafter, current draft proposals concerning cross-border company migration (e.g. the KPMG Proposal, and the 1998 EC Draft Proposal for a Fourteenth Company Law Directive on the Transfer of the Registered Office or the De Facto Head Office of a Company from One Member State to Another are examined against the background of EC law and private international law principles.

Maastricht, Netherlands   STEPHAN RAMMELOO
October 2000

Acknowledgements

The author wishes to thank the *Wetenschapscommissie* (Research Committee) of the Universiteit Maastricht, Netherlands for financially supporting my research project and the Max Planck Institut für ausländisches und Internationales Privat- und Wirtschaftsrecht in Hamburg (Germany) for enabling me to undertake research. The author also expresses his gratitude to Nicole Kornet for revising the manuscript, as well as Prof. Dr. Caroline Forder and Mrs. Wies Rayar for their useful linguistic comments and moral support, Prof. Dr. Harm-Jan de Kluiver and Prof. Dr. Hildegard Schneider for being inspiring discussion partners, Gabriele Iermano of the Università degli studi di Napoli Frederico II (Italy) for providing me with Italian materials, and Mrs. Margriet van Woerden of the Private Law department of the Universiteit Maastricht for preparing the manuscript before it was sent to the publisher.

Outline Table of Contents

Detailed Table of Contents

Table of Cases

European Court of Justice

ALPHABETICAL

NUMERICAL/CHRONOLOGICAL

International Court of Justice

National Cases

Canada

Belgium

France

Germany

Italy

United Kingdom

United States

Table of International Treaties and Conventions

EC SECONDARY LEGISLATION

NATIONAL LEGISLATION

Abbreviations

AA	*Ars Aequi*
AC	Appeal Cases, English Law Reports
AG	—Aktiengesellschaft
	—Advocate General
AJCL	*American Journal of Comparative and International Law*
AktG	Aktiengesetz
art. Article	
AWD	Außenwirtschaftsdienst des Betriebsberaters
BayOLG	Bayerisches Oberstes Landesgericht
BB	Betriebsberater
BCLC	Butterworth Company Law Cases
BGBl.	Bundesgesetzblatt
BGE	Entscheidungen des Schweizerischen Bundesgerichts
BGH	Bundesgerichtshof
BGHZ	Entscheidungen des Bundesgerichtshofes in Zivilsachen
BJM	*Basler Juristischer Mitteilungen*
BV	Besloten Vennootschap
BVBA	*Besloten Vennootschap met Beperkte Aansprakelijkheid*
CA	Court of Appeal
C de C	Cour de Cassation
cf.	compare
ch.	chapter
Ch.	Chancery Division
Civ.	Cour de Cassation, chambre civile
CLC	Commercial Law Cases
CLC Act	Conflict of Laws Corporations Act 1998 (*Wet Conflictenrecht Corporaties, Netherlands*).
CLJ	*Cambridge Law Journal*
Clunet	*Journal de Droit International*
CMLR	*Common Market Law Review*
co	company
Cod. civ.	Codice civile (Italy)
Com.	Cour de cassation, chambre commerciale
cons.	consideration

D.	*Recueil Dalloz (Dalloz-Sirey)*
DB	*Der Betrieb*
Dir.com.degl.sc.int.	Diritto Communiatario e Degli Scambi Internazionali
DLR	Dominion Law Reports
DnotZ	*Deutsche Notarzeitung*
DWiR	*Deutsches Zeitschrift für Wirtschaftsrecht*
ECJ	European Court of Justice
EC Law	European Community Law
ECR	Report: Decisions of the European Court of Justice
edn.	edition
ed(s).	editor(s)
EEIG	European Economic Interest Grouping
EFTA	European Free Trade Association
e.g.	*exempli gratia*
EGBGB	Einführungsgesetz zum Bürgerlichen Gesetzbuch
ELJ	*European Law Journal*
ELR	*European Law Review*
EM	Explanatory Memorandum
et seq.	and the following (pages)
EuR.	*Zeitschrift für Europarecht*
EuZW	*Europäische Zeitschrift für Wirtschaftsrecht*
EWG	Europäische Wirtschaftsgemeinschaft
EWiR	Entscheidungen zum Wirtschaftsrecht
n	footnote
Foro It.	Foro Italiano
Gazz. Uff.	Gazzetta Uffiziale
Giur Com.	*Giurisprudenza Commerziale*
Giur. It.	*Giurisprudenza Italiana*
GmbH	Gesellschaft mit beschränkter Haftung
GmbHG	Gesetz betreffend Gesellschaften mit beschränkter Haftung
GP	Gazette du Palais
i.a.	*inter alia*
ibid.	ibidem
ICJ	Judgments of the International Court of Justice
ICLQ	*International Comparative Law Quarterly*
id.	*idem*
i.e.	*id est*

ILM	International Legal Materials
IPRax	*Praxis des Internationalen Privat- und Verfahrensrechts*
IPRG	*Gesetz zur Reglung des Internationalen Privatrechts*
IPRspr.	Die deutsche Rechtsprechung auf dem Gebiete des Internationalen Privatrechts im Jahre

JBL	*Journal of Business Law*
JCP	*Juris-classeur Périodique (Semaine juridique)*
JT	*Journal des Tribuneaux*
JTDE	*Journal des Tribuneaux. Droit Européen*
JuS	*Juristische Schulung*
JutD	*Juridisch up to date*
JW	*Juristische Wochenschrift*
JZ	*Juristenzeitung*

KB	King's Bench Law Reports
KG	—Kammergericht
	—Kommanditgesellschaft
Kh.	Rechtbank van Koophandel

L.	Loi
LG	Landgericht
LR	Law Reports
Ltd.	Private limited company (England)

| MDR | *Monatschrift für Deutsches Recht* |
| MJ | *Maastricht Journal of European and Comparative Law* |

NILR	*Netherlands International Law Review*
NIPR	*Nederlands Internationaal Privaatrecht*
NJ	*Nederlandse Jurisprudentie*
NJB	*Nederlands Juristenblad*
NJW	*Neue Juristische Wochenschrift*
NV	—Naamloze Vennootschap
	—Tijdschrift voor de Naamlze Vennootschap
NVIR	Nederlandse Vereniging voor Internationaal Recht (Dutch International Law Association)

OHG	Offene Handelsgesellschaft
OJ	Official Journal of the European Communities
OLG	Oberlandesgericht
	—Obligationenrecht (Swiss Civil Code)
	—Ondernemingsrecht

p(p).	page(s)
PFFC Act	Pro-Forma Foreign Companies Act 1998 (*Wet op de Formeel Buitenlandse Vennootschappen*, Netherlands)
plc	Public limited company
QB	Law Reports. Queen's Bench Division of the High Court
QC	Queen's Counsel
RabelsZ.	*Rabels Zeitschrift für Ausländisches und Internationales Privatrecht*
Rb	Rechtbank (Dutch district court)
RDS	*Revue suisse de jurisprudence (SJZ)*
R(ec).	*Receuil*
Rev cr.d.i.p.	*Revue Critique de Droit International Privé*
Rev.Soc.	*Revue des Sociétés*
Rev.Trim.Dr.Eur.	*Revue Trimestielle de Droit Européen*
RG	Reichsgericht
RGZ	Entscheidungen des Reichsgerichts
Riv.dir.int.	*Rivista di Diritto Internazionale*
Riv.dir.int.priv.proc.	*Rivista di Diritto Internazionale Privati e Processuale*
RIW/AWD	*Recht der Internationale Wirtschaft. Außenwirtschaftsdienst des Betriebsberaters*
RPS	*Revue Pratique des Sociétés*
RSJ	*Revue Suisse Jurisprudentielle*
RTDE	*Revue Trimestielle de Droit Européen*
R.v.St.	Raad van State (State Council: Belgium or Netherlands)
S.	*Sirey, Receuil général des lois et arrêts*
s	section
SA	Société Anonyme
Sarl	Société à Responsabilité Limitée
SchwJbIntR	*Schweizerisches Jahrbuch für Internationales Recht*
SE	*Societas Europea*
SEW	Sociaal Economische Wetgeving—Tijdschrift voor Europees en economisch recht
SJR	Schweizerische Juristenzeitung
SJZ	*Schweizerische Juristenzeitung*
Spa.	società per azioni
Srl.	società a responsabilità limitata
ss	sections
Stbl.	Staatsblad (Netherlands Official Gazette)

subs	subsection
TLR	*Times Law Reports*
Trb.	Tractatenblad van het Koninkrijk der Nederlanden (Netherlands: official Gazette for publication of international treaties)
TRV	*Tijdschrift voor Rechtspersoon en Vennootschap*
TVR	*Tijdschrift voor Rechtsvergelijking*
TVVS	*Tijdschrift voor Vennootschappen Verenigingen en Stichtingen*
UNICE	Union of Industrial and Employers' Confederations of Europe
UWG	*Bundesgesetz gegen den unlauteren Wettbewerb*
vol.	volume
W	*Weekblad van het Recht*
WLR	Weekly Law Reports
WM	Wertpapier-Mitteilungen. Zeitschrift für Wirtschafts- und Bankrecht
WPNR	Weekblad voor Privaatrecht, Notariaat en Registratie
ZEuP	*Zeitschrift für Europäisches Privatrecht*
ZfRVgl.	*Zeitschrift für Rechtsvergleichung, Internationales Privatrecht und Europarecht*
ZGB	Zivilgesetzbuch
ZGR	*Zeitschrift für Unternehmens- und Gesellschaftsrecht*
ZHR	*Zeitschrift für das Gesamte Handels- und Wirtschaftsrecht*
ZPO	Zivilprozeßordnung
ZSR	*Zeitschrift für Schweizerisches Recht*
ZVerglWiss.	*Zeitschrift für Vergleichende Rechtswissenschaft*

Part 1

The Legal Status of Foreign Companies: The Present State of European Law

1

Cross-Border Company Relationships in Europe: Main Features

I. INTRODUCTION

It is beyond dispute now that corporations have replaced states as the most important makers of waves in the world's economy. It is also firmly established that with
the increasing globalisation of that economy corporations operate in many cases
far beyond the borders of the country that presided over their birth.[1]

A continuing process of economic globalization has provoked profound
changes in the conduct of business and trade and the reactions of states to
those changes. Today more than ever, market players realize that entering
into business transactions with 'foreigners' involves more than a mere
exchange of goods and services. A more dynamic attitude is called for,
with either active participation in foreign undertakings, or even the total
transfer of an enterprise from one country to another. This is not simply a
matter of making more profits. Freedom of establishment and the abolition of national barriers bring intensified competition. Consequently, company managers are urged to take daring initiatives: a complete transfer of
business undertakings might well turn out to be necessary in order to survive.[2] Strategies like these become more attractive with the realization that
further enlargement of the EU is drawing near.

Versatile legal instruments should enable businessmen to penetrate
new markets. But those businessmen who show willingness to accept this
challenge will find themselves placed in an awkward position. Granting

---

[1] Drury (1998) 165. Cf., in a comparable sense, Lutter (2000) 1: '*Unternehmen sind die
Motoren des europäischen Binnenmarkts*'.
[2] Drury (1999) 354 et seq. observes: '[t]his is where the problems can begin. Once major
decisions about the company as a whole are taken regularly in another jurisdiction there is a
possibility that the courts in the host state of the foreign operations would decline to recognize the whole company as valid, and possibly treat it as something which did not have corporate personality and in consequence as something which no longer possesed limited
liability. If potential losses were the main cause of concern, the last thing the controllers of the
company would want to lose is limited liability.' Cf. ch 6 III 1, below.

freedom of establishment to *legal* foreign persons is likely to have a heavier impact on a legal order than welcoming *natural* foreign persons. Consequently, companies operating across borders will experience considerable differences in treatment (rigid or lenient) between company law regimes of the still expanding number of the EU member states. These differences are due to the fact that authorities of (non-)industrialized States take a rather ambiguous position: each seeks to balance the goal of stimulating economic growth by welcoming foreign investors against other aims such as creditor protection, worker co-determination, fair and equal competition on domestic markets, tax revenue policies, etc.[3] Of all types of legal relationships, companies in particular confront legal professionals with problems of a 'multi-party' character. It is therefore important to realize that any concept used to 'recognize'[4] foreign equivalents of domestic company forms presupposes that all the interests of those involved are weighed against each other properly.

II. THE MULTI-PARTY NATURE OF COMPANY RELATIONSHIPS: AREAS OF LAW INVOLVED

Multi-party relationships frequently give rise to conflicting interests. As regards companies, some examples are colliding substantive company law interests, shareholders' and debenture holders' value interests, creditor protection, worker co-determination, social security and tax law policies.[5] The costs and benefits to society must be balanced: a state which is overly generous to the foreign companies conducting business activities on its territory may have an influx of foreign investors, but this benefit might also be outweighed by costs, such as abuses, or even fraud, committed by those in charge of the foreign company's management. Once state authorities allow foreign companies to have management and control offices on their territory, they may occasionally find themselves confronted with companies whose foreign status appears to be purely fictitious.[6]

---

[3] Wouters/Schneider (eds) *Current issues of cross-border establishment of companies in the European Union* (1995) gives the reader a good impression of today's European company law trends and problems from a comparative angle. Part I: Conflict of laws dimension: recognition of foreign companies and cross-border transfer of the corporate seat; Part II: Tax and corporate law aspects; Part III: Labour law aspects; Part IV: Insolvency and fiduciary duties; Part V: The process of formulating corporate law rules: harmonisation *versus* competition between jurisdictions. See further Buxbaum/Hopt (1988); Edwards (1999); Hopt (1998); European Business Law (1991); and Wiesner (1998).

[4] The definition of 'recognition' is highly confusing and is explained in ch 2 I 2, below.

[5] See Lutter (2000) 1 et seq.

[6] More detail below: ch 2 II 3, ch 6 II 1 (Delaware and other 'pro-forma' foreign companies), ch 4 II 1 (the Dutch experience of *Formeel Buitenlandse Vennootschappen*), and ch 4 II 3 (Swiss law on 'fictitious' foreign legal persons, notably the Liechtenstein *Anstalt*).

Thus EC activity in respect of company law applies the public policy balance, well known in the national context, to the creation and functioning of the Internal Market. The essential elements are, on the one hand, the creation of a climate favourable for corporate enterprises and, on the other, the provision of equivalent standards of protection for those dealing with companies.[7]

While exploring company law in Europe today, one will find that the wide range of internal and external company interests repeatedly leads to an *ad hoc* approach. The following non-exhaustive catalogue of relevant law sources underscores that there is no such thing as a vast, coherent, and exhaustive set of 'European' company law rules. Instead, areas of EC law which have been harmonized coincidentally seem to amalgamate with elements of national substantive law (cf. *inter alia* company, nationality, taxation, labour, and social security law), and national conflict of law rules:

—Primary EC law: e.g. articles 43, 44, 46, 48, 65, 234, 293, and 308 (previously articles 52, 54, 56, 58, 73m, 177, 220, and 235) of the EC Treaty;[8]
—Secondary EC law:
   (i)   Draft proposal for a *Societas Europea* (SE);[9]
   (ii) European Economic Interest Grouping (EEIG);[10]
   (iii) EC Company Law Harmonisation Programme;[11]
   (iv) European labour law.[12]

---

[7] Richards (1991) 1.

[8] These provisions are discussed in ch 2 IV, and, in particular the Treaty of Amsterdam (entered into force: 1 May 1999) in ch 6 I 2 and III 1, below.

[9] As a consequence of the fact that worker co-determination is highly controversial, the draft proposal for a *Societas Europea* appears to have been stuck in a blind alley for nearly three decades now: not for the first time, the Davignon Committee tried to reanimate this project in May 1997. Subsequently, under the chairmanship of Luxembourg, a draft proposal for a directive was elaborated. This proposal established a link between the 'European company' and the European Works Council on the basis of Directive 94/45 EC. But the opposing views have apparently not undergone drastic changes since 1972. Once more, even the combination of an optional application of a *Societas Europea* and several 'menus' regarding the co-determination regime, could not count on the mercy of all member states! See ch 2 I 3 and ch 6 I 2, below.

[10] *Report*, p. 23. OJ L 199 of 31 July 1985: see ch 6 III 2, below. As regards administrative and judicial supervision procedures, the EEIG also inspired proposals concerning intra-community company mobility (i.e. cross-border seat transfers): ch 6 III 2, below.

[11] The company law harmonization programme is far from finished. For an impression of the status of all (draft) directives: Wiesner (1998) 619 et seq.; Hopt (1999); Edwards (1999); and ch 6 I 2, below.

[12] See Directive 94/45 of 22 September 1994, OJ 1994 L 254/64, concerning the European Works Council. Note that there is a close relationship between labour law and company law at both EC and national levels: considerable differences exist between member states as regards the level of worker co-determination in business undertakings. One may think of powers and duties of employees as members of (one or two-tier) management and supervisory boards, cf. the vehement resistance of the German judiciary and doctrine against the setting aside of *Arbeitnehmermitbestimmung* by replacing the German *Gesellschaftsstatut* with any foreign company law: ch 4 III 1, below. To a large extent, this also explains why the draft for

Apart from EC law, other areas of law are involved as well:
—(inter)national tax law;[13]
—national laws on social security;[14]
—private international law rules concerning the law applicable to foreign legal persons of the legal orders involved;[15]
—'Neighbouring' private international law rules and substantive law on contract, formal validity, tort, etc.;[16]
—private international law rules on jurisdiction resulting from the Brussels Convention on Jurisdiction and the Enforcement of Judgments in Civil and Commerical Matters (including the total range of Accession Treaties and the Parallel Lugano Convention);[17]
—national mandatory legislation restricting the scope of private international law rules;[18]
—national laws concerning the nationality or citizenship of natural and legal persons;[19]
—national laws concerning the protection of the company's name or trade;[20]
—national laws on civil procedure.[21]

a 5th Company Directive on the functioning of organs has been in a dead-end street for about two decades now: ch 6 I 2, below.

[13] cf. the consequences of EC law, e.g. the ECJ cases of *Avoir Fiscal* and *Haliburton*, ch 2 IV 2, below.

[14] See for the influence of EC law on national sickness insurance benefit programmes for company directors, ECJ *Segers*, ch 2 IV 2, below.

[15] See Part 2 below, in which the private international law rules of 'incorporation' and 'real seat' law families are compared.

[16] e.g. pre-incorporation contracts, company formation requirements (e.g. a notary deed), liability of managing directors: rather than to the proper law of the company, these matters *ratione materiae* may be submitted to the proper law of either a contract, formal validity, or tort. See ch 4 below, II and III, for the precise scope of the proper law of the company and the demarcation problems mentioned briefly here.

[17] Of importance here is the avoidance of a proliferation of litigation arising from multi-party and cross-border company activities, cf. the ECJ *Powell Duffryn* judgment, on art. 2 in conjunction with art. 53 and arts. 16 and 17 of the Brussels Convention on Jurisdiction and the Enforcement of Judgments in Civil and Commercial Matters. See ch 2 IV 2 and ch 6 II 1, below.

[18] As a result of these rules, 'pro-forma' foreign companies which have their management and control centre in 'incorporation' countries and exclusively conduct their business there (e.g. the Netherlands and Switzerland) experience a particularly high degree of legal uncertainty and unpredictability: see ch 4 II 1 and 3, below. 'Real seat' countries on the contrary are troubled less by this problem, as will be seen.

[19] Parallels between the 'birth' and 'death' of natural persons and corporations are drawn in several legal orders. Cf. the common law approach, (ch 4 II 2 below) and the French concept of a company's 'nationality' and its relationship with diplomatic protection, (ch 4 III 2 below). The nationality of natural persons is relevant at another level as well, namely that of ('possible enemy') shareholders.

[20] cf. references to this issue in art. 157 of the 1987 Swiss Private International Law Code: ch 4 II 3, below.

[21] Of paramount importance is the status of foreign companies in court proceedings: should these companies be accorded *ius standi in iudicio* (the right to appear in court proceedings) or not? See ch 4 II 1 and 3, below.

This is by no means a complete record of 'European' company law *cum annexis*.[22] Thus, an image is created of a rather coincidental, disintegrated range of involved areas of the law. The interdisciplinary nature of today's company law developments in Europe is likely to influence the underlying conceptual premises as well: this requires an open-minded, integrated approach, balancing all internal and external company interests.

III. AN INTEGRATED APPROACH OF EC LAW AND PRIVATE INTERNATIONAL LAW

The foregoing demonstrates that any attempt by either private international law or EC law alone to tackle the problem of recognition of foreign companies and their precise status is doomed to fail. Disputes arising from cross-border company relationships are known for their complicated nature: in particular the multi-party feature of this area calls for adequate treatment of all the different kinds of disputes which emerge. This should be carried out by a co-ordinated use of EC law, private international law concerning both the proper law of the company and international jurisdiction, substantive company and civil procedural law, tax law, social security law, labour law, contract, or tort law concepts. The risk of disharmonious consequences should therefore be counteracted whenever possible, for example avoiding inconsistent court decisions by concentrating disputes in a single legal order.[23] This is only one of the reasons why an integrated law approach is indispensable.

In Part 1 the following matters are touched upon: (i) what theories about the legal treatment of foreign companies have been elaborated so far? And (ii) is it relevant for the cross-border mobility of a company whether the law of an EC member state or that of a non-EC country applies? Given that the core concept of traditional theories in private international law on the legal concept of the mutual recognition of foreign legal persons was rooted in the nineteenth century, or perhaps even earlier, it is intriguing to consider whether, at the crossroads of EC law and conflict of laws, those theories

---

[22] Recent overview of related matters (banking law, insurance etc.) in Wiesner (1998). Cf. The European Private Company? (1995), notably the contributions from a comparative angle contained therein (Dutch, Italian, French, German, Spanish, Greek, Belgian, US American law), *inter alia* concerning incorporation and government control, criminal control, limited liability, capital requirements, liability of directors and shareholders, protection of minority members, etc.; and Drury/Hicks (1999) 429 et seq.

[23] The ECJ *Powell Duffryn* judgment, ch 2 IV 2, below, focuses *inter alia* on the equal treatment of shareholders settled in a number of European countries, forms an instructive example of weighing their common interest against the interests of others.

[24] Largely from a retrospective point of view: what has or has not been achieved so far is mainly rooted in the 'pre Amsterdam' era. Part 3 of this book takes the Treaty of Amsterdam as a basis for further debate.

have been influenced by, or at least adequately respond to current perceptions of EC law. To that end, EC law and private international law are dealt with consecutively in the first and second part of this book.[24] Finally, Part 3 seeks to establish a synthesis between the disciplines of EC law and private international law in order to respond adequately to today's developments in Europe's cross-border company relationships.

2

Recognition Theories: Private International Law Treaties and EC Law

I. INTRODUCTION

Considering that the EC law era started nearly half a century ago, one would expect EC law to provide tools enabling cross-border freedom of establishment for companies. However, the legal status of foreign companies and their cross-border manoeuvrability used to belong to the exclusive domain of private international law specialists. Their attempts to define 'foreign' companies and the rights conferred upon them culminated in two opposing recognition theories, commonly referred to as the 'incorporation' theory and the 'real seat' theory. Methodological links between EC law and private international law still exist today, in that the text of the basic provisions on the freedom of establishment of natural and legal persons contained in articles 43 and 48 of the EC Treaty is more or less rooted in those traditional recognition theories. Before analysing these provisions of the EC Treaty, it is therefore necessary to consider the origins and the functioning of both recognition theories. Attention is then given to attempts at reconciliation based on private international law and EC law.

1. A PRELIMINARY REMARK: 'RECOGNITION'

A concise treatment of the existing theories on the mutual recognition of foreign companies requires that the term 'recognition' be clarified. For a considerable period, it was uncertain whether states:

> ought to recognise foreign corporations at all. In both Europe and the United States, in the last century, views were put forward to the effect that a company, being a creature of the legal system which created it, can have no existence outside the ambit of that law.[1]

Precisely what 'recognition' means can easily be misconceived if one does not take into account that it covers two disparate legal concepts. When we speak of 'recognition' of a foreign company in a *narrow* sense, we consider that foreign company as a legal subject, i.e. a bearer of rights and duties, nothing more and nothing less.[2] This concept says nothing about the proper law of the company: the law applicable to company matters still needs to be ascertained. Thus, methodologically speaking, the conflict of laws task of determining the *lex societatis* is clearly preceded by the matter of recognition. By contrast, 'recognition' in a *broad* sense encompasses the ultimate outcome of the process of finding the proper law of the company: in other words, the status of a company (legal person or not) is defined by the *lex societatis*, rather than the *lex fori*. In this broad concept, matters such as formation, structure, functioning of organs, dissolution, and winding up are all governed by the (possibly foreign) proper law of the company.

As will be seen, a conclusive answer as to which of these concepts is taken as the point of departure can often be formulated only after a thorough examination of the court decisions and learned writings of the legal order involved. The same applies to (reports of) multilateral and bilateral (draft) treaties. We will find, however, that the 'being' of a company (i.e. its possession of rights and duties) is now hardly ever contested.[3]

---

[1] Drury (1998) 176.

[2] cf. (among many others) Großfeld (1974) 344; Rabel (1960) 132 et seq.; Vlas (1999) 4 et seq.; and Sonnenberger/Großerichter (1999) 725. This notion was closely linked to 'concession theory of corporate personality': Drury (1998) 176. The narrowed notion of 'bearership of rights and duties' also formed the starting point of several (draft) proposals for multilateral treaties (see below). According to the Mercantilism doctrine, foreign companies owe their existence and legal capacity to a concession granted to them by their own sovereign power; it remains to be seen, however, whether that will be acknowledged by sovereign authorities of other legal orders as well. Sandrock (1989) 507, underlines that the refusal to give foreign companies such a grant was essential to the Mercantilism doctrine.

[3] cf. Behrens (1989) 358: '*Die Rechtsfähigkeit einer Gesellschaft ist (. . .) keineswegs territorial beschränkt. Sie erstreckt sich nach Maßgabe des Kollisionsrechts ohne weiteres auch über die Grenzen des Gründungsstaates hinaus. (. . .) ob dabei nun verlangt wird, daß im Gründungsstaat auch der Geschäftssitz liegt (Sitztheorie) oder nicht (Gründungstheorie), wird die Gesellschaft auch außerhalb des Gründungsstaates als Rechtssubjekt behandelt.*' In the second (comparative) part of this book, further notice is given to national conflict of law concepts, *inter alia* having regard to what the notion of 'recognition' of foreign companies precisely stands for.

2. THE 'REAL SEAT' THEORY

Origins: main features

At present, there are two contrasting conflict of law theories as regards the recognition of foreign legal persons:[4] the 'incorporation' theory and the 'real seat' theory. The 'real seat' theory[5] probably dates back to the middle of the nineteenth century.[6] According to this theory, the law of the country where the company has its 'real' seat (i.e. its management and control centre) is the law applicable to company relationships.

Conceptually speaking, this approach is synonymous with what is commonly referred to as the 'objective proper law' test: those in charge of the company's management are not free to choose the law which governs company law relationships (*lex societatis*). For example, a business undertaking in Germany making use of the legal form of an English private limited company will not be recognized as such. Party autonomy thus being excluded, the legal order to which the company is deemed to be 'most closely connected', or more precisely, the location of the company's 'real seat', has to be identified.

Essential to this theory are the sanctions applicable if the formation requirements of the country where the company has its real seat are not satisfied. Possible consequences are the following: (i) the company as such is no longer considered to be a legal subject, and (ii) its managers are deprived of the most important company benefit, namely restricted liability.[7] At first glance, the identification of a company's real seat may seem a

[4] Notwithstanding the fact that the following applies to legal persons in general, I shall refer in the following to 'companies', since these entities form the *pièce de résistance* of this discourse.

[5] This doctrine is commonly referred to as the *'theorie du siège réel'*, or *'siège social'* in France; *Sitztheorie* in Germany; *leer van de werkelijke zetel* in the Netherlands; and *teoria della sede (effetiva)* in Italy. The precise meaning of these notions cannot be isolated from their national law contexts (see Part 2 of this book).

[6] It is difficult to trace the origins of this theory: Sandrock (1989) 505 et seq. It allegedly originates from the concept of sovereign states attempting to control their territories (cf. the ideas of e.g. Herder, Mancini). Coupled with the control concept, 'nationality' became the predominant connecting factor in the conflict of laws, for both natural and legal persons. As the nationality concept no longer tolerated that a company be *'l'homme de plusieurs maîtres'*, companies had to submit themselves to a sole sovereign power, namely the state on whose territory their strategic centre was located. Together with the concept of mercantilism, this control-oriented concept eventually culminated in today's restrictive policy of precluding foreign companies (i.e companies duly established and incorporated abroad) from having their real seat in a domestic territory. Cf. *inter alia* Behrens (1988) 512 et seq.; Rabel (1960); and Vlas (1999) 6 et seq. for further information. For a common law perception of the civil law based 'real seat' doctrine, cf. Clarke (1991) 162 et seq.

[7] See Behrens (1988) 517. He does not accept that the concept of personal liability is directly based on the generally applicable presumption that any formation of a foreign company should be considered as a form of abuse of the law, as this rigid approach would be incompatible with a modern and flexible European Single Market.

feasible task: in a number of situations this 'real seat' is obvious. However, how should multinational companies (i.e. companies increasingly getting involved with several legal orders) be treated? The generic formula of the 'real seat' does not seem to furnish adequate responses to this phenomenon: most legal systems adhering to the 'real seat' doctrine tend to consider the 'management and control centre' to be the company's 'real seat'. It is clear, however, that this centre does not necessarily coincide with what is commonly referred to as the company's main *business* (or exploitation) centre (e.g. production plants).[8]

The 'real seat' theory basically functions as a double-edged sword: it affects both companies incorporated under a foreign system of law but having their real seat on domestic territory, and companies incorporated under domestic law having their management and control office abroad. Both the former and the latter category are considered to have failed formation requirements. This rigid principle is often mitigated though, with the help of the private international law escape device of *renvoi* or remission: real seat countries allow companies to have their management and control office abroad, provided that the conflict of law rules of the country where the real seat is situated adhere to the 'incorporation' theory.[9]

The 'real seat' theory has always been predominantly influenced by control policies.[10] However, protagonists of decisive factors that have become obsolete—for example, the law of the place where the company contract was concluded, or the law of the place where shares were issued[11]—were less concerned with the complexity of modern society's cross-border multi-party company relationships than state authorities are today.[12] Nowadays, it is generally assumed that business activities conducted on the territory of the state where the 'foreign'[13] company *de facto* resides should be supervised effectively. Hence, a brief retrospective view is indispensable here, to demonstrate that the 'real seat' theory is more or less rooted in sentiments that deliberately place the emphasis on 'foreigner

---

[8] See Part 2, below.

[9] German law is an example of this 'non-receprocity' principle, cf. Großfeld/König (1992) 433, with further notice, and ch 4 III 1, below. Much the same applies to Italian conflict of laws: ch 4 III 3, below.

[10] Drobnig (1990) 326, quoting Hausmann, describes the legal order which is predominantly interested in its mandatory law being obeyed, as a *Wächteramt* (safeguard).

[11] Vlas (1982) 43, quoting other law sources, summarizes a plenary catalogue of decisive factors that are now considered obsolete. An open-ended conflict rule (finding the proper law by examining all relevant factors case by case) was still being suggested at the dawn of last century by F. Despagnet (1909) 168, quoted by Vlas (1982) 34. Vlas' recommendation to contemporary private international law specialists is to leave Pandora's box closed.

[12] cf. the ECJ judgment in *Powell-Duffryn*, ch 2 IV 2, below.

[13] 'Foreign' should be understood in a broad sense here, namely (1) a company incorporated under the law of another legal system, and/or (2) a company having its management and control centre beyond the borders of the country where the main business activities are conducted.

control'. At the same time, the nationality of *natural* persons controlling the company was deemed to be of considerable importance.[14] Relics of this theory can be found in English as well as French court decisions.[15] It has been argued, though, that even apart from situations of war,[16] attributing decisive weight to 'nationality' as a means of determining to which legal order the company is most closely connected may turn out to be perilous.[17] *A fortiori* it would be highly controversial under EC law to stress the need to control companies for no other reason than that natural persons in charge of the management of such companies are foreign nationals.[18] Today, control theories of this kind are no longer considered to be adequate tools to find the proper law of the company. Neither can this archaic concept be tolerated under EC law.[19] It can only be relied on subsidiarily, namely in situations of war.

Despite its flaws, the 'real seat' doctrine has never been seriously at risk.[20] However, given that the 'real seat' theory potentially frustrates cross-border company mobility in 'Europe', the critical observer must be alert as to whether or not the 'real seat' theory is ultimately incompatible with EC law.[21]

Pros and cons

What many theories have in common is that they exist for want of something better. Legal theories seem to share this fate. The pros and cons of the

[14] Even today, some remains of this 'foreigner control' theory can still be traced at European law level, see ch 2 IV 1, below.

[15] UK: *Daimler Co. Ltd. v Continental Tyre and Rubber Co. (Great Britain) Ltd.* [1916] 2 AC 307 (HL): subsidiary of German company; all members of the management board and nearly all shareholders were Germans. Under the 1914 Trading with the Enemy Act people were '*prima facie* to be regarded as a friend, but [the Court] will assume an enemy character if its agents or the persons *de facto* in control of its affairs are resident in an enemy country'. For France: cf. the *Remington* case, ch 4 III 2, below.

[16] cf. Vlas (1982) 46 and (1999) 6 et seq., with further notice, deprecating the ill-defined character of this concept: nationality (or domicile of choice) of whom in particular? The (majority) of the management (supervisory?) board members, or the (majority) of the company's shareholders? Neither is this a stable instrument in the case of a changing leadership.

[17] This is so, irrespective of whether the construed nationality of a legal person or the genuine nationality of natural persons who appear to be in charge of the company is under discussion, cf. both the French and Italian experience as regards the combined proper law test, i.e. the '*siège réel (social)*' ultimately being based on notions of 'nationality' of the company, ch 4 III 2 and 3. Comparative analysis and overall conclusions in ch 3 below.

[18] Neither is it permitted to place natural persons in charge of a company in a detrimental position for the sole reason that the company appears to be incorporated in another country (ECJ *Segers* judgment, see ch 2 IV 2, below).

[19] Wouters (1996/97) 39, convincingly argues that, apart from the foregoing, the acceptance of the control theory would lead to discriminatory treatment of the managing directors of a capital company (which after all is a legal person) compared to the—irrelevant—'nationality' of a partner in a firm.

[20] But see (ECJ *Centros*) below. [21] Behrens (1988) 500.

'real seat' theory have been described frequently.[22] Its positive values are as follows:

The 'real seat' theory justifies the application of no system of law other than that which is predominantly interested. It follows from the normative wording of the decisive factor underlying this conflict of law rule, that there is (nearly) always a genuine link between the cosmopolitical facts and the system of law applied thereto. Consequently, and this is deemed to be the overwhelming strength of the 'real seat' doctrine, nearly all possible forms of abuse of a foreign system of law by those in charge of the company's management are effectively precluded: the 'real seat' theory thus stands for equal treatment and the protection of fair competition.[23]

At the same time, however, this focus on control appears to be the major weakness of the 'real seat' doctrine: particularly in a globalizing business world it is often difficult to determine where a company actually has its 'real' seat.[24] Ultimately, the need for protective measures is likely to function as a guideline in the process of ascertaining the proper law of the company.[25] Nevertheless, this appears to be one of the intrinsic flaws of the 'real seat' doctrine: business undertakings cannot be expected to operate in only one market on a continuing basis. For instance, capital markets, employment markets, and consumer markets are not necessarily concentrated within the same territory. Furthermore, it may turn out to be problematic to determine the company's 'real and only' seat,[26] or to elaborate a conflict rule capable of embracing all the relevant connecting factors.[27]

---

[22] A more detailed comparative analysis of how it functions in the German, French, and Italian conflict of law systems is given in ch 4 III below.

[23] See, among many others, Behrens (1988) 512.

[24] Lots of problems were unveiled by Ebenroth/Bippus (JZ, 1988) 678 et seq.: (i) the 'real' seat cannot be deduced from the articles of association; (ii) how to find the real seat when a company's management office appears to be decentralized?; (iii) how to define a 'ranking list' of (more or less) important (members of) organs and what is the status of the shareholders' meeting and/or production plant? Although the latter cannot be manipulated, it is common for production plants to be situated in several countries; and what about (iv) a *Doppelsitz* (dual management and control office)? Open-ended formulas (e.g. closest relationship) or rebuttable presumptions can only be utilized at the expense of legal certainty. As will be seen, the catalogue of factors determining a company's 'real' (*sic*) seat may also serve as an instrument to find out whether under the EC Treaty one may speak of 'establishment' pursuant to art. 52 JO 58: see ch 2 IV 2, below.

[25] See Behrens (1988) 512.

[26] See Behrens (1988) 513. EC law confronts us with the extra dimension of primary and secondary establishment: Sonnenberger/Großerichter (1999) 729, 731, say that the problem in defining a company's 'real seat' reappears on the level of secondary establishment: a company duly established in one EC member state, while exclusively operating in another through a branch. This also has consequences for bogus branches of foreign companies, wishing to transfer their headquarters into the territory of another EC member state through the back door. Cf. the debate on ECJ *Centros*, below.

[27] cf. Großfeld (1986) 353: *'ein Kollisionsnorm die auf das Ganze des Unternehmens zielt'*. It must be mentioned that this problem could be circumvented to a certain extent by restricting the material scope of the proper law of the company in favour of other conflict of law

Moreover, the company could even be confronted with nullity, for example when it is incorporated under the law of one country, but has its management and control centre in another country, whose legal order, adhering to the 'real seat' theory, denies its existence. Furthermore, perhaps it feels less 'realistic' for German counterparts to contract with a foreign company 'at least' having its real seat in Germany, than to do business with a foreign company not having any 'contact centre' in or ties with Germany at all,[28] not to mention the problem of the *Doppelsitz* (double residence).[29] From a public international law perspective, the view has even been put forward that the 'real seat' doctrine is incompatible with the European Convention on Human Rights.[30] Finally, the economic mobility of companies, planning to move their headquarters to another country, is seriously thwarted, because cross-border transfers entail a compulsory *Statutenwechsel* (change in the proper law of the company).[31] The worst-case scenario is that of unintended dissolution and winding-up of the company.[32] Today, more than ever, the Single Market is likely to suffer from an overly rigid application of the 'real seat' theory with all its consequences. Needless to say, freedom of establishment is a prerequisite for accomplishing a Single Market.[33]

provisions (e.g. related to contracts, torts, etc.). This can only be done, however, at the cost of a certain loss of coherence.

[28] In this sense, Knobbe-Keuk (1990) 328.

[29] See Eyles (1990) 100 et seq. Such a company would have dual nationality. For 'bipatrid' companies cf. the consequences of the Belgian *Lamot* doctrine, ch 4 II 1 and ch 6 III 1, below. But then, the non-discrimination goal of arts. 52 and 58 of the EC Treaty would be seriously thwarted.

[30] From a German perspective, Meilicke (1992) 578, 579, referring to a judgment of the French Cour de Cassation of 12 November 1990, Rev. des soc. 1992, p. 133: the French Supreme Court held that the French Act of 30 May 1857, on the basis of which foreign associations were to be recognized only after having received a *diplomatic* permit, was not consistent with arts. 6(1) and 14 of said Convention. (The case was about the non-recognition of a Liechtenstein *Anstalt*. A diplomatic permit was not granted.) However, the word 'recognition' should undoubtedly be understood in a narrow sense here (i.e. bearership of rights and duties), whereas today in most real seat countries such 'recognition' is no longer withheld from foreign subjects. Furthermore, Meilicke argues that any denial of a foreign company's existence would be contrary to investment treaties, as concluded between, for example, Germany and the USA, and Spain and other states. This view was contested by Ebke (1998) 212, who asserts that both the 1857 Act and the French Supreme Court judgment only concern the *ius standi* of aliens. This has nothing to do with conflict of laws and substantive company law.

[31] When compared to natural persons again, one could say that under the 'real seat' theory migrating companies lose their nationality, or domicile of origin.

[32] This is, however, by no means a hard and fast rule. As will be shown in ch 4 III, below, a sliding scale of rigid measures are taken by real seat countries: from inexorable application of the 'real seat' theory with all its (undesired) legal consequences (compulsory dissolution and winding up), to a more lenient and permissive attitude in order to avoid the burden of compulsory winding up, using either conflict of law or substantive law-oriented escape devices.

[33] Sandrock (1989) 506 et seq. condemns the negative impact of this theory on free competition and the *'kostenspielige gesellschaftsrechtliche Umgründung'* (expensive transformation of a foreign company into a company form allowed under the law of the 'real seat' country) which as yet, even under EC law, seems not to be prohibited (see below).

3. THE 'INCORPORATION' THEORY

Origins: main features

In contrast to the 'real seat' theory, the 'incorporation' theory[34] stands for a subjective proper law test. Pursuant to this theory,[35] the company is governed by the law according to which it is duly established. In other words, those in charge of the company's management are free to choose which legal system applies to its company law relationships (*lex societatis*). This is so, regardless of whether an existing company decides to transfer its real seat to the 'incorporation' country while maintaining its status, or whether, 'out of the blue', the company is duly established under a foreign system of law. If, according to the system of law chosen, the company has met the formation requirements, the company is recognized anywhere.[36] If, for example, the English company referred to in the above section on the real seat theory decided to settle not in Germany but in the Netherlands, it could conduct activities on behalf of an English private limited company. English substantive law on matters such as formation, structure and functioning of organs, dissolution, and winding up will be respected by the Dutch legal order, since the Netherlands adhere to the 'incorporation' theory. From a conflict of law perspective, it can be said that the 'incorporation' theory, at least in its purest form, stems from the principle of party autonomy.[37]

Although a company normally has its registered office in the country under whose law it is established, this is not compulsory under each system of law adhering to the 'incorporation' theory; according to, for example, Swedish law, a company is subject to the law of the country where it is registered after its formation. (It should not be overlooked, though, that in a number of situations the proper law will coincide with the law of registration, simply because under many systems of law the registration itself

---

[34] This doctrine is commonly referred to as *theorie du siège statutaire* in France, *Gründungstheorie* in Germany, *leer van de statutaire zetel/incorporatieleer* in the Netherlands and *teoria della sede statutaria* (or: *dell'incorporazione*) in Italy. For a general comparative historical view: Rabel (1960).

[35] Rudiments of this recognition theory can be found in ancient law journals and English law books, cf. Foote (1882) 465 et seq. and (1914). According to Vlas (1982) 49 and (1999) 11, the 'incorporation' theory came into being long before the 'real seat' theory. He touches upon the English case of *Henriques v Dutch West India Co.* (1728) LD Raym 1532. It can be doubted, however, whether this judgment is an acceptance of the 'incorporation' theory as we know it today: this case appeared to be about the *ius standi in iudicio* of the West India Company in English court proceedings, rather than the law applicable to cross-border company relationships.

[36] Knobbe-Keuk (1990) 327, observes that: '*Aus der Gründungstheorie folgt: Einmal anerkannt—überall anerkannt*' (once recognized, a company is recognized everywhere).

[37] Detailed information—notably on the exceptions to this principle—in ch 4 II 1, below.

forms part of the formation requirements.)[38] Likewise, a company may appear to have no registered office at all. Common belief, however, is that it is the *lex societatis*, and not the registered office, which is the decisive factor. This principle is also set forth in treaties.

Pros and cons

The 'incorporation' theory is highly attractive for legal as well as economic reasons. Legally speaking, ascertaining the proper law is uncomplicated: the decisive factor—the law according to which the company is established—is of a formal nature, offering the highest amount of legal certainty and predictability.[39] Further inquiries into the location of the 'main' management or business centre are no longer needed.[40] Nor do 'decentralized' companies that operate on a cross-border scale affect legal certainty and predictability. Aside from this, economic trade is fostered by the lenient and liberal character of the 'incorporation' theory. This theory is undisputedly best suited to the common interest of accomplishing the Single Market.[41] It favours the recognition of foreign companies, without encroaching upon their internal organization and functioning. Even the cross-border migration of a company's management and control office without loss of identity is possible. Here there are parallels between legal persons and natural persons: natural persons also do not lose their status when they cross state frontiers.[42]

However, the major strength of this recognition theory appears also to be a serious drawback. It is hardly surprising that those in charge of the company's management are expected to choose the company regime they consider to be more 'generous'. Opponents of the 'incorporation' theory therefore believe that it provokes a rat-race to keep up with economic

[38] Grasmann (1970) 251. Cf. Dutch case-law: unpublished judgment of the Rotterdam District Court of 30 June 1992, quoted by Vlas (*Rechtspersonen*, 1993) 6, ordering that a company established under the law of Delaware should also have its registered office in that state. The Court further observed that such a company cannot have its registered office in the Netherlands, for the reason that this is not tolerated under the law of Delaware, being the proper law of the company. Likewise, Zwolle District Court 1 November 1995, *NIPR* 1996 144 (further at ch 4 II 1, below). See also Vlas (1999) 7 et seq., quoting Rotterdam District Court 20 August 1993, *NJ* 1994, 356.

[39] Drury (1998) 168 et seq.

[40] Vlas (1999) 8, observes that this theory is better equipped to meet modern society's communication standards than the 'real seat' theory: a company may reside exclusively in a purely 'virtual context' (e.g. on the Internet) as long as it is duly formed in accordance with the incorporation statute. Although the company's management and control centre may be disconnected from the 'real' (!) world, I would be inclined to say it is for the proper law of the company whether to acknowledge an exclusively 'virtual' registered office, or not.

[41] Previously, 'countries with a long-standing commercial maritime tradition' already benefited from the 'incorporation' theory, as 'an open attitude to trade is expected to be met with reciprocity': Edwards (1999) 335 n 6, referring to I.G.F. Cath.

[42] Vlas (1999) 8.

competition. Those who commonly speak of the 'Delaware effect', or 'syn-drome',[43] dislike the phenomenon of companies incorporated under the law of either the US state of Delaware or any other state which has a rep-utation for its lenient company law regime.[44]

It makes quite a difference, though, from which perspective the Delaware syndrome is looked at. Originally, the non-industrial state of Delaware was clearly interested in increasing tax revenues. Businessmen from all over the United States were particularly interested in incorporat-ing and registering their company in Delaware at the cost of annual regis-tration fees, for the reason that the Delaware company law regime was relatively lenient and flexible. The 'popularity quote' of Delaware com-pany law was the result of a rat-race between mainly the states of New Jersey and Delaware.[45] This rat-race was held for no other purpose than to attract businessmen, as a result of which tax revenues of the states involved increased considerably. In the absence of detailed federal com-pany law (cf. the 1933 Securities Act and the 1934 Securities Exchange Act), the law of Delaware merely contains 'default' provisions, which will apply only in so far as the articles of association do not provide otherwise.

Considered in a European[46] context, the Delaware effect has a mirror image. Due to ECJ case-law, national treasuries from EC member states benefit far less from annual incorporation fees paid by foreign companies having their registered office on their territory.[47] Instead, businessmen profit from the Delaware effect in other ways. For example, in the Netherlands, compared to the mass of formation requirements of a Dutch

[43] cf. recently Ebke (1998) 207 et seq.; and Drury (1998) 165 et seq.

[44] cf. *Delaware Laws* (September 1996 edn). Literature: Carey (1974) 663; W. Carey/M.A. Eisenberg (1995); Fischel (1982) 913; Winter (1989) 1526.

[45] For a short historical overview of this 'law beauty competition', cf. Drury (1998) 184 et seq. He quotes Bebchuk (1992) 1437: 'Delaware is at present the domicile of more than half of all Fortune 500 companies and more than 40 per cent of all companies listed on the New York Stock Exchange. It is also the leading destination of companies that reincorporate: Delaware attracted eighty-two per cent of publicly traded firms that reincorporated in the past three decades and ninety per cent of the New York Stock Exchange-listed companies that reincor-porated between 1927 and 1977.' Cf. de Wulf (1999) 322.

[46] Of course, we may not overlook the enormous differences in attitude towards Delaware companies in the UK, Ireland, and the Netherlands on one hand, and the large group of 'real seat' countries on the other.

[47] Case 71/91 and 178/91 *Ponente Carni Spa* [1993] ECR 1947. The Court observed: '(1) (a)rticle 10 of Council Directive 69/335/EEC of 17 July 1969 concerning indirect taxes on the raising of capital must be interpreted as prohibiting, subject to the derogating provisions of Art. 12, an annual charge due in respect of the registration of capital companies even though the product of that charge contributes to financing the department responsible for keeping the register of companies. (2) Article 12 of the Directive must be interpreted as meaning that duties paid by way of fees or dues referred to in Article 12(1)(e) may be payment collected by way of consideration for transactions required by law in the public interest such as, for exam-ple, the registration of capital companies. The amount of such duties, which may vary according to the legal form taken by the company, must be calculated on the basis of the cost of the transaction, which may be assessed on a flat-rate basis.'

Besloten Vennootschap (approximately the Dutch equivalent of a private limited company)[48] the benefits are clear. The formation of a Delaware corporation (or any other foreign company) can be considered as mere 'adminstrative red tape', no declaration of no objection (i.e. an inquiry into the pasts of those who will be in charge of the company's management) is required by the Justice Department; there no are minimum capital requirements; accounting and auditing are not subject to EC directives; the registration of shareholders is not obligatory;[49] etc.[50] Provided that a legal order adheres to the 'incorporation' theory, it is only logical for 'local' businessmen to incorporate their company under a more lenient foreign law, for the sole purpose of circumventing stricter company law provisions at home.[51] Some are prepared to qualify this behaviour as fraudulent. But it must be kept in mind that making use of facilities offered by the 'incorporation' theory cannot as such be condemned as unlawful, in spite of the fact that company managers can ultimately be held liable for misconduct. On the contrary, this appears to be the essence of the 'incorporation' theory. Corresponding with this, the 'incorporation' theory is often inspired by macro-economic policies of states: an influx of foreign investors is likely to raise the employment rate. In particular the aftermath of World War II inspired states to transform their rural economies into industrialized ones.[52]

The fear that it would be highly tempting for legal orders to 'sell' their company law system to (local or foreign) businessmen too hastily has been frequently expressed. This mechanism of 'inter-state legal competition' is part of the Delaware effect. To quote Judge Brandeis, 'the race was not one

---

[48] It is not surprising that the Delaware effect particularly caught the attention of commentators in those legal orders that (i) adhere to the 'incorporation' theory, whilst (ii) their domestic company law is strictly regulated (e.g. the Netherlands). van den Braak/Huiskes (1992) 1165; Brood (1989); Debets (1987); and van Velzen (1995). For detailed information, see ch 4 II 1, below. Contrary to the development in the Netherlands, in the United Kingdom, which after all is an 'incorporation' country too, relatively little attention is given to the Delaware effect: the second condition (notably as regards the *private* limited company) appears not to be fulfilled in the company law of the United Kingdom.

[49] Note that pursuant to s. 351 of the Delaware General Corporation Law ('management by stockholders') shareholders can operate as managing directors. By virtue of subs (3) 'the stockholders of the corporation shall be subject to all liabilities of the directors'. But under the circumstances, it will be difficult to trace them without the assistance of the Secretary of State. Cf. however Carey/Eisenberg (1995) 737 et seq., with reference to the duties of controlling shareholders.

[50] cf. however, recent important legislative restrictions to the 'incorporation' theory in the Netherlands, ch 4 II 1, below.

[51] Drury (1998) 186, speaks of 'business proprietors seeking a benign jurisdiction in which to incorporate their enterprise'.

[52] This economically biased policy was explicitly put forward in both the Netherlands (ch 4 II 1) and Switzerland (ch 4 II 3). Italy took another position: the same policy was adhered to, but without being prepared to be at the mercy of these foreign investors. This resulted in a *sui generis* approach: see ch 4 III 3 below.

of diligence but of laxity'.[53] On the other hand, it has been shown that many legal orders, while balancing the costs and benefits to society, stick to stringent formation and capital requirements, accounting and auditing standards, and worker co-determination.[54] As will be seen, it even happens that well known 'incorporation' countries put an end to excessive use, or even abuse, of the 'incorporation' theory.

II. RECONCILIATORY ATTEMPTS: DOCTRINE AND CASE-LAW

1. THE *DIFFERENZIERUNG* CONCEPT

Combining the best of both worlds

One may safely conclude from the foregoing that in their purest form, both theories on the recognition of foreign legal persons stand for an all-or-nothing choice.[55] In other words, one single legal system should govern all company law issues. As Rabel put it: 'The essential incidents of the activities of any legal entity are controlled by one municipal law, a single ubiquitous personal law, parallel to the statute personal of individuals. (. . .) This law governs existence, capacity, internal structure, external legal relations, modifications of the charter and dissolution of the legal entity'.[56] Managers of foreign companies are thus either given total freedom to choose the proper law of the company ('incorporation' theory), no matter which links exist between the company and the *lex societatis*, or they are submitted to the relentless principle that a company is governed by the law of the country on whose territory it has its central management and control office. If the latter principle applies, businessmen can only avoid

---

[53] *Louis K. Ligget Co. v J.M. Lee*, 288 US 517 (1933), 77 L ed. 3, 558 et seq.

[54] As a consequence of the fact that worker co-determination is highly controversial, the draft proposal for a *Societas Europea* appears to have been in a dark alley for nearly three decades now: not for the first time, the Davignon Committee tried to reanimate this project in May 1997. Subsequently, under the chairmanship of Luxembourg, a draft proposal for a Directive was elaborated. That proposal established a link between the 'European Company' and the European Works Council on the basis of Directive 94/45 EC. But the opposing views do not seem to have undergone drastic changes since 1972. Once more, even the combination of an optional application of a *Societas Europea* and several 'menus' as regards the co-determination regime, could not count on all member states. For more detailed information, see *inter alia* Winter (1998) 14 et seq.

[55] As will be seen, it is much easier to restrict the 'incorporation' theory without giving up its core concept, than to adjust the 'real seat' theory without losing its essence. See ch 4 II 1, below. Cf. however ch 2 IV 2 (ECJ *Centros*).

[56] Rabel (1960), vol. II, 3. Drury (1998) 168, ironically adds that '(w)hile most states agree on the desirability of (. . .) a single municipal law, there is little agreement on the selection of the connecting factor which links a company to a particular legal system'.

personal liabilities by opting for one of the types of legal person envisaged by the law of the country on whose territory they operate.

For a considerable time, doctrinal attempts were undertaken to drive proponents of the two opposing theories towards reconciliation. As a consequence of the fact that it is impossible for two extremes to meet, learned writers were more or less forced to give up the principle of one single proper law governing all matters of company law relationships. The well known attempts at reconciliation are briefly considered next.

The concept of *Differenzierung*

Grasmann, who is considered to be the *auctor intellectualis* of the *Differenzierungslehre*,[57] advocated a splitting of the proper law of the company, such that company law matters should no longer be decided according to a single proper law. He introduced a threefold company law conflict rule. In his opinion, the following conflict rules are constantly competing: the *Vornahmestatut* (the *lex loci actus*, or law of the country on whose territory the company organs conduct activities), the *lex causae* (the law governing transactions between the company and third parties) and, finally, the *lex societatis* (the law according to which the company is established). None of these conflict rules must be given decisive weight in advance. Instead, the applicable law is to be found on the basis of a case-by-case approach, in which emphasis is placed on the specific needs of the commercial business world, in particular the protection of third parties entering into business transactions with the company. Case-by-case, decisive weight should be given to the conflict rule, which alternatively favours the business world or third party protection. Affairs regarded as purely internal are, for example, the company's formation, the rights and duties of the company's organs and its members, and the dissolution and winding up of the company. Obviously, these matters are likely to fall within the material scope of the *lex societatis*, the outside world not being affected at all. It is, however, more complex to submit external affairs to one of the remaining two conflict rules. Representation and capital protection, for example, are deemed to be subject to the *lex loci actus*. If doubts exist as to whether the topic under discussion should be regarded as external or internal, the various interests at stake should be examined. As far as the legal status or capacity of the company is concerned, two situations are to be clearly distinguished: the company is deemed to be subject to the *lex loci actus* if the company has legal capacity under that system of law but not under the *lex societatis*; vice versa, the legal capacity attributed to the company by the law under which it is incorporated remains unaffected when the company

---

[57] Grasmann (1970). See further, Ebenroth/Bippus (JZ, 1988) 677 et seq.

lacks legal capacity under any other proper law. This combined test clearly best suits the business world's interests.

Criticism

Not surprisingly, Grasmann's theory met with disapproval.[58] First, the distinction between 'internal' and 'external' affairs may turn out to be highly artifical. One complaint often heard is that gathering capital in order to create a company's fund involves both internal and external company matters. Furthermore, it is confusing for the outside world to find that the company is subject to several proper laws, none of which, however, can be presumed to apply. Remedies for these problems cannot be expected to emanate from substantive law notions.

2. The *Überlagerung* concept

Basic concept

The *Differenzierungstheorie* and the concept of *Überlagerung* were both elaborated by German scholars. Like Grasmann, Sandrock[59] defended the view that the principle of a single proper law governing all company matters should be set aside.[60] Unlike the *Differenzierungstheorie*, however, the *Überlagerungstheorie* prescribes the alternative application of either the 'incorporation' theory or the 'real seat' theory in advance.[61] Formation matters are governed by the law of incorporation. So are other issues regarding external company law relationships. However, if companies do not have their real seat in the country where the company is established, company creditors, shareholders, and other third parties can occasionally rely on the application of mandatory law provisions of the country where the company's real seat is situated. Like the *Differenzierungstheorie*, several systems of law may apply; contrary to the first theory, however, there is

---

[58] Grasmann's theory is now considered obsolete, so it will not be dealt with extensively. The *Differenzierungslehre* was commented on by *inter alia* Rabel (1960) and Sandrock (1989); see also, from the German angle, ch 4 III 1, below. From a Dutch perspective, cf. Coenen and Vlas, referred to in ch 4 II 1, below.

[59] Sandrock (1978). The general concept of this theory was taken from US federal law. For further notice and comments, Großfeld/König (1992) 436; and Sack (1990) 353 et seq.

[60] Neither is there good reason to stick adamantly to the concept of a single nationality (see I 3, above) attaching to the legal person throughout its lifetime: Sandrock (1989) 512.

[61] A theory developed by the Dutch scholar Vlas (1982) 62 et seq., should be mentioned briefly here. This theory of the *maatschappelijke prioriteit* (the principle of social priority) contains elements of both Sandrock's *Überlagerung* concept and the general private international law concept of mandatory law provisions. Since the theory elaborated by Vlas directly influenced Dutch law, it is set out in ch 4 II 1, below.

no room for a *cumulation* of applicable laws to the issue at stake.[62] It has been said that German courts were inspired by Sandrock's concept of *Überlagerung*, while taking account of the draft EC Convention on the Mutual Recognition of Companies.[63] In addition, attempts were made to place this theory at the heart of article 56 of the EC Treaty.[64] Furthermore, remnants of this theory can allegedly be found in the Netherlands, because this legal order recently adjusted the 'incorporation' theory to accommodate the goal of combating the abuse of foreign companies.[65] The *auctor intellectualis* of the *Überlagerung* concept concludes from the ECJ decision in *Centros*[66] that the ECJ is shifting towards the acceptance of that theory.[67]

Criticism

Like other theories which try to combine the best of both worlds, Sandrock's theory has been condemned for creating a *Normenmix*[68] at the cost of predictability and legal certainty.[69] Moreover, judgments as to which substantive law provisions should be regarded as mandatory, and therefore capable of setting aside the law of the 'Incorporation' country, are at best highly arbitrary. Even the search for a single proper law of the company will lead to demarcation problems (see Part 2 below). It will only be possible to ascertain the precise scope of the proper law of the company after a thorough examination of borderline cases.

3. 'DELAWARE' AND 'PRO-FORMA FOREIGN' COMPANIES

It would be wrong to think that the 'real seat' countries are only worried about foreign undertakings settling on their territory. Those legal orders which adopt the 'incorporation' theory may feel an even stronger urge to

---

[62] In this respect, the 'Überlagerung' concept can be compared to the 'Kombinations-theorie' which was elaborated by Zimmer, commented on by Behrens (1999) 324: the 'incorporation' theory should be applied to those companies having real ties with the 'Incorporation' country. Pro-forma foreign companies, however, should be submitted to the 'Real Seat' theory.

[63] e.g. KG Berlin, *RIW* 1990, p. 496, commented by Großfeld/König (1992) 436. See for further information, ch 2 IV 1, below.

[64] Ch 2 II 1, below.   [65] Ch 4 II 1 below.

[66] Case C–212/97; [1999] CMLR 551.   [67] Sandrock (1999) 1337 et seq. See IV 2, below.

[68] Großfeld/König (1992) 436. Cf. Ebenroth/Einsele (1988) 217 et seq., comparing the legal practice of the United States of America with Germany. Sack (1990) 356, predicts a better future for the concept of *Überlagerung*, claiming that it would be more feasible if the paramount controversies between substantive company law of the member states were to diminish. But this seems to be wishful thinking. For a comparison of Sandrock's *Überlagerungstheorie* and the doctrine of social priority elaborated by the Dutch scholar Vlas, see ch 4 II 1, below.

[69] What has been said above about the *Differenzierungstheorie* also applies generally to Sandrock's *Überlagerungstheorie*.

combat the abuse of a host state's 'generosity'. Long before 'European' attempts to restrict abuse of foreign companies were undertaken,[70] American courts had already confronted the 'Delaware syndrome'. Although, under the 'incorporation' theory the law of the state of incorporation basically applies to all company law issues, there are exceptions to the rule. This was illustrated by the case of *Western Airlines Inc. v Sobieski*, decided by the Californian Court of Appeal.[71] Western Airlines, a company incorporated in Delaware, took over the shares of a California corporation by way of a share exchange. The corporation did more business in California than in any other state, and apparently did none in Delaware.[72] However, under California's Blue Sky law a permit was required from the State Corporations Commissioner. The Californian Court held that this law should be enforced, at least for the benefit of the California stockholders.[73] Local law provisions can thus frustrate the incorporation statute and restrict liberal policies.[74] Although in quite a different manner, legal orders in Europe also 'considered the relative merits of the place of incorporation and real seat theories, and changed (their) rules in consequence',[75] as will be seen.

III. RECONCILIATORY ATTEMPTS: PRIVATE INTERNATIONAL LAW

1. THE 1956 DRAFT TREATY OF THE HAGUE CONFERENCE ON THE MUTUAL RECOGNITION OF THE LEGAL PERSONALITY OF COMPANIES

So far, both the 'incorporation' theory and the 'real seat' theory have been set forth in bilateral[76] and multilateral (draft) conventions. Notably, multilateral conventions are of a compromisory nature: they usually reflect the struggle to combine the best of both worlds by trying to reconcile gaps

---

[70] See below.

[71] *Western Airlines Inc. v Sobieski*, 191 Cal.App. 2d399, 12 Cal.Rprt 719 (1961), and cases quoted by Drury (1998) 171.

[72] For parallels between this case and the Dutch Bill of Parliament of 1 January 1998 concerning the *Wet puur formeel buitenlandse vennootschappen* (Pro-Forma Foreign Companies Act) see ch 4 II 1, below.

[73] Drury (1998) 171, quoting R. Leflar, who is of the opinion that the virtue of having internal corporate affairs settled by one single law, for the sake of unity of operation, is evident, but it is hard to see why Delaware should have any better claim to dominance, on facts such as these, than California.

[74] See Drury (1998) 188 et seq.

[75] ibid. More detail below, in ch 4 II 1 (Netherlands) and II 3 (Switzerland). From a European point of view (Single Market), see ch 6 II 1, below.

[76] Since bilateral conventions are closely connected with the legal orders involved, they receive special treatment in Part 2 below, on comparative law. Where there are ramifications at European law level, this is noted.

which may be unbridgeable. To date, only one attempt appears to have been fruitful.[77] Other projects are no longer expected to become law. Nor are they regularly applied on an anticipatory basis by national courts.[78] For this reason, they are not dealt with extensively here.

The European Community dates back to the mid-1950s. During the same era, the Hague Conference on Private International Law elaborated a draft treaty on the mutual recognition of the legal personality of companies.[79] The main motive behind this could have been: 'we have chosen not to choose'.[80]

Pursuant to the Treaty regime, 'recognition' of a foreign company should be understood in a narrow sense: it means only that the foreign company is to be considered as a legal subject, i.e. a bearer of rights and duties. Nothing was said yet about the proper law of the company: the law applicable to company law matters would still have to be ascertained.[81]

It seems that the draft treaty firmly establishes the 'incorporation' theory (article 1), although this conflict rule is immediately followed by a 'corrective' provision in article 2: a contracting state whose law has adopted the 'real seat' theory may not recognize a company's legal personality if its real seat is situated in the territory of that state or in another contracting state adhering to the 'real seat' theory.

It is also interesting that, in spite of the fact that the Convention as such never entered into force,[82] the 'implementation' bill was passed by the Dutch Parliament. According to this bill, 'the Netherlands is not a country whose law recognises the *siège réel* as defined in article 2 of (the draft of the Hague Treaty)'.[83]

---

[77] The European Convention on the Recognition of the Legal Personality of International Non-governmental Organisations (Strasbourg) of 24 April 1986, cf. European Treaty Series nr. 124, which was elaborated under the auspices of the Council of Europe. Date of entry into force: 1 January 1991. Without any reservations, this Treaty pays homage to the 'incorporation' theory (art. 2). Once a company is endowed with legal personality in the country of its registered office, this legal personality is recognized in all contracting states (Belgium, Greece, Austria, Portugal, Slovenia, the United Kingdom, and Switzerland).

[78] See ch. 4 below. There are, however, exceptions to the rule: see IV 1, below.

[79] *Actes et documents de la Septième Session*, 367–71. According to art. 11 of the Treaty, eleven ratifications of the Contracting States were required. As a matter of fact, only the Netherlands, Belgium, and France ratified. See for further references *i.a.* Henriquez (1961); Hoogstraten, (1967) III; Vlas (1982) 85; and, from retrospective point of view, (1999) 14; and Wouters (1996/97) 583 et seq. For a comparative analysis of the draft treaty of the Hague conference and its EC counterpart, see IV 1, below.

[80] Philip (1956) 327. This motif preceding the chapter on the draft treaties of the Hague conference and the EC, was quoted by Vlas (1982) 85.

[81] See I 2, above, The 'minimum' concept also follows from the fact that, under the Treaty, the contracting states remain free to restrict the rights of foreign companies on condition that the *ius standi in iudicio* is not infringed (draft art. 5).

[82] See the remark made by Drury (1998) 182, that this Convention is currently 'gathering dust'.

[83] It would, however, be incorrect to conclude from this implementation bill that the Dutch courts voluntarily applied the entire set of conflict rules of the draft Hague

IV. RECONCILIATORY ATTEMPTS: EC LAW

1. EC TREATY EX ARTICLES 52, 58, AND 220

Hidden conflict rules: non-discrimination

As regards mutual recognition of foreign companies in the EU, there is a close relationship between EC law and private international law. This is demonstrated by the fact that the question was raised, whether a *versteckte* (hidden) *European* conflict rule could be found beneath the surface of article 58.[84] The first paragraph of this provision clearly reveals the well known conflicting theories concerning companies:

(1) Companies or firms formed in accordance with the law of a Member State and having their *registered office, central administration or principal place of business* within the Community shall, for the purpose of this Chapter, be treated in the same way as natural persons who are nationals of Member States.

This relationship prompted writers to ask whether or not the 'discriminatory' 'real seat' theory should be condemned under the EC Treaty.[85] However, this should not be concluded too hastily: just because this theory is less hospitable to foreign companies than the 'incorporation' theory does not mean that the 'real seat' theory is in itself 'discriminatory'. Foreign and domestic companies are subjected to identical rules under the 'real seat' theory.[86] All companies should comply with the substantive company law of the state on whose territory their management and control office is located: in other words, all companies are expected to have their real seat in the territory of the state according to whose law they are established. This is so, regardless of the legal order—domestic or foreign—from which the company originates.[87] Therefore, if the 'real seat' theory is not discriminatory, the next question is whether the 'real seat' theory possibly forms a non-discriminatory restriction, incompatible for other reasons with the EC Treaty. Pursuant to a cross-border seat transfer, the company has to give up its 'nationality' (i.e. *lex societatis*) and accept the 'nationality' of another

Treaty. Compared to the Treaty, the Dutch bill merely took a relatively firm position with regard to one of the existing recognition theories. For the legal consequences of the unilateral conflict approach chosen by the Dutch legislator before the 1998 CLC Act entered into force, see in detail Rammeloo (1995) 53, and ch 4 II 1, below.

[84] cf. Sandrock/Austmann (1989) 250. The existence of these conflict rules beneath the surface of arts. 52 and 58 is denied by de Wulf (1999) 321. This matter is considered further in IV 2, below.

[85] In this respect, reference is often made to Behrens (1988) 499 et seq.

[86] ibid., underlining that the real seat conflict rule does not differentiate between 'domestic' and 'foreign' companies but is applied 'allseitig' (on a mutual basis).

[87] ibid., 518.

member state adhering to the 'real seat' doctrine, therefore a conflict arises and this has been criticized more than once.[88]

Equal treatment of natural and legal persons

According to another view the freedom of establishment of legal persons in other EC member states is already accomplished. To start with, article 52 reflects the dynamic process which is expected ultimately to culminate in the accomplishment of the Single Market:

(1) Within the framework of the provisions set out below, restrictions on the freedom of establishment of nationals of a Member State in the territory of another Member State shall be abolished by progressive stages in the course of the transnational period. Such progressive abolition shall also apply to restrictions on the setting up of agencies, branches or subsidiaries by nationals of any Member State established in the territory of any Member State.
(2) Freedom of establishment shall include the right to take up and pursue activities as self-employed persons and to set up and manage undertakings, in particular companies or firms within the meaning of article 58, under the conditions laid down for its own nationals by the law of the country where such establishment is effected, subject to the provisions of the Chapter relating to capital.

Article 52 must be read in conjunction with article 58, which states:

(1) Companies or firms formed in accordance with the law of a Member State and having their registered office, central administration or principal place of business within the Community shall, for the purpose of this Chapter, be treated in the same way as natural persons who are nationals of Member States.
(2) 'Companies or firms' means companies or firms constituted under civil or commercial law, including co-operative societies, and other legal persons governed by public or private law, save for those which are non-profit making.

An appropriate starting point for debate would be that once a company is duly formed in accordance with the law of an EC member state, its existence is no longer doubted: the *ideelle Zielrichtung* (i.e. the policy)[89] allegedly underlying the EC Treaty at least presupposes a 'minimum' recognition. However, prior to the definition of the precise extent of freedom offered to legal persons under the articles 52 and 58,[90] it is necessary

---

[88] Behrens (1988) takes the view that this hostile attitude cannot be justified by simply referring to the 'neutral' character of the 'real seat' doctrine. This complaint often appears in writings on European law and conflict of laws; more detail in IV 2 and, from a national law perspective, ch 4 III 1, below. (Germany, a special position is taken by *inter alia* Roth). The discussion also influences attempts to regulate intra-community seat transfers: ch 6 III, below.

[89] Eyles (1990) 96.

[90] It is highly questionable whether this is possible. Eyles (1990) 84, underscores that over the past four decades the literal wording of these provisions was never amended. Arts. 52 and 58 should therefore be interpreted against a dynamic background of a rapidly developing Single Market. Behrens (1988) 508, wonders what the precise reach of art. 52 is: does it merely

to examine the anthropomorphic approach to companies,[91] in the sense that parallels are frequently sought between *natural* and *legal* persons[92] and the troublesome concept of 'nationality'. Does the EC Treaty treat companies as if they were natural persons, considering that the fundamental principle of freedom of establishment applies to both natural persons ('nationals') and legal persons (undertakings, in particular 'companies or firms') of the member states?

Although this analogous reasoning may seem attractive at first glance, natural persons can for several reasons hardly be compared to their legal counterparts. The private international law concept of endowing companies with a 'nationality' carries intrinsic flaws.[93] This concept is not suited to designating the 'close connection' between companies and EC member states: it is not the 'nationality' which concerns the authorities, but the rights—more precisely, the right of establishment—conferred upon such 'European' companies.[94] Furthermore, it cannot be ignored that from a political point of view the 'nationality' of foreign companies, i.e. their recognition, is also a delicate matter because it can be used either to attract or chase off foreign investors.[95] Last but not least, cross-border company relationships would be severely hampered by a fundamental divergence between civil law and common law: as Clarke put it, 'in company law, questions raising conflicts of law points are concerned primarily with the *three* key concepts of nationality, domicile and residence'.[96] Nevertheless, the drafters of the EC Treaty never gave in to those who advocated the

prohibit discriminatory treatment, or does it also affect non-discriminatory restrictions which potentially affect the freedom of establishment? Although the notion of 'discrimination' was interpreted in a broad sense by the ECJ, Behrens reaches the conclusion that, contrary to the area of 'services', non-discriminatory restrictions fall outside the scope of art. 52.

[91] Clarke (1991) 162, *i.a.* refers to the 'birth and death' of legal persons under UK law, p. 168. Cf. ch 4 II 2, below.

[92] Behrens (1988) 498 et seq. for further general information.

[93] At present, the 'nationality' of a company as decisive factor in private international law is considered as obsolete in most legal orders. Cf. its relative durability in French private international law (combination of the *siège social* of the company and the *nationalité des personnes morales*): ch 4 III 2, below.

[94] Wouters (1996/97) 126, quoting Y. Loussouarn: *'Le problème dit de la "nationalité" des sociétés se présente rarement à l'état pur. Il est toujours posé soit à propos d'un problème de conflits des lois, soit d'un problème de jouissance des droits. On recherche en effet le lien d'allégeance unissant la société à un Etat déterminé, soit pour découvrir quelle est la loi qui doit la régir, soit pour préciser si elle doit bénéficier sur le territoire d'un pays des droits dont la jouissance est réservée aux nationaux et qui sont de ce fait, refusés aux sociétés étrangères comme aux personnes physiques étrangères'* Rev.Tr.Dr.Comm 1959 246.

[95] cf. the opposing industrial policies of the Netherlands, attempting to turn post-war agricultural society into a modern industrialized nation by welcoming foreign investors (ch 4 II 1 below) and the more hesitant attitude of France: Wouters (1996/97) 127. More detail in ch 4 III 2, below.

[96] Clarke (1991) 161.

insertion of the 'control theory'[97] into article 58.[98] As a compromise, secondary establishment should be real and genuine: article 52 requires 'agencies, branches or subsidiaries by nationals of any Member State' to be 'established in the territory of any Member State'. The setting up and, in particular, the registration of branches of a company duly formed in accordance with the law of another member state, although it conducts no business in that member state, nevertheless gave rise to countervailing measures by national authorities.[99]

Registered office, central administration, or principal place of business

Leaving the problematic parallels between natural and legal 'nationals' behind, a superficial reading of article 58 inspires optimism: it prescribes that as long as (i) 'companies or firms (are) formed in accordance with the law of a member state and (ii) (have) their registered office, central administration *or* principal place of business within the Community'[100] in order to (iii) pursue business activities, then those companies should be treated in the same manner as natural persons who are nationals of member states. Many writers agree that the factors contained in article 58 offer a margin of manouevrability to companies; it is not necessary that both the

[97] This notion, particularly underlying the 'real seat' doctrine, was explained in ch 2 I, above. Consequently, authorities of the member states must refrain from making use of this instrument. If not, they violate the non-discrimination provision of art. 52 of the EC Treaty.

[98] cf. Eyles (1990) 88 et seq., who dissents from Bleckmann. The latter rejects the freedom of establishment for natural persons from non-EC countries, participating in capital companies that have their seat on 'European' territory. Wouters (1996/97) 127, observes that initially, a French–Italian proposal added a third subs to art. 58, allowing member states to refuse freedom of establishment to companies that were *'soumises à une influence prépondérante exercée par des ressortissants d'un Etat tiers ou des capitaux étrangères à la Communauté'*. Wouters 129, however, underpins the importance of an open market, accessible to investors from non-EC countries (e.g. Japan, USA), as these market players also contribute to a prospering European market. In a comparable sense Eyles (1990) 89, 90, preferring a clear-cut distinction between the company and its managing directors. He admits, however, that it is not certain whether these 'third-country directors', like their counterparts from EC countries, should benefit from e.g. sickness benefits under art. 52 of the Treaty (cf. the *Segers* judgment, IV 2, below). This is a logical consequence of the *Nebeneinander veschiedener Rechtsträger* (the co-existence of natural and legal persons as beneficiaries of different rights under the EC Treaty).

[99] See IV 2, below.

[100] Emphasis added. These connecting factors reflect the two theories on the recognition of foreign companies. The third notion even explicitly pays tribute to the Italian concept of *l'ogetto principale dell'impresa*, as laid down in art. 25 of the 1995 Code on Private International Law: ch 4 III 3, below. Edwards (1999) 339, observes that '(t)hese three alternative requirements have been interpreted by some commentators as abandoning the real seat theory in favour of the incorporation theory on the basis that, since the three requirements are alternative and have equal weight, a company with its registered office but not its real seat in the Community would fall within the definition. (. . .) It seems likely that the alternatives were included to satisfy all Member States, whichever theory they applied, rather than a view endorsing one of the prevailing theories at the expense of the other.'

company's incorporation seat *and* its real seat (i.e. central administration or principal place of business) are situated on EC territory.[101] Freedom of establishment comprises both the right to conduct business in a member state, entailing the right to primary establishment, and the right to set up agencies, branches, or subsidiaries (secondary establishments) for companies settled in an EC member state already.[102] These branches may, however, engender problems of their own: how should foreign companies, which claim freedom of *secondary* establishment, by setting up a branch in the territory of an EC member state, while this bogus 'branch' is nothing but the company's headquarters, be dealt with?[103]

Companies or firms

The impression might arise that founders of a company are free to choose their 'favourite' company form, as long as this form is provided for under the law of *one* of the EU member states.[104] Then, no other conclusion would be justified than that after a battle of many decades the 'incorporation' theory (which would undeniably best meet the goal of accomplishing the Single Market) has driven the 'real seat' theory out of the EC Treaty. Moreover, article 58 is drafted extremely widely ('companies *or firms*'[105]). But it is precisely this wide scope which hides irreconcilable concepts and causes problems.[106] To date, there is no case-law from the European Court

[101] See Wouters (1996/97) 147 et seq., with further notice. The liberal attitude of the Treaty towards companies having only their *registered* office within the EC met with notable criticism, cf. Loussouarn and Everling, quoted by Wouters 149. This kind of 'freedom' should, however, not be overestimated: first, freedom of establishment can hardly be profited from if the real seat is not on the territory of one of the other EC member states; secondly, the risk of fraud is reduced to a large extent, if one takes into account that most member states adhere to the 'real seat' theory.

[102] Primary establishment (*Hauptniederlassung; établissement principal*) and secondary establishment (*sekundäre/abgeleitete Niederlassung; établissement secondaire*). These rights were further elaborated by the General Programme for the abolition of restrictions on freedom of establishment of 1960, OJ English Special Edition, Second Series IX, 7. According to this Programme, the right to set up agencies, branches, or subsidiaries only exists in so far as their activity shows a genuine and continuous link with the economy of a member state. Detail in Eyles (1990) 38 et seq., with further notice, and the opinion of Advocate General La Pergola in ECJ *Centros*: Case C–212/97 [1999] ECR I–1459. (See IV 2, below.)

[103] Described by Sonnenberger/Großerichter (1999) 730, as companies 'coming in through the back door'. Cf. the debate on ECJ *Centros*.

[104] The words 'registered office, central administration *or* principal place of business within the Community' suggest a considerable amount of freedom of choice for those establishing a company. This view was defended three decades ago by, *inter alia*, Drobnig, (1966/67) 117; and Koppensteiner (1971), commented on by Behrens (1988) 501. More recently, Timmermans (1984) 38 et seq. and the ECJ *Segers* judgment, see IV 2, below.

[105] Emphasis added.

[106] cf. Edwards (1999) 338 et seq. Wouters (1996/97) 30 et seq., points at what has been described as the '*manque (. . .) de rigueur terminologique*' of art. 58. Apparently, art. 58 was the result of mere compromising. He advocates an extensive interpretation of art. 58, as a result of which all entities classified as companies and firms under their national law are

of Justice concerning the precise scope of article 58(2). It is noteworthy that the expression 'companies or firms' more or less envisaged the companies and firms provided under the law of the—initially six—civil law member states, whilst common law notions were left out of the debate at that time. The equivalents of 'companies and firms' mentioned are therefore by no means to be considered as representative in today's context.[107]

Primary establishment: 'recognition'

It cannot be denied that doctrine also provoked optimism. At the dawn of the EC era, the extended scope of article 58 had already raised the question whether the recognition debate was made redundant by the provisions of articles 52 and 58. Some authors took the view that it would be highly contradictory to create a far-reaching freedom of establishment which would later be made subject to (national) private international law rules concerning the recognition of companies duly formed in another member state.[108] Others emphasized that articles 52 and 58 must be considered merely as 'programme' provisions, which outline a general policy direction, rather than as a direct basis of rights for (physical or legal) individuals.[109] Is it, though, reasonable to conclude that article 58 imposes the 'Incorporation'

considered as beneficiaries of said provision. In the case of a lack of legal personality or even capacity, the question how such an entity should be able to enjoy the freedom of establishment must be answered by the proper law of the company. Semi-public (non)-profitable organizations belong to a special subcategory. On the *'organismes d'intérêt public'* and the *'économie sociale'*, see Wouters (1996/97) 72, with detailed information. According to Richards (1991) 3, this is a 'rather grey area'.

[107] cf. the pattern characteristic of the Swiss Federal Code on Private International Law, ch 4 II 3, below. Since this monograph concentrates on the recognition of foreign capital companies, I refer to Wouters (1996/97) 31, 61 et seq., for detailed information on this subject. He argues that, in conformity with the ECJ case-law on free movement in other areas, a non-restrictive approach should be taken as the point of departure for further debate, since one of the fundamental Treaty provisions is at stake.

[108] cf. Wouters (1996/97 579 et seq., *i.a.* quoting Beitzke, Everling, and Loussouarn. Others shared this liberal view: cf. Drobnig (1966/67) 117; Koppensteiner (1971), noticed by Behrens (1988) 501; and Timmermans (1984) 38 et seq. It must not be overlooked, though, that the expression 'recognition' provokes misinterpretations, as it may cover various concepts: a 'maximal' concept (i.e. including the applicability of the foreign *lex societatis*), or a 'minimal' concept (meaning that a foreign company is considered to be a legal subject, i.e. a bearer of rights and duties, the *lex societatis* however not yet being decided over). Whereas Beitzke (referred to by Wouters (1996/7) 579 et seq.) speaks of companies having the right to 'conclude contracts' or to 'appear before Courts', it is conceivable that 'recognition' is used here in a 'minimal' sense. Cf. the relationship between arts. 58 and 220 of the Treaty, below.

[109] cf. Wiedemann and Staudinger-Großfeld, quoted by Behrens (1988) 501. Note, however, the end of the transition period (1 Jan. 1970) and the ECJ judgment in Case 2/74 (*Reyners*), on the basis of which art. 52 was given direct effect: from that time on, individuals could invoke this provision in (national) court proceedings. Großfeld (1986) 352, and Ebke (1987) 250, however, took the view that art. 58 still requires a *sui generis* approach. Behrens believes that, since art. 52 is no longer to be understood as a mere *Programmsatz*, it is no longer certain that harmonization of company law is a *sine qua non* for the recognition of companies from other member states.

theory on all member states at the expense of the 'real seat' theory? In subsequent ECJ judgments, this view has occasionally been sustained.[110]

It should then be asked whether the conclusion that article 52 in conjunction with article 58 of the EC Treaty prohibit member states from applying the 'real seat' theory is incompatible with another Treaty provision. Article 220 obliges member states to enter 'as far as necessary' into further negotiations on *inter alia* the following company law subjects: (i) the *mutual recognition of companies or firms within the meaning of the second paragraph of article 58;* (ii) the retention of legal personality in the event of transfer of their seat from one country to another; and (iii) the possibility of mergers between companies or firms governed by the law of different countries.[111] Like their fellow private international law researchers, European law specialists adopted distinctions: they took the view that the word 'recognition' in article 220 means 'minimum' recognition, so that a foreign company is considered to be a legal subject, i.e. a bearer of rights and duties, although its *lex societatis* is not established.[112] In this context, it is understandable that this 'minimum' recognition concept also concerned the drafters of the EC Treaty, in the sense that they had an eye to the private international law concept of the nineteenth century: legal persons are after all 'constructions' of the human mind which need explicit 'recognition' from (foreign) authorities.[113] Nowadays, the mere existence of foreign companies is beyond debate, and this preliminary matter of recognition is absorbed by the conflict of law rules prescribing either the 'real seat' or the 'incorporation' theory. As will be seen, however, all efforts to accord recognition to at least the companies of other member states in 'Europe' have so far not been very successful.[114] Neither are businessmen entitled to derive any rights directly from article 220.[115] This may

---

[110] e.g. Behrens (1988) 501 and Timmermans (1984) 39, took the view that the 'real seat' doctrine infringes upon the freedom of establishment as provided for under arts. 52 and 58. A conclusive answer can only be given after thorough examination of ECJ case-law, IV 2, below. Drobnig (1990) 191, is surprised by the fact that especially German doctrine was troubled by uncertainty as to whether arts. 52 and 58 contain a (hidden) conflict of law rule; other member states' commentators have remained silent on this subject.

[111] Emphasis added.

[112] Private international law specialists were also troubled by this confusing concept: see I 2, above. Wouters (1996/97) 573, 579, quotes G. Beitzke, who in his capacity as an official reporter underscored that, in spite of the fact that the fundamental duty to recognize companies from other Member States had been the central premise, the drafters of the Treaty cautiously inserted in art. 220 the obligation to negotiate further on this subject, in that it prescribes these negotiations 'as far as (they are) necessary', Bonn 1962, 4958/IV/62-N, 48 et seq. Drobnig (1990) 186, concludes from this assertion that art. 220 is nothing more than a 'Programmsatz, und dazu noch ein bedingter'.

[113] ibid. 189. Cf. the historical private international law developments in e.g. the Netherlands, ch 4 II 1 below (notably the *Moguntia* case), and France, ch 4 III 2, below (notably the 1857 Act, concerning recognition by *décret*).

[114] IV 1, below.

have worried few people at the beginning of the EC era, because in those days all member states still adhered to the 'real seat' theory.[116] However, today more than ever, the need to find an answer to this problem is increasing.[117]

Secondary establishment

The EC Treaty contains an explicit provision concerning secondary establishments: pursuant to article 52, first paragraph of the Treaty, this right comprises the 'setting up of agencies, branches or subsidiaries by nationals of any Member State established in the territory of any Member State'.[118] Although the Treaty does not define these three concepts, there is a certain *communis opinio*: whereas a 'subsidiary'[119] is an entity having legal personality distinguishable from the legal personality of the parent company, a 'branch' is an 'office' forming part of the legal entity of the principal establishment of the company.[120] The only difference between a 'branch'[121] and an 'agency'[122] is that the managers of a branch have a more dependent status. In this respect, the European Court of Justice observed that 'when the grantee of an exclusive sales concession is subject neither to the control nor to the direction of the grantor, he cannot be regarded as being at the head of a branch, agency or other establishment of the grantor within the meaning of article 5(5)' of the Brussels Convention on

---

[115] Case 137/84 *Ministère Public v Mutsch* [1985] ECR 2681. Formerly, German scholars paid attention to the scope of art. 220 in relation to art. 58: whereas e.g. Behrens (1988) 506, argued that art. 220 had been countered by the liberal wording of art. 58, others, e.g. Ebenroth/Eyles (1988) 12, Ebke (1987) 245, and Großfeld (1986) 351, took the opposite view: that the 'real seat' doctrine was not affected by the EC Treaty.

[116] As far as Dutch law is concerned, it was unclear whether, prior to the 1959 Implementation Act (*Uitvoeringswet*) which accompanied the 1956 (draft) Treaty of the Hague Conference on the Mutual Recognition of Companies, the 'incorporation' theory was adhered to already: cf. Rammeloo (1995) 52 and ch 4 II 1, below. Furthermore, not until 1973 did other 'incorporation' countries (the United Kingdom and the Republic of Ireland) join the EC.

[117] At present, at least three member states—the United Kingdom, the Netherlands, and Ireland—apply the 'incorporation' theory. The Scandinavian countries (Denmark, Finland, and Sweden) also apply a species of the 'incorporation' theory: cf. Wouters (1996/97) 599 for further information. Furthermore, the urge to solve this problem has grown, now that the Single Market is in a far more progressive stage than four decades ago.

[118] cf. *i.a.* Eyles (1990) 38 et seq., 101 et seq.; Wouters (1995) 103; and (1996/97) 191 et seq., with detailed information.

[119] French: *filiale*; German: *Tochtergesellschaft*; Italian: *filiale*; Dutch: *dochtervennootschap*. A parent company and its subsidiary are mutually linked by control of the former over the latter. The descriptions and criteria laid down in the Seventh Council Directive on consolidated accounts are often referred to. 'Control' implies e.g. (a majority of) voting rights in the subsidiary, the right to appoint or dismiss directors thereof, etc.

[120] cf. the corresponding opinion of the Advocate General La Pergola on ECJ *Centros*, Case C–212/97 [1999] ECR I–1459; *CMLR* (1999) 566 et seq. and IV 2, below.

[121] cf. French: *succursale*; German: *Zweigniederlassung*; Italian: *succursale*; Dutch: *bijkantoor*.

[122] cf. French: *agence*; German: *Agentur*; Italian: *agenzia*; Dutch: *agentschap*.

Jurisdiction and Recognition and Enforcement of Foreign Judgments in Civil and Commercial Matters.[123] What these notions have in common is that:

the concept, of a branch, agency or other establishment implies a place of business which has the appearance of permanency, such as the extension of a parent body, has a management and is materially equipped to negotiate business with third parties so that the latter, although knowing that there will if necessary be a legal link with the parent body, the head office of which is abroad, do not have to deal directly with such parent body but may transact business at the place of business constituting the extension.[124]

An analysis of the case-law of the European Court so far seems to justify the conclusion that the following two essential criteria describe what constitutes a 'branch' or 'agency': (i) submission to the control of a foreign principal and, taking into consideration the *Blanckaert* formula, (ii) the authority of the representative to conclude transactions on behalf of this principal. It should be taken into account that these interpretations basically refer to the Brussels Convention on Jurisdiction and Recognition and Enforcement of Foreign Judgments in Civil and Commercial Matters. Nevertheless, there seems to be good reason to assume that they also influenced article 52 of the Treaty of Rome.[125]

The 1968 draft EC treaty on the mutual recognition of companies

EC Treaty Basis

Like the 1956 draft treaty on the mutual recognition of the legal personality of companies, the 1968 EC draft treaty on the mutual recognition of companies[126] is known for its ambiguous nature. This is explained by two factors: (i) doubts had been expressed as to whether the issue of recogni-

---

[123] Case 14/76 *De Bloos Bouyer* [1976] ECR 1497.

[124] cf. also ECJ interpreting 'a dispute arising out of the operations of a branch, agency or other establishment', as laid down in art. 5.5 of the Brussels Convention on Jurisdiction and the Enforcement of Judgements in Civil and Commercial Matters, Case 33/78 *Somafer-Ferngas* [1978] ECR 2183. This autonomous interpretation was reiterated in e.g. Case 139/80 *Blanckaert & Willems* [1981], 819: was a German *Vermittlungsvertreter* a 'branch' under art. 5 of the Brussels Convention? This depends on (i) whether the representative is subordinated to instructions, (ii) whether he is free to represent several competing firms, and (iii) whether he is actively involved in the execution of the transactions. Art. 5.5 was not applicable in this case. Case 439/93, *Lloyd's Register of Shipping* [1995] I–961. For further, see Wouters (1995) 103, n 7; and (1996/97) 192, who emphasizes that under the Brussels Convention these notions demand a restrictive interpretation (exception to art. 2: *forum rei* principle), at least when compared to the fundamental character of art. 52.

[125] Wouters (1996/97) 197, adds that these definitions are based on common principles of civil procedural law of the member states.

[126] Signed in Brussels on 29 February 1968, Bull. EG suppl. 2–1969. An *Explanatory Report* was written by B. Goldman, *Rev.Trim.Dr.Eur.* 1968 405–23. Except for the Netherlands, this Treaty was ratified by the 'original' member states, i.e. Germany, France, Belgium, Italy, and

tion of companies resulted directly from the liberal wording of article 58 of the EC Treaty,[127] and (ii) the content of the conflict rules of the 1968 draft treaty.

As pointed out above, the notion of 'recognition' contained in article 220 of the EC Treaty is far from clear.[128] Nevertheless, this provision was the foundation of the 1968 draft treaty. Achieving a single market was deemed to be possible only after abolishing the impediments which flow from different national concepts of precisely what constitutes the 'recognition' of foreign companies, including conditions, borders, etc.[129]

Main features: a half-hearted compromise

Apart from its weak institutional basis, the fundamental flaws of the 1968 draft treaty follow from the fact that the efforts to reconcile the two recognition theories were completely vain. The image which appears is one of a half-hearted compromise. To begin with, draft articles 1 and 2 appear to prescribe the 'incorporation' theory:

1: Companies under civil or commercial law, including co-operative societies, established in accordance with the law of a Contracting State which grants them the capacity of persons having rights and duties, and having their statutory registered office in the territories to which the present Convention applies, shall be recognised as a right.

2: Bodies corporate under public or private law, other than the companies specified in article 1, which fulfil the conditions stipulated in the said article, which have as their main accessory object an economic activity normally exercised for reward, and which, without infringing the law under which they were established, do in fact continuously exercise such activity, shall be recognized as a right.

However, these provisions are immediately neutralized by draft articles 3 and 4, which both offer room for the 'real seat' theory:

3: Notwithstanding the foregoing, any Contracting State may declare that it will not apply the present Convention to any of the companies or bodies corporate specified in articles 1 and 2 which have their real registered office outside the

Luxemburg. Although, formerly, new member states committed themselves to the 1968 draft treaty, its ratification is no longer expected: Wouters (1996/97) 592 and n 2848: further negotiations were cancelled. In November 1993 the Netherlands formally withdrew the ratification Act, cf. Vlas (*TVVS* 1994) 16 and (1999) 16. For literature and further references see *i.a.* Diephuis/Timmermans, (1980) Drobnig (1967) 93; Perrin (1969) 64; van Alkemade (1968) 189; and, for a more retrospective analysis, Vlas (1993) 12 and Wouters (1996/97) 573 et seq.

[127] cf. the foregoing section, focusing on the debate concerning the relationship between arts. 58 and 220 of the EC Treaty.
[128] On the concepts of 'minimum' and 'maximum' recognition, see I 2, above. Furthermore, the drafters of art. 220 were criticized for copying the archaic private international law concept of the 19th century, namely that it followed from the fictitious character of a legal person that such an entity, when operating beyond national borders, required an explicit 'recognition permit' by foreign authorities: see I 4, above.
[129] Wouters (1996/97) 581 et seq. gives further information.

territories to which the present Convention applies, if such companies or bodies corporate have no genuine link with the economy of one of said territories.

4: Any Contracting State may also declare that it will apply any provisions of its own legislation which it deems essential, to the companies or bodies corporate specified in articles 1 and 2 having their real registered offices on its territory, even if these have been established in accordance with the law of another Contracting State. The supplementary provisions of the legislation of the state making such a declaration shall apply in only one of the following cases:

  (i) If the memorandum and the articles of association so permit, if necessary by an express general reference to the law in accordance with which the company or body corporate has been established.

  (ii) If the memorandum or the articles of association so permit, the company or body corporate fail to make clear that it has actually exercised its activity for a reasonable time in the Contracting State in accordance with the law under which it was established.[130]

Draft article 4, to be read in conjunction with articles 1 and 2, would have led to the combined application of two systems of law. Companies duly established under the law of one member state but having their management and control office in another would have been prevented from escaping those mandatory law provisions normally applied to their 'domestic' counterparts. Obviously, this risks the courts being confronted with the dangerous task of applying the substantive company law rules of two legal orders simultaneously: what was said above about the private international law theories of *Differenzierung* and *Überlagerung*[131] applies here as well.[132] Furthermore, it would be an understatement to say that provisions such as draft article 4, which grant discretionary powers to member states, would not contribute to the achievement of a renewed European *ius commune*.[133] Apart from the fact that this would seriously endanger the harmonization programme, article 7—which is believed to favour own nationals—would also be discriminatory under article 52 of the EC Treaty.[134] Last but not least, this EC project has had a paralysing effect on

---

[130] Such reservations were indeed made by Germany, France, and Italy, as they feared that it would become too easy for subsidiaries of American parent companies in the Netherlands to settle in Europe. Vlas (1999) 18 (with further notice) takes the view that Dutch company law can now be described as strict.

[131] See section II 1, above.

[132] This approach was denounced as being schizophrenic: Vlas (1982) 95, quoting J.C. van Oven's opinion on the '*Spaltungstheorie*'. More recently (1999) 19, Vlas mentions the objections of the *Nederlandse Commissie Vennootschapsrecht*, the Dutch expert committee on company law: how to handle the appointment of a member of the management board when one of the proper laws (plural) of the company requires such appointment to be made by the shareholders' meeting, the other system of law requiring that it is for the supervisory board to decide whether or not the managing director should be appointed? Yet, the Goldman report decided not to refrain from such dualism of proper laws, now that the alternative of non-recognition of foreign companies as foreseen in art. 2 of the Hague recognition Treaty was deemed to be worse.

[133] Wouters (1996/97) 595.

the freedom of establishment, in the sense that even in the early 1990s it continued to inspire German courts to observe that reluctance to recognize foreign companies is not contrary to EC law![135]

The EC draft treaty versus *the Hague Conference draft treaty*

It is intriguing that in the early 1960s an EC treaty on recognition was deemed necessary, whilst in 1956 (just one year before the EC Treaty of Rome was signed) the draft treaty of the Hague Conference had seen the light. This duality of treaties arose partly because (i) the EC attempt was shaped with an eye to the functioning of the Single Market, and (ii) its scope is narrower than the Hague draft treaty (associations and foundations being excluded), whereas (iii) public legal persons had been excluded from the scope of the Hague draft treaty.[136] Nowadays, however, the point of departure of both draft treaties, that the matter of recognition was a preliminary question unconnected to the *lex societatis*, is considered obsolete. Although the EC 1968 draft treaty has occasionally been applied by national courts, its ultimate impact on the further development of the Single Market was not welcomed.[137] It has been condemned as 'a typical, but extreme, example of Community fudge which, in the event, satisfied no one'.[138]

[134] ibid.

[135] ibid. 594 et seq., discussing two cases: OLG *Zweibrücken*, 27 June 1990, *IPRax* 1991 406 and KG Berlin 13 June 1989, *NJW* 1989 3100. In the *Zweibrücken* case the Court held that non-recognition of a foreign company was not contrary to EC law, now that—even apart from art. 220 and the ECJ *Daily Mail* judgment (below)—the 1968 draft EC treaty on the recognition of companies never came into force. Earlier, the KG Berlin decided similarly, observing that Germany had made the reservation pursuant to draft art. 4 of said draft treaty. Cf. proposals to facilitate intra-community company transfers emanating from the dialogue between EC law and private international law: ch 6 II, below.

[136] Wouters (1996/97) 583. The last two arguments in particular do not convince Wouters: he argues that associations and foundations also take part in economic transactions. On the other hand, partnerships also fell within the scope of the 1968 draft EC treaty. Art. 1 should be read in conjunction with art. 8: these provisions did not require that the beneficiaries were given legal personality under the proper law of the company. Cf. in particular with an eye to free movement of partnerships in Europe today, Rammeloo (*Dossier* 1999) 80. Cf. Vlas (1999) 17, and Edwards (1999) 338. As far as *public* legal persons having their seat in the territory of a member state are concerned, Wouters argues that it would have been easier to apply the Hague Recognition Treaty analogously.

[137] cf. the Italian Supreme Court in *Guerra v de Plano Trust*, 28 July 1977, *Rev. cr.d.i.p.* 1979 658: recognition of foreign companies denied on the basis of art. 9.2 of the 1968 draft treaty. According to Wouters (1996/97) 592, this 'anticipatory' (!) application of the draft treaty is to be qualified as 'paralegal *ius commune*'.

[138] Clarke (1991) 164.

The Convention on Jurisdiction and Enforcement of Judgements in Civil and Commercial Matters

Legal basis

Unlike, for example, contractual relationships, a company relationship has a complicated, multi-party character: its organs (e.g. shareholders' meeting, management board, and in civil law-oriented countries a separately operating supervisory board), individual members, creditors, employees, national social security and tax authorities, all have an interest in the company's prosperity. This is likely to generate problems with regard to the settlement of disputes emerging from the cross-border operations of companies. Furthermore, searching for solutions to neutralize the unbridgeable controversy between the 'real seat' doctrine and the 'incorporation' theory is like trying to square the circle.

Furthering the Single Market was one of the central goals underlying article 220 of the EC Treaty, to be achieved *inter alia* by obliging member states to negotiate on the recognition of judgments in civil and commercial matters. This resulted in the Brussels Convention on Jurisdiction and the Enforcement of Judgments in Civil and Commercial Matters. In fact, this Convention reaches beyond imposing specific duties on the member states: it not only provides for the recognition and enforcement of judgments of other member states, but also contains a set of jurisdiction rules. (As a consequence, the Brussels Convention has been characterized as a *traité double*, a double-sided Convention.) The same principle applies to the four subsequent Accession Treaties,[139] the total set of Conventions completed the range of International Civil Procedure in EC/EFTA countries.[140]

---

[139] See ch 6 II 1, below.

[140] Convention on Jurisdiction and the Enforcement of Judgements in Civil and Commercial Matters, Brussels, 27 January 1968, amended by later Conventions of Accession. For up-to-date information see loose-leaf editions (available in all member states), e.g. Droz, *Compétence Judiciaire* (France), Geimer-Schütze, *EuGVÜ* (Germany), Vlas, *losbl. BRv., Verdragen, EEX* (Netherlands), etc. Unless provided otherwise, the Jurisdiction and Enforcement Convention (incl. the Accession Treaties) are hereafter referred to as the Brussels Convention. The EEC/EFTA Parallel Convention of 16 September 1988 is often referred to as the Lugano Convention. Although not entirely identical to the Brussels Convention, the set of jurisdiction rules contained therein is more or less similar to the Brussels Convention. Disparities between 'Brussels' and 'Lugano' may arise from the fact that when it comes to obeying the interpretations of the Brussels Convention by the ECJ, the contracting states of Lugano are of course free to (dis)obey these interpretations. For the moment, there seem to be no striking disparities between Brussels and Lugano as regards company law relationships. However, see the suggestions for reform in ch 6 II 1, below.

Jurisdiction: 'real seat' versus 'incorporation' forum

As regards the jurisdiction rules, parallel to the absence of a commonly accepted *lex societatis*, there is also no such thing as a *forum necessitatis*, or proper forum for company law relationships. Instead, recourse should be had to articles 2 and 53, and articles 5, 16, and 17 of the Convention. Article 2 is the starting point for the jurisdiction search, as it delimits the formal scope of the Convention. It operates on a non-discriminatory basis:

Subject to the provisions of this Convention, persons domiciled in a Contracting State shall, whatever their nationality, be sued in the Courts of that State.

Unfortunately, however, article 2 cannot be applied directly to legal persons, for the simple reason that their 'domicile' still needs to be defined. There is no uniform, autonomous interpretation of this notion under the Convention; article 53 reads:

For the purposes of this Convention, the seat of a company or other legal person or association of natural or legal persons shall be treated as its domicile. However, in order to determine that seat, the Court shall apply its rules of private international law.

In order to determine whether a trust is domiciled in the Contracting State whose Courts are seised of the matter, the Court shall apply its rules of private international law.[141]

Thus, the everlasting trench war between the 'incorporation' theory and the 'real seat' theory reappears at the level of international competence. Since national courts are explicitly permitted by the Brussels Convention to apply their own rules of private international law, a *Gleichlauf* (i.e. the application of the *lex fori* as the proper law of the company) will usually result. Occasionally, however, positive as well as negative jurisdiction conflicts may present themselves. A company incorporated under English law but with its real seat on Belgian territory represents the first situation: both an English court (incorporation seat in the UK) and a Belgian court (real seat situated in Belgium)[142] will accept international jurisdiction under articles 2 and 53 of the Convention. A company incorporated under the law of Belgium with its real seat on Dutch territory is an example of a

[141] Note that, for the purpose of this Convention, in the UK Civil Jurisdiction and Judgments Act 1982 it was necessary to define a 'seat', since this notion was previously unknown.

[142] This is by no means an academic exercise. Cf. the Belgian Supreme Court and the famous *Lamot* judgment of 12 November 1965, *RW* 1965/66 874 et seq. and *RIW* 1984 1489 et seq. This case was considered from a European and private international law point of view by Wouters (1996/97) 632 et seq. Subsequent to this landmark case, a number of company seat transfers, notably from the United Kingdom or the Netherlands to Belgium, took place, predominantly for tax law purposes. In this respect *Lamot* considerably resembles the ECJ *Daily Mail* case (ch 2 IV 2, below). Both cases are given more attention in the context of seat transfers, ch 6 III 1, below.

negative competence conflict: neither the Belgian (real seat of the company situated abroad), nor the Dutch courts (registered office of the company situated abroad)[143] will accept international competence.[144] Remedies must then be taken from the broader context of the Convention, for example Section 8, notably article 21, formulating rules for related actions and/or pending cases. Even the exclusive jurisdiction rule of article 16(2) is troubled by the controversy between both recognition theories:

The following Courts shall have exclusive jurisdiction, regardless of domicile: (. . .)
2. in proceedings which have as their object the validity of the constitution, the nullity or dissolution of companies or other legal persons or associations of natural or legal persons, or the decisions of their organs, the Courts of the Contracting State in which the company, legal person or association has its seat.

The solution to a positive jurisdiction clash, as described above, should be taken from article 23:

where actions come within the exclusive jurisdiction of several Courts, any Court other than the Court first seized shall decline jurisdiction in favour of that Court.[145]

Article 17 (prorogation, choice of jurisdiction) of the Convention provides a partial solution to the problems just described. As will be demonstrated, the European Court of Justice deemed a choice of forum as prescribed by the articles of association of a company to be a form of prorogation of jurisdiction allowed for under that provision.[146]

Recognition and enforcement of foreign judgments

As for the third title (Recognition and Enforcement) of the Brussels Convention, no recognition provision was elaborated specifically for company law matters. It has been asked whether article 28 might empower authorities of a member state to deny the recognition of a foreign judgment, for the reason that this judgment would be contrary to the exclusive jurisdiction rules of section 5, in particular article 16(2). It goes without saying, however, and without reservation, that the Convention, notably

---

[143] At least on the basis of the Brussels Convention. They are likely to accept jurisdiction on the basis of a national *forum actoris* rule (i.e. a long-armed statute), pursuant to national Codes on Civil Procedure, if the company is a defendant residing in a non-'Brussels' country.

[144] Situations like these may occur: since Belgian conflict of law rules accept the instrument of *renvoi* (remission), a transfer of the real seat of a Belgian company does not necessarily lead to its dissolution and winding up. Cf. court decision commented on from a Belgian perspective by Lenaerts (1988) 110 and (1989/90) 906; and, from a Dutch perspective by Bellingwout (1997) 202.

[145] cf. Rammeloo (1995) 434, for further information

[146] Case 214/89, *Powell Duffryn plc v Wolfgang Petereit* [1992] ECR 1755. Detail on this case in ch 2 IV 2, below.

article 53, explicitly refers to the private international law of the forum.[147] It is worth mentioning, though, that in the course of developing Accession Treaties to the Brussels Convention, serious attempts are also being made to bridge the opposing seat theories.[148]

2. ECJ DECISIONS

The ECJ case of *Segers*

The facts

The facts underlying the *Segers* case[149] were the following. From 1980 Mr Segers, a Dutch national, ran a commercial undertaking known as Free Promotion International which had its registered office in the Netherlands. Wishing to extend his activities, he decided to transform his business into a limited liability company. To his mind, the formation of a Dutch BV would take too long. Besides, Mr Segers thought the designation 'Ltd.' was more attractive than the Dutch equivalent 'BV'. He therefore decided to take the following measures: in April 1981 the private limited liability company Slenderose Limited, with its registered office in London, was formed in accordance with English law. In June 1981 Mr Segers and his wife took over that company, each holding an equal number of shares. In July 1981 Mr Segers incorporated his 'converted' one-man business, Free Promotion International, whose registered office was in the Netherlands, as Slenderose Limited, a subsidiary of that company. At the same time, he became a director of Slenderose. In practice, all of Slenderose's business was conducted by its subsidiary in the Netherlands. In July 1981, in order to obtain sickness insurance benefits, Mr Segers registered as sick with the Dutch *Bedrijfsvereniging*, the association responsible for sickness insurance benefits. That body, however, refused his claim on the grounds that he did not have an employment contract with Slenderose and that he was consequently not subordinate to an employer. (The Dutch *Ziektewet* provided that any person in a subordinate position in relation to another person, an employer, is insured.) After proceedings before the court of first instance, Mr Segers appealed to the *Centrale Raad van Beroep*. The *Raad* observed that a company director who holds 50 per cent or more of the shares must be deemed to work for that company in a position subordinate to it. The Association argued that this case-law applied to directors of companies whose registered office was in the

---

[147] See Vlas (1999) 86. The court of the member state where the recognition should be effected is simply obliged to tolerate a divergent qualification of the company's 'seat'.

[148] See ch 6 II 1, below.

[149] Case 79/85 *Segers v Bedrijfsvereniging voor Bank- en Verzekeringswezen, Groothandel en Vrije Beroepen* [1986] ECR 2375.

Netherlands, but excluded directors of a company incorporated under any foreign system of law.

Preliminary questions

The *Centrale Raad van Beroep* stayed proceedings and referred the following questions to the European Court of Justice for a preliminary ruling:

(1) Do the principles of freedom of establishment within the EEC and freedom to provide services within the EEC—in particular the last sentence of article 52 read with article 58 of the EEC Treaty and the last sentence of article 60 read with article 66 of the Treaty—mean that, when deciding whether there is an insurance obligation under Netherlands social security legislation, Netherlands courts may not make any distinction between the director/major shareholder of a private company incorporated under Netherlands law and a director/major shareholder of a private company incorporated under the laws of another member state, even if the foreign company clearly does not carry out any actual business in the other member state concerned but carries on business only in the Netherlands?

(2) If that question must be answered in the negative, does Community social security law (in particular, article 3(1) of regulation no. 1408/71) or any other provision of Community law prohibit such a distinction?

ECJ judgment

The Court, *inter alia*, observed the following:

13. The question submitted to the Court concerns a case in which the refusal to grant benefits is based not on the nationality of the director but on the location of the registered office of the company which he directs. However, as far as companies are concerned, it should be recalled that according to the judgment of the Court of 28 January 1986 (Case 270/83 *Commission v France* [1986] ECR 273) the right of establishment includes, pursuant to Article 58 of the EEC Treaty, the right of companies or firms formed in accordance with the law of a Member State and having their registered office, central administration or principal place of business within the Community to pursue their activities in another Member State through an agency, branch or subsidiary. With regard to companies, it should be noted that it is their registered office in the abovementioned sense that serves as the connecting factor with the legal system of a particular state, as does nationality in the case of natural persons.

14. In that respect the Court would observe that a company which has been formed in accordance with the law of another Member State and which conducts its business through an agency, branch or subsidiary in the Member State in which it seeks to establish itself cannot be deprived of the benefit of the rule set out above.

The Court reached the conclusion that distinct treatment based solely on the fact that the company has its registered office in another Member State would deprive article 58 of all meaning, and continued as follows:

15. It is established that entitlement to reimbursement of sickness costs pertains to a person and not to a company. However, the requirement that a company formed

in accordance with the law of another Member State must be accorded the same traetment as national companies means that the employees of the company must have the right to be affiliated to a specific social security scheme. Discrimination against employees in connection with social security protection indirectly restricts the freedom of companies of another Member State to establish themselves through an agency, branch or subsidiary in the Member State concerned.

Support for this proposition was found *inter alia* in the above-mentioned General Programme for the abolition of restrictions on freedom of establishment of 1960, as well as in earlier ECJ decisions.

The Court further established that article 58 only requires that a company is duly formed under the law of another Member State and has either its registered office, central administration, or principal place of business within the Community. The fact that the company conducts its business solely in another member state is immaterial (consideration 16). Neither does the need to combat fraud justify different treatment of the employee on the basis of article 56 of the Treaty, concerning public policy, public security, or public health (consideration 17).

The Court therefore ruled:

The provisions of Articles 52 and 58 of the EEC Treaty must be interpreted as prohibiting the competent authorities of a Member State from excluding a director of a company from a national sickness insurance benefit scheme solely on the ground that the company in question was formed in accordance with the law of another Member State, where it also has its registered office, even though it does not conduct any business there.

Critical observations

Freedom of establishment: misinterpretations

As pointed out earlier,[150] a superficial reading of article 52 in conjunction with article 58 of the EC Treaty might give the false impression that freedom of establishment for legal persons is already firmly established, and that further action programmes are therefore no longer required. The *Segers* judgment appeared not to be capable of removing misinterpretations like these. On the contrary, a retrospective view shows us that it caused even greater confusion: it has been erroneously argued that pursuant to *Segers* the 'real seat' theory was expelled. This conclusion seems premature. How then is the *Segers* decision to be brought into line with such Treaty provisions as article 220, *inter alia* obliging member states to regulate the mutual recognition of foreign companies? Even if the Court had decided that *Segers* should be considered as a turning point, after

---

[150] IV 1, above.

which the 'real seat' theory was no longer recognized under the EC Treaty, it is unlikely that article 220 would have been left unnoticed, with no explicit consideration.

The facts were essential here: Mr Segers was a director of a company incorporated under the law of *England*. The real seat of this company happened to be situated in the *Netherlands*.[151] When Mr Segers applied for a sickness insurance benefit, his application was refused by the Dutch authorities, *inter alia* because he appeared to be the director of a company incorporated under foreign law. The Court, however, following the opinion of the Advocate General, stated that under the articles 52 and 58 a director of a company cannot be deprived of a national sickness insurance benefit scheme for the sole reason that the company was incorporated in another member state, even though the company does not conduct any business there.

Considered from the perspective of the freedom of establishment of *legal* persons under the EC Treaty, *Segers* can hardly be considered as a landmark judgment. Rather than explicitly *imposing* the 'incorporation' theory upon all member states (to the detriment of the 'real seat' theory), the Court was *confronted* here with a constellation of facts, which involved the legal orders of two EC member states (the United Kingdom and the Netherlands) whose private international law systems had both adopted the 'incorporation' theory independent from, and prior to, EC law.[152] Since the *Segers* case appeared to have ties with the national conflict of law rules of both the United Kingdom and the Netherlands—nothing more, nothing less—it is obvious that there was no need at all for the Court to introduce the more liberal concept of the 'incorporation' theory. But neither was this liberal concept imposed upon all other member states (see above).[153] Had this been the case, the Court would undoubtedly have initiated such an overwhelming breakthrough explicitly. Taking these observations into consideration, we can no longer conclude that the *Segers* case is shocking: it is logical for the Court to rule that once foreign companies are permitted to conduct business in one EC member state, directors of such companies—in their capacity as *natural* persons—ought not to be deprived of (here: sickness insurance) benefits provided under the law of

[151] The subsidiary Free Promotion International Company Ltd.

[152] This is often overlooked, cf. Eyles (1990) 346, complaining that the fundamental weakness of the *Segers* decision lies in the '*sanktionslose Statutenwechsel*' (unsanctioned change in the proper law of the company). Although there are no European law instruments to regulate transformations of this kind as yet, such instruments are simply not needed when two incorporation countries are involved.

[153] Indeed the *Segers* judgment provokes premature conclusions: as a matter of fact, two incorporation countries were involved, whereas the majority of EC member states adhere to the 'real seat' theory. But closer reading of the case also reveals that the ECJ had no reason whatsoever to spend any time on the matter of *recognition* of foreign *companies*, since the preliminary proceedings were unrelated to that issue.

another member state. In conclusion, *Segers* was about non-discrimination against *natural*, not *legal* persons.[154] Furthermore, the judgment must be read in the context of *social security law*, rather than that of conflicts of law regarding companies.[155]

The ECJ case of *Daily Mail*

The facts

The facts in the *Daily Mail* case[156] were the following. The UK Income and Corporation Taxes Act 1970 subordinates companies resident in the United Kingdom to corporation tax. Companies residing outside the United Kingdom, even those incorporated under English legislation and having a registered office there, however, are generally liable to tax only on income arising in the United Kingdom. For the purposes of corporation tax, the definition of 'residence' is defined in section 482(7):

A body corporate shall be deemed (. . .) to be resident or not to be resident in the United Kingdom according as the central management and control of its trade or business is or is not exercised in the United Kingdom.

Section 482(1) also regulates company transfers from the United Kingdom to another legal order:

Subject to the provisions of this Section, all transactions of the following classes shall be unlawful unless carried out with the consent of the Treasury, that is to say: (a) for a body corporate resident in the United Kingdom to cease to be so resident.

Such consent may, on the basis of section 482(2), be given specifically, or, if given generally, be revoked by the Treasury, and may in any case be absolute or conditional. *Daily Mail* and General Trust plc (hereafter to be referred to as *Daily Mail*) was the applicant in the main proceedings: it is a limited company incorporated under English law whose registered office is in London. For the purposes of the case, the company is also 'resident' there. On 1 March 1984, *Daily Mail* submitted to the tax authorities an application for consent under section 482(1) of the 1970 Act, with a view to transferring its residence to the Netherlands. In order to effect that transfer, (i) all board meetings were planned to be held in the Netherlands;

---

[154] Advocate General Darmon, however, stressed that in the case before him, separate treatment was based on the company's residence, rather than on the nationality of any natural person involved: p. 2377.

[155] In this respect there are parallels between *Segers* and Case 270/83 *Commission v France* [1986] ECR 273: both judgments prohibit unequal treatment of own nationals and nationals of other member states (in the areas of social security law and tax law) for the sole reason that a company has its registered office in another member state. Detailed information in Zisowsky (1994).

[156] Case 81/87 *R v HM Treasury and Commissioners of Inland Revenue, ex p Daily Mail and General Trust plc* [1988] ECR 5483.

(ii) two persons resident in the Netherlands would replace two members of the board residing in the UK, as a result of which only two of the eight directors would be resident in England; (iii) an office for book-keeping and administration were permanently to be rented in the Netherlands; (iv) a bank account would be opened in the Netherlands, and (v) *Daily Mail* would be registered with the Netherlands Chamber of Commerce.

All this would result in liability for Netherlands corporate tax. Furthermore, *Daily Mail* would no longer be liable for capital gains tax and advance corporation tax in the United Kingdom, although the company would remain liable for income tax in the United Kingdom.[157] Subsequent negotiations between the Treasury and *Daily Mail* culminated in a letter of 1 April 1986, in which *Daily Mail* declared that in order to provide services to third parties, it would establish a branch in the Netherlands even in advance of transferring its residence there. The letter also stated that even without the consent of the Treasury *Daily Mail* was entitled to transfer its residence to the Netherlands under article 52 of the Treaty and asked for confirmation of that proposition of unconditional consent before 31 May 1986. On 24 June 1986 *Daily Mail* brought an action before the Queen's Bench Division of the High Court of Justice, essentially for a declaration that it was entitled to transfer its residence to the Netherlands under article 52 of the Treaty without the consent provided for under section 482(1) of the Income and Corporation Taxes Act 1970, or, in the alternative, that it was entitled under article 52 of the Treaty to the unconditional consent of the Treasury.

Preliminary questions

By an order of 6 February 1987, the national court decided to stay proceedings and referred the following questions to the Court of Justice for a preliminary ruling:

(1) Do Articles 52 and 58 of the EEC Treaty preclude a Member State from prohibiting a body corporate with its central management and control in that Member State from transferring without prior consent or approval that central management and control to another Member State in one or both of the following circumstances, namely where:

(a) payment of tax upon profits or gains which have already arisen may be avoided?

(b) were the company to transfer its central management and control, tax that might have become chargeable had the company retained its central management and control in that Member State would be avoided?

(2) Does Council Directive 73/148/EEC give a right to a corporate body with its central management and control in a Member State to transfer without prior consent or approval its central management and control to another Member State in

---

[157] For substantial information on tax calculations, read the report of the hearing (n 156 above).

the conditions set out in Question 1? If so, are the relevant provisions directly applicable in this case?

(3) If such prior consent or approval may be required, is a Member State entitled to refuse consent on the grounds set out in Question 1?

(4) What difference does it make, if any, that under the relevant law of the Member State no consent is required in the case of a change of residence to another Member State of an individual or firm?

ECJ judgment

First question

Having taken notice of various diverging opinions,[158] the Court (cons. 15) emphasized once again, that freedom of establishment is one of the fundamental principles of the Community and that the provisions of the Treaty guaranteeing that freedom have been directly applicable since the end of the transitional period for both Community nationals and companies referred to in article 58. The Court continued:

16. Even though those provisions are directed mainly to ensuring that foreign nationals and companies are treated in the host Member State in the same way as nationals of that State, they also prohibit the Member State of origin from hindering the establishment in another Member State of one of its nationals or of a company incorporated under its legislation which comes within the definition contained in Article 58. As the Commission rightly observed, the rights guaranteed by Articles 52 et seq. would be rendered meaningless if the Member State of origin could prohibit undertakings from leaving in order to establish themselves in another Member State. In regard to natural persons, the right to leave their territory for that purpose is expressly provided for in Directive 73/148, which is the subject of the second question referred to the Court.

17. In the case of a company, the right of establishment is generally exercised by the setting up of agencies, branches or subsidiaries, as is expressly provided for in the second sentence of the first paragraph of Article 52. Indeed, that is the form of establishment in which the applicant engaged in this case by opening an investment management office in the Netherlands. A company may also exercise its right of establishment by taking part in the incorporation of a company in another Member State, and in that regard Article 221 of the Treaty ensures that it will receive the same treatment as nationals of that Member State as regards participation in the capital of the new company.

18. The provision of United Kingdom law at issue in the main proceedings imposes no restriction on transactions such as those described above. Nor does it stand in the way of a partial or total transfer of the activities of a company incorporated in the United Kingdom to a company newly incorporated in another Member State, if necessary after winding up and, consequently, the settlement of the tax position of the United Kingdom company. It requires Treasury consent only where such a company seeks to transfer its central management and control

---

[158] cf. the following section.

out of the United Kingdom while maintaining its legal personality and its status as a United Kingdom company.

19. In that regard it should be borne in mind that, unlike natural persons, companies are creatures of the law and, in the present state of Community law, creatures of national law. They exist only by virtue of the varying national legislation which determines their incorporation and functioning.

20. As the Commission has emphasised, the legislation of the Member States varies widely in regard to both the factor providing a connection to the national territory required for the incorporation of a company and the question whether a company incorporated under the legislation of a Member State may subsequently modify that connecting factor. Certain States require that not merely the registered office but also the real head office, that is to say the central administration of the company, should be situated on their territory, and the removal of the central administration from that territory thus presupposes the winding-up of the company with all the consequences that winding-up entails in company law and tax law. The legislation of other States permits companies to transfer their central administration to a foreign country but certain of them, such as the United Kingdom, make that right subject to certain restrictions, and the legal consequences of a transfer, particularly in regard to taxation, vary from one Member State to another.

21. The Treaty has taken account of that variety in national legislation. In defining, in Article 58, the companies which enjoy the right of establishment, the Treaty places on the same footing, as connecting factors, the registered office, central administration and principal place of business of a company. Moreover, Article 220 of the Treaty provides for the conclusion, so far as is necessary, of agreements between the Member States with a view to securing inter alia the retention of legal personality in the event of transfer of the registered office of companies from one country to another. No convention in this area has yet come into force.

22. It should be added that none of the directives on the co-ordination of company law adopted under Article 54(3)(g) of the Treaty deal with the differences at issue here.

23. It must therefore be held that the Treaty regards the differences in national legislation concerning the required connecting factor and the question whether—and if so how—the registered office or real head office of a company incorporated under national law may be transferred from one Member State to another as problems which are not resolved by the rules concerning the right of establishment but must be dealt with by future legislation or conventions.

24. Under those circumstances, Articles 52 and 58 of the Treaty cannot be interpreted as conferring on companies incorporated under the law of a Member State a right to transfer their central management and control and their central administration to another Member State while retaining their status as companies incorporated under the legislation of the first Member State.

25. The answer to the first part of the first question must therefore be that in the present state of Community law Articles 52 and 58 of the Treaty, properly construed, confer no right on a company incorporated under the legislation of a Member State and having its registered office there to transfer its central management and control to another Member State.

26. Having regard to that answer, there is no need to reply to the second part of the first question.

Second question

27. In its second question, the national court asks whether the provisions of Council Directive 73/148 of 21 May 1973 on the abolition of restrictions on movement and residence within the Community for nationals of Member States with regard to establishment and the provision of services give a company a right to transfer its central management and control to another Member State.
28. It need merely be pointed out in that regard that the title and provisions of that Directive refer solely to the movement and residence of natural persons and that the provisions of the Directive cannot, by their nature, be applied by analogy to legal persons.
29. The answer to the second question must therefore be that Directive 73/148, properly construed, confers no right on a company to transfer its central management and control to another Member State.

Third and fourth questions

30. Having regard to the answers given to the first two questions referred by the national Court, there is no need to reply to the third and fourth questions.

The Court therefore rules:

(1) In the present state of Community law, Articles 52 and 58 of the Treaty, properly construed, confer no right on a company incorporated under the legislation of a Member State and having its registered office there to transfer its central management and control to another Member State.

(2) Council Directive 73/148 of 21 May 1973 on the abolition of restrictions on movement and residence within the Community for nationals of Member States with regard to establishment and the provision of services, properly construed, confers no right on a company to transfer its central management and control to another Member State.

Critical observations

Tax law purposes: financial solidity of EC member states

For more than just one reason, the *Daily Mail* judgment has been regarded as a landmark decision. Therefore, its consequences need to be considered thoroughly. Like earlier cases decided by the European Court of Justice, *Daily Mail* is rather complicated: matters of company law (including conflict of law rules) and tax law (or social security law) frequently merge.[159] This is due to the fact that decision makers in companies are expected to maximize the benefits offered to them by a Single Market, by strategically

---

[159] See the first consideration of Advocate General Darmon's opinion: 'where company law meets tax law'. With regard to EC law and company law, in particular German tax law: Behrens (1989) 355.

synergizing the effect of various legal and socio-economic factors. Although within the total framework of (EC) law this market behaviour is by no means reprehensible, there is a limit to everything. The dispute in *Daily Mail* concentrated primarily on the question whether the transfer of a company could be subject to the consent of national (English) tax authorities. Tax law still remains the domain of the individual member states. The Court:

has almost no express Community law provision which can serve as a touchstone for national tax rules impeding a company's right of establishment. In the absence of legislation, the Court can only approach the compatibility of national tax rules with Community law from the perspective of their impact on the freedom of establishment as safeguarded by article 52 juncto article 58 EC.[160]

Whereas it followed from earlier case-law—'avoir fiscal'[161]—and subsequent cases—e.g. *Commerzbank*[162] and *Haliburton Services*[163]—that member states were precluded from promulgating legislative measures that would place a disproportionate burden on the freedom of establishment

---

[160] Wouters (1995) 111: so far, efforts to harmonize aspects of corporate tax law based on article 100 of the Treaty have been unsuccessful.

[161] Case 270/83 (1986) ECR, 303. Insurance companies having both registered office and subsidiaries in France; benefits from a shareholder's tax credit (*avoir fiscal*) in respect of dividend on shares which they hold in French companies, whereas this benefit was denied to branches and agencies established in France by insurance companies registered in another member state. Discrimination and violation of art. 52 of the Treaty. Although 'the possibility cannot altogether be excluded that a distinction based on the location of the (seat) of a company or the place of residence of a natural person may, under certain conditions, be justified in an area just as tax law' (cons. 19), this was not the case here: otherwise, these foreign companies would have been forced to set up a subsidiary in France, thus restricting their freedom under art. 52 to choose the appropriate legal form in which to pursue their activities in another member state, which freedom must not be limited by discriminatory tax law provisions.

[162] Case 330/91 *Commerzbank AG* [1993] ECR I–4017. The UK Income and Corporation Taxes Act 1970 granted compensation ('repayment supplement') to companies receiving repayment of overpaid taxes, provided that these companies were resident in the UK for tax reasons. Commerzbank AG, a German company, was refused such compensation, for the sole reason that it conducted business in the UK through the intermediary of its London branch. The Court held that the UK legislation was not in compliance with arts. 52 and 58, condemning both overt discrimination on the basis of the nationality or, in the case of a company, its seat, and covert discrimination, which by other criteria of distinction, leads in fact to the same results. 'Although it applies independently of a company's seat, the use of the criterion of fiscal residence (. . .) is liable to work more particularly in the disadvantage of companies having their seat in other Member States. Indeed, it is most often those companies which are resident for tax purposes outside the territory of the Member State in question' (cons. 15).

[163] Case 1/93 *Haliburton Services BV v Staatssecretaris van Financiën* [1994] ECR I–1137. Tax relief granted by Dutch corporate tax law for transfers connected with internal organization of groups of companies under the condition that the companies involved are Dutch NVs or BVs, being members of a group whose holding is also one of these forms. Haliburton Services GmbH (Germany) sold a part of its undertaking to Haliburton BV and claimed that tax provision to be discriminatory, and prohibited by arts. 6, 52, and 58. The Court held that the Dutch tax law provision rendered the transaction less profitable to the transferor.

of legal persons pursuant to articles 52 and 58, the *Daily Mail* case reveals the other side of the coin.

Bearing in mind the common interest of the financial strength of the member states, the outcome in *Daily Mail* is not surprising: 'had the Court struck down the United Kingdom tax law here by allowing *Daily Mail* to transfer its headquarters, the Treaty rules on establishment could have become a favourite refuge for international tax planners'.[164] Undeniably, this would have culminated in vast numbers of 'tax-motivated transfers' of corporate seats.[165] This is probably why *Daily Mail*, when compared to cases such as *Haliburton* or *Commerzbank*, is a borderline case, in as much as the freedom of establishment under the Treaty is made to form an impediment to the tax legislation of the member states.

Amalgamation of tax law and company law

The tax law interests are plain and clear. But it is highly questionable why the Court opted to 'reformulate' a purely tax law matter into a question of international *company* law, conflict of law problems as such not being involved at all.[166] In the words of Clarke, 'United Kingdom Conflict Rules regarding winding-up of companies remain, in large measure, untouched by Community law developments'.[167] However, many writers took the view that the European Court of Justice (reluctantly?) opted for rescuing the 'real seat' theory from its (premature?) demise.[168]

---

[164] Wouters (1995) 127, who ironically adds that this can hardly have been the intention of the authors of the Treaty. Clarke (1991) 167, comments that 'by Section 66 and Schedule 7 of the Finance Act 1988, a company incorporated in the United Kingdom is now regarded, with some exceptions, as a resident there for taxation purposes, *even if the central management and control is elsewhere*. The residence of a company incorporated abroad will, however, for tax purposes continue to be determined by reference to the place where its central management and control is exercised' (emphasis added). For more information on UK tax law and the *Daily Mail* case, see Bentley (1991) 171 et seq.

[165] ibid. Cf. Ebke (1998) 209, who speaks of 'quota hopping'.

[166] Behrens (1989) 354, even reproaches the Court for simply having denied a freedom of establishment to companies in general, notwithstanding the fact that the preliminary proceedings concentrated on another issue. In other words, the real issue was not really given an answer. In a comparable sense, Knobbe-Keuk (1990) 333; Timmermans (1991) 69; and Wouters (1995) 128. Critical observers are troubled by this 'reformulation' of the quintessence. Sack (1990) 353, concludes from the fact that, *since* the ECJ did not ban the 'real seat' theory from the EC Treaty regime, the requirement of Treasury authorization was not *prohibited* under the Treaty *either* (emphasis added). It must not be overlooked, however, that there is good reason to assume that the Court deliberately addressed this matter in order to remove the confusion which had arisen from its earlier *Segers* judgment (see IV 2, above).

[167] Clarke (1991) 167.

[168] Großfeld/König (1992) 435; and Knobbe-Keuk (1990) 331, for further information. The obsolete character of the 'real seat' theory had been questioned prior to the *Daily Mail* judgment by e.g. Ebke (1987) 247. Others, e.g. Sandrock/Austmann (1989) 253, on the contrary, tried to play down the consequences of the *Daily Mail* judgment. They observed that the ECJ, rather than appreciating the 'real seat' theory, was confronted with substantial dissimilarities between the company law policies of the member states. More or less in the same sense, Knobbe-Keuk (1990) 325; and Behrens (1989) 354, the latter believing that, instead of

It has been argued that possibly less radical options were also available as well: a synthesis was sought between article 56(1) of the EC Treaty[169] and the *Überlagerungstheorie*.[170] This theory rejects the traditional view that a legal person can only have one nationality. In the words of Sandrock, a servant can obey more than one master. Thus, further integration of the Single Market would be enhanced by a more effective use of (human) capital.[171]

Needless to say, both legally and economically speaking, the interests at stake for both *Daily Mail* and the Treasury were considerable. Neither is it surprising that 'the parties to the main proceedings (took) entirely opposite views'[172] on the question whether the transfer of the management of a company constitutes 'establishment' within the meaning of the Treaty. The applicant (*Daily Mail*), argues that the planned transfer falls within the scope of establishment: support for this view was sought *inter alia* in the General Programme for the abolition of restrictions on freedom of establishment. The applicant claimed, more particularly, that the real seat should be considered as sufficient to permit the existence of a 'real and continuous link' with the economy of that state, thus constituting 'establishment' within the meaning of the Treaty. This view was contested by the United Kingdom, who said a change of residence does not imply a change of economic activities, especially 'since a company wishing to conduct economic activity in another Member State can do so through secondary establishments'.[173] The Commission took the view that it is for national law to decide whether a company may transfer its residence without being wound up. According to Advocate General Darmon the problem should be expressed 'in different terms'. What exactly constitutes the central management of a company 'is difficult to pin down'. Even designations as to where the management board resides are not satisfactory, because 'owing to the progress made by means of communication, it is no longer necessary to arrange formal board meetings'. In this respect, he

prescribing the 'real seat' theory, the Court leaves it to the member states to opt for one or other recognition theory. He regrets that the judgment was given 'too soon'. This view was clearly disapproved by Großfeld/König (1992) 435: to their enormous relief, the 'real seat' doctrine has, at least for the time being, been saved. They even suggest additional remedies (defences?) against the 'incorporation' theory.

[169] Sandrock (1989) 513, invokes the *Polizeivorbehalt*. Art. 56 reads as follows: 'The provisions of this Chapter and measures taken in pursuance thereof shall not prejudice the applicability of provisions laid down by law, regulation or administrative action providing for special treatment for foreign nationals on grounds of public policy, public security or public health'. Although admittedly this provision has an eye on natural persons, Sandrock asserts that it could be used analogously to replace (parts of) the *lex societatis*, prescribed by the 'real seat' theory.

[170] See II 2, above.

[171] Sandrock (1989) 512. See ch 2 II 2, above, and ch 6 I 2, below, in particular the theory of 'comparative economic advantage'.

[172] These words were used by the Advocate General Darmon, cons. 6.   [173] Ibid.

refers to the telephone, telex, telecopier, and the soon to be introduced on-line board meetings.

A 'formal legal assessment' has no relevance to the real relation between the board and the centre of the company. Therefore, in order to find out whether the transfer of the management centre constitutes an 'establishment' within the meaning of the Treaty, a 'range of factors' should be taken into consideration. In order to determine whether one may speak of a genuine[174] establishment under the EC Treaty, the customary list of connecting factors which are to be balanced to ascertain a company's real seat again plays an essential role.[175] If the outcome of this inquiry is positive, the next question is whether national authorities are allowed to make a transfer subject to authorization. It is interesting that, when compared to the Court decision, the Advocate General chose not to reformulate a purely tax law matter into a question of international company law, conflict of law problems as such not being involved; instead he made a clear-cut distinction between the admissibility of an authorization prior to the transfer on the one hand, and the settlement of a company's tax liability before transferring its central management to another member state on the other.

Disentangling tax law and company law matters

As far as the *Daily Mail* judgment is concerned, first and foremost it is noteworthy that the Court explicitly refers to the national conflict of law rules of the member states involved on the status of foreign companies. This approach is adequate: whilst the circumstances of the earlier *Segers* case had led to mistaken interpretations of the judgment (see above) the legal orders involved in *Daily Mail* were again the United Kingdom and the Netherlands. The Court considered it to be a premise ('it is apparent') of national law 'that *under United Kingdom company legislation* a company (. . .) incorporated under that legislation and having its registered office in the United Kingdom, may establish its central management and control outside the United Kingdom without losing legal personality or ceasing to be a company incorporated in the United Kingdom' (cons. 3). Dutch legislation reflects the same principle: '. . . whose legislation does not prevent foreign companies from establishing their central management in the

---

[174] In the opinion of the Advocate General, this is not the case, for example, when the effect of the transfer is that the company ceases to be subject to legislation which would otherwise apply to it (cons. 9).

[175] The Advocate General *inter alia* mentions: the residence of principal managers; the place at which general meetings are held; the place at which administrative and accounting documents are kept; the place at which the company's principal financial activities are carried on, in particular, the place at which it operates a bank account; the (main) production plant, etc. See I 2, above.

Netherlands' (cons. 6).[176] Only afterwards are the preliminary questions dealt with. Meanwhile, it is highly intriguing that the *Daily Mail* case was about the freedom of *departure*, rather than the freedom of establishment in a more classical sense. It therefore presents a mirror image of the more common case of a company applying for approval to enter the territory of a sovereign state.[177]

EC law on freedom of establishment and private international law: the status quo

The matter of the recognition of companies is excluded from Community law 'as it now stands'.[178] In other words, freedom of establishment is moulded by *national* conflict of law rules.[179] Consequently, the obligation laid down in article 293 (previously article 220) of the Treaty to negotiate further 'as far as necessary' is by no means deprived of its relevance.[180] At least, after the *Daily Mail* judgment, member states are not permitted to deny the *existence* of a company which is duly incorporated under the law of another member state, or to deny it access to its territory.[181] In the meantime, conducting business beyond national borders presupposes that either the requirements set by those member states which adhere to the 'real seat' theory (still the largest group) will have to be obeyed, or recourse should be had to the right of *secondary* establishment.[182] It is remarkable that, considering primary establishment is still the prerogative

---

[176] Behrens (1989) 360, convincingly concludes from the foregoing that '*ohne Not*' (i.e. without being forced to by the facts), the Court considered the *company* conflict rules of the United Kingdom and the Netherlands.

[177] cf. in a broader context (including the mirror image of the return to the member state after an earlier departure), Wouters (1996/97) 444 et seq.

[178] Note, however, the adamantly dissenting view of Drobnig (1990) 193 et seq.: art. 58 contains a '*versteckte Kollisionsnorm*' (a hidden conflict rule) which—even after *Daily Mail*—prescribes the 'incorporation' theory, on condition, though, that mandatory (company) law provisions of the member state where the company has its real seat are respected. This highly EC-law spirited approach comes near to the reconciliatory attempts undertaken by private international law doctrine; see II 1 and 2 above on *Überlagerung* and *Differenzierung* theories. In a comparable sense Behrens (1994) 17, asserts that EC law at least implicitly symphathizes with the 'incorporation' theory. The inquiry by Wouters (1996/97) 607 et seq., demonstrates that both the real seat and the registered office of the company appear in secondary EC legislation. De Wulf (1999) 321 is not prepared to accept the existence of any such hidden conflict rules. It cannot be denied, however, that the freedom of establishment of legal persons has at least proved to be 'sensitive' to conflict of law theories (Sonnenberger/Großerichter (1999) 726).

[179] Sandrock/Austmann (1989) 250. If we recall the discussion in IV 1, above, in the words of Eyles (1990) 352, there is no such thing as a 'European' conflict of law rule.

[180] See IV 1, above.

[181] Wouters (1996/97) 137. Transcribed to the well known private international law recognition theories, this stands for the 'minimum requirement' of foreign companies. As a matter of fact, the company is a bearer of rights and duties, but the proper law of the company is not addressed: the *lex societatis* still remains to be ascertained. See I 2, above.

[182] i.e. on the level of a subsidiary, agency or branch, cf. Behrens (1991) 97, and IV 1, above.

of national authorities, the use of agencies or branches may perhaps be a loophole.[183] For example, bearing in mind that the control theory is excluded from article 58,[184] it is even possible under the Treaty to set up an English private limited company with a branch in Germany, all of the company's members being German nationals. This appeared to be the situation underlying the *Landshuter Druckhaus* judgment.[185]

The right of secondary establishment is, however, reserved for companies formed in accordance with the law of a member state, provided that there is an economic link between the member state and the overseas territory.[186]

Neverthless, member states are not entirely free to do as they please.[187] Indeed, the Court emphasizes that 'it should be borne in mind that, unlike natural persons, companies are creatures of the law and, *in the present state of Community law*, creatures of *national* law. They exist only by virtue of the varying national legislation which determines their incorporation and functioning' (cons. 19, emphasis added). The Court concluded that neither the differences in national legislation concerning the required connecting factor (registered office or management and control centre) nor the question which of these factors can be transferred, and if so how, are problems which are resolved by Community law, and therefore they need to be dealt with by future legislation or conventions (cons. 23). In the meantime, there is the 'under-estimated quality'[188] of the Court's observation that the Treaty not only imposes obligations on the host state, but also:

prohibits the member state of origin from hindering the establishment in another state of one of its nationals or of a company incorporated under its legislation

---

[183] cf. ECJ *Centros*, and IV 2, above.

[184] See IV 1, above. Nevertheless, the control theory reappears in certain areas, e.g. aviation, navigation, broadcasting, and financing: Wouters (1996/97) 134 et seq.

[185] cf. Ebke (1987). It is noteworthy that his contribution preceded the *Daily Mail* case; cf. further Großfeld/König (1992) 434; Wouters (1996/97) 130 et seq., commenting on the *Landshuter Druckhaus* case, BayOLG 18 September 1986, WM 1986, p. 1557. Wouters observes that art. 52 even applies to situations of nationals who return to their own member states. As this case predated the ECJ *Daily Mail* judgment, the Bavarian Appeal Court hesitated over its position on the question whether the 'real seat' theory applicable in Germany was in compliance with art. 58 of the Treaty. The Bavarian Court held: '*Muß danach die Niederlassungsfreiheit nach artt. 52, 59 EWGV geprüft werden, so ist zu erwägen, daß nach art. 58 Abs. 1 EWGV möglicherweise ein satzungsmäßiger (statutarischer) Sitz genügt; das ist die Auffassung der Gründungstheorie*'. Even after the *Daily Mail* judgment, Sandrock (1989) 511, welcomed the doubts expressed at an earlier stage by the BayOLG: in his opinion, the 'real seat' doctrine and the EC Treaty are 'at daggers drawn'.

[186] cf. Wouters (1996/97) 150, on the General Programme on freedom of establishment. The precise status of this Programme, however, remains unclear: ibid. 151.

[187] Knobbe-Keuk (1990) 332, says we cannot simply ignore the *Daily Mail* judgment. We could at least try to interpret it as '*gemeinschaftsverträglich*' (in the spirit of the Union). See ch 6 I 1, below.

[188] Wouters (1995) 127.

which comes within the definition contained in article 58.[189] As the Commission observed with good reason, the rights guaranteed by articles 52 et seq. would be rendered meaningless if the member state of origin could prohibit undertakings from leaving in order to establish themselves in another member state (cons. 16).[190]

This minimum standard has given a new impetus to the debate about whether and how Community rules should facilitate cross-border transfers. As will be seen,[191] legal orders adhering to the 'real seat' doctrine often prescribe the compulsory dissolution and winding up of a company as soon as it decides to transfer its headquarters from one country to another. It may be asked, however, whether these consequences are compatible with the aforementioned minimum standard: real seat countries could also facilitate these transfers by taking away the disproportionate barrier of compulsory winding up of the company.[192] A workable alternative is that immigrating companies, in the interest of the shareholders and the creditors of the company, could be transformed into a domestic equivalent legal form, while retaining their identity.[193] Some writers, however,

---

[189] See Part 3 below, notably on the dialogue between EC law (freedom of establishment, freedom of departure) after the entry into force of the Treaty of Amsterdam on 1 May 1999 and private international law (*Statutenwechsel*, i.e. change in the proper law of the company).

[190] Wouters (1995) 127 says this is in line with a tendency in the area of free movement of persons and services, as the Court interprets Treaty provisions as prohibiting member states from impeding the free movements of its own nationals, such as by not recognizing professional qualifications acquired in another member state, or by restricting the use of an academic title obtained in another member state: cf. Case 19/92 *Krause v Land Baden-Württemberg* [1993] ECR I–1663.

[191] See Part 2 below for a comparative analysis at the level of private international law of some member states; for an integrated approach to EC and private international law: ch 6 III, below.

[192] In the opinion of Advocate General Darmon, however, '(i)t is generally accepted that the winding up required by national legislation as a condition for the migration of the company is *not* contrary to Community law' (emphasis added). This is explained by the fact that it would be highly paradoxical if a member state not requiring winding up were placed by Community law in a less favourable fiscal position precisely because its legislation on companies was more consistent with Community objectives in regard to establishment.

[193] Current German law has been condemned for being far too *mobilitätsfeindlich* (hostile to cross-border transfers in general). Cf. Behrens (1991) 97, on OLG *Zweibrücken NJW* 1990 3092 (Luxembourg public company entering German territory); ibid. (1998) 353; and Roth (1995) 31, with regard to BayOLG 7 May 1992, *ZIP* 1992 842, *IPRax* 1992 389; cf. Großfeld/ König (1991) 380 and 406; and Ebke (1998) 211: even when the following conditions are fulfilled foreign companies may not register in Germany (cf. s 36 et seq. and 45 AktG): (i) according to the conflict of laws of Luxembourg, companies can transfer their head office to another country while retaining their identity, and (ii) the structure of the transferring company is in keeping with German law. *Neugründung* (re-establishment) of the company under German law is inevitable. A plea for a teleological, or more precisely: less restrictive interpretation of German law with an eye to the *'zukünftige Rechtsfortbildung der Europäischen Gemeinschaft'* was relentlessly rejected by the Court. The same rigid position was taken by OLG Hamm 30 April 1997, *EuZW* 1998 31: even under the Maastricht Treaty the Court refused to initiate preliminary proceedings before the ECJ. Further details in ch 4 III 1, below (seat transfers). Contrary to this, constructive solutions were created in Belgian law (the *Lamot* doctrine, ch 6 III 1, below) and even the legislation of a non-EU country, notably arts. 161 and 163 of the Swiss Federal Code on Private International Law: ch 4 II 3, below.

believe that these problems are negligible: no theory exists without costs.[194] The ultimate challenge here is to harmonize the requirements set by EC law, on the one hand, and by national conflict of law rules of both the state of departure and the state of re-establishment of the company on the other.[195]

Provisional conclusions

The *Daily Mail* judgment leaves the critical observer with a feeling of disappointment: *Roma locuta, causa finita*, it seems.[196] Although tax law objectives may justify the final outcome,[197] in essence *Daily Mail* has been regretted as a setback for both European and private international law developments.[198] Had the Court decided differently, it might have exposed itself to the severe reproach of having usurped its authority since, apart from tax law interests, the traditional substantive discrepancies between nationally oriented notions of company law demand a European legislative process which has the consent of all member states.[199] In other words, the *Daily Mail* judgment leaves us with many questions, but perhaps not with a total vacuum in European law.[200]

The ECJ case of *Powell Duffryn v Petereit*

Facts

The ECJ judgment in *Powell Duffryn v Petereit*[201] illustrates the confusing entanglement of EC law and private international law, as well as national substantive company law notions. The facts were the following. In a series of share issues in 1979, 1981, and 1982, Powell Duffryn plc, a company incorporated under English law, acquired registered shares in IBH-

---

[194] Großfeld/König (1992) 433: '*Dieser Kerngedanke der Sitztheorie ist heute noch gültig; er wird durch Kritik an Randfragen nicht erschüttert*'.

[195] See ch 6 II, below.

[196] Sandrock/Austmann (1989) 250; Roth (1995) 41: 'judicial restraint (. . .) without limiting the direct effect of art. 52 EC more than is absolutely necessary'. From a comparative point of view, Sandrock (1989) 511 even suggests reiterating preliminary proceedings on this subject once again. In his opinion this would be justified, since (i) *Daily Mail* was about tax law, rather than (private international) company law, and correspondingly, (ii) the compatibility of the 'real seat' theory with the EC Treaty had not been (explicitly) questioned. Some writers even assume that the 'real seat' theory is a *Theorie auf Zeit* (predestined to perish) e.g. Großfeld/König (1991) 380. They assume that gradually the *Überlagerungstheorie* (see 2 II above) will take the place of the 'real seat' theory in its purest form.

[197] See Behrens (1989) 361: '*Die Entscheidung des Gerichtshofs vermag nicht zu befriedigen. Das Ergebnis läßt sich rechtfertigen.*'

[198] cf. among many others Schmitthoff (JBL 1988) 454 et seq.; Drobnig (1990) 203; and Sandrock/Austmann (1989) 250.

[199] Rammeloo (1995) 51.

[200] These provisional conclusions are the starting point for further investigations in ch 6 II 1, below.

[201] Case 214/89, *Powell Duffryn plc v Wolfgang Petereit* [1992] ECR 1755.

Holding AG, a company governed by German law. After the first issue, the 1980 IHB's general shareholders' meeting, in which Powell Duffryn participated, adopted a resolution with acclamation, to insert the following clause to the articles of association:

By subscribing for or acquiring shares or interim certificates the shareholder submits, with regard to all disputes between himself and the company or its organs, to the jurisdiction of the Courts ordinarily competent to entertain suits concerning the company.

As a result of a compulsory winding up, IBH went into liquidation in 1983. Petereit, as trustee of IBH-Holding AG, claimed the remaining sums owed on the (registered) shares purchased by Powell Duffryn, as well as restitution of dividends unduly distributed.

Preliminary questions

The *Landgericht* declared itself competent on the grounds of the jurisdiction clause in the articles of association. Powell Duffryn contended that, pursuant to article 2 of the Brussels Convention on Jurisdiction and the Enforcement of Judgments in Civil and Commercial Matters, the only competent court was that of the place of residence of the defendant (the court of the country where Powell Duffryn was established, i.e. the United Kingdom). The *Oberlandesgericht* appealed for a preliminary ruling on article 17 of the Brussels Convention. In essence, the questions were the following:

(1) Does a clause in the Articles of Association of a company (as referred to) constitute an 'agreement' within the meaning of article 17, and does the answer depend on whether the shareholder subscribes to a share issue or acquires existing shares?;
(2) If the answer to the first question is in the affirmative, then
    (a) does subscription for, and acceptance of, shares by means of a written declaration of subscription, on the occasion of an increase in capital of a company comply with the formal requirements prescribed by article 17, namely that it must be 'in writing or evidenced in writing'?;
    (b) has the requirement that the dispute must fall within those 'which may arise in connection with a particular legal relationship', defined in the same article been met?; and
    (c) does the choice of forum also affect claims with regard to paying up shares, and restitution of dividends unduly distributed?

ECJ judgment

First question
Having analysed the divergent opinions[202] and compared the different legal systems of the contracting states, the Court observed that the rela-

---

[202] cf. the following section.

tionship between a limited company and its shareholders may be either of a contractual nature, or of a *sui generis* (or regulatory) character. The phrase 'agreement conferring jurisdiction' in article 17 should therefore be interpreted independently or should be deemed to refer to the internal law of one or the other of the states concerned. The Court observed that none of these options should be chosen to the exclusion of the others, an appropriate choice is only possible in relation to each provision of the Convention, in the light of full effectiveness in relation to the objectives of article 220 of the EEC Treaty. It is deemed important, however, that the uniformity of rights arising out of the Convention be guaranteed.[203] The Court continued:

14. Therefore, and as the Court ruled on similar grounds in relation to the words 'matters relating to a contract' and other terms in article 5 of the Convention serving as criteria for determining a special jurisdiction, the concept of an agreement conferring jurisdiction in article 17 should be regarded as an independent concept.
15. In this connection it should be observed that, when required to interpret the words 'matters relating to a contract' in article 5 (. . .), the Court held that the obligations imposed on a person in his capacity as a member of an association must be regarded as contractual obligations because membership of an association created between the members close links of the same kind as those which are created between the parties of a contract.
16. In the same way the ties existing between the shareholders of a company are comparable to those between the parties to a contract. The formation of a company is an expression of a community of interests among the shareholders in the pursuit of a common goal. In order to attain this aim, each shareholder has, in relation to the other shareholders and the company bodies, rights and obligations which are set out in the company's articles of association must be regarded as a contract governing at one and the same time relationships between the shareholders and the company.

The Court concluded from this that a jurisdiction clause in the articles of association is indeed an 'agreement' within the meaning of article 17, which binds all shareholders, regardless of whether an individual is opposed to it or not, or whether he became a shareholder after the clause was accepted. By becoming and remaining shareholder, a member agrees to submit to all the provisions of the articles of association and the resolutions passed by company bodies,[204] even if he does not agree with them. This assessment is followed by a crucial consideration:

20. A different interpretation of article 17 of the Convention would lead to the multiplication of grounds of jurisdiction for disputes arising from one and the same legal and factual relationship between the company and its shareholders and would infringe the principle of legal certainty.

---

[203] Cons. 11–13.
[204] Provided that these instruments are in conformity with the relevant national law.

Second question, subsection (a)
As for the formal conditions of article 17 of the Brussels Convention, the
Court once more underlined that they have the function of ensuring that
the parties' consent is evidenced. But then the Court emphasised that this
case cannot be compared to those decided previously:

25. However, it must be stressed that the situation of shareholders in relation to a
company's articles of association, which expresses a community of interests
among the shareholders in the pursuit of a common goal, differs from that referred
to by the judgment cited above (*Colzani-Rüwa*[205], SR), which is that of a party to a
contract of sale in relation to the general conditions of sale.
26. First of all, it should be observed that, in the legal systems of all the Contracting
States, company articles of association are in writing. Furthermore, in the company
law of all those states it is accepted that the articles of association play a special part
in that they are the basic instrument governing the relationship between a shareholder and the company.
27. The next point to be noted is that, regardless of how the shares are acquired,
any person who becomes a shareholder in a company knows, or ought to know,
that he is bound by the company's articles of association and amendments which
are made to them by the company bodies in conformity with the relevant law and
the articles themselves.

The Court thus reached the conclusion[206] that shareholders are deemed to
be aware of any jurisdiction clause, provided that the articles of association are 'lodged at a place which is accessible to the shareholders, such as
the company's registered office, or are kept in a public register'.

Second question, subsection (b)
Pursuant to article 17, jurisdiction clauses also have to be sufficiently designated, meaning that the choice of forum may not reach beyond the settlement of disputes which have arisen or may arise 'in connection with a
particular legal relationship'. The Court started by observing that this
restriction on the freedom to choose a forum is intended to limit the effect
of such an agreement on disputes originating from the legal relationship
with which the agreement was concluded. In other words, parties should
not be caught by surprise, in the sense that the choice of forum would govern any dispute arising from whatever (past or future) legal relationship
with their counterparts. The Court observed that a jurisdiction clause in
the articles of association fulfils this requirement 'where it covers disputes
which have arisen or which may arise in connection with relationships
between the company and its shareholders as such'. However, 'the question whether, in the particular case, the jurisdiction clause should be given

---

[205] Case 24/76 [1976] ECR 1831, [1977] *CMLR* 345.   [206] Cons. 28 and 29.

this meaning, is a question of interpretation which should be left to the national Court'.[207]

Second question, subsection (c)
It is questioned here whether the jurisdiction clause applies to the disputes which have been referred to. The Court decided:

36. On this point it should be observed that the interpretation of the clause conferring the jurisdiction which has been relied upon before the national court is a matter for that court.
37. Consequently the reply (. . .) should be that it is for the national court to construe the jurisdiction clause relied upon before it in order to determine which disputes are within its ambit.

The Court therefore ruled:

(1) A clause conferring jurisdiction on the Courts of a Contracting State to entertain disputes between a company limited by shares and its shareholders, inserted into the statutes of such company and adopted in accordance with the provisions of the applicable national law and the statutes, constitutes an agreement conferring jurisdiction within the meaning of Article 17 of the Brussels Convention.
(2) Irrespective of the manner of acquisition of shares, the formal requirements laid down in Article 17 must be considered to be complied with in regard to any shareholder, where the clause conferring jurisdiction contained in the statutes of the company and those statutes are lodged in a place to which the shareholder may have an access or are entered in a public register.
(3) The requirement that a dispute must arise in connection with a particular legal relationship within the meaning of Article 17 is satisfied if the clause conferring jurisdiction in the statutes of a company may be interpreted as referring to the disputes between the company and its shareholders as such.
(4) It is for the national court to interpret the clause conferring jurisdiction invoked before it, in order to determine which disputes fall within its scope.

Critical observations

The multi-party nature of company relationships: related law

Although the *Powell Duffryn* judgment does not specifically focus on the EC law framework regarding the freedom of establishment of (legal) persons (articles 52 and 58 of the EC Treaty), its significance lies in the Court's interdisciplinary legal reasoning: as pointed out in the foregoing section, unlike other cases, *Powell Duffryn* demonstrates the struggle to regulate cross-border company relationships at the crossroads of EC law and company law (both substantive law and conflict of laws) of the EC member states.

In the course of the compulsory winding up and liquidation procedure of the holding company incorporated under German law and residing in

---

[207] Cons. 30–34.

Germany, the shareholders were ordered to pay up their (registered) shares. One of these shareholders, Powell Duffryn plc, residing in England, denied that it was bound by the jurisdiction clause, declaring that all disputes between shareholders and IBH-Holding AG were to be settled before a German court. The European Court of Justice was requested to give preliminary rulings on article 17 of the Brussels Convention on Jurisdiction and Recognition and Enforcement of Foreign Judgments in Civil and Commercial Matters. This would involve the difficult task of keeping the following legal areas in concert with each other: (i) the EC Treaty; (ii) private international law rules in the (EC) Brussels Convention on Jurisdiction and Recognition and Enforcement of Foreign Judgments in Civil and Commercial Matters, and (iii) notions underlying substantive EC company law, not to mention the EC law harmonization programme in the field of company law. On top of this, as compared with contract law, company law fundamentally involves 'multi-party'[208] relationships. In the *Powell Duffryn* case, the shareholders appeared to be settled throughout Europe. Inconsistent Court decisions, resulting from a cross-border proliferation of jurisdiction, should be avoided at all costs.

Exclusive jurisdiction: prorogation of forum

Article 16(2) in conjunction with articles 53 and 17 of the Brussels Convention are analysed first. As pointed out earlier, there can be no doubt that the exclusive jurisdiction rule of article 16(2), excluding the parties' right to prorogation,[209] does not apply here, because the issue at stake has nothing to do with 'the validity of the constitution, the nullity or dissolution of companies (. . .) or the decisions of their organs'. Nor is it a case on 'proceedings relating to the winding up of insolvent companies', which are excluded from the scope of the Brussels Convention.[210]

Turning to article 17, which is the legal basis for choice of jurisdiction, it should be noted that prior to the *Powell Duffryn* judgment, jurisdiction clauses in the articles of association of a company were hardly ever heard of.[211] The examination of the requirements of article 17 compels us to deal

---

[208] Polak *CMLR* (1993) 412. In his opinion, 'scattered litigation' will lead to cumbersome proceedings pursuant to arts. 21 and 22 (*lis pendens*—related actions) of the Brussels Convention.

[209] Petereit even argued that on the grounds of art. 5(3) of the Brussels Convention, jurisdiction of the German Court was also to be based on tort actions. Perhaps even more remarkable was that this was denied by the national court on the merits of specific circumstances in this particular case: in the Court's view, the Holding did not suffer a loss of assets. On the contrary, Petereit's claim would bring economic benefit to the company.

[210] Art. 1.2. Cf. Gaudemet-Tallon (1992) 535: '*une action de droit commun, exercée certes à l'occasion de la faillite, mais qui n'est pas substantiellement affectée par celle-ci*'.

[211] Hamel/Lagarde/Jauffret (1980) 383 et seq.: '*les actionnaires français d'une société étrangère sont liés par une clause des statuts attribuant compétence à la juridiction étrangère*'. In a comparable sense Geimer (1989) 886, although advocating an extrapolation of art. 222 of the

with various topics separately. First and foremost, the case must have an international character.[212] Furthermore, as a general premise there must be genuine consensus between the parties. This is a matter of contract law, therefore excluded from the scope of both the Brussels and the Rome Contracts Conventions.[213] The latter, however, is often applied by way of analogous reasoning. In addition, article 17 of the Brussels imposes both substantive and procedural requirements on a jurisdiction agreement. As the former category did not give rise to any interpretation problems,[214] *Powell Duffryn* in particular focused on the procedural requirements. Building further on earlier case-law (*Peters v ZNAV*), the Court observed that the 'agreement' spoken of in article 17 should be interpreted autonomously and that the relationship between a company and its shareholders is 'contractual'.[215]

Harmonization policies: substantive law considerations

There are currently some intriguing questions, and perhaps even changes afoot. In the first place, the classification of a relationship between a company and its shareholders as an 'agreement' is by no means uncontroversial: the Court daringly 'harmonizes' opposing company law concepts in the EC member states as to whether this relationship is of a 'contractual', rather than an 'institutional', nature.[216] Furthermore, it must be asked whether this construed relationship between substantive company law notions and conflict of laws is aimed at protecting specific groups of litigants. Taking into consideration that the Brussels Convention also represents modern conflict of laws, this is not surprising (cf. the protection of

German *Zivilprozeßordnung (Gerichtsstand der Mitgliedschaft)*, a jurisdiction rule written for purely internal situations.

[212] Wouters (1996/97) 641, quoting Vlas: although company law matters of a purely internal nature do not fall within the scope of the Brussels Convention, this condition is addressed already if just one shareholder is resident abroad.

[213] Choice of jurisdiction has been excluded from the 1980 European Convention on the Law applicable to Contractual Obligations on the basis of art. 1(2)(d).

[214] The substantive requirements laid down in art. 17 are: (i) the court chosen must be in one of the contracting states; (ii) at least one of the parties must be domiciled there; and (iii) the case must have an international character.

[215] Case 34/82 *Peters v ZNAV* [1983] ECR 987, on the payment due because of a membership relation between an association and its members: 'contractual obligation' under art. 5 of the Brussels Convention.

[216] cf. Rammeloo (1995): the ECJ is 'skating on thin ice'. Vandeginste (1992) 250, takes the view that the procedural rules of the Brussels Convention are contaminated by substantive law of the member states. Polak *CMLR* (1993) 415, denounces the ECJ's 'persuasive approach'. The suggestion of Advocate General Tessauro, however, that there was a consensus (*'volonté sociale'*) between the collective shareholders, replacing the will of individual shareholders, was not adopted by the Court. Gaudemet-Tallon (1992) 537, fears that the Court has lost itself in an unconvincing and ambiguous *'démarche'*, which will presumably not receive much support, and that *'on s'éloigne beaucoup du fondement consensuel sur lequel repose l'article 17'*. Wouters (1996/97) 58, thinks further discussion will be unfruitful, as this controversy is outdated.

consumers, insured parties, and employees). Prior to *Powell Duffryn*, no such protection had been introduced for shareholders as a specific group. However, it appears that gerrymandering, changing boundaries in order to enhance the protection of so-called weaker parties, is inserted by the authoritative words of the Court. Of course, the uniform treatment of shareholders—which would fit perfectly within the notion of ex article 54(3)(g)[217] of the EC Treaty—would be of pre-eminent importance. But protection lies far beyond this aim because this presupposes that a shareholder is to be considered as a 'weaker' party. Indeed, a privileged position for shareholders was advocated. Such a position has been compared to that of insurance policy-holders (Section 3 of the Brussels Convention), consumers (Section 4), and employees (arts. 5 and 17).[218] But shareholders definitely fall outside this category. They are hardly a homogenous group: it is highly doubtful whether institutional investors, such as Powell Duffryn, deserve the same level of protection as private investors. So it is doubtful whether the latter group, entering a (cross-border operating) economic market for speculative reasons, deserve protection at all. Any sweeping jurisdiction rule, either prohibiting the choice of forum to the 'disadvantage' of the shareholders, or allowing it only after a dispute has arisen, seems inappropriate here. Inserting a substantive yet arbitrary criterion, differentiating between institutional and 'consumer' shareholders, would harm the procedural law interest of the Brussels Convention in providing concrete jurisdiction rules. Furthermore, the introduction of substantive law notions would seriously jeopardize the 'concentration rather than proliferation' policy of the Brussels Convention.

Neither is *Powell Duffryn* to be characterized as a standard case if we look at the formal requirements prescribed by article 17. Contrary to the strict interpretation set forth in its earlier case-law, the Court deemed that a choice of forum in the articles of association is in compliance with article 17, notably that the agreement was 'in writing or evidenced by writing',[219] and irrespective of when and how the shares were acquired. In the light of

---

[217] Art. 54 served as a basis for the harmonization programme in the field of company law. It prescribes the following: '(1) Before the end of the first stage, the Council shall, acting unanimously on a proposal from the Commission and after consulting the Economic and Social Committee and the European Parliament, draw up a general programme for the abolition of existing restrictions on freedom of establishment within the Community (. . .) (3) The Council and the Commission shall carry out the duties devolving upon them under the preceding provisions in particular: (. . .) g. by co-ordinating to the necessary extent the safeguards which, for the preservation of interests of members and others, are required by Member States of companies or firms within the meaning of the second paragraph of art. 58 with a view to making such safeguards equivalent throughout the Community.'

[218] See Gaudemet-Tallon (1992) 538, underpinning the interests of *'les petits actionnaires épargnants'*, who are totally unaware of 'something' called 'articles of association'.

[219] cf. earlier judgments: Case 25/76 *Segoura v Bonakdarian* [1976] ECR 1851 (oral agreement, later confirmed in writing); Case 71/83 *Tilly Russ* [1984] ECR 2417 (the mere communication of jurisdiction on the back of a bill of lading was not sufficient).

the foregoing, it is puzzling why the Court did not opt for analogous reasoning, since article 17(2) (jurisdiction conferred on Courts by a trust instrument) could have been applied here.[220]

Conclusions

The Court's policy to shift away from a proliferation of closely connected disputes under the Brussels Convention was understandable and justifiable. Streamlining multi-party relationships by concentrating the settlement of disputes in a single court, notably the chosen *forum societatis*, favours equal (fair?) treatment of all shareholders, and at the same time prevents mutually incompatible court decisions. The advantages thus produce 'full effect'.[221] However, one may well ask whether this down-to-earth approach is based on 'pithy argumentation'[222] for the mere sake of pragmatism. Nor is it to be expected in the near future that cases like *Powell Duffryn* will in future also be decided on the basis of the *Gleichlauf* principle (i.e. that the *lex societatis* of the forum is applied).[223] This can easily be explained by the fact that *Powell Duffryn* was about a company (IBH-Holding AG) incorporated under German law, having both its registered office and its management and control centre on German territory.[224] *Quid iuris*, however, if the company's real seat and registered office are not both in the country of the designated court, but the articles of association contain a clause similar to that in *Powell Duffryn*? Then judicial practice will be as usual: courts will turn to article 53 of the Brussels Convention in order to assess whether, according to the private international law rules of the forum, the court has jurisdiction.[225] A final conclusion must be that even after *Powell Duffryn* there is still no single appropriate *forum societatis* under the Brussels Convention.

The ECJ case of *Centros*

Facts

Questions were raised in the proceedings between *Centros Ltd.*, a private limited company registered on 18 May 1992 in England and Wales, and

---

[220] Rammeloo (1995) 433, quoting Geimer (1989) 886: '*wie achtlos die Verfasser des Übereinkommens (. . .) die Frage von Gerichtsstandsklauseln übergangen haben*'.

[221] Polak *CMLR* (1993) 415.

[222] Vandeginste (1992) 250. Wouters (1996/97) 60, opposes this view: he believes that it is the common interest (*intérêt commun; gemeinsamer Zweck*) rather than the classical notion of *affectio societatis*, which is appropriate to reconcile notions from national origins.

[223] This was suggested by Polak *CMLR* (1993) 419.

[224] Note that the *Segers* case did not present a clash between the two recognition theories either: the parties involved, the United Kingdom and the Netherlands, both adhere to the 'incorporation' theory (see IV 2, above).

[225] Rammeloo (1995) 434.

Erhvervs- og Selskabsstyrelsen, the Trade and Companies Board ('the Board') under the authority of the Danish Department of Trade, concerning that authority's refusal to register a branch of Centros in Denmark.[226] It is clear from the documents in the main proceedings[227] that Centros had not traded since its formation.[228] Since United Kingdom law imposes no requirement on limited liability companies as to the provision for and the paying up of a minimum share capital, Centros's share capital, which amounted to £100, had neither been paid up nor made available to the company. It was divided into two shares held by Mr and Mrs Bryde, Danish nationals residing in Denmark. Mrs Bryde was a director of Centros, whose registered office was situated in the United Kingdom, at the home of a friend of Mr Bryde. Under Danish law Centros, as a 'private limited company', is regarded as a foreign limited liability company. The rules governing the registration of branches (*filialer*) of such companies are laid down by the *Anpartsselskabslov* (Law on Private Limited Companies). In particular, article 117 provides:

1. Private limited companies and foreign companies having a similar legal form which are established in one Member State of the European Communities may do business in Denmark through a branch.

During the summer of 1992, Mrs Bryde requested the Board to register a branch of Centros in Denmark. The Board refused on the grounds *inter alia* that Centros, which did not trade in the United Kingdom, was in fact seeking to establish in Denmark not a branch, but a principal establishment, and was seeking thereby to circumvent the national rules concerning, in particular, paying up minimum capital of DKK 200,000 by Law No. 886 of 21 December 1991. Centros brought an action against the decision. In those proceedings, Centros maintained that, since it was lawfully formed in the United Kingdom, it was entitled to set up a branch in Denmark under article 52 in conjunction with article 58 of the Treaty. According to Centros, the fact that it had never traded in the United Kingdom since its formation had no bearing on its right of freedom of establishment. In its *Segers* judgment, the Court had ruled that articles 52 and 58 of the Treaty prohibited the competent authorities of a member state from denying a company director national sickness insurance benefit solely on the ground that the company had its registered office in another member state, even though it did not conduct any business there. In *Centros*, the Board submitted that

---

[226] Case C–212/97 [1999] ECR I–1459; [1999] *CMLR* 551. Cf. 'Proceedings of the Court of Justice and the Court of First Instance of the European Communities' 8–12 March 1999, no. 07/99, p. 1, and [1999] *CMLR* 551 et seq.

[227] cf. considerations 2–12 of the ECJ judgment.

[228] In the words of Advocate General La Pergola, [1999] *CMLR* 556: 'The company has been dormant since its formation and has never done any business'.

its refusal to grant registration was not contrary to articles 52 and 58 of the Treaty since the establishment of a branch in Denmark appeared to be a way of avoiding Danish national rules on the provision for and the paying up of minimum share capital. Furthermore, its refusal to register was justified by the need to protect private or public creditors and other contracting parties, and by the need to prevent fraudulent insolvencies.

Preliminary question

1. By order of 3 June 1997 [. . .] the Danish Höjesteret referred to the Court for a preliminary ruling under art. 177 of the Treaty a question on the interpretation of Articles 52, 56, and 58 of the Treaty [. . .]:

   13. Is it compatible with Article 52 of the EC Treaty, in conjunction with Articles 56 and 58 thereof, to refuse registration of a branch of a company which has its registered office in another Member State and has been lawfully founded with company capital of £100 (approximately DKK 1,000) and exists in conformity with the legislation of that Member State, where the company does not itself carry on any business but it is desired to set up the branch in order to carry on the entire business in the country in which the branch is established, and where, instead of incorporating a company in the latter Member State, that procedure must be regarded as having been employed in order to avoid paying up company capital of not less than DKK 200,000 (at present DKR 125,000)?

ECJ judgment

Considerations 15–22 focused on the fundamental and preliminary question whether or not branches benefit from the freedoms guaranteed by articles 52 and 58 of the Treaty:

15. As a preliminary point, it should be made clear that the Board does not in any way deny that a joint stock or private limited company with its registered office in another Member State may carry on business in Denmark through a branch. It therefore agrees, as a general rule, to register in Denmark a branch of a company formed in accordance with the law of another Member State. In particular, it has added that, if Centros had conducted any business in England and Wales, the Board would have agreed to register its branch in Denmark.

16. According to the Danish Government, Article 52 of the Treaty is not applicable in the case in the main proceedings, since the situation is purely internal to Denmark. Mr and Mrs Bryde, Danish nationals, have formed a company in the United Kingdom which does not carry on any actual business there with the sole purpose of carrying on business in Denmark through a branch and thus of avoiding application of Danish legislation on the formation of private limited companies. It considers that in such circumstances the formation by nationals of one Member State of a company in another Member State does not amount to a relevant external element in the light of Community law and, in particular, freedom of establishment.

17. In this respect, it should be noted that a situation in which a company formed in accordance with the law of a Member State in which it has its registered office

desires to set up a branch in another Member State falls within the scope of Community law. In that regard, it is immaterial that the company was formed in the first Member State only for the purpose of establishing itself in the second, where its main, or indeed entire, business is to be conducted (see, to this effect, *Segers* paragraph 16).

18. That Mrs and Mrs Bryde formed the company Centros in the United Kingdom for the purpose of avoiding Danish legislation requiring that a minimum amount of share capital be paid up has not been denied either in the written observations or at the hearing. That does not, however, mean that the formation by that British company of a branch in Denmark is not covered by freedom of establishment for the purposes of Articles 52 and 58 of the Treaty. The question of the application of those articles of the Treaty is different from the question whether or not a Member State may adopt measures in order to prevent attempts by certain of its nationals to evade domestic legislation by having recourse to the possibilities offered by the Treaty.

19. As to the question whether, as Mr and Mrs Bryde claim, the refusal to register in Denmark a branch of their company formed in accordance with the law of another Member State in which its has its registered office constitutes an obstacle to freedom of establishment, it must be borne in mind that that freedom, conferred by Article 52 of the Treaty on Community nationals, includes the right for them to take up and pursue activities as self-employed persons and to set up and manage undertakings under the same conditions as are laid down by the law of the Member State of establishment for its own nationals. Furthermore, under Article 58 of the Treaty companies or firms formed in accordance with the law of a Member State and having their registered office, central administration or principal place of business within the Community are to be treated in the same way as natural persons who are nationals of Member States.

20. The immediate consequence of this is that those companies are entitled to carry on their business in another Member State through an agency, branch or subsidiary. The location of their registered office, central administration or principal place of business serves as the connecting factor with the legal system of a particular State in the same way as does nationality in the case of a natural person.[229]

21. Where it is the practice of a Member State, in certain circumstances, to refuse to register a branch of a company having its registered office in another Member State, the result is that companies formed in accordance with the law of that other Member State are prevented from exercising the freedom of establishment conferred on them by Articles 52 and 58 of the Treaty.

22. Consequently, that practice constitutes an obstacle to the exercise of the freedoms guaranteed by those provisions.

The next question is whether the provisions of articles 52 and 58 cannot be relied on if the company has been set up with no other reason than to circumvent the application of the national law governing formation of

---

[229] The Court explicitly refers to *Segers* (paragraph 13), Case 270/83 *Commission v France* [1986] ECR 273 (paragraph 18), Case C–330/91 *Commerzbank* [1993] ECR I–4017 (paragraph 13), and Case C–264/96 *ICI* [1998] I–4695 (paragraph 20).

private limited companies (abuse of freedom of establishment). The Court observed as follows:

24. It is true that according to the case-law of the Court a Member State is entitled to take measures designed to prevent certain of its nationals from attempting, under cover of the rights created by the Treaty, improperly to circumvent their national legislation or to prevent individuals from improperly or fraudulently taking advantage of provisions of Community law.[230]

25. However, although, in such circumstances, the national courts may, case by case, take account—on the basis of objective evidence—of abuse or fraudulent conduct on the part of the persons concerned in order, where appropriate, to deny them the benefit of the provisions of Community law on which they seek to rely, they must nevertheless assess such conduct in the light of the objectives pursued by those provisions (*Paletta II*, paragraph 25).

26. In the present case, the provisions of national law, application of which the parties concerned have sought to avoid, are rules governing the formation of companies and not rules concerning the carrying on of certain trades, professions or businesses. The provisions of the Treaty on freedom of establishment are intended specifically to enable companies formed in accordance with the law of a Member State and having their registered office, central administration or principal place of business within the Community to pursue activities in other Member States through an agency, branch or subsidiary.

27. That being so, the fact that a national of a Member State who wishes to set up a company chooses to form it in the Member State whose rules of company law seem to him the least restrictive and to set up branches in other Member States cannot, in itself, constitute an abuse of the right of establishment. The right to form a company in accordance with the law of a Member State and to set up branches in other Member States is inherent in the exercise, in a single market of the freedom of establishment guaranteed by the Treaty.

28. In this connection, the fact that company law is not completely harmonised in the Community is of little consequence. Moreover, it is always open to the Council, on the basis of the powers conferred upon it by Article 54(3)(g) of the EC Treaty, to achieve complete harmonisation.

29. In addition, it is clear from paragraph 16 of *Segers* that the fact that a company does not conduct any business in the Member State in which it has its registered

---

[230] The Court explicitly refers to earlier judgments: 'in particular, regarding freedom to supply services, Case 33/74 *Van Binsbergen v BedrijfsverenigingMetaalnijverheid* [1974] ECR 1299 (paragraph 13), Case C–148/91 *Veronica Omroep Organisatie v Commissariaat voor de Media* [1993] ECR I–487 (paragraph 12), and Case C–23/93 *TV 10 v Commissariaat voor de Media* [1994] ECR I–4795 (paragraph 21); regarding freedom of establishment: Case 115/78 *Knoors* [1979] ECR 399 (paragraph 25), and Case C–61/89 *Bouchoucha* [1990] ECR I–3551 (paragraph 14); regarding the free movement of goods: Case 229/83 *Leclerc and Others v 'Au Blé Vert' and Others* [1985] ECR 1 (paragraph 27); regarding social security: Case C–206/94 *Brennet v Paletta* [1996] ECR I–2357, '*Paletta II*' (paragraph 24); regarding freedom of movement for workers: Case 39/86 *Lair v Universität Hannover* [1988] ECR 3161 (paragraph 43); regarding the Common Agricultural Policy: Case C–8/92 *General Milk Products v Hauptzollamt Hamburg-Jonas* [1993] ECR I–779 (paragraph 21); and regarding company law: Case C–367/96 *Kefalas and Others v Greece* [1998] ECR I–2843 (paragraph 20)'.

office and pursues its activities only in the Member State where its branch is established is not sufficient to prove the existence of abuse or fraudulent conduct which
would entitle the latter Member State to deny that company the benefit of the provisions of Community law relating to the right of establishment.

30. Accordingly, the refusal of a Member State to register a branch of a company
formed in accordance with the law of another Member State in which it has its registered office on the grounds that the branch is intended to enable the company to
carry on all its economic activity in the host State, with the result that the secondary
establishment escapes national rules on the provision for and the paying up of a
minimum capital, is incompatible with Articles 52 and 58 of the Treaty, insofar as
it prevents any exercise of the right freely to set up a secondary establishment
which Articles 52 and 58 are specifically intended to guarantee.

The final question was 'whether the national practice in question might
not be justified for the reasons put forward by the Danish authorities'.[231]
The Court observed the following:

32. Referring both to Article 56 of the Treaty and to the case-law of the Court on
imperative requirements in the general interest, the Board argues that the requirement that private limited companies provide for and pay up a minimum share
capital pursues a dual objective: first, to reinforce the financial soundness of those
companies in order to protect public creditors against the risk of seeing the public
debts owing to them become irrecoverable since, unlike private creditors, they cannot secure those debts by means of guarantees and, second, and more generally, to
protect all creditors, whether public or private, by anticipating the risk of fraudulent bankruptcy due to the insolvency of companies whose initial capitalisation
was inadequate.

33. The Board adds that there is no less restrictive means of attaining this dual
objective. The other way of protecting creditors, namely by introducing rules making it possible for shareholders to incur personal liability, under certain conditions,
would be more restrictive than the requirement to provide for and pay up a minimum share capital.

34. It should be observed, first, that the reasons put forward do not fall within the
ambit of Article 56 of the Treaty. Next, it should be borne in mind that, according
to the Court's case-law, national measures liable to hinder or make less attractive
the exercise of fundamental freedoms guaranteed by the Treaty must fulfil four
conditions: they must be applied in a non-discriminatory manner; they must be
justified by imperative requirements in the general interest; they must be suitable
for securing the attainment of the objective which they pursue; and they must not
go beyond what is necessary in order to attain it.[232]

35. Those conditions are not fulfilled in the case in the main proceedings. First, the
practice in question is not such as to attain the objective of protecting creditors
which it purports to pursue since, if the company concerned had conducted busi-

---

[231] Cons. 31.
[232] The Court explicitly refers to case C–19/92 *Krause v Land Baden-Württemberg* [1993]
ECR I–1663 (paragraph 32), and Case C–55/94 *Gebhard v Consiglio dell'Ordine degli Avvocati e
Procuratori di Milano* [1995] ECR I–4165 (paragraph 37).

ness in the United Kingdom, its branch would have been registered in Denmark, even though Danish creditors might have been equally exposed to risk.

36. Since the company concerned in the main proceedings holds itself out as a company governed by the law of England and Wales and not as a company governed by Danish law, its creditors are on notice that it is covered by laws different from those which govern the formation of private limited companies in Denmark and they can refer to certain rules of Community law which protect them, such as the Fourth Council Directive 78/660/EEC of 25 July 1978 based on Article 54(3)(g) of the Treaty on the annual accounts of certain types of companies (OJ 1978 L 222, p. 11), and the Eleventh Council Directive 89/666/EEC of 21 December 1989 concerning disclosure requirements in respect of branches opened in a Member State by certain types of company governed by the law of another State (OJ 1989 L 395, p. 36).

37. Second, contrary to the arguments of the Danish authorities, it is possible to adopt measures which are less restrictive, or which interfere less with fundamental freedoms, by, for example, making it possible in law for public creditors to obtain the necessary guarantees.

38. Lastly, the fact that a Member State may not refuse to register a branch of a company formed in accordance with the law of another Member State in which it has its registered office does not preclude that first State from adopting any appropriate measure for preventing or penalising fraud, either in relation to the company itself, if need be in co-operation with the Member State in which it was formed, or in relation to its members, where it has been established that they are in fact attempting, by means of the formation of the company, to evade their obligations towards private or public creditors established on the territory of a Member State concerned. In any event, combating fraud cannot justify a practice of refusing to register a branch of a company which has its registered office in another Member State.

The Court therefore rules:

It is contrary to Articles 52 and 58 of the EC Treaty for a Member State to refuse to register a branch of a company formed in accordance with the law of another Member State in which it has its registered office but in which it conducts no business where the branch is intended to enable the company in question to carry on its entire business in the State in which that branch is to be created, while avoiding the need to form a company there, thus evading application of the rules governing the formation of companies which, in that State, are more restrictive as regards the paying up of a minimum share capital. That interpretation does not, however, prevent the authorities of the Member State concerned from adopting any appropriate measure for preventing or penalising fraud, either in relation to the company itself, if need be in co-operation with the Member State in which it was formed, or in relation to its members, where it has been established that they are in fact attempting, by means of the formation of a company, to evade their obligations towards private or public creditors established in the territory of the Member State concerned.

Critical observations

Incompatibility of the 'real seat' theory with the EC treaty? Misinterpretations

What are the ramifications of the *Centros* decision for the freedom of establishment of legal persons in Europe? A number of German commentators seem to be convinced that this ruling means that member states are obliged to relinquish the *Sitztheorie* (i.e. 'real seat' theory).[233] Their view seems to be strengthened by the fact that the judgment is *'vom Plenum des EuGH gefällt worden'* (decided by a *plenary* session of the ECJ).[234] From now on, natural and legal foreign persons alike should be welcomed in Germany or any other member state of the European Union; the latter category would no longer have to worry about adjusting their structure to the company laws of the state of establishment. Germany had better get used to *'Gesellschaften mit ausländischem Rechtskleid'*, companies established abroad, having their real seat on German territory.[235] But then one might ask whether current attempts to draft a Fourteenth Council Directive on the Transfer of the Registered Office or the *De Facto* Head Office of a Company from One Member State to Another[236] is completely redundant.[237] Of course, this remark does not make sense: apart from the fundamental question—'real seat' or 'incorporation' theory?—the complexity of cross-border company seat transfers in itself requires a harmonized procedure, the aim of which is to safeguard the interests of all parties involved.[238]

However, for three reasons, I beg to differ with the view of those who are convinced that the 'real seat' theory is no longer compatible with the

---

[233] *Centros* is said to have provoked widespread debate cf. the tenor of the comments by Sedemund/Hausmann (1999) 810 et seq.: '*Abschied von* Daily Mail? (A Farewell to *Daily Mail?*)'; Meilicke (1999) 627 et seq.: '*EuGH kippt Sitztheorie* (ECJ subverts "real seat" theory)'; Sonnenberger/Großerichter (1999) 724: '*Die Gesellschaft steht im Sinne des Art. 48 EGV natürlichen EG-Staatsangehörigen gleich und kann sich in vollem Unfang auf die Niederlassungsfreiheit berufen*'; ibid., 725: '. . . *weitreichende Konsequenzen für (. . .) materielles und internationales Gesellschafts-, Gläubiger- und Verkehrsschutzrecht*'; Sandrock (1999) 1337, 1341: '*ein Etappensieg für die Überlagerungstheorie. Der Stein ist ins Rollen gekommen*'; '*Hinsichtlich (. . .) EG-angehörige Gesellschaften (. . .) ist die Sitztheorie Rechtsgeschichte*'. In the same sense de Wulf (1999) 318: 'As a consequence of *Centros*, one particularly radical way to combat abuse of freedom of establishment, i.e. the German version of the "Real Seat" theory, can no longer be maintained.' More moderate conclusions were drawn by Behrens (1999) 331; Ebke (1999) 656 et seq.; Ulmer (1999) 662 et seq.; and Vlas (2000). Cf. further Borges (2000), Ebke (2000), Roth (2000), and Zimmer (2000).

[234] Meilicke (1999) 627, and Sandrock (1999) 1341.

[235] Meilicke (1999) 628.   [236] See ch 6 III 2, below.

[237] de Wulf (1999) 321, also stresses that *Centros*, although favouring freedom of establishment, neither facilitates a free choice of the proper law of the company, nor creates an instrument to transfer a company's seat from one EC member state to another.

[238] In spite of ECJ *Centros*, Lutter (2000) 13, surprisingly, adheres to the view that the registration of a branch of a duly established private limited company would be frustrated by the fact that under German law this English company would be denied *Rechtsfähigkeit* (capacity).

EC Treaty. First, the Court did not explicitly consider the 'real seat' theory. Secondly, one should distinguish between primary and secondary forms of establishment. Finally, there is a considerable difference between the principled refusal to register branches or subsidiaries of fictitious or pro-forma foreign companies, on one hand, and perhaps more moderate kinds of penalties for not having complied with national (company) laws of a member state on the other.

Absence of ECJ considerations regarding recognition theories

Since any serious attempt to relinquish the 'real seat' theory would indeed have a revolutionary impact on *'die Grundlagen des internationalen Gesellschaftsrechts'* (i.e. fundamental premises underlying cross-border company law), one could hardly expect the Court to remain silent on this matter.[239] At the same time, the absence of explicit ECJ considerations undoubtedly gives rise to the risk of speculative reasoning, attributed to the ECJ by many writers.[240] Like ECJ *Segers*, writers seem to be confused once again, as the facts underlying *Centros* arose in two 'incorporation' countries, namely the United Kingdom and Denmark.[241] One thing can be learnt from ECJ *Daily Mail* is that obiter dicta[242] far from contributing to legal certainty, create uncertainty, simply because they are not suited to deal with a problem in detail.[243] It is crucial for the proper functioning of a Single Market that neither foreign companies nor their secondary

[239] In the opinion of Vlas (2000) 339, however, this is easy to explain: although the Danish authorities took the view that the branch should *de facto* be considered as a primary establishment (cons. 7), the preliminary question focused exclusively on secondary establishment (cons. 18). This also explains why the ECJ did not refer to ECJ *Daily Mail*.

[240] Vlas (2000) 339, ironically observes that many commentators seem to have the gift of exegesis. Ebke (1999) 660. Both de Wulf (1999) 319, and Sonnenberger/Großerichter (1999) 722, re-emphasize that the ECJ based its decision exclusively on EC law, and in no way on conflict of law theories. Sonnenberger/Großerichter (1999) 726, reiterate that ECJ *Daily Mail* on the other hand justified the conclusion that national conflict of law rules concerning legal persons prevailed over EC law on freedom of establishment for legal persons. Sandrock (1999) 1340 et seq., firmly expresses the belief that company law conflict rules are done with. Although the ECJ did not explicitly consider the conflicting recognition theories, in his view this clearly follows from the *'Entscheidungsgründen'*. Henceforth, the national conflict of law rules of EC member states, in as much as they pay homage to the 'real seat' theory, should no longer frustrate cross-border company seat transfers.

[241] See Ebke (1999) 658 (for further information) and 660, Sonnenberger/Großerichter (1999) 722, and de Wulf (1999) 319. In this respect, there is great similarity between the ECJ cases *Centros* and *Segers* (see below): (i) both cases were about secondary establishment; (ii) both the United Kingdom and the Netherlands already adhered to the 'incorporation' theory.

[242] cf. ECJ *Daily Mail*, cons. 23: '(i)t must therefore be held that the Treaty regards the differences in national legislation concerning the required connecting factor and the question whether—and if so how—the registered office or real head office of a company incorporated under national law may be transferred from one Member State to another as problems which are not resolved by the rules concerning the right of establishment but must be dealt with by future legislation or conventions.'

[243] Ebke (1999) 661.

establishments be denied the freedom of establishment.[244] It is, of course, quite another question whether these primary or secondary establishments are subject to restrictive legislative measures of EC member states, and if so, to what extent these measures are allowed under the EC Treaty.

Freedom of secondary establishment

Secondary establishments fundamentally benefit from freedom of establishment under the EC Treaty. Pursuant to Treaty article 52, first paragraph, prohibitions on restrictions to the freedom of establishment of nationals of a member state 'shall also apply to restrictions on the setting up of *agencies, branches or subsidiaries*[245] by nationals of any Member State established in the territory of any Member State'.[246] It is likely that businessmen prefer to use foreign *private* limited companies, *public* limited company types being more strictly regulated.[247] Considering that Centros was duly established as a private limited company in the United Kingdom, it was entitled to set up a branch in Denmark. This right is clearly confirmed by the wording of the ECJ judgment.[248] This is understandable: geographically speaking, the Single Market is quite a large area, as a result of which entrepreneurs cannot do without a network of local agencies, branches, and subsidiaries. The essential question is: what would remain of this fundamental freedom if secondary establishments could be denied registration under the national law of a member state just because (i) the 'foreign' company does not conduct any (economic) activity in the country where it is duly established, and (ii) that foreign company—including its branch or agency—were presumed to have been set up exclusively to circumvent national company laws. Another question is whether under these circumstances national authorities may place restrictions on this fundamental right.

National measures restricting fundamental freedoms: conditions

The rigidity of the Danish national provision to discourage branches of pro-forma foreign companies brings us to the second topic. A refusal to

---

[244] cf. in this sense de Wulf (1999) 319, who argues that the existing differences between the company law regimes of the EC member states do not provide an excuse for refusing to register a company duly established in another member state. In his view, however, it is remarkable that the ECJ (cons. 28) shows a degree of impatience, observing that 'it is always open to the Council, on the basis of the powers conferred upon it by art. 54(3)(g) of the EC Treaty, to achieve complete harmonization'.

[245] All following emphases added.   [246] More details in IV 1, above.

[247] See Ulmer (1999) 662, who observes that it would not have made any sense for the Danish couple to use a public limited company for their purposes. Lutter (2000) 7, emphasizes that today more than ever company law features disparities between public and private companies.

[248] cf. cons. 15–22, above. Lutter (2000) 9, says that small and medium-sized companies should be encouraged by the consequences of this decision: setting up a branch is far less complicated than establishing a subsidiary company.

register a company's branch ultimately constitutes an obstacle to the exercise of the freedoms guaranteed by articles 52 and 58 of the Treaty:

The fact that Mr and Mrs Bryde formed the company Centros in the United Kingdom for the purpose of avoiding Danish legislation requiring that a minimum amount of share capital be paid up does *not*, however, mean that the formation by that British company of a branch in Denmark *is not covered by freedom of establishment for the purposes of Article 52 and 58 of the Treaty*. The question of the application of those articles of the Treaty is *different* from the question whether or not a *Member State may adopt measures* in order to prevent attempts by certain of its nationals to evade domestic legislation by having recourse to the possibilities offered by the Treaty.[249]

In other words, a member state is entitled to:

take measures designed to prevent certain of its nationals from attempting, under cover of the rights created by the Treaty, improperly to circumvent their national legislation or to prevent individuals from improperly or fraudulently taking advantage of provisions of Community Law.[250]

Of eminent importance, however, is that such measures should be taken 'in the light of the objectives pursued by those provisions'. The Court reiterates that national measures which tend to hinder or make less attractive the exercise of fundamental freedoms guaranteed by the Treaty must fulfil *four* conditions: (i) they must be applied in a non-discriminatory manner; (ii) they must be justified by imperative requirements in the general interest; (iii) they must be *suitable for securing the attainment of the objective* which they pursue;[251] and (iv) they must *not go beyond what is necessary in order to attain it*.[252] Notably, the third requirement appears not to be fulfilled since in the observation of the Court, 'if the company concerned had conducted business in the United Kingdom, its branch *would* have been registered in Denmark, even though Danish creditors might have equally been exposed to risk'.

The ECJ case of *Segers*[253] again requires consideration. As has been explained, the decision in *Segers* did not prohibit further application of the 'real seat' theory; once foreign companies are permitted to conduct business in an EC member state, *directors* of such companies, in their capacity as *natural* persons, ought not to be deprived of (here: sickness insurance) benefits provided under the law of another member state. In other words, *Segers* was about non-discrimination between *natural*, not *legal*, persons. In the context of *Centros*, the importance of *Segers* lies predominantly in the fact that:

---

[249] Cons. 18.   [250] Cons. 24.   [251] Cons. 34.   [252] Cons. 34.
[253] Case 79/85 *Segers v Bedrijfsvereniging voor Bank- en Verzekeringswezen, Groothandel en Vrije Beroepen* [1986] ECR 2375. See IV 2, above.

a company formed in accordance with the law of a Member State in which it has its registered office desires *to set up a branch* in another Member State *falls within the scope of Community law*. In that regard, it is *immaterial* that the company was formed in the first Member State *only for the purpose of establishing itself in the second, where its main, or indeed entire, business is to be conducted* (see, to this effect, Segers).[254]As a consequence:

companies are entitled to carry on their business in another Member State through an agency, branch or subsidiary. The location of their registered office, central administration or principal place of business serves as the connecting factor with the legal system of a particular State in the same way as does nationality in the case of a natural person.[255]

In addition:

it is clear from paragraph 16 of *Segers* that the fact that a company does not conduct any business in the Member State in which it has its registered office and pursues its activities only in the Member State where its branch is established is not sufficient to prove the existence of abuse or fraudulent conduct which would entitle the latter Member State to deny that company the benefit of the provisions of Community law relating to the right of establishment.[256]

What can we conclude from the above? An emphatic refusal to register a fictitious foreign company's branch must be overkill. But then it should be asked whether under the EC Treaty any other kinds of remedies are allowed to counter the problem of pro-forma foreign companies (including their secondary establishments) attempting to circumvent (rigid) domestic company laws.

Other measures: the Dutch Pro-Forma Foreign Companies Act of 1998

In its observations, the Court stated:

it is possible to adopt measures which are *less restrictive*, or which interfere less with fundamental freedoms, by, for example, making it possible in law for public creditors to obtain the necessary guarantees.[257]

In this respect, Member States are by no means precluded from

adopting any appropriate measure for *preventing or penalising fraud*, either in relation to the company itself, (. . .) *or in relation to its members*, where it has been established that they are in fact attempting, by means of the *formation* of the company, to *evade* their obligations *towards private or public creditors*.[258]

The italicized phrases at first sight seem to leave the door open for the approach, introduced by the Dutch 1998 Pro-Forma Foreign Companies (PFFC) Act. Section 1 of this Act, which contains specific conflict of law

---

[254] Cons. 17.   [255] Cons. 20.   [256] Cons. 29.   [257] Cons. 37.
[258] Cons. 38 and 39.

rules, defines pro-forma foreign companies as follows: 'In this Act a pro-forma foreign company means a capital company with legal personality incorporated under a law other than Dutch law, which conducts its business entirely or almost entirely in the Netherlands without having any further real tie with the state under whose law it was incorporated'. Creditors of pro-forma foreign companies are deemed to deserve protection: the provisions of sections 2 et seq. contain additional 'formation' (e.g. minimum capital)[259] and disclosure requirements, the non-compliance of which results in joint and several liability of those in charge of the company's management for transactions entered into by the company. Although this Act basically influences the primary establishment of pro-forma foreign companies, having their headquarters in the Netherlands, there is no reason to assume that, for example, 'real seat' countries are precluded from taking comparable measures against secondary forms of establishments (e.g. branches) of foreign companies having their primary establishment abroad. Instead of completely refusing the registration of a foreign company's branch, the Danish legislator could also subject managers of (the branch of) a foreign company to the penalty of personal liability for non-compliance with the minimal capital requirements of Danish company law. The method pursued by the Dutch legislator (personal liability of company directors) comes closer to the penalties imposed by EC Company Law Harmonization Directives.

However, the method pursued by the Dutch legislator also has flaws. The Dutch legislator is said to have taken up the challenge of fighting abuses of (pro-forma) foreign companies too enthusiastically: the catalogue of duties contained in the Dutch PFFC Act (see II 1 above) might also turn out to be discriminatory[260] against directors of foreign companies, as

---

[259] Of course, these requirements are not real 'formation' requirements in the usual sense: the question whether formation requirements are indeed complied with is to be answered exclusively by the proper law of the company. In the context used here, all that is meant is that if pro-forma foreign companies do not comply with certain mandatory law provisions of Dutch company law, the penalty will be joint and several liability of those in charge of the company's management.

[260] Schutte-Veenstra (1999), 229. Vlas (2000), 339 et seq., however, observes that pursuant to art. 4 subs. 5 and art. 5 subs. 3, art. 4 of the Dutch 1998 Pro-Forma Foreign Companies Act 1998 does not apply to a company subject to the law of another EC member state or a state which is a party to the Agreement on the European Economic Area of 2 May 1992 and to which the Second, Fourth and Seventh Company Law Directives are also applicable. Van den Braak (2000), 352 et seq., on the contrary, concludes from cons. 20 of the *Centros* decision that art. 48 (ex art. 58) of the EC treaty imposes on EC member states to acknowledge the 'incorporation' theory. She explicitly advocates that companies from other EC member states be 'recognized' in a broad sense (see ch 2 I 1, above). Subsequent to the matter of the company's recognition, the (non)-compliance of national restrictive measures must be examined. As regards the Dutch Pro-Forma Foreign Companies Act 1998, she distinguishes two categories of national legislation: national measures that frustrate freedom of establishment (e.g. several registration requirements, minimum capital requirements) and those national measures that do not inflict upon freedom of establishment as such (e.g. tortious liability of company

compared to duties imposed upon directors of Dutch companies. Perhaps it would be advisable (i) to apply several articles of the Dutch company law code (contained in the second book of the Dutch Civil Code) by analogous application; (ii) to all (i.e. not only pro-forma) foreign companies.[261] Nothing less, but—and this is essential—nothing *more* either. It has also been argued that article 56 of the EC Treaty (i.e. art. 46, formerly art. 56, of the EC Treaty) does not justify measures against companies from other EC member states, solely because they must be considered as *pro-forma* foreign.[262] Article 56 requires that 'public policy' be seriously jeopardized.[263] It has even been put forward that pursuant to ECJ *Centros* it is fundamentally prohibited to impose any minimum capital requirement on (branches of) companies established in other EC member states.[264] I beg to differ on this matter. The precondition that 'national measures must be justified by imperative requirements in the general interest'[265] was not followed by any overall conclusion that capital requirements *as such* are not suited to protect company creditors. In my opinion, the Court solely condemns the *penalty of non-registration* of the company's branch as a consequence of not having complied with member states' national company laws on capital requirements. There is no reason to assume that punishing non-compliance with capital requirements by imposing personal liability on

managers resulting from national substantive laws). Only the first category is compulsorily to be answered in accordance with the law of the EC member state where the company is duly incorporated.

[261] See Van den Braak, (2000) 352 et seq.

[262] cf. the view expressed by the Commission, rendered by Advocate General La Pergola, (1999) *CMLR* 562: 'on the one hand (. . .) *Centros* was simply exercising the right of establishment in the Member State that offered the most favourable conditions in respect of the paid-up capital requirements, a procedure which (. . .) is exactly one of the objectives freedom of establishment is designed to achieve. (. . .) On the other hand, (. . .) the Member State in which it is sought to set up a secondary establishment may impose conditions for the registration of the branch based on its domestic rules and designed to secure for persons in its own territory who enter into relations with the foreign company a greater measure of protection than is afforded by that company's memorandum of association. In the present case it appears at least probable, if not certain, that the Danish rules on paying up capital achieve the declared objective of protecting public creditors. With respect to that objective, the Commission considers however that it is disproportionate to refuse permission for the secondary establishment purely and simply on a presumption of intent to circumvent the laws currently in force. Such refusal cannot be justified on the grounds mentioned on art. 56.' Advocate General La Pergola also advocates that art. 56 should be 'interpreted strictly. It cannot be invoked in support of economic aims' (ibid. 565).

[263] Schutte-Veenstra (1999) 229, *inter alia* quoting ECJ Case 36/75, *Rutili* [1975] ECR 1219; Timmermans (1988) 328; and De Wulf (1999) 320. Cf. the observation made by the United Kingdom, [1999] *CMLR* 558, rendered by Advocate General La Pergola: 'the restriction on the right of establishment resulting from the Companies Board's decision cannot be justified on purely economic grounds, which are not covered by art. 56'. This view was opposed by the Danish Companies Board, the Danish government, and French and Swedish authorities (ibid. 560). German writers, however, seem to differ on this matter; see below.

[264] De Kluiver (1999) 528; Van den Braak (2000) 354.   [265] Cons. 34.

company managers is altogether prohibited under the EC Treaty.[266] Moreover, this reasoning seems to be more in line with the 2nd Company Law Directive on Co-ordination of Capital of Companies:[267] although this Directive basically applies to *public* companies,[268] it would hardly make sense to assume that the concept of minimum capital as an instrument to protect company creditors is fundamentally useless for *private* company types. Last but not least, it has been questioned whether the Dutch 1998 PFFC Act is incompatible with secondary EC law (i.e. the company law harmonization programme) for other reasons.[269]

Decisions after ECJ Centros: *is the 1998 PFFC Act compatible with the EC Treaty?*

It is interesting to note that the question of the compatibility of the Dutch 1998 PFFC Act and the ECJ case of *Centros* prompted the cantonal court of Groningen (Netherlands) to initiate preliminary proceedings in a case concerning a private limited company incorporated in the United Kingdom, whilst solely conducting business in the Netherlands. The preliminary question concentrates on the issue whether the duties that pursuant to articles 2 et seq. PFFC Act are imposed upon pro-forma foreign companies, as defined in art. 1 of this Act, comply with articles 43 and 48 of the EC Treaty.[270]

Other measures: the German approach

According to German commentators, the consequences of ECJ *Centros* are the following. Even if the *Sitztheorie* (i.e. 'real seat' theory) has not been officially abandoned by the Court,[271] companies duly established in any other EC member state can no longer be denied *Rechtsfähigkeit* (capacity) by German authorities;[272] neither should registration of (branches of) said

---

[266] See Vlas (2000) 340.

[267] 13 December 1976 (77/91 EEC), OJ 1977 L 26/1.

[268] This is not altered by the fact that e.g. the Netherlands also applies this Directive to the Dutch *Besloten Vennootschap* (private company limited by shares).

[269] See ch 6 II 1, below.

[270] Local district court Groningen 19 October 1999, *NJkort* 1999, 94 (*Kamer van Koophandel en Fabrieken Groningen v Vennootschap naar buitenlands recht Challenger Trading Co. Ltd.*), officially registered at the ECJ as C–410/99. Although preliminary proceedings were cancelled because this company appeared in June 2000 to be no longer registered, similar cases may be expected soon.

[271] Behrens (1999) 325. However, Sandrock (1999) 1341, deduces the following from *Centros*: (i) the application of the traditional German conflict of law theory ('real seat' doctrine) to companies from other EC member states is no longer permitted; (ii) nor can it be applied to companies duly established in a legal order with which Germany has concluded a bilateral treaty, on the basis of which the 'incorporation' theory prevails (see ch 4 III 1, below); but (iii) the 'real seat' theory remains unaffected when companies from other countries are involved. The first category supposedly leaves room for the application of the *Überlagerungstheorie* (see II 2, above).

[272] Behrens (1999) 323 et seq.; Meilicke (1999) 627; de Wulf (1999) 319; and Lutter (2000) 13.

companies be refused. For example, the refusal to register a branch of an English postbox company by the Bavarian Court of Appeal[273] is considered to be incompatible with EC law.[274] Furthermore, branches of foreign companies must be able to register as *Eigentümer in das Grundbuch* (owners of immovable property).[275] The nightmare vision of foreign companies 'invading' Germany does not seem to be realistic. ECJ *Centros* does not preclude German courts from taking other kinds of measures, such as holding directors of these companies liable for non-compliance with German company law requirements on capital requirements.[276] In the view of Ulmer, a *'Differenzierung nach Gefährdungspotential'* (classification by potential risk) should form the basis for further debate.[277] Subjecting the *Innenverhältnisse*, the relationship between the company and its organs, to the chosen foreign proper law of the company should not meet with any objection. The law on *Mitbestimmung*, worker co-determination, on the other hand, is said not to be touched upon by *Centros* either.[278] Finally, capital requirements have always been of pre-eminent importance to German company law. In that respect, it is interesting to note that there is an increasing appreciation of other instruments, such as the English concept of wrongful trading, whereas on the other hand doubts concerning *Minimumkapital* are no longer concealed.[279] Apart from that, any *Betrügerei* (fraudulent behaviour) should be counter-attacked by introducing the penalty of personal liability *'beim Handeln mittels einer inländischen Zweigniederlassung unter Schädigung inländischer Gläubiger'* (in a case of acting on behalf of a branch to the detriment of domestic creditors).[280] Piercing the corporate veil functions as a last resort; either English law, or

---

[273] BayOLG 26 August 1998, *DB* 1998, pp. 2318 et seq., commented on by Sedemund/Hausmann (1999) 810.

[274] de Wulf (1999) 319 and Sonnenberger/Großerichter (1999) 729, reach the same conclusion.

[275] Meilicke (1999) 627; and Sonnenberger/Großerichter (1999) 730.

[276] The *'Kombinationstheorie'* was suggested as an alternative by Zimmer, commented on by Behrens (1999) 324: the 'incorporation' theory should be applied to those companies having real ties with the 'incorporation' country. Pro-forma foreign companies, however, should be subject to the 'real seat' theory.

[277] Ulmer (1999) 662 et seq. In the same sense, Sonnenberger/Großerichter (1999) 730.

[278] ibid. 663: *'Eine Nichtanerkennung der Komplementärfähigkeit der ausländischen GmbH aus gründen der Mitbestimmungsumgehung müßte daher aus der Sicht des Centros-Urteils Bestand haben.'* He expresses his sacrosanct belief, that any amendments thereto under a foreign proper law of the company would not even pass the German test of *ordre public*.

[279] Ulmer (1999) 664: while comparing the company laws of the EC member states on minimum capital requirements (e.g. German GmbH: DM 50,000; Portugal DM 70,000; Austria: approximately DM 30,000; Netherlands: 40,000 Dutch guilders), he considers the differences *'als nicht so gravierend, wie es auf den ersten Blick erscheinen darf'* (not so problematical as it may have appeared). Lutter (2000) 9 et seq., advocates the extension of the Second Directive on Co-ordination of Company Law on Capital of Companies to private company types.

[280] Ulmer (1999) 664. Legal basis for liability is s 823.2 BGB (Civil Code), in combination with the proper German law of a tort.

German law on *Haftung wegen eindeutiger Unterkapitalisierung* (liability resulting from non-compliance with minimum capital requirements) could serve as a basis to fight abuses underlying the ECJ *Centros* case.[281] On the other hand, it has been doubted whether it is still legitimate to submit managers of a non-German company residing on German territory to *unbeschränkte Haftung der Gesellschafter* (unrestricted personal liability).[282] Altogether, it remains to be seen whether the Danish device—multiple purpose trip: combining a holiday in the UK with the setting up of an English private limited company—will become popular.[283]

After ECJ Centros: *is the German* Sitz *theory compatible with the EC Treaty?*

On 30 March 2000 the German Federal Supreme Court ordered preliminary proceedings at the ECJ in order to establish whether the German *Sitztheorie* (real seat theory) is in compliance with the EC Treaty.[284] The facts underlying this case were as follows. The plaintiff, a *Besloten Vennootschap* (i.e. the Dutch equivalent of a private limited company) which was duly incorporated and registered at the Commerce Chamber of Amsterdam in the Netherlands had its management and control office on German territory. Both company managers of this *Besloten Vennootschap* (BV) were German nationals with residence in Germany. Prior to the transfer of the management and control centre of the BV from the Netherlands to Germany, a contract was concluded between the plaintiff and the defendant, obliging the defendant to rebuild immovables in Düsseldorf that were owned by the plaintiff. As the defendant failed to perform his duties arising from contract, the BV started court proceedings against the defendant. As German private international law prescribes that a legal person's capacity is submitted to the *Personalstatut* (i.e. the proper law of the company), this proper law has to be found by giving decisive weight to the *tatsächlicher Sitz—Hauptverwaltung* (the management and control centre) of the company.[285] As a consequence of the fact that the Dutch BV had its *Sitz* (i.e. management and control office) on

---

[281] Ulmer (1999) 665. Cf. Sonnenberger/Großerichter (1999) 724, referring to others.

[282] ibid. 730. Cf. the Dutch alternative, contained in the 1998 PFFC Act, above.

[283] Ulmer (1999) 664. Roth (2000) 155, observed that if the real seat theory 'were to be replaced by the incorporation theory special spatially determined rules would have to be developed, leading to a mix of foreign company law with parts of German company law' (cf. workers' co-determination).

[284] Beschluß vom 30. März 2000—VII ZR 370/98. At the time of conclusion of the manuscript, there was no official record of this judgment yet. The following is based on the 'Bundesgerichtshof. Mitteilung der Pressestelle' (i.e. Press-report of the Federal Supreme Court, issued on 5 April 2000, http://www.uni-karslruhe.de/-BGH/entinfo.htm), and on the Appeal Court judgment (OLG Düsseldorf: decision from 10 September 1998), which ultimately gave rise to the BGH judgment. These lower court proceedings were analysed by Ebke (2000), 203 et seq.

[285] See Ebke (2000), 203, with further references.

German territory, however without being incorporated as a German legal person, the German LG (i.e. lower court) withheld the plaintiff *Rechtsfähigkeit* (i.e. capacity). As a consequence thereof, the BV was deemed to lack *Parteifähigkeit* too (i.e. *ius standi*, capacity to appear in court proceedings) on the basis of §§ 50 and 543 ZPO.[286] The court explicitly observes that, notwithstanding the fact that the plaintiff must be regarded as an existent company under the law of the Netherlands,[287] this does not preclude German courts from applying the real seat theory in its severest consequences. Neither is this in the view of the court prohibited under the EC Treaty.

The BGH expresses its concern, that the real seat theory seeks to safeguard the interests of company creditors and company members alike. The incorporation theory would therefore lead to applicability of the system of law which ultimately provides for the weakest possible protection of the aforesaid interests. The following preliminary questions were referred to the ECJ by the German Federal Supreme Court: does the abovementioned reasoning (application of the Real Seat theory) infringe upon the freedom of establishment which is granted by articles 43 and 48 of the EC Treaty?[288] Does freedom of establishment impose the duty upon authorities of EC member states to apply the incorporation theory to companies duly incorporated in other EC member states as it is being done in other EC member states? Accordingly, matters of *Rechtsfähigkeit* (capacity) would also have to be submitted to the law under which the company has been duly incorporated, if subsequent to its formation the company transferred its management and control office to the territory of another EC member state.

Notwithstanding the fact that, like ECJ *Daily Mail*, this case is about the cross-border transfer of a company's management and control office from one EC member state to another, the following aspects may not be overlooked. Contrary to ECJ *Daily Mail*, the heart of the matter is about company law, not tax law. Furthermore, the facts in this case are centred around the freedom of establishment, rather than the freedom of departure of legal persons. When compared to ECJ *Centros*, primary rather than secondary establishment is at stake here. The two issues that arise in the BGH-case must be clearly disentangled. The first matter has regard to the *Rechtsfähigkeit* (capacity) of companies having their management and control centre in another European member state than that where they are

---

[286] Zivilprozeßordnung, i.e. the German code on civil procedure.

[287] The plaintiff underscored that the Netherlands adhere to the incorporation theory, as a consequence of which under art. 4 of the German EGBGB (reference back) the BV should not be denied capacity to appear in court proceedings.

[288] The Federal Supreme Court underscores that this matter has not been clarified in the previous ECJ *Daily Mail* and *Centros* judgments.

incorporated. Closely linked thereto is the *Parteifähigkeit* (i.e. the right of legal persons to appear in court proceedings) in the EC member state where their real management and control office is located, notwithstanding their incorporation in another member state. The second matter, which needs to be answered independently, is that of the system of law which ultimately applies to these companies.[289]

As regards the *ius standi*, i.e. the right to appear in court proceedings, it is highly remarkable that this case is about a Dutch company type which is resident on German territory, not acting as a defendant but as a *plaintiff*. In an inverse situation, that is if claims had been brought *against* the Dutch *Besloten Vennootschap*, the opponent of the BV would have had the alternative to take action against the managers of the BV in their status as partners of e.g. an *Offene Handelsgesellschaft*.[290] In the foregoing situation, however, the Dutch BV, coming in from another EC member state, has no possibility at all to initiate court proceedings before a German court, simply because its 'existence' is denied by German authorities. Reasoning in the spirit of ECJ *Centros*, one could argue that it would be contrary to the EC Treaty to apply the real seat theory in its severest consequences: withholding capacity and *ius standi* from either secondary or primary establishments of legal persons that are duly established in another EC member state would in its effects closely resemble a refusal by national authorities of EC member states to register (branches of) companies incorporated in other EC member states. In my opinion, it is not unlikely that the ECJ reaches at the conclusion that the aforesaid measure emerging from German national law disproportionally hinders the access to the European Market. Quite another matter, however, is whether from now on real seat countries (e.g. Germany or France) should relinquish their attitude and are obliged to grant companies from other EC member states the same treatment as companies are entitled to in incorporation countries (e.g. the United Kingdom and the Netherlands), or whether perhaps it shall remain possible for the former group of countries to submit companies from other EC member states to legislative measures that are also imposed upon own nationals. There seems to be no clear-cut answer to this question imposing itself. The progressive stage at which the European Market is, however, challenges the ECJ to take a position.

It is noteworthy that the goals and methods pursued by the Dutch legislator—e.g. the 1998 PFFC Act—are more or less comparable to German legislation: detailed disclosure prescriptions function as a *'hinreichende*

---

[289] Note that the discussion reminds us of the precise meaning of the word 'recognition' of foreign companies ('minimum' and 'widened' recognition), which has been dealt with in ch 2 I 1 above.

[290] See ch 4 III 1, below.

Warnfunktion' (warning to company creditors).[291] It must be recalled once again, however, that it is not completely clear what is permitted and what is not under the EC Treaty. None of the German writings considered explicitly expressed the view that the EC Treaty fundamentally opposes restrictive measures; indeed Ulmer explicitly rejects the idea of incompatability of the complete range of aforementioned German measures with the EC Treaty.[292]

Cross-border company seat transfers after *Centros*

An interesting position was taken by de Wulf.[293] Following *Centros*, a distinction should be made between the transfer of only a company's *headquarters* to another EC member state on one hand, and the cross-border transfer of a company's *business activities* on the other. Whereas the former situation does not constitute *establishment* under the EC Treaty, the latter situation, in his view, essentially permits companies to invoke freedom of establishment, as a result of which even *primary* establishment is granted under the EC Treaty.[294] One should not overlook, however, that de Wulf basically denies the existence of the hidden conflict rules underlying articles 52 and 58 of the EC Treaty.[295]

The future: the race to the bottom reconsidered

It has been argued that after *Centros*, the national legislators of EC member states face the complicated task of reconsidering their national laws.[296] Should we prepare again for a race to the bottom? This fear has been countered. Unlike for example American states, European member states do not have such clear interests in starting a regulatory competition. Although they remain interested in attracting foreign investors (companies in particular), these interests are believed to be outweighed by tax law, as well as social law interests. de Wulf points to the following factors: (i) instruments such as 'incorporation fees' and annual 'franchise taxes', to be paid by companies established in for example Delaware, are not similar in Europe;[297] (ii) efforts to avoid a 'race to the bottom' in the USA primarily concern the interests of shareholders, rather than those of the

---

[291] See ch 4 III 1, below referring *i.a.* to ss 13.2 and 19 Handelsgesetzbuch (Commercial Code), s 4 GmbHG (Private Company Law Code).

[292] Ulmer (1999) 665. Cf. criticism of the Dutch 1998 PFFC Act, and the views of *i.a.* Schutte-Veenstra (1999) 229, above.

[293] de Wulf (1999) 321 et seq.

[294] de Wulf, however, admits that in everyday practice this is highly complicated, since such a transfer does not extricate companies from re-incorporating under the law of the country of re-establishment.

[295] See IV 1, above.   [296] cf. Sonnenberger/Großerichter (1999) 727 et seq.

[297] cf. comments in I 3, above.

management board,[298] whereas European legal orders concentrate on the protection of company creditors; (iii) last but certainly not least, it has been argued that the attraction of the Delaware company law regime is explained by its reputation for high-quality standards (including the know-how of specialized company lawyers and judges, etc.).[299]

Conclusion

Contrary to the view advocated particularly amongst German writers, it remains uncertain whether ECJ *Centros* precludes EC member states from retaining the 'real seat' theory. It would be an exaggeration to call the *Centros* judgment 'revolutionary', in the sense that *'wesentliche Grundlagen des Internationalen Gesellschaftsrechts (sind) erschüttert'*.[300] ECJ *Centros* (merely?) limits national restrictive legislative measures. Furthermore, both 'incorporation' and 'real seat' countries may have legitimate interests in taking legislative measures to prevent their nationals from circumventing national company laws. They are allowed to take such measures provided, however, that they do not constitute a disproportionate hindrance to the freedom of establishment for companies or their agencies, branches, or subsidiaries. Dutch and German writers seem to differ, however, on the extent to which national measures are allowed under the EC Treaty.

---

[298] According to de Wulf (1999) the US state of Delaware is primarily concerned with its own interests (tax income revenues) and the interests of shareholders, possibly to the detriment of company creditors, who are mostly established outside Delaware.

[299] de Wulf (1999) 322 et seq., quoting Roberta Romano. For a more general view of competing national legislators in the field of EC company law: Merkt (1995) 553 et seq.

[300] Sedemund/Hausmann (1999) 810.

3

Provisional Conclusions

I. FREEDOM OF ESTABLISHMENT FOR COMPANIES: A LEGAL VACUUM

The preceding inquiry into the mobility of legal persons in Europe justifies no other conclusion than that, despite high expectations, the outcome for the time being is poor. Until now neither EC law nor private international law has shown itself capable of elaborating the versatile legal instruments needed to tackle the problem of deficient cross-border company mobility.

II. PRIVATE INTERNATIONAL LAW

Long before the EC law era, private international law was already divided on what has been described as everlasting warfare between the 'incorporation' theory and the 'real seat' theory. According to the 'incorporation' theory, a company is governed by the law according to which it is (duly) established, whereas the latter theory prescribes that the law of the country where the company has its real seat (i.e. its management and control centre) is applicable to company relationships. Thus, the 'incorporation' theory stands for party autonomy while the 'real seat' theory stands for an objective proper law test.

In considering a period of more than a century, a critical observer will find that all efforts ever undertaken to bring about satisfactory international regulation of the matter of mutual recognition of foreign legal persons have been in vain. Neither international organizations (in particular the Hague Conference on Private International Law), nor doctrine (cf. the reconciliatory concepts of *Überlagerung*, *Differenzierung*, *maatschappelijke prioriteit*, etc.) have managed to create a breakthrough. As a consequence, cross-border company jurisdiction, the determination of the proper law of the company, and recognition and enforcement of foreign judgments related thereto, are all affected by this controversy. The fact that all attempts to end the warfare have failed can be explained as follows. Of all the available legal vehicles through which to conduct business, companies tend to be the most attractive form. As a consequence of this, the pursuit of economic markets depends largely on whether only domestic or also foreign company forms are allowed to conduct business on a state's territory. This is of predominant importance, because considerable differences exist between the company law regimes of different states. Rather than simply trying to ascertain the closest 'geographical' relationship, each of the competing private international law recognition theories reflects major national economic policies of the legal orders on whose territories companies operate. These national policies may either stress the encouragement of industrialization by attracting foreign investors, or the need to 'control' foreigners by obliging them to opt for a domestic company form. The former policy is likely to lead to acceptance of the 'incorporation' theory, whereas the latter is best safeguarded by the 'real seat' theory.

III. PRIVATE INTERNATIONAL LAW AND EC LAW: THE INTERRELATIONSHIP

The interrelationship between private international law and EC law is steadily intensifying. Ascertaining the 'proper law' of the company is no longer a unifocal process of trying to find the closest (geographical) relationship with a legal order. Today, more than ever, we are conscious of the fact that, apart from the above described economic impact of recognition theories on economic markets, EC law comprises (overt or 'hidden') conflict rules. An analysis of both legal disciplines on a complementary basis is therefore required. From a retrospective view, it can be said that, occasionally, the two legal disciplines even carry identical flaws: any analogy which over the years has been construed between natural and legal persons (e.g. 'birth' and 'death' of a company) by both EC law and private international law specialists may seem attractive, but in practice this approach turns out to be artificial and highly problematic.

IV. PRIMARY EC LAW

Thus far, neither of the two opposing private international law recognition theories has been imposed upon EC member states by articles 43 and 48 (ex arts. 52 and 58) of the EC Treaty. However, recent developments deserve contemplation. The German BGH initiated preliminary proceedings to put an end to uncertainty whether the German *Sitztheorie* (i.e. real seat theory) still complies with the EC Treaty. Even if European law as it now stands still permits EC member states to adhere to the real seat theory, this does not mean that the authorities of EC member states are entirely free to apply this theory in all its severest consequences. They should at least refrain from sustaining national law provisions that form a disporportionate hindrance to companies planning to cross borders. They should even go beyond this minimum standard, as they are obliged to accommodate their national laws to further cross-border company mobility.

The incorporation theory, being far more appropriate to promote cross-border company mobility than its counterpart, seems to be compatible with the EC Treaty. However, due to different treatment of 'genuine' and 'pro-forma' foreign companies in the Netherlands, its compatibility with EC law has explicitly been doubted as well. Notwithstanding the fact that preliminary proceedings concerning the compatibility of the Dutch Pro-Forma Foreign Companies Act 1998 were cancelled, similar cases are expected to give rise to preliminary proceedings in the near future.

V. SECONDARY EC LAW

The Treaty on the European Union (including the Treaties of Maastricht and Amsterdam) provides no clear guidance on freedom of establishment for legal persons. Consequently, recourse must be had to secondary EC law. Prior to the piecemeal Company Law Harmonization Programme, there was still a (common?) belief that an overall settlement of the recognition matter was possible. However, the 1968 EC draft treaty on the mutual recognition of companies, which was based on article 220 of the EC Treaty, ultimately shared the fate of its Hague Conference counterpart, and did not become law either. What both legislative projects had in common was that their failure was predetermined by the frequently criticized compromising and impractical character of the drafts.

Since then, the general belief has taken hold that the complicated matter of the precise status granted to foreign companies and the exercise of rights by those companies cannot simply be reduced to one single recognition principle, covering all imaginable cross-border company relationship matters. Recognition of foreign companies was deemed to be more feasible after a piecemeal harmonization of company law in Europe. To that end, a rather ambitious Company Law Harmonization Programme was initiated. Although several of the directives were implemented in the national legislation of member states, many other directives never progressed beyond the status of drafts. For several decades now, those draft directives attempting to regulate the heart of the matter (e.g. the Fifth Company Law Directive on the functioning of company organs) carry the seeds of disruption. To a large extent, this also explains the stalling of the draft proposal for a *Societas Europea*.

VI. MULTI-PARTY NATURE AND MULTIPLE INTERESTS

European company law developments thus seem to have run up a blind alley. To a large extent, this is explained by the complexity of the subject-matter involved. Cross-border migration of natural persons is hardly comparable to the migration of companies. Frequently, disputes involving companies are of a compound nature: matters of primary and secondary European law, company law (including conflict of laws), the law on nationality of natural and legal persons, tax law, labour law, social security law, etc. become entangled. The multi-party nature of company relationships includes both internal and external relationships: company organs (e.g. the shareholders' meeting, the management board, and in civil law countries, often the supervisory board) individual shareholders, creditors, debenture holders, and employees, all have their own specific interests in the company's prosperity. Also, the impact of company cross-border mobility on the economy of EC member states exceeds that of natural persons.

In this respect, the *Powell Duffryn* judgment is a landmark case, in that it sufficiently demonstrates that the settlement of disputes arising from cross-border operating companies requires an integrated EC law and private (international) law approach. The additional value of this judgment lies predominantly in its interdisciplinary reasoning: *inter alia* the search for uniform interpretation of notions such as 'contract' (article 5) and 'agreement' (article 17) in the Brussels Convention has been realized with the help of substantive law notions. Furthermore, the link with the harmonization programme in the area of company law (ex article 54(3)(g) of the EC Treaty) is brought into line with both substantive company law and private international law concepts. However, the final outcome, which was achieved at the cost of the authoritative (persuasive?) powers of the ECJ, seems to be insufficient to overcome the enduring conflict between the 'incorporation' and the 'real seat' theory.

VII. PRIMARY AND SECONDARY ESTABLISHMENT: FIGHTING OR PREVENTING FRAUD

Following the EC case of *Centros*, member states are not allowed to refuse the registration of a branch set up by a company duly formed in another member state. Such refusal is contrary to ex articles 52 and 58 of the EC Treaty. Any assumption that, due to *Centros*, the 'real seat' theory is no longer acknowledged under the EC Treaty seems at least premature. Member states are, however, not precluded from taking other, less restrictive measures to fight or prevent fraud. There is a clear relationship between *Centros* and the kind of measures promulgated by the Dutch 1998 PFFC Act. Dutch and German writers seem, however, to differ on the extent to which national measures are permitted under the EC Treaty. It is for the ECJ to decide whether the Dutch Pro-Forma Foreign Companies Act on one hand, and German *Sitztheorie* on the other comply with articles 43 and 48 of the EC Treaty or not.

Part 2

The Present State of Private International Law: A Comparative Analysis

4

'Incorporation' Countries versus 'Real Seat' Countries

I. INTRODUCTION

The overall impression one gets after having read the preceding chapters is that a paradoxical situation exists: a rapidly developing Single Market on one hand, and authorities of national legal orders either tending to limit the liberal concept of the 'incorporation' theory, or even adamantly holding onto the 'real seat' (*siège réel*) theory on the other. Undoubtedly, contrasting perceptions at national level (i.e. the legal and economic policies of the individual EC member states) may be held responsible for that. However, in-depth attention will now be given to the law of six legal orders (one of them being a non-EU country), three of which adhere to the incorporation theory, the others being representatives of the real seat theory.

General recognition of companies by all EC member states on a reciprocal basis is not to be expected soon (see Part 1 above). A closer look at the private international law developments of a group of Member States is therefore necessary. First, the three legal orders in Europe which at present pay homage to the incorporation theory are explored. Apart from the Netherlands and the United Kingdom, Switzerland, although not (yet?) a member of the European Union,[1] also deserves a closer look. As will be

---

[1] Currently, however, several degrees of 'intensified contacts' between Switzerland and the European Union (including possible future membership) are being contemplated; for more detailed information see ch 4 II 3 below.

seen, Swiss authorities, like their counterparts in the Netherlands, try to balance conflicting objectives: the liberal principle of the incorporation theory is important from the point of view of welcoming foreign investors; the need to combat abuses of this lenient regime may, however, be seen as a drawback, compelling Swiss authorities to limit their generous attitude towards foreign companies. There is another good reason to extend the inquiry to Switzerland: the Swiss 1987 Code on Private International Law contains a set of detailed conflict rules and substantive law provisions on the recognition of foreign companies and cross-border company seat transfers. Perhaps this sophisticated set of rules may turn out to be eligible for transcription by, or at least to inspire, the EC legislator.[2]

Today more than ever, the multi-party character of company relationships creates new challenges. As the *Powell Duffryn* judgment[3] shows the impact on the socio-economic sphere of notably the state in whose territory the company's 'seat' (either central managment and control office, or registration office) resides. When compared to, for example, 'common' contracts, company affairs are characterized by coinciding, and more frequently conflicting, interests of shareholders, management (and supervisory) boards, employees, debenture holders, company creditors, national treasury departments, social security authorities, etc. It is therefore conceivable that the authorities of the majority of member states let the 'real seat' doctrine prevail over party autonomy (i.e. the incorporation theory). This concern has been put forward repeatedly by doctrine and by the judiciary of Germany, France, and Italy, being representatives of the real seat law family.

II. 'INCORPORATION' COUNTRIES

1. THE NETHERLANDS

Historical development

The ambiguity of the 'recognition' concept
It was not until the mid-1950s that Dutch law put an end to ambiguity regarding the recognition of foreign companies. In the absence of codified

---

[2] See ch 4 II 3 and ch 6 III below.
[3] See ch 2 IV 2 above.

rules on conflict of laws, the preceding era reflected hesitation: courts and doctrine alike showed aloofness towards companies incorporated under a foreign system of law but having their real place of business on Dutch territory. Learned writers[4] either based their views on ill-defined definitions of the notion of 'seat', or manifestly paid tribute to the concept of the real seat theory: contrary to Asser, who refrained from any attempt to define a company's 'seat',[5] Kosters estimated the company's seat to be the place where *'de leiding der zaken geschiedt'*, i.e. where the central management is situated.[6] Case-law also reflected ambiguity: 'incorporation' theory and real seat theory each had their own protagonists.[7] For several reasons the few[8] decisions of the Dutch Supreme Court in this area did not provide real guidance. Although mentioned often, the case of *UNRRA*[9] is unsuitable to establish a firm position: the recognition in the Dutch court of the *lichaam* ('body', or 'entity') of the UNRRA, which was established by co-operation between several member states to protect the interests of war victims, had nothing to do with Dutch law concerning the recognition of foreign legal persons, now that *public*, not private international law (i.e. the formation of a UN body by means of a treaty) was at stake. Thus, the dispute about whether or not the Dutch Supreme Court in 1863 had accepted

[4] For a bird's-eye view of Dutch doctrinal concepts in those days, see Cohen Henriquez (1961) 38–44 and Vlas (1999) 4 et seq.

[5] T.M.C. Asser, *Schets van het Internationaal Privaatrecht* (1880) 135, mentions *'de zetel'* (seat), without giving any definition. Neither can any answer be deduced from the context: (actual) place of business, place of central management, or perhaps even the place where the company had been incorporated?

[6] J. Kosters, *Het Internationaal Burgerlijk Recht in Nederland* (1917) 659.

[7] Courts seemed to sit on a fence. In favour of the incorporation theory were e.g.: cantonal court Boxtel 20 December 1859, W 2361 (insurance company La Belgique duly incorporated in Belgium, therefore to be considered as a company having legal personality in Belgium); Court Amsterdam 13 August 1869, W 3149; Court Rotterdam 11 September 1922, NJ 1924, p. 167. In favour of the real seat theory: Court Almelo 30 October 1901, W 7736; Court Amsterdam 22 April 1910, W 9159; Court of the Hague 12 May 1925, NJ 1926, p. 63; Court Roermond 3 May 1934, NJ 1935, p. 253 (citing Kosters, see n 6 above). Hesitatingly, Court Rotterdam 19 June 1913, NJ 1913, p. 1067 (held: since the company Surie & Sons was incorporated in England, which turned out also to be its place of actual business, the question concerning the validity of formation should be answered in accordance with English law).

[8] An explanation for the relatively small number of Supreme Court judgments on conflict of laws is that the 'Wet op de Rechterlijke Organisatie' (Judicial Organization Act) was revised in 1963; prior to this Act, the SC was not authorized to review uncodified areas (of which Dutch private international law at that time formed an outstanding example). Since in 1963 the scope of section 99 of this Act was widened ('legislation' was replaced by the expression 'law') the supervisory function of the Supreme Court was no longer restricted to written legislation; from then on case-law and doctrine were included as well.

[9] HR 19 May 1950, NJ 1951, 150, commented on by Vlas (1999) 27.

the incorporation theory[10] remained unresolved. Opposing views of this judgment stemmed from the question of how the word 'recognition' should be interpreted: was it to be understood as an implied designation of the company's own rules (i.e. recognition in a broad sense)? Or did it mean simply recognition of the company as a bearer of rights and duties, after which the *lex societatis* would still have to be ascertained (i.e. the narrow sense)?[11] Doubts were not removed by the Dutch Supreme Court, which merely observed that Moguntia was not obliged to apply for a *Koninklijke Bewilliging* (Royal Assent), which in those days was still prescribed by article 36 of the Dutch Commercial Code. The Supreme Court ordered that (i) the King's sovereignty cannot have extraterritorial effect, and (ii) the matter before the court touched upon the formal validity of acts, which is governed by article 10 of the *Wet Algemeene Bepalingen* (General Provisions Act). According to that provision, formal requirements of the place of formation had to be complied with. Article 36 was therefore not considered to be applicable to foreign companies (i.e. companies duly established abroad).[12] However, the highest Court remained silent on the essential matter of how to ascertain the company's own rules.

The 1959 Act of Parliament: the turning point

Although the 1956 Draft Treaty of the Hague Conference on the Mutual Recognition of the Legal Personality of Companies never officially acquired the status of 'law',[13] the Dutch Act which was promulgated by Parliament on the *enforcement* of that Treaty did enter into force.[14] It was concluded from the literal wording of the Act that the incorporation theory undoubtedly applied in the Netherlands. According to the Act: *'Nederland is niet een land, welks wet de werkelijke zetel in aanmerking neemt als bedoeld in Article 2 van* [the draft of the Hague Treaty]'.[15] This turning point

---

[10] HR 23 March 1866, W 2781 (*Moguntia AG Mainz, Germany v NV Trajectum Zeist, NL*).

[11] See ch 2 I 2 above.

[12] Vlas (1982) 74 considers foreign companies 'invading' the territory of the Netherlands: in everyday practice the Justice Department, while handing out the so-called 'declaration of no objection' which was—and still is—required for the formation of a Dutch NV (and now also a BV), never obliged the NV to have its *central place of management* in the Netherlands. The *registered office* of a Dutch NV or BV, however, must always be situated in the Netherlands: cf. articles 67.3 and 177.3 of the Company Law Code, contained in the second book of the Dutch Civil Code.

[13] See ch 2 III 1 above.

[14] *Uitvoeringswet* van 25 juli 1959, Staatsblad 1959, 256. This law entered into force on 7 October 1959.

[15] 'The Netherlands *is not a legal order* which recognizes the real seat within the meaning of article 2 of [the draft of the Hague Treaty]' (author's transl.) It is of paramount

was inspired predominantly by economic policies.[16] First, the Dutch market would thereby become more attractive to potential foreign investors.[17] Furthermore, there was a certain element of reciprocity: maintaining the real seat theory[18] was believed to be highly detrimental to *Dutch* enterprises operating on *foreign* markets. Besides, foreign subsidiaries of Dutch companies operating on Dutch territory would also suffer from a (too) rigid application of the real seat doctrine by Dutch authorities.[19]

In spite of the fact that the Dutch government ultimately opted to abandon the real seat theory, doubts had not been removed entirely. The negatively drafted formula which was adopted by the abovementioned 1959 *Uitvoeringswet* (Act of Parliament) at least enabled authorities to place restrictions or reservations on the application of the 'incorporation' theory in the future. If necessary, the Dutch government nevertheless retained powers to alter its attitude towards foreign legal persons, since the Hague Treaty as such never entered into force.[20]

Interregional company law relationships

After 1959 Dutch courts approached the incorporation theory with a benevolent attitude.[21] Exceptions to this general position reflect the idea of

importance to note that the conflict rule enshrined in this *Uitvoeringswet* was (i) unilaterally drafted, and (ii) formulated as a denial; thus, it implicitly created discretionary powers (cf. 'reservations', still permitting Dutch authorities to supress any future abuses of a foreign company law by restricting the incorporation principle; see below).

[16] cf. more generally Edwards (1999) 335 (and ch 2 I 3 above).

[17] cf. Timmerman (1999) 156 and Vlas (1999) 24.

[18] Note that in those days the real seat theory was still being adhered to in the draft for a Benelux Code on Private International Law (see below).

[19] Vlas (1999) 24.

[20] The then Minister of Justice expressed the view that, despite the fact that the *Uitvoeringswet* was so closely linked to the Convention, this would not mean that the Netherlands would be obliged to stick to a system of recognition enshrined in a Convention, if that Convention was suspended afterwards. See Handelingen Tweede Kamer (1959) 2003 and 2004; Vlas (1982) 74, and (1993) 17 and 18.

[21] cf. Appeal Court of The Hague 29 February 1980, *NJ* 1980, 608 (assessment of international competence of the Dutch Court, not of the proper law of the company: company incorporated in Liberia having actual place of business in France); Court of Amsterdam 6 April 1982, WPNR 1985, p. 817 (also on the issue of competence: the winding-up of a company having its real seat in the Netherlands but incorporated under English law must be ordered by the English court). HR 11 November 1988, *NJ* 1989, 606 (foreign companies, i.e. those incorporated abroad, need not be registered in the Netherlands). Several court decisions merely covered the situation of foreign companies whose actual places of business corresponded with the law of incorporation. Consequently, these judgments are less aposite for the purpose of clarifying Dutch law: cf. recently, Court Zutphen 29 December 1988, *NIPR* 1989, 277; Appeal Court Amsterdam 22 November 1990, *NIPR* 1991, 128 (access to Dutch Court of companies incorporated abroad allowed).

fairness rather than a fundamental rejection of the incorporation theory.[22] Since 1990, one could even impute an explicit and unconditional acceptance of the incorporation theory to the Dutch Supreme Court, since it was held that 'the structure as well as the organization of the company and the functioning of its organs are to be subordinated to the system of law according to which the company was formed'.[23] One should bear in mind, however, that private international law of the Dutch Antilles, not a conflict of Netherlands laws, was at stake here.[24]

The year 1998 appeared to be another turning point, as will be seen. A *pars pro toto* codification of private international law rules concerning foreign legal persons was accomplished in that year.[25] The framework of a general Codification on Private International Law, including a chapter on legal persons, will be given brief attention first.

Towards a general codification of private international law?

Historical context

Attempts to codify the private international law of the Netherlands date back to the end of the nineteenth century, with the establishment in 1897 of the State Expert Committee on Private International Law.[26] The end of World War II marked the beginning of a new era involving harmonization

---

[22] HR 8 November 1957, *NJ* 1960, 629, HR 17 June 1966, *NJ* 1966, 374, and HR 27 June 1969, *NJ* 1969, 365, *NJ* 1970, 190/191 (*Carl Zeiss Stiftung*). These cases were aimed at restricting the unacceptable effects of confiscation measures. The Carl Zeiss Jena Stiftung was established in 1899. In the aftermath of World War II it suffered confiscation measures taken by the authorities of Eastern Germany. However, it was held that a confiscation measure ordered by the Russian authorities against Carl Zeiss Jena could not affect the continuing (independent) existence of 'Carl Zeiss Heidenheim' (being situated in former Western Germany), the latter body corporate being considered as legal successor of 'Carl Zeiss', according to the law of its *real* seat, i.e. the law of Western Germany at that time.

[23] HR 20 April 1990, *NJ* 1991, 560 (*Natco*), commented on by Vlas (1996) 463 (author's transl.). There was no genuine conflict between the two recognition theories, considering the fact that the company incorporated in accordance with the law of the Dutch Antilles also had its real seat there: see Vlas, (1993) 22 and (1999) 22. Remarkably, the inquiry concerning the irrevocability of a proxy given by the general meeting of shareholders could just as well have been considered as an issue to be settled by the proper law of *contract* (cf. hereafter, the material scope of the company's own rules).

[24] The (company) law codes of the separate territorial units of the *Koninkrijk der Nederlanden* (i.e. the Kingdom of the Netherlands including the Dutch Antilles and the island of Aruba in the Caribbean) are not (yet) identical: as a matter of fact, the former Dutch 1928 Company Law Act still applies *mutatis mutandis* in the overseas territories.

[25] See ch 4 II 1 below.

[26] The status of this State Expert Committee has recently been formalized by a Bill of Parliament, being referred to as the *Wet van 14 februari 1998, houdende regeling van de samenstelling en de werkzaamheden van de Staatscommissie tot voorbereiding van de te nemen maatregelen ter bevordering van de codificatie van het internationaal privaatrecht, ingesteld bij koninklijk besluit van 20 februari 1897, Stcrt. 1897, nr. 46 (Wet op de Staatcommissie voor het internationaal privaatrecht), Stb. 1998, 208.*

efforts on a cross-border scale. Under the auspices of Benelux, the economic union of Belgium, the Netherlands, and Luxembourg, conflict of law specialists drew up a draft code on the conflict of laws. This code was meant to replace the few written conflict of law provisions of the three legal orders involved. In the Netherlands no written conflict rule concerning foreign companies had so far been enacted.

The provision enshrined in article 3 of the 1951 version of the draft Benelux code still corresponded with the then prevailing recognition theory: the existence of a legal person and its representative organs were to be governed by the law of the state of its seat, i.e. the place where the central management (*hoofdadministratie*) was situated. However, this provision was deleted from the 1969 version of the draft code: no satisfying answers were found to (i) the recognition of companies incorporated under the law of a Benelux member state having their real seat abroad, and (ii) the recognition of companies, incorporated under the law of third countries, having their real seat on the territory of a Benelux state. The abolition of article 3 preceded the abrogation of the entire codification project in 1975.[27]

Piecemeal codification

Post-war Europe became conscious of the fact that draft regulations for international treaties had so far been dropped or at least shelved.[28] As a consequence of this, Dutch conflict of law experts tried to revive attempts to bring about a Private International Law Code on a national level. As regards the conflict rule concerning legal persons, the main goal was to replace the aforementioned negative formula of the *Uitvoeringswet* of 1959 with a more complete and coherent set of rules. To this end, three complementary initiatives were implemented in the 1980s:

(1) a General Code on Private International Law, including a chapter on the status and treatment of foreign legal persons;
(2) the *Wet Conflictenrecht Corporaties* (Conflict of Law Corporations Act); and
(3) the *Wet op Formeel Buitenlandse Vennootschappen* (Pro-Forma Foreign Companies Act).

As a member of the *Staatscommissie IPR* (governmental expert committee on Private International Law), Strikwerda explains that the Dutch legislator had been inspired by conflict of law codifications of the 1980s in other

---

[27] *19e Rapport Commun des gouvernements belge, neerlandais et luxemburgeois au Conseil Interparlementaire consultatif de Benelux au sujet de la cooperation entre les trois états en matière d'unification de droit, Doc. 159/I et annexe.* The total failure ('ein Requiem') of the Benelux draft code was analysed by H.U. Jessurun d'Oliveira, *RabelsZ.* 1975 224. From a retrospective angle, see also Strikwerda (1997) 26.

[28] cf. Part 1 above.

European countries (notably Austria, Germany, and Switzerland). The 'pre-draft' for a general Private International Law Code, originally meant to be a paper for further debate, was made public in August 1992 by the Ministry of Justice (subdivision Private Law).

Recently, however, the idea gained momentum that, first and foremost, specific parts of private international law should be codified step by step; thereafter, these *pars pro toto* codifications should be consolidated and concentrated (i) in an additional (10th) book of the Civil Code of the Netherlands, as well as (ii) in the Code on Civil Procedure.[29] The text of the 'pre-draft' is therefore not set out here in detail.

Freedom of incorporation: abuses and remedies

Liberal 'incorporation' theory versus *a rigid substantive company law regime*

Although the entry into force of a General Code on Private International Law is not to be expected in the near future, the Dutch legislator felt the need to fight the abuse of foreign companies. As emphasized above, the paramount reason for the endorsement of the incorporation theory in the Netherlands is to encourage the free flow of commerce. This goal is to be enhanced, *inter alia*, by favouring establishment by foreign investors wanting to penetrate the Dutch market. Free entrepreneurship and a liberal attitude towards the recognition of foreign companies go hand in hand.

For a long time, the incorporation theory has been applied in its purest form in the Netherlands: until 1 January 1998, the company's own rules, chosen by the founders of the company, were not subject to any legislative or judicial limitations; neither a *bona fide* and legal choice nor a genuine relationship between the system of law under which the company is incorporated and the Netherlands was required. Consequently, the strategy of domestic entrepreneurs to conduct their business while making use of a more generous system of company law was by no means reprehensible, let alone fraudulent. Economic competition may even compel businessmen to join the notorious 'race for the bottom'.[30] However, of all countries paying homage to the incorporation theory, the Netherlands had the best reason to fear abuses.[31] The coincidence of a liberal incorporation doctrine coupled with rigid local company laws concerning the formation of a Dutch NV or BV[32] has been criticized as being schizophrenic.

---

[29] Strikwerda (1997) 26. Cf. further the special issue of *NIPR* 1994, entirely devoted to the 'pre-draft'. To some extent, the provisions concerning corporations influenced the current 1998 CLC Act: see below.

[30] See ch 2 I 3 and II 3 above.

[31] See Roelvink (1987); Siemer/Helmig (1987); and Vlas, *The Fight against Pseudo-Foreign Corporations* (1994) 308 et seq. and (1999) 28 et seq.

[32] Read the mandatory prescriptions of section 4 (formation of legal entities in general) in conjunction with sections 64 (NVs) and 175 (BVs) et seq. of the second book of the Dutch Civil

Abuse of Dutch company types

Over the years, temptation grew to circumvent rigid Dutch company law by simply incorporating a company under a less stringent foreign system of law.[33] Cohen Henriquez ironically rendered the picturesque example of the '. . . local window cleaner in the small village of Appingedam in the Northern rural district of the Netherlands, exclusively being engaged in business activities in (this region of) the Netherlands, making use of the legal form of an English private limited company'.[34] Indeed, this paradoxical legal attitude is a classic example of flaunting the imperfection . . .[35]

As stressed before: businessmen cannot be reproached for seeking to combine the best of both worlds. But they should not commit fraudulent behaviour. This is likely to be the case when a company is set up with the intention of letting the company go bankrupt to the detriment of its creditors. In the early 1980s creditors frequently suffered from abuse, particularly by Dutch private companies (BVs). In those days, Dutch company law had inadequate remedies to fight *mala fide* businessmen. Three Bills of Parliament (*Misbruikwetten*),[36] one of them implemented in sections 138 and 248 of the second book of the Dutch Civil Code,[37] the other two amending the law on company tax and social security charges,[38] were

Code: there is a set of formation requirements which must be complied with (notary deed signed by a civil law notary, a certificate of no objection by the Dutch Justice Department, and minimal capital requirements). Since the handing out of the certificate of no objection by the Justice Department can take a while, entrepreneurs often enter into pre-incorporation transactions on behalf of the (not yet existing) company (commonly referred to as NV or BV 'i.o' (*in oprichting*), to be understood as 'in formation'; see ss 93 for NVs and 203 for BVs).

[33] As will be seen (conflict of laws of the United Kingdom, ch 4 II 2 below), other systems of law which adopt the incorporation theory are troubled far less by these kind of problems, simply because businessmen are hardly likely to feel the masochistic urge to exchange their liberal local company law regime for a more rigid foreign system of law.

[34] Cohen Henriquez (1982) 265 et seq.

[35] cf., more recently, Vlas, *The Fight against Pseudo-Foreign Corporations* (1994) 310. While paying attention to other notorious cases, he is sceptical as well: 'Sometimes foreign companies are founded as "shelf-companies" by another foreign company and then sold to Dutch entrepreneurs. Some Dutch companies even act as a founder of foreign companies, under the slogan "A Delaware company incorporated in Holland".'

[36] Bills of Parliament from 4 June 1981 (Stb. 370), 21 May 1986 (Stb. 276), and 16 May 1986 (Stb. 275).

[37] The fundamental principle enshrined in these provisions follows from the first sentence: 'On the involuntary liquidation of a company limited by shares, each managing director shall be jointly and severally liable to the estate for the amount of the liabilities to the extent that these cannot be satisfied out of the liquidation of the other assets if the management has manifestly performed its duties improperly and if it is plausible that this is an important cause of the involuntary liquidation.' For a complete English text edition, see H.C.S. Warendorf/R.L. Thomas, *Companies and Other Legal Persons under Netherlands Law and Netherlands Antilles Law* loose-leaf edition, Deventer.

[38] The attention focused on malpractice (notably fraud) committed in the construction trade; a considerable number of *koppelbazen* (*mala fide* labour brokers) tackled the problem of taxes and high social security charges simply by not paying them.

necessary to counter this form of malpractice. Pursuant to these legislative measures, company directors, as well as others in charge of the company's management can be held jointly and severally liable for debts of the company if (i) the company's winding-up in a case of insolvency is a consequence of misconduct, and (ii) obligations arising from tax law and social security law are not satisfied.

Incorporation theory: abuse of foreign company types

Mala fide businessmen thus confronted with efficient tools to combat the abuse of—mainly—*Besloten Vennootschappen* (the Dutch equivalent of private limited companies) created other escapes: an easy way out appeared to be to set up a company in a foreign legal form. As a matter of fact, the incorporation theory invited them to do just that.[39] Apart from being lenient,[40] some foreign company law regimes turned out to be even more profitable for those businessmen worried by the records of their criminal pasts (fraud): a *Verklaring van geen bezwaar* (declaration of no objection), issued by the Dutch Justice Department, is a *conditio sine qua non* for establishing a Dutch NV or BV.[41] It precluded these businessmen from establishing another Dutch company for a specified period of time.

Even so, businessmen were not *totally* exempted from personal and joint liability under foreign company law regimes. Several Dutch mandatory law provisions apply regardless of whether the company is incorporated under Dutch or foreign law. In the first place the scope of the above-cited section 138 was explicitly expanded to cover *'een naar buitenlands recht opgerichte rechtspersoon'* (any legal person that has been established abroad).[42] Furthermore, it should not be overlooked that legislation at the crossroads of company law and labour law, such as the *Wet op de Ondernemingsraden* (Act on Worker Co-determination), as well as legislation on accounting and auditing and section 6 of the Dutch Code of Commerce (containing the duty to keep up the accounts for everyone who runs an undertaking) apply equally to foreign entities.

---

[39] See the previous section.

[40] Swift procedure, minimum costs, no minimum capital requirements, no notary expenses, etc.

[41] Sections 64 and 175 of the second book of the Dutch Civil Code contain the complete set of formation requirements for NVs and BVs (Dutch Public and Private Limited Companies, limited by shares); see also above.

[42] Although subs. 11 was added to s 138—which basically governs the liability of company managers for debts of *public* companies—it has never been doubted that it also applies to *private* company types; after all, it appeared that the latter category of (small) foreign companies was highly attractive to businessmen. For detail see Roelvink (1986) 87 et seq. and Vlas (1999) 140 et seq.

In spite of that, the proposed measures did not reach far enough in the eyes of many.[43]

In the early 1980s Vlas elaborated the doctrine of the *maatschappelijke prioriteit* (social priority rules).[44] Mandatory law rules in private international law should adjust the incorporation theory. Dutch provisions in Book 2 of the Civil Code ought not to be applied, however, if the (foreign) law of incorporation would offer sufficient protection to creditors of the company. Unlike the doctrine of mandatory law, the social priority doctrine has the following features: (1) it deals with company law, rather than quasi-public law; (2) even if the proper law of the company turns out to be that of the Netherlands, Dutch *lois d'application immédiate* may turn out not to be applicable, and vice versa; and (3) Dutch social priority rules may be applied to Dutch companies having their management and control office in, for example, New York. Although there are certain similarities between Vlas' social priority rules doctrine and Sandrock's *Überlagerungstheorie*[45] the latter concept allegedly 'leads to legal uncertainty and to the alternating application of the "siège réel" and "incorporation" principles'. In the theory of the superaddition (*Überlagerung*) the relationship between the company and one of its creditors can be governed by the law of the real seat, whereas the relationship between the company and another creditor can still be governed by the law of incorporation. Furthermore, this theory leads to the application of all mandatory rules of the law of the real seat instead of the law of incorporation.[46]

Counter-attack: the 1998 CLC Act in conjunction with the 1998 PFFC Act

In 1992 the *Commissie Vennootschapsrecht* (the Company Law Expert Committee)[47] was established. The general feeling was that the incorporation theory should not be totally abandoned. Instead, the gap between the nearly unrestricted freedom of incorporation and unpopular rigid local law was to be bridged by extending more mandatory domestic law

[43] Broad attention was given to the abuse of what became known as 'pseudo-', or 'pro-forma foreign' companies, notably private limited company types (e.g. the Delaware corporation, the English private ltd. co., etc.). See e.g. Roelvink (1986), Debets (1987), Siemer/Helmig (1987), Bellingwout (1993), van den Braak/Huiskes (1992), and, with further references, Vlas (1999) 30 et seq. For a comparative analysis of 'tramp' or 'pro-forma foreign' companies (i.e. USA, Netherlands, Switzerland) see R. Drury, 'The Regulation and Recognition of Foreign Corporations: Responses to the "Delaware Syndrome" ', CLJ (1998) 165 et seq. (discussed in ch 2 II 3 above).

[44] Vlas (1982), *The Fight Against Pseudo-Foreign Corporations* (1994) 312 et seq., and (1999) 32.

[45] For this theory, I refer to ch 2 II 2 above.

[46] Vlas *The Fight Against Pseudo-Foreign Corporations*, n 44 above 314 and Coenen (1993) 1272 et seq.

[47] Stcrt. 23 November 1992, nr. 227. Cf. Uniken Venema (1992). Previously (November 1990), the view was taken that for the time being there was no need for further infringements of the incorporation theory. Subs. 11 of s 138 (which was to be abolished in 1998, see below) was deemed to be effective.

provisions to foreign companies. Although lower Dutch courts had previously been willing to apply Dutch mandatory company law provisions (notably sections 69 and 180 of the second book of the Dutch Civil Code[48]) to pro-forma companies as well,[49] this application of Dutch law was explicitly overruled by the Dutch Supreme Court.[50] Subsequent to the SC *Texelse Visser* judgment, lower courts refrained from other analogies that would possibly also have been tried if the Supreme Court had not been so clear on this subject.[51] The road of *ius curia novit* thus being blocked, it was commonly felt that legislative attempts should be made to provide for the application of several mandatory Dutch company law provisions[52] to foreign companies.

After intensive debates, the legislative deficit has finally been remedied: we can say that, particularly with an eye to the need to fight the abuse of

[48] These provisions *inter alia* place a duty upon company directors of Dutch NVs and BVs (i.e. public as well as private companies limited by shares) (i) to register the company properly and (ii) to comply with minimum capital requirements, with the sanction of joint and several liability for debts of the company.

[49] cf. the *Romca* case, District Court Breda 21 September 1982, *NJ* 1984, 283. For a summary of this case see Vlas *The Fight Against Pseudo-Foreign Corporations* n 44 above 311 and (1999) 32. New York corporation Romca Inc., had its management and control centre in the Netherlands. Formerly, one of the directors had been director of a Dutch company of the same name; that Dutch company had been declared insolvent. The Court observed that since Romca Inc. had not been duly registered in the Register of Companies of one of the Chambers of Commerce in the Netherlands, the company's directors were jointly and severally liable for the company's debts according to sections 69 and 180 of book 2 of the Dutch Civil Code. The Court underscored that third parties ought to know the directors' powers and the extent of the company's solvency.

[50] HR 11 November 1988, *NJ* 1989, 606. For a description of the case see Vlas (1999) 33. A Dutch oil trading company sold gas oil to a fisherman, who lived on the Dutch island of Texel. The oil trading company sent several bills for oil deliveries to the fisherman at his residence on Texel, addressing them to a Danish private company limited by shares, an *Anpartselskab* (ApS). The fisherman refused to pay the bills for the reason that the ApS had been the contracting party. For alleged economic reasons he had conveyed his fishing boat to the ApS, which had been established especially for this purpose. The District Court of Alkmaar decided in conformity with the aforementioned *Romca* case; the Court of Appeal of Amsterdam, however, denied that the ApS should be registered in accordance with the Dutch Trade Register Act. The Supreme Court explicitly held that the articles 69 and 180 of the Dutch Civil Code apply solely to Dutch companies, even if the 'foreign' company enters Dutch jurisdiction.

[51] District Court Leeuwarden 7 June 1995, *NJ* 1995, nr. 657. Pro-forma foreign company (i.e. a company incorporated under the law of Delaware, having its management and control office exclusively in the city of Dokkum in the Netherlands). No requirement to pay up shares, now that, contrary to Dutch company law, there is no such requirement under the law of Delaware.

[52] e.g. ss 178 (minimum capital requirements under the penalty of personal and joint and several liability of directors of the company), 139, and 150 (publication; account and auditing). The ratio of these provisions lies in the need to protect company creditors. Some protection of employees had been realized already, as the WOR (Worker Co-determination Act) applies, regardless of the (foreign) legal form of the company. Neither the special inquiry procedure (ss 344 et seq.), nor the *structuurregime* for large companies (ss 152 and 262 et seq. for NVs and BVs) are deemed to be compatible with a foreign proper law of the company: see Vlas *The Fight Against Pseudo-Foreign Corporations* n 44 above 316 and (1999) 136 and 148 et seq.

foreign companies, a piecemeal codification has recently been accomplished. On 1 January 1998 two Bills of Parliament entered into force. One of them, commonly referred to in the Netherlands as the WCC,[53] contains general conflict rules for foreign legal persons.[54] According to section 1(1), '(i)n this Act the following terms shall mean: (a) corporation: partnerships, companies, associations, co-operatives, mutual insurance societies, foundations, and other bodies which operate externally as an independent unit or organization, and interest groups; (b) officer: a person who without being a constituent body of the corporation, is vested with representative authority under the law governing such corporation and its articles or the agreement establishing the interest group. (2) A corporation which, under its agreement or deed of establishment, has its corporate seat or registered office, or, in the absence thereof, its external centre of activities on the date of establishment in the territory of the state under the laws of which it is established, shall be governed by the law of that state.' Pursuant to article 7, '(t)he Act of 25th July 1959, Statute Book 256 for the implementation of The Hague Convention of 1st June 1956 with regard to the recognition of the legal personality of foreign companies, associations and foundations is hereby repealed'.

Another Act, known as the WFBV,[55] settles the problem of the *'formeel buitenlandse vennootschappen'* (i.e. companies of a purely pro-forma foreign character). The 1998 CLC Act is given wider material scope in that the conflict rules contained therein also apply to entities not endowed with legal personality.[56] Sections 1–6 of the PFFC Act impose significant duties on managing directors of pro-forma foreign companies. This set of mandatory rules, however, applies solely to *formeel buitenlandse rechtspersonen* (*pro-forma* foreign companies, which have no other genuine ties with a country, apart from formation and incorporation. This means that 'genuine' foreign companies remain unaffected by this piece of legislation. One has to remember though, that *all* foreign companies—whether pro-forma foreign or not—remain subject to section 5 of the 1998 CLC Act. This

[53] *Wet Conflictenrecht Corporaties*; the recommended English translation is: Conflict of Laws Corporations Act (CLC Act): H.C.S. Warendorf/R.L. Thomas, *Companies and Other Legal Persons under Netherlands Law and Netherlands Antilles Law* n 37 above. Cf. Vlas (1999) 3, with further references.

[54] Bills of Parliament of 17 December 1997, Stb. 698 and 699. Cf. Bellingwout (1992); van den Braak/Huiskes (1992); Kleman (1995); Strikwerda (1997) 229; Uniken Venema (1992); Vlas (1998) and (1999) 20 et seq.; and Wezeman (1995). Surprisingly, at least according to Vlas (1998) 53, the regulation of pro-forma foreign companies attracted more attention from the academic world, whereas the fundamental principle enshrined in the *Wet Conflictenrecht Corporaties* is of higher importance to the Dutch private sector.

[55] *Wet Formeel Buitenlandse Vennootschappen*; the recommended English translation is: Pro-Forma Foreign Companies Act (hereinafter referred to as the 1998 PFFC Act): H.C.S. Warendorf/R.L. Thomas, see n 53 above.

[56] e.g. partnerships: see Vlas (1998) 53 and (1999) 160 et seq. for further information.

provision more or less copied the former section 138(11) of the second book of the Dutch Civil Code: '(1) Notwithstanding the provisions of sections 2 and 3, sections 138 and 249 of Book 2 of the Civil Code shall, if the corporation is declared bankrupt in the Netherlands, apply or be of corresponding application to the liability of directors and supervisory board members of a corporation governed by foreign law pursuant to section 2 or section 4 and subject to the levy of corporate income tax in the Netherlands. Persons charged with the management of the business conducted in the Netherlands shall be liable as directors. (2) The court which declares the bankruptcy has jurisdiction in respect of any claims arising from the provision in the first subsection.' The fundamental principle enshrined in the sections 138 and 249 can be found in the first sentence: 'On the involuntary liquidation of a company limited by shares, each managing director shall be jointly and severally liable to the estate for the amount of the liabilities to the extent that these cannot be satisfied out of the liquidation of the other assets if the management has manifestly performed its duties improperly and if it is plausible that this is an important cause of the involuntary liquidation.'[57]

The 1998 PFFC Act: main features

Section 6 of the CLC Act explicitly states that '(t)his Act shall not affect the provisions of the Pro-Forma Foreign Companies Act'.[58] Section 1 of the latter defines pro-forma foreign companies as follows:[59] 'In this Act a pro-forma foreign company means a capital company with legal personality incorporated under a law other than Dutch law, which conducts its business entirely or almost entirely in the Netherlands without having any further real tie with the state under whose law it was incorporated. In this section the countries forming part of the Kingdom of the Netherlands are considered as states.' Creditors of purely pro-forma foreign companies are deemed to be worthy of protection: the provisions of sections 2 et seq. contain additional 'formation'[60] and disclosure require-

---

[57] As s 5 1998 CLC Act explicitly copies s 138 of the second book of the Dutch Civil Code, subs. 11 of s 138 was abolished (s 8 1998 CLC Act) on 1 January 1998. Vlas (1999) 143, takes the view that it is irrelevant whether or not the proper law of the company also provides equivalent measures.

[58] This is why Boele-Woelki (1995) 2655 et seq. and Vlas (1999) 35, advocate a consolidated incorporation of both the 1998 CLC Act and the 1998 PFFC Act in a future tenth book of the Dutch Civil Code, to be devoted to the Private International Law of the Netherlands.

[59] The wording of s 76, subs. 1 of the draft Code on Conflict of Laws is slightly different but its core concept is similar to that of the *Commissie Vennootschapsrecht*'s proposal.

[60] Of course, these requirements should by no means be understood as 'formation' requirements in the usual sense: the question whether or not formation requirements are complied with is answered exclusively by the proper law of the company. In the context used here, nothing else is meant than that if pro-forma foreign companies do not comply with certain mandatory law provisions of Dutch company law, the penalty will be joint and several liability of those in charge of the company's management.

ments. Section 2(1) reads: 'The directors of a pro-forma foreign company must give notice for registration in the commercial registry that the company falls within the definition in section 1 and deposit at the commercial registry an officially certified copy, or a copy certified by a director, of the Dutch, French, German or English text of the incorporation deed and the articles, if set out in a separate deed. They must also give notice for registration of the register in which, and the number under which, that company has been registered and the date of first registration. They must further notify for registration the name, personal data, if it relates to a physical person, and the address of the holder of all of the shares in the capital of the company or of the joint owner of matrimonial joint property, if all of the shares in the capital of the company constitute part thereof, without taking into account the shares held by the company or its subsidiaries. The directors of a pro-forma foreign company must notify the commercial registry of any change in what must legally be registered in the commercial registry with mention of the date on which such change took effect. Whatever must be performed pursuant to this Act may not take place by proxy. (2) The commercial registry referred to in the first subsection is the commercial register kept by the chamber of commerce and industry authorised pursuant to sections 6 and 7 of the Commercial Register Act 1996.'

Pursuant to section 3(1), '(a)ll papers, printed documents and announcements to which a pro-forma foreign company is a party or which it issues, with the exception of telegrams and advertisements, must clearly list the full name and legal type of the company, its corporate seat and the place of establishment of the enterprise owned by it and, if it must be registered in a register under the law applicable to it, the register, the identification number of its registration and the date of its first registration. It must also state under which number the company is registered in the commercial register and that the company is a pro-forma foreign company. It shall be prohibited to use an indication in any written papers, documents or notices which contrary to the truth imply that the enterprise belongs to a Dutch legal person. (2) If the capital of the company is mentioned, it must in any event state the issued amount and the paid-up part thereof. (3) If the company continues to exist after its winding up, the words 'in liquidation' (*in liquidatie*) must be mentioned after its name.'

Capital requirements and provisions concerning the registration of a certificate that the company complies with those requirements are taken from section 4(1): 'The issued and paid-up part of the capital of a pro-forma foreign company must at least be equal to the amount of the minimum capital referred to in section 178, subsection 2 of Book 2 of the Civil Code at the time when the company first falls within the definition in section 1.[61] (2) When the company first falls within the definition of section 1, its shareholders' equity must amount to at least the minimum capital referred to in subsection 1. (3) Simultaneously with the notice referred to in section 2, subsection 1 the directors must deposit at the commercial registry referred to in that section a certificate of a registered accountant or accountant-administrative consultant stating that the company complies with the provisions of subsections 1 and 2. The second and third sentence of section 204a, subsection 2 of Book 2 of the Civil Code shall apply, *mutatis mutandis*. The certificate shall relate to a date no earlier than five months from the date on which the company first falls within the definition in section 1. (4) The directors shall be liable jointly and severally, together with the company for any legal act binding on the company performed during their management in a period prior to compliance with the provisions of section 2, subsection 1 and subsections 1 to 3 inclusive of this section, or in any other period in which subsection 1 is not complied with or the shareholders' equity falls below the amount referred to in subsection 1 as a result of distributions to share-holders or by a repurchase of shares. (5) Subsections 1 to 4 inclusive shall not apply to a company subject to the law of any Member State of the European Union or of a state which is a party to the Agreement on the European Economic Area of 2 May 1992 and to which is also applicable the Second Directive no. 77/91 EEC of the Council of European Communities of 13 December 1976 on the co-ordination of safeguards required in Member States from companies referred to in Article 58, second paragraph of the Treaty, in order to protect the interests both of the participants in these companies and of third parties with regard to the incorporation of companies limited by shares and the maintenance and change of their capital for the purpose of harmonising such safeguards (OJ EC L26).'

Additional accounting and auditing requirements are contained in section 5(1): 'Save for subsection 2, section 10 of Book 2 of the Civil Code shall apply, *mutatis mutandis*, to a pro-forma foreign company. The obligations referred to therein shall be imposed on the directors of the company. (2) Each year, within six months after the end of the financial year, save where this period is extended by up to six months by an authorised resolution adopted in special circumstances, the directors shall prepare annual accounts and an annual report. Part 9 of Book 2 of the Civil Code shall apply, *mutatis mutandis*, to the annual accounts and annual report and the other information, provided publication pursuant to section 394 of that Book is made by the deposit at the commercial registry referred to in sec-

---

[61] The amount of money needed for a private company's incorporation is fixed at 40,000 Dutch guilders. For a thorough description of all the ins and outs see Vlas (1999) 41 et seq.

tion 2, subsection 2.[62] (3) Subsection 2 shall not apply to a company subject to the law of any member state of the European Union or of a state which is a party to the Agreement on the European Economic Area of 2 May 1992 and to which is also applicable the Fourth Directive no. 78/660/EEC of the Council of European Communities of 25 July 1978 on the basis of Article 54, paragraph 3(g) of the Treaty with regard to the annual accounts of certain types of companies. (OJ EC L222) and the Seventh Directive no. 83/349/EEC of the Council of European Communities of 13 June 1983 on the basis of Article 54, paragraph 3(g) of the Treaty on the consolidated annual accounts (OJ EC L193). (4) Each year prior to 1 April the directors must file for deposit at the commercial registry proof of registration in the register where the company must be registered according to the law applicable to it. Such proof may not have been issued more than four weeks prior to the date of filing.'

Pursuant to section 6, directors shall be jointly and severally liable for any misleading information emanating from account and auditing reports: 'Sections 249 and 260 of Book 2 of the Civil Code shall apply to pro-forma foreign companies, *mutatis mutandis.*'

Local managers and men of straw should heed section 7: 'For application of sections 2 to 6 inclusive, persons charged with the day-to-day management of the enterprise owned by the company shall be deemed to be directors of the company.' Pursuant to sections 9 and 10, non-compliance with the Act also results in criminal law penalties.

The PFFC Act: pros and cons

What are the merits of this piece of legislation? The company creditors may be protected effectively, but the courts will have to face the extremely complex task of defining exactly which company 'types' are aimed at,[63] and which of them will be defined as 'pro-forma foreign'.[64] Because the draft committee took the view that the incorporation theory should not be entirely substituted by the real seat theory, the characterization problem of exactly what a company's real seat is reappears in a second stage: precisely when do exceptions to the—after all still prevailing—incorporation principle apply? The definition of what has to be considered as a pro-forma

---

[62] Apart from criminal law sanctions—Section D of the *Wet Economische Delicten* (Economic Crimes Act) is applicable: ss 999 and 1000 of the Code on Civil Procedure authorize the Enterprises Division of the Amsterdam Court of Appeal to prescribe alterations in accounting proceedings.

[63] Vlas (1999) 36 emphasizes that even though s 1 speaks of 'capital companies', the German GmbH, whose capital is not necessarily divided into shares, is covered as well.

[64] The Minister of Justice estimated that about 4,000 'foreign' (caseload!) companies operating in the Netherlands can be expected to fall within the scope of the Bill: Vlas (1989) 54 and (1999) 31.

foreign company perhaps provides a glimpse of what is to come.[65] Since all relevant connecting factors can only be weighed *after formation* and often even *after business activities*, the benefits that might result from fighting abuse by foreign companies can only be achieved by sacrificing predictability.[66] This project has been criticized for its schizophrenic dualism (two systems of law governing company relations).[67] Perhaps, those in charge of company activities in the Netherlands wishing to avoid being held personally liable should voluntarily comply with the mandatory provisons in advance. The balance of costs and benefits would then still be positive, since neither the requirement of preformation supervision by the Ministry of Justice, nor the inquiry procedure (sections 344 et seq.) apply to companies incorporated under foreign law, irrespective of whether those companies are deemed to be merely pro-forma foreign.

What precisely remains attractive in a foreign company law regime? Notably, small and medium-sized business enterprises, which are purely 'homeward bound' can hardly be expected to prefer foreign company forms, now that the paramount reason to set up such companies (capital requirements; creditor interests) seem to have vanished. The popularity of the English private limited company (or the Danish ApS), at least from a company law perspective, might diminish. Nevertheless, it remains to be seen whether the Dutch legislative initiative is in conflict with EC law.[68]

---

[65] Which of the connected factors should be given decisive weight? Head office of the company; seat of (majority) shareholders; amount of participation, or other aspects? Cf. Coenen (1993) 1275: it is not certain whether the real seat of the company depends upon the location of the head office, the actual place of business, or whether company tax law should be considered as a decisive factor. Even if a conclusive answer were available, there is an element of quantity: a line must be drawn to decide what exactly forms 'the essential part'. This sophistic problem is known as the Sorites proof: when will a heap of gravel cease to be a heap? Vlas (1999) 37 even seems prepared to accept that a window-cleaning company incorporated abroad but operating in the Netherlands as well as in the nearest cross-border Belgian district falls within the scope of the PFFC Act all the same.

[66] The Dutch legislator could also have preferred the approach pursued by s 5 of the 1998 CLC Act: the proposed mandatory rules would then apply to *each* foreign company (irrespective of whether a company is to be considered as a genuine or a pro-forma foreign company). *Mutatis mutandis* Stille (1998) 63, who even advocates abandoning the incorporation theory totally in favour of the 'real seat' theory. However, this alternative would make the good suffer for the bad: see Drury (1998), above.

[67] Bellingwout (1992) 680 et seq, criticized the half-hearted compromise of the (then) draft proposal. For methodological reasons, he doubts whether the incorporation theory is compatible with the measures that have now become binding rules. Instead, as a tool for creditor protection, a black list of 'notorious foreign companies' operating in the Netherlands should be drawn up and published by Dutch authorities. One could of course question the impact of such a witch-hunt; is it for courts to decide, and which criteria should be used?

[68] Conclusive answers, in so far as they can be formulated, can only be reached by means of a dialogue between EC law and private international law; meanwhile, it is remarkable that it has been explicitly questioned whether the Dutch *Wet op de puur formeel buitenlandse vennootschappen* (PFFC Act) might be incompatible with the EC Treaty: see ch 2 IV 2. (ECJ *Centros*, see also following text and ch 6 II 1 below.)

The right to primary and secondary establishment: the PFFC Act and the ECJ case of Centros

Fifteen months after the entry into force of the Dutch 1998 PFFC Act the ECJ was requested to make a preliminary ruling under ex article 177 of the EC Treaty by the Danish *Höjesteret* in proceedings between Centros Ltd and Erhvervs- og Selskabsstyrelsen.[69] The Dutch PFFC Act is about the *primary* establishment of companies established in accordance with a foreign system of law, having their management and control centre on Dutch territory; the ECJ judgment primarily focuses on the *secondary* establishment of a foreign company in Denmark. There is, however, a certain relationship between the Dutch PFFC Act and the case before the ECJ: both the Dutch and the Danish authorities were concerned with people conducting business on Dutch, or Danish, territory, with the intention of circumventing rigid domestic company law requirements (for example, regarding minimum capital). The main concern for the Dutch authorities was that the incorporation theory leads to abuses: notably those (*mala fide*) businessmen who were no longer permitted by the Justice Department to set up a company were given an escape mechanism of setting up a company in another member state. Needless to say, this 'foreign' company would conduct business exclusively in the Netherlands. On 1 January 1998, the above described PFFC Act made this loophole less attractive. Danish authorities attempted to refuse the registration of a *branch* of a foreign company (Centros Ltd, a private company limited by shares under English law), which had been set up by Danish nationals exclusively conducting business in Denmark and for no other purpose than to circumvent rigid Danish company law capital requirements. In the view of the ECJ, the Danish authorities, in refusing to register the branch of Centros Ltd, had gone a step too far: such a fundamental refusal is contrary to ex articles 52 and 58 of the EC Treaty. The Court further observed: '(t)hat interpretation *does not*, however, *prevent* the authorities of the member state concerned from adopting any *appropriate* measure for *preventing or penalizing fraud, either* in relation to the *company itself*, if need be in co-operation with the member state in which it was formed, *or in its relation to its members*, where it has been established that they are in fact attempting, by means of the formation of a company, to *evade* their obligations towards private or public creditors established in the territory of the member state concerned.'[70]

Allegedly, the Dutch legislator took up the challenge to fight abuses by (pro-forma) foreign companies too enthusiastically: the catalogue of

---

[69] Case C–212/97 [1999] ECR I–1459; CMLR 551. See ch 2 IV 2 above.
[70] Cons. 38. (emphasis added).

duties contained in the Dutch PFFC Act[71] appears to discriminate[72] against directors of foreign companies, when compared to duties imposed upon directors of Dutch companies. Perhaps it would be preferable (i) to apply several sections of the Dutch company code (contained in the second book of the Dutch Civil Code) by way of analogous application; (ii) to *all* (i.e. not solely or pro-forma) foreign companies. Nothing less, but—and this is essential—nothing *more* either. It has been argued further that article 56 of the EC Treaty (i.e. the current provision of article 46 of the EC Treaty) does not justify measures against companies from other EC member states solely because they must be considered as *pro-forma* foreign. Article 56 requires that public policy is seriously jeopardized.[73] It has even been suggested that pursuant to the ECJ case of *Centros* it is fundamentally prohibited to impose any minimum capital requirement on (branches of) companies that are established in other EC member states.[74] However, I beg to differ on this matter. The precondition that 'national measures must be justified by imperative requirements in the general interest'[75] was not followed by any overall conclusion that capital requirements *as such* are not suited to protecting company creditors. In my opinion, the Court solely condemns the *penalty of non-registration* of the company's branch as a consequence of not having complied with national company laws of the member states concerning capital requirements. There is no reason to assume that punishing non-compliance with capital requirements by introducing personal liability of company managers is prohibited under the EC Treaty.[76] Moreover, this way of reasoning seems to be more in concert with the 2nd Company Law Directive on co-ordination of the capital of companies:[77] even though this Directive basically applies to *public* companies,[78] it would hardly make sense to assume that the concept of minimum capital as an instrument to protect company creditors would be fundamentally useless for *private* company types. Last but not least, it has been questioned whether the Dutch 1998 PFFC Act is incompatible with secondary EC law (i.e. the company law harmonization programme) for other reasons.[79] In this respect, it is interesting to note that the compatibility of the Dutch 1998 PFFC Act with the *Centros* case roused the cantonal

[71] See section II 1 above.

[72] Schutte-Veenstra (1999) 229, and Van den Braak (2000) 147 et seq. See ch 2 section IV 2 above.

[73] Schutte-Veenstra (1999) 229, *inter alia* quoting ECJ Case 36/75, *Rutili* [1975] ECR 1219, and Timmermans (1988) 328. German writers, however, seem to differ on this matter: see III 1 below.

[74] de Kluiver (1999) 528; Van den Braak (2000) 354.   [75] Cons. 34.

[76] *Mutatis mutandis* in the same sense: Vlas (1999) 53.

[77] 13 December 1976 (77/91 EEC), OJ 1977 L 26/1.

[78] This is not altered by the fact that, for example, the Netherlands also applies this Directive to the Dutch *Besloten Vennootschap* (i.e. private company limited by shares).

[79] See ch 6 II 1, below.

court of Groningen (Netherlands) to initiate preliminary proceedings in a procedure concerning a private limited company incorporated in the United Kingdom and conducting business solely in the Netherlands. The preliminary question is whether the duties that articles 2 et seq. PFFC Act impose upon pro-forma foreign companies, as defined in article 1 of this Act, comply with articles 43 and 48 of the EC Treaty.[80]

The scope of the applicable law

Basis: 1998 CLC Act

Despite restrictive measures emanating from the 1998 PFFC Act, the incorporation theory must still be taken as the starting point. As regards the precise material scope of the proper law of the company, it may be questioned whether any issues are left to the *lex fori*, the proper law of a contract, or to any other system of law which appears not to be the law of the country where the company is incorporated. To answer these questions, a survey of the most important issues will be conducted.

The 1998 CLC Act envisages a wide range of 'entities': according to section 1 the term 'corporation' includes '. . . partnerships, companies, associations, co-operatives, mutual insurance societies, foundations, and other bodies which operate externally as an independent unit or organization, and interest groups.'

Section 3 contains a catalogue of issues that fall within the scope of the proper law of the legal person (*corporatie*). As a matter of fact, the 1998 CLC Act does not break with tradition.[81] This is not surprising, if one takes into consideration that the incorporation theory has basically been sustained.

Scope of the proper law of the company

Under section 3 of the 1998 CLC Act, '(t)he law governing a corporation shall extend, in addition to its establishment, in particular to the following subject matters: (a) the possession of legal personality or the power to be the subject of rights and obligations, to perform legal acts, and to act at law;[82]

---

[80] Cantonal court Groningen 19 October 1999, NJkort 1999, 94 (*Kamer van Koophandel en Fabrieken Groningen v Vennootschap naar buitenlands recht Challenger Trading Co. Ltd.*), officially registered at the ECJ as C–410/99. However, because this company appeared no longer to be registered in May 2000 it is unlikely that the preliminary proceedings will be continued.

[81] An overview is rendered by Vlas (1999) 23 and 111–160.

[82] ibid. 77 et seq. This complies with case-law preceding the CLC Act: see Appeal Court Amsterdam 22 November 1990, *NIPR* 1991, nr. 128 and Appeal Court 's-Hertogenbosch 15 May 1991, *NIPR* 1993, nr. 116. Cf. however Appeal Court Amsterdam 26 September 1996, *NIPR* 1998, nr. 119: denial of *ius standi* of the English company Rainbow, since prior to Court proceedings the registration of this company had been removed, which resulted in a loss of legal personality and therefore dissolution under English law. Rainbow claimed a 'reasonable period' in which to remedy this omission (analogous application of section 21 of the second book of the Dutch Civil Code) which allegedly resulted from 'coincidence rather than

(b) the internal regulation of the corporation[83] and all subject matters related thereto;[84] (c) the representative authority of constituent bodies and officers of the corporation;[85] (d) the liability of directors, supervisory board members, and other officers in that capacity as regards the corporation; (e) the question who, jointly with the corporation, is liable for any acts by which the corporation is bound pursuant to an authority such as that of an incorporator, partner, shareholder, member, director, supervisory board member, or other officer of the corporation; (f) the termination of the existence of the corporation.'[86]

substantial problems'. The Appeal Court, however, rejected this argument for two reasons: (i) any risk resulting from choosing a foreign proper law of the company must be borne by Rainbow; (ii) *in casu* the provision invoked cannot be applied anyway, since the 'reasonable period' only applies until the company is dissolved.

[83] Vlas (1999) 111: fundamental company law issues such as the appointment, dismissal, suspension, and functioning of members of the management board as well as the supervisory board are governed by the incorporation law. Cf. Court Leeuwarden 7 June 1995, NJ 1995, nr. 657: formation of company; contribution in kind governed by proper law of the company. Doubts have been expressed as to whether the law of incorporation or the *lex loci actus* as prescribed by art. 10 of the *Wet houdende Algemeene Bepalingen* (the General Provisions Act) applies to formal validity. The incorporation of a company in accordance with Dutch law should always comply with the compulsory prescriptions of ss 64 (NV, public company) and 175 (BV, private company): see Vlas (1999) 117 for further information. Subs 2 of these provisions *inter alia* demands a notary deed executed in the presence of a Dutch notary public, excluding the escape device of an informal and private arrangement. Neither the formation of a Dutch company in accordance with a foreign *lex loci actus*, nor any such formation by a foreign public notary is permitted.

[84] cf. Vlas (1999) 123 et seq. The relationship between shareholders and company is basically governed by the incorporation law. The status of membership, dividend rights, adjournments and conduct (e.g. quorum and resolutions), the liability of (subsequent) shareholders for the amount due on issued shares are matters that usually fall within the scope of the applicable law. On whether registered shares may be transferred freely or not, see ibid. 127. Multi-party relationships require uniformity and predictability (equal treatment) of, for example, voting agreements between shareholders, no matter how contractually biased these relationships may be. However, in order to protect the shareholder, the transfer of bearer shares will be governed by the law of the place where the shares are disposed of: the *lex rei sitae* principle, according to (analogous application of) section 7 of the Dutch law, *Wet houdende Algemeene Bepalingen* applies here.

[85] Transactions concluded by organs of the company and others representing the company were explicitly excluded from the material scope of the Hague Convention of 14 March 1978 on the Law applicable to Agency (art. 3 (a)). Dutch case-law adopted an identical rule. This exemption can be explained by the fact that cross-purposes (conflict of laws *versus* harmonization attempts) originating from EC law, more specifically the first EC Council Directive on Company Law of 9 March 1968 contains detailed rules on the 'validity of obligations entered into by a company' (s. II).

[86] Cantonal court The Hague 9 April 1992, *NIPR* 1992, nr. 282: the winding-up order of an English court does not affect the (continuing) existence of a Dutch BV in the Netherlands, as a consequence of which the registration in the Trade Register of the Dutch Chamber of Commerce that the company had been dissolved must be considered as *contra legem*. For the application of the mandatory law provision of the former provision s 138(11) of the second book of the Dutch Civil Code, see Appeal Court Amsterdam 12 Dec 1994, *NJ* 1996, nr. 43: bankruptcy of SARL, a French private company limited by shares. Accounts and auditing records over the previous four months were missing. Managing directors held liable for *'faute commise dans la gestion'* (misconduct). Cf. also Appeal Court Arnhem 25 April 1995, *NJ* 1995,

Contractual matters

Further inquiry reveals exceptions. Although the formation and existence of a company, to begin with, are governed by the proper law of the company, rather than being considered as matters of contract,[87] the latter may apply to the so-called *voorovereenkomst* ('pre-formation contract', i.e. the contract paving the way for the formation of a company).[88] But then again, there is no concrete rule which provides sufficient certainty and predictability.[89] A clear distinction should be made between pre-incorporation *agreements to establish a company*, and company founders who enter into legal transactions with third parties *on behalf of the company* (*vennootschap 'in oprichting'*, i.e. pre-incorporation *contracts*). The extent to which the founders of the company are personally liable for acts conducted in the name of the future company are governed by the law of incorporation.[90]

Tort matters: piercing the corporate veil

A thin line divides company matters from tort matters in both substantive law and conflict of laws. Several topics must be examined cautiously. It follows clearly from the wording of article 3 of the 1998 CLC Act that the liability of company organs (i.e. manager, supervisory board members and others) is basically submitted to the law according to which the company is incorporated.[91] There are, however, exceptions to this rule. According to Dutch substantive law on this point, the question whether tortious behaviour has to be imputed to the legal person involved depends

nr. 600 and Court Rotterdam 15 April 1994, *NIPR* 1994, nr. 436. Note that art. 138.11 was replaced on 1 January 1998 by art. 5 1998 CLC Act: see ch 4 II 1, above.

[87] Vlas (1999) 116. This also corresponds to the fact that the topic of company formation was excluded from the scope of the Rome Convention on the law applicable to Contractual Obligations from 1980 (art. 1 subs. 2 sub (e) and the offical report of the Convention).

[88] The *Report* written by M. Giuliano/P. Lagarde is clear on this subject: all acts conducted by or contracts that envisage contractual obligations between those who intend to establish a company are unaffected by the exclusion of s 1 subs. 2 sub (e).

[89] Vlas (1999) 112 et seq., observes that the court might give preference to the law of the place of habitual residence of the contracting parties, supposing that there is a common residence. On the other hand, decisive weight could also be given to the law with reference to which the company will be incorporated. The attraction of this suggestion lies in its predictability. As it does not affect the structure or organization of the company in itself, it could even be acceptable to those legal systems adhering to the real seat theory.

[90] Vlas (1999) 114. Cf. also District Court Utrecht 30 July 1997, *NIPR* 1998, nr. 138 (subsequent to Court Utrecht 18 January 1995 and Appeal Court Amsterdam 26 September 1996): whether a person must be held liable for a transaction concluded on behalf of a German GmbH depends on whether at the time the contract was concluded the company already existed. If the answer to this question is affirmative, it must be ascertained whether the contracting person as well as the GmbH must be held liable in case the company was not registered at the time of the conclusion of the contract. Both issues must be answered in accordance with German law.

[91] See above.

ultimately on the open-ended issue of whether *maatschappelijk verkeer* (social perceptions) actually deem that behaviour to be tortious.[92] The foreign proper law of the company might, however, restrict this criterion in the sense that only the members and not the employees of a legal person can commit a tort. According to everyday practice, the question whether the applicable law extends also to tort rules is often a matter of secondary qualification.

As far as misleading information contained in a prospectus prepared for the issuing of capital is concerned, it has been suggested that the actions of individual shareholders can be based on the proper law of the tort.[93] It should be recalled that, pursuant to section 6 of the 1998 PFFC Act, directors are jointly and severally liable for any misleading information emanating from accounting and auditing reports: 'Sections 249 and 260 of Book 2 of the Civil Code shall apply to pro-forma foreign companies, *mutatis mutandis.*'

Basically, it is exclusively for the proper law of the company to decide whether or not organs of the company enjoy the privilege of limited liability, whether they must be held liable for the company's debts, or whether the 'corporate veil must be lifted'. Two situations should be clearly distinguished: (i) personal liability of the shareholders and company managers for the company's debts, and (ii) the opposite situation of a company being liable for debts arising from 'non-company' (i.e. private) transactions entered into by these persons.[94] As regards the first situation, sections 138 and 248 of the second book of the Dutch Civil Code may apply on the basis of section 5 the 1998 CLC Act, irrespective of the otherwise applicable law. These provisions, however, do not cover the entire range of *doorbraak* (piercing the veil) cases, but only cases of bankruptcy. How then should other situations be dealt with? Several solutions have been advocated: either the proper law of the company, or the law governing the (contractual?) relationship between the company and its creditors, or per-

---

[92] Vlas (1999) 147.

[93] Vlas (1999) 121, quoting the following cases: HR 20 December 1985, NJ 1986, 231: liability for misleading information in a prospectus of an NV incorporated in the Dutch Antilles implicitly based on Dutch law; District Court Utrecht 23 July 1997, JOR 1998, 62: Dutch law applicable, the prospectus having been published in the Netherlands. Note, however, that the first judgment is concerned with private inter*regional*, not inter*national* law.

[94] This phenomenon is commonly described as an *omgekeerde doorbraak* (i.e. an inverse piercing of the veil).

[95] cf. Vlas (1999) 138 and 143. Kokkini-Iatridou (1982) 142, however, opposed by Vlas (*The Fight Against Pseudo-Foreign Corporations* 1994) 320 and (1996) 460, takes a firmer position: 'The question whether the corporate veil can be lifted is also governed by the law of incorporation.' Vlas, on the other hand, argues that his view is supported by the fact that the Pro-Forma Foreign Companies Act (see section II 1, above) does not create a general rule for lifting the corporate veil either. Cf. further on this subject Struycken (1981); Polak (1989). van Dongen (*Identificatie*, 1995) 303, even suggests applying the system of law which 'best favours' the interests of the company creditor.

haps even the *lex fori* might be applied.[95] The interest of equal treatment (i.e. the right of all creditors to sue board members personally, regardless of which particular law governs the relationship between individual creditor and company) could call for a splitting of the proper law. Consequently, the question whether board members are liable would be submitted to the law of incorporation. An affirmative answer would submit the conditions of fault, damage, and cause to the law of the place where the damage (e.g. misleading publication) occurred. Note that the foregoing leaves open the possibility of suing also the company or its members under the common conflict of laws rule of tort.[96] As regards the inverse situation of a company being liable for debts or arising from 'non-company' (i.e. private) transactions entered into by shareholders and company managers, case-law on this point is lacking. It can be argued, however, that this phenomenon closely resembles a *vereenzelviging* (i.e. the identification of the company as a 'tool' of, for example, a majority shareholder, hiding behind the corporation).[97]

Seen from a private international law perspective, the insider trading problem has been described as a wasteland.[98] Several suggestions have been made as to how to tackle this type of misconduct.[99] The conflicting treatment of external liability, i.e. the liability of the seller/buyer who is aware of an approaching exchange-rate fluctuation affecting the market value of shares towards his counterpart calls for appropriate measures. The eligibility of several systems of law has been defended: either the *lex societatis*,[100] or the proper law of the contract, or the law of the place where the abuse of inside information took place, or the law of the stock exchange may apply.[101]

Borderline issues

Both the dispute settlement procedure for Dutch BVs (the Dutch equivalent of private limited companies) and the general inquiry procedure for Dutch corporations provided by part 8 of the second book of the Dutch Civil Code (articles 335 et seq. and 344 at seq.) apply solely to *Dutch* companies. Section 3 of the 1998 CLC Act does not explicitly extend the scope

---

[96] Vlas (1999) 144, speaks of a *'quasi-doorbraak'* ('quasi-piercing'). He refers to HR 9 December 1988, *NJ* 1989, 203 and HR 4 October 1991, *NJ* 1992, 247 (refusal by managing director of a Greek company to perform the company's contractual duties; basis for action in tort?).

[97] Vlas (1999) 145 et seq. (quoting various court decisions) emphasizes, however, that only the legal personality may be set aside in exceptional circumstances. Cf. Appeal Court Amsterdam 20 June 1979, *NILR* 1980, p. 252; Appeal Court the Hague 23 May 1989, *NIPR* 1988, 184, although neither of these explicitly consider conflict of laws.

[98] At least this is the impression of Vlas, (1999) 147 et seq.   [99] ibid.

[100] This would however lead to an artificial rupture, since the legal effects of the transaction usually appear at the stock exchange.

[101] In the absence of such a location, perhaps recourse should be had to the proper law governing the contractual relationship between the buyer and the seller.

of the proper law of the company to these issues. As regards the settlement of disputes,[102] it has been argued that an action undertaken by a group of shareholders should be submitted to the proper law of the company, consequently the Dutch dispute settlement procedure cannot be applied to foreign companies.[103] Apart from the fact that the *Ondernemingskamer* (Corporate Division) of the Amsterdam Court of Appeal lacks competence if the company has its registered office outside Dutch territory,[104] according to Vlas, courts will have to restrict the scope of articles 344 et seq. to Dutch companies, since these provisions are deemed to be so closely connected with Dutch legal persons that it is not appropriate to apply them to foreign corporations having their real seat on Dutch territory.[105]

Although capital prescriptions are basically governed by the proper law of the company (section 3 of the 1998 CLC Act)[106] contributions in cash or in kind might necessitate the application of the *lex rei sitae* principle.[107] As far as *certificering van aandelen* (voting trusts) are concerned, the relationship between the voting trust (i.e. an administration office) and the company is governed by the law of incorporation; however, the relationship between the adminstration office and the individual stakeholders is to be considered as a contractual relationship, and is therefore governed by the proper law of a contract, as provided for in the Rome Contracts Convention of 1980 (see above).

As regards the transfer of shares in a Dutch NV or BV, sections 86 and 196 of the second book of the Dutch Civil Code apply. Foreign law will apply to the ability to transfer shares in a company incorporated elsewhere. Again, contractual aspects are governed in conformity with the proper law of the contract, i.e. the Rome Contracts Convention. Thus, the contracting parties may choose the applicable law concerning the material validity of the transfer contract (article 3 of the Convention),[108] whereas the formal validity of the contract falls under the scope of article 9, which

---

[102] The importance of this procedure is explained by the fact that under Dutch law, shareholders of a Dutch BV cannot transfer their shares freely. Instead, they depend on a form of consent from either other shareholders, or other company organs. In a case of conflict, there is a good chance that each will become the other's prisoner. This situation can only be resolved with the help of an adequately regulated court proceeding.

[103] Vlas (1999) 148.

[104] ibid 150, referring to art. 16(2) of the Brussels Convention and s 995 of the Dutch Code on Civil Procedure.

[105] ibid 149 et seq.   [106] ibid 121.

[107] ibid 122. This is illustrated by the example of a contribution in kind in a Dutch BV of immovable property in Germany. While the contribution issue must be dealt with in accordance with Dutch company law, the transfer of the immovable property is governed by the (German) *lex rei sitae*.

[108] Vlas (1999) 122. In the absence of such a choice, the law of the country where the party who at the time of conclusion of the contract is to effect the characteristic performance habitually resides will apply, unless the contract is more closely connected with another country (art. 4, subss. 2 and 5).

makes a distinction between situations in which both parties are domiciled in the same country (when the law of the place where the contract was concluded applies) and situations in which they are domiciled in different countries (in which case the law of either the place where the contract was concluded or of the domicile of one of the parties to the contract or the proper law of the contract applies). The same principle applies to the mortgage or assignment of shares in security, including a lien on shares, irrespective however of the nature of the shares (e.g. registered or bearer). If the articles of association prohibit sureties of these kinds then no further recourse to any equivalent forms of sureties under foreign law is admissible. The incorporation law governs the question of how far any such surety will affect registration or voting rights.[109] On 22 December 1998 a draft Conflict of Laws Bill concerning rights *in rem* was presented jointly by the *Staatscommissie voor Internationaal Privaatrecht* (the government expert committee on private international law) and the *Koninklijke Notariële Beroepsorganisatie* (the organization of public notaries) to the Minister of Justice of the Netherlands. The proposal contains conflict of law rules governing the transfer of registered shares and bearer shares and the relationship between the relevant actors (e.g. shareholders, company, and others).[110]

To a certain extent, splitting the proper law may appear to be necessary in the case of voting by proxy. Although Dutch law submits the admission and the precise content of a proxy to the law of incorporation,[111] it can be presumed that the internal legal relationship between the authorizing party and his/her counterpart is governed by its own proper law of (contractual) representation.[112]

Although the 'existence, structure, and organization' are all governed by the proper law of the company, the Rome Contracts Convention (notably article 6) applies to employment contracts of organ members, as well as to a *Selbstkontrahierung*, a contract between two companies (or partnerships), concluded by a natural person who is director of both companies.[113]

---

[109] ibid 127 et seq.

[110] This document will not be dealt with extensively here. See for further information Vlas (1999) 129 et seq.

[111] HR 20 April 1990, *NJ* 1991, 560 (*Natco*). Vlas (1999) 125 et seq., considers that the permit to represent the company by proxy, the precise content of that instrument, and its formal validity are all governed by the proper law of the company.

[112] Vlas (1999) 126, excluding this matter from both the Rome Contracts Convention 1980 and the Hague Convention on the Law Applicable to Agency from 1978.

[113] cf. Vlas (1999) 136, quoting Appeal Court The Hague 27 November 1987, *NIPR* 1988, 393. Cf. also Court Alkmaar 12 December 1985, *NIPR* 1986, 300, concerning a management contract between a company and a director, to be governed by the chosen law, in the absence of which the law of domicile of the director is decisive, provided that the law of incorporation does not prohibit such agreements.

Section 3(c) of the 1998 CLC Act provides that company representation falls within the scope of the proper law of the company.[114] Company representation was excluded from the material scope of the Hague Convention of 14 March 1978 on the Law applicable to Agency.[115] However, powers to represent the company which are given by company organs to another who is not the 'representative authority of constituent bodies and officers of the corporation' are not excluded from the scope of that Convention.[116] Situations in which an individual acts *ultra vires* on behalf of and in the name of the company are also not excluded from the scope of the Convention.[117] It has been noted that a clash between conflict of laws and EC law (notably the First Company Law Directive) is to be avoided. There is, however, no such clash when bona fide third parties enter into transactions with the company, while being unaware of the limitations on the powers of representation under the law of incorporation, when those limitations are unknown to the law of the place of conclusion of the transaction. As a result, to appeal to such limitations by the company is not possible. By analogy, an appeal to the *ultra vires* doctrine by the company under the same circumstances is also likely to fail.[118]

As for international competence, the court of the country on whose territory the company has its seat usually accepts international jurisdiction. According to articles 2 and 53 of the Brussels Convention on the Jurisdiction and Recognition and Enforcement in Civil and Commercial Matters, to be read in conjunction with Dutch law—section 10(2) of the first book of the Dutch Civil Code—the statutory (i.e. incorporation) seat is the decisive connecting factor.[119]

[114] This section speaks of: '. . . (c) the representative authority of constituent bodies and officers of the corporation'. Cf. earlier case-law: Appeal Court 9 February 1937, *NJ* 1937, 992; Appeal Court Amsterdam 25 May 1989, *NIPR* 1989, 422; District Court Arnhem 12 September 1996, *NIPR* 1997, 348.

[115] See above.

[116] cf. District Court Assen 12 January 1988, *NIPR* 1988, 355: Dutch law applicable to the questions (i) whether a 'non-officer' of the company could represent a Dutch BV; and (ii) whether any representation restrictions should be accepted by the German counterpart of the company. Application of the Hague Convention of 14 March 1978 on the Law applicable to Agency on an anticipatory basis.

[117] Vlas (1999) 135.

[118] In this respect, Vlas (1999) 135 links this classical conflict rule with art. 5 of the ILA-Draft Convention Relating to Companies (Hamburg 1960): 'I. In contract, the (personal) law of the company governs the power of the company to act and the authority of the organs to act for the company. II. However, if a contract entered into by an organ of the company in a country other than that of the company's personal law—whether the organ is temporarily or permanently residing there—and the other party ought not reasonably to have known about the restrictions on the powers of the company or the authority of the organ, the company is bound by the said contract if the powers of the company or the authority of the organ are not similarily restricted by the law of the place where the contract is entered into.'

[119] cf. again preceding case-law, Appeal Court Amsterdam 11 July 1996, *NIPR* 1997, nr. 369: dissolution and winding up of eight Dutch BVs (i.e. equivalent form of private ltd. co.) at the request of the Dutch Public Prosecutor, although all companies had their real seat

Seat transfers

Transfer of management and control centre

Though formulated in a low spirit, the *Daily Mail* judgment[120] is still the starting point when it comes to defining the precise extent of freedom of establishment granted to companies in Europe today. The ECJ refrained from setting aside national conflict rules of the member states that adhere to the 'real seat' theory.

Again, the overall picture can only be deduced from piecemeal legislation. To begin with, the 1998 CLC Act did not bring about fundamental changes in Dutch private international law concerning companies.[121] Section 4 of the 1988 CLC Act reads as follows: 'If a corporation with legal personality transfers its seat or registered office to another country and the law of the state of the original seat and that of the state of the new seat recognize, on the date on which the seat or registered office is transferred, the continued existence of such body as a legal person, its continued existence as a legal person shall also be recognized under Dutch law. From the time of transfer of the seat or registered office the law of the state of the new seat or registered office shall govern the matters referred to in section 3, save where, under that law, the law of the state of the original seat or registered office continues to be applicable.'[122] The *raison d'être* of the 'incorporation' theory lies predominantly in the fact that companies incorporated under a particular system of law are allowed to have their centre of management and control on the territory of another state. Vice versa, the same principle applies to a foreign company planning to settle in the Netherlands: such a company is not subject to dissolution procedures under the law of the Netherlands.[123] Where one would expect a Dutch NV or BV to transfer its

(management and control office) in Spain. Acceptance of international jurisdiction based on the fact that the BV was incorporated and registered (i.e. domiciled in the sense of s 10(2) of the first book of the Dutch Civil Code) in the Netherlands. However, cf. Court of Amsterdam 1 July 1992, *NIPR* 1992, nr. 439: plaintiff residing in the Netherlands. Despite the fact that the defendants (two companies) were incorporated in Liberia and had their real seat in Greece, the Court accepted jurisdiction on the basis of the *forum auctoris* principle (i.e. the long-armed statute) emanating from art. 126, subs. 3 of the Dutch Code on Civil Procedure.

[120] Case 81/87 *R v HM Treasury and Commissioner of Inland Revenue, ex p Daily Mail* [1988] ECR 5483. See above, ch 2 IV 2.

[121] See above, ch 4 II 1. For comments, cf. *i.a.* Vlas (1999) 8 and 9; van Boeschoten (1993); Bellingwout (1997).

[122] Official English versions of these Acts: H.C.S. Warendorf/R.L. Thomas, *Companies and Other Legal Persons under Netherlands Law and Netherlands Antilles Law* loose-leaf edition, Deventer.

[123] cf. Timmerman (1999) 152. It is of course quite another question whether an 'in-moving' company is allowed to adopt the legal form of a Dutch NV or BV company on a strictly *voluntary* basis. For the quite different position under German law, see III 1, below). Van den Braak (1994) 678 et seq., assesses the conditions for such a transformation on the basis of analogous application of the domestic substantive company law provision of section

management and control centre to another incorporation country, it is striking to find that such transfers, notably to Belgium, although being a *'real* seat' country, are relatively popular.[124] Article 179 of the Belgian *Vennootschapswet* (Company Act) submits any foreign company—even if it is incorporated elsewhere—having its real seat on Belgian territory to the law of Belgium. Belgian law is willing to tolerate such an 'in-moving' company only on condition that it satisfies Belgian legal requirements. Surprisingly, such a company is not necessarily subject to dissolution and winding-up under Belgian law. This is due to the 'Lamot' doctrine,[125] pursuant to which five conditions must be complied with: (i) the absence of *fraus legis*; (ii) all the requirements of the law of the emigration country must be met; (iii) the continuing existence of the legal person must also be allowed under the law of the emigration country; (iv) the immigration country must not oppose the continuing existence of the legal person; and finally (v) the structure of the company should be fundamentally compatible with the law of the immigration country, i.e. 'essential' changes in the company structure cannot be tolerated. Bellingwout comments that a cross-border seat transfer from an incorporation country (the Netherlands) to a 'real seat' country (Belgium), without loss of identity, is possible.[126] This means *inter alia* that the management board has to pass a resolution, and at the same time amend its articles of association, in order to adopt the form of a Belgian BVBA.[127]

Transfer of registered office

Seen from a Dutch perspective again, apparently insurmountable problems arise as soon as a company incorporated under Dutch law decides to transfer its *registered office* to another country.[128] Before the 1998 CLC Act entered into force, it was generally accepted that unless both the 'emigration' country and the country of re-establishment explicitly authorize such

---

18 of the the the second book of the Dutch Civil Code. Cf. the countervailing view of Yarzagaray (1995) 671 et seq.: the internal law provision cannot be used for for *cross-border* transformation procedures.

[124] Bellingwout (1997) 203 et seq.

[125] Cass., 12 November 1956, Pas., 1966, I, p. 336, R.P.S. 1966, p. 136. Cf. *in extenso* III below.

[126] Bellingwout (1997) 204. It should not be overlooked that the lack of loss of identity might also result in 'dual nationality' of the company (i.e. Dutch *and* Belgian). Bellingwout, however, believes that this is not necessarily incompatible with Dutch law.

[127] For a detailed description of the transfer procedure (e.g. role of the general meeting, amendment of articles of association, alteration of name 'BV' to 'BVBA', capital nomination in Belgian currency, 'assistance' of Belgian public notary, etc) and comments thereto, see Jacob (1993) 879 et seq., Wouters (1996/97) 632. Cf. further ch 6 III 1 below.

[128] See Timmerman (1999) 152 for further information. Any decision to transfer the registered office of a Dutch NV or BV company abroad would be null and void, since it clearly follows from the third subsection of either section 66 (NV), or section 177 (BV) of the Dutch Company Code (incorporated in the second book of the Dutch Civil Code) that the registered office of the said companies must be situated in the Netherlands.

kinds of transfers (i.e. by an Act of Parliament), the corresponding amendment of the articles of association was considered null and void, since sections 177(3) (public company) and 286(3) (private company) demand that the registered office of each company incorporated under Dutch law must be in the Netherlands (*'de zetel moet zijn gelegen in Nederland'*).[129] The example usually referred to by Dutch authors is that of the *NV Indonesische Aardoliemaatschappij*: the registered office of that company was transferred from the Netherlands to the Republic of Indonesia and was indeed legally authorized by an Act of Dutch Parliament.[130] The transfer of the registered office of the Compania Shell de Venezuela Limited from Ontario (country of incorporation) to the Netherlands is an example of the inverse situation.[131]

Interregional company seat transfer

To date, Dutch law allows for an inter*regional* transfer of a company's registered office, i.e. from the Netherlands territory in Europe to the Kingdom's overseas territory in the Caribbean (the Dutch Antilles and the island of Aruba) or vice versa.[132] Immediate threat of war or revolution, for example, may urge a company to do so, in order to avoid confiscation of the company's assets.[133]

International company seat transfer in case of emergency

Legislation allowing an international 'departure' of the company's registered office from the Netherlands has recently entered into force. A distinction should be made between normal and emergency situations.

As observed above, normal situations are governed by section 4 of the 1998 CLC Act: 'If a corporation with legal personality transfers its seat or registered office to another country and the law of the state of the original

---

[129] cf. Bellingwout (1997) 202. However, it is theoretically possible for a legal system to allow a company to be incorporated under a system of law other than that of the country of registration.

[130] *Wet* (Bill of Parliament) of 28 October 1959, Stb. 386. However, for political reasons its Indonesian counterpart never came into force: see Vlas (1999) 9.

[131] This transfer was sanctioned by two Acts of Parliament ('Bill concerning Compania Shell de Venezuela Limited' of 18 May 1973 and its Dutch counterpart '*Wet* (Bill of Parliament) of 23 January 1974', Stb. 22). For detail see Vlas (1985) 167.

[132] Act of the Kingdom on the Voluntary Transfer of the Seat of Legal Persons; Act of 9 March 1967, Stbl. 1967, 161, last amended in 1997 and in force since 1 January 1998. There is also an Act of the Realm on the Transfer of the Seat of Legal Persons and Institutions by the Government; Act of 9 March 1967, Stbl. 1967, 161, last amended in 1993. For the official English versions of these Acts, see H.C.S. Warendorf/R.L. Thomas, *Companies and Other Legal Persons under Netherlands Law and Netherlands Antilles Law* Loose-leaf edition, Deventer.

[133] cf. Sanders/Westbroek (1998) 609. Thus the company acquires the status of *Aruba Naamloze Vennootschap*, a public company limited by shares. There is no equivalent of a *Besloten Vennootschap* (i.e. a private limited company) under the laws of Aruba and the Dutch Antilles.

seat and that of the state of the new seat recognize, on the date on which the seat or registered office is transferred, the continued existence of such body as a legal person, its continued existence as a legal person shall also be recognized under Dutch law. From the time of transfer of the seat or registered office the law of the state of the new seat or registered office shall govern the matters referred to in section 3, save where, under that law, the law of the state of the original seat or registered office continues to be applicable.'[134] However, it must not be overlooked that section 4 envisages only transfers *buitenom*, i.e. transfers of a company's registered office from one third country to another, the Netherlands not being directly involved.[135] The underlying ratio of section 4 is that the Dutch legal order is affected as soon as (i) the transferred company has assets on Dutch territory, or (ii) the company is involved in court proceedings in the Netherlands.[136]

The transfer of a company's registered office to or from the Netherlands is only foreseen in emergency situations and therefore calls for special legislation.[137] The second category of transfers, those to third countries, functions on a complementary basis, in that it offers an additional escape where even the overseas territories of the Kingdom of the Netherlands do not provide a safe haven.[138]

Draft for a General Private International Law Code

The conflict of law provision in section 74 of the draft proposal for a *General* Code on Private International Law also acknowledges the transfer of the company's incorporation seat beyond national borders:

Indien een rechtspersoonlijkheid bezittende corporatie haar statutaire zetel verplaatst naar het buitenland en het recht van de Staat van de oorspronkelijke zetel en dat van de Staat van de nieuwe zetel op het tijdstip van de zetelverplaatsing beide het voortbestaan van de corporatie als rechtspersoon erkennen, blijft zij ook naar Nederlands recht als rechtspersoon voortbestaan. Na de zetelverplaatsing beheerst het recht van de Staat van de nieuwe zetel de in Section 73 bedoelde onderwerpen, behoudens voorzover ingevolge dat recht daarop het

---

[134] Section 4 does not provide detailed instructions on how to accomplish a cross-border seat transfer; instead, it must be considered as a mere *Programmsatz* (fundamental principle). Cf. ch 6 III, below.

[135] Vlas (1999) 9.

[136] ibid. 10. Cf. for the international context of this topic ch 6 III 2, below.

[137] cf. two different 'escape routes':

—Voluntary Transfer of Seat to *Overseas Regions* (i.e. the Caribbean territories of the Kingdom of the Netherlands) Acts: Acts of 9 March 1967, (Stbl. 1967 161 and 162);

—Voluntary Transfer of Seat to *Third* Countries Act: Act of 13 October 1994, Stbl. 1994, 800, in effect since 23 November 1994. For the English version see H.C.S. Warendorf/R.L. Thomas, *Companies and Other Legal Persons under Netherlands Law and Netherlands Antilles Law* loose-leaf edition, Deventer.

[138] cf. Sanders/Westbroek (1998) 609. The number of countries acknowledging in-moving transfers of this kind appears to be small, cf. Delaware, New Brunswick (Canada), and New South Wales (Australia).

recht van de oorspronkelijke zetel van toepassing blijft. (Where a legal person's registered office is transferred to another country and the law of both the state of former residence and the state of new residence recognize the continuing existence of the legal person's status and legal personality at the moment of transfer, Dutch law will also acknowledge the continuing identity of the legal person involved. After the seat transfer the law of the state of 'immigration' will apply to the issues mentioned in Section 73 of the Draft Code, except for those issues to which, according to the law of the 'immigration' state, the law of the state of original residence will remain applicable.)

However, this draft provision provoked disapproval, because it remains unclear whether a universal or a unilateral scope was envisaged. Apparently, the provision applies exclusively to Dutch companies, moving '. . . *naar het buitenland*' ('abroad'); but then again, the text has neutral wording, in that it refers to 'the state of original residence', instead of 'the Netherlands'. No doubt, the latter expression seems more suitable to emphasize again that a unilateral scope is envisaged by the drafters. If, on the contrary, the provision were to function universally, the risk of confusion could simply be removed by replacing the expression *naar het buitenland* (abroad) with the more neutral expression '*naar een ander land*' ('to another country').[139] If this is the case, the provision should be understood in the broadest sense. It would then cover the following situations: (i) a company's seat transfer from the Netherlands to a third country, (ii) a company's seat transfer from a third country to the Netherlands, and finally (iii) a company's seat transfer from one third country to another.[140] Further confusion could be caused by the fact that the provision merely states that under the conditions referred to the company will be recognized as a legal person; it remains uncertain whether this legal entity will continue to exist without the need to change its identity, or whether it will need to be transformed into an equivalent Dutch company form, i.e. an NV or BV. It should be emphasized that the acceptance of the 'incorporation' theory by the Netherlands does not in itself offer an answer of any kind, since the problem is not simply one of recognition of a foreign company having its real head office in the Netherlands, but the (opposite) specific issue of the transfer of the registered office into the Netherlands.[141]

---

[139] In this sense van Boeschoten (1993) 25. Cf. in this respect comments on s 4 of the 1998 CLC Act, above.

[140] Polak (*WPNR* 1993) 758, describes the third category as a transfer 'going round the town'.

[141] Van Boeschoten (1993) 26, prefers the solution provided in the Swiss Code on Private International Law (more detail at II 3, below): companies entering the Dutch legal sphere by registration in the Netherlands should adapt themselves (i.e. transform) to Dutch company law. In the same sense, Polak *WPNR* (1993) 758.

2. ENGLAND

Historical development

Continuity of the incorporation principle

English private international law concerning foreign legal persons is charcterized by an undeniable endorsement of the 'incorporation' theory. By comparison with their foreign fellow academic writers, it is striking that English conflict of laws specialists hardly ever seemed to be troubled by a clash between the 'incorporation' theory and the 'real seat' theory. In fact, the absence of any extended debate is striking for continental observers:[142] 'in company law, questions raising conflicts of law points are concerned primarily with the three key concepts of nationality, domicile and residence. In both English and Scots conflict rules, the nationality of a company is determined by the law of the country in which it is incorporated and from which it derives legal personality. (. . .) In the conflict rules of both England and Scotland, (. . .) traditionally the concentration has been on the factors of registration and incorporation.'[143] Obviously, neither Parliament nor the courts have ever felt the urge to introduce corrective measures to ensure equal competitive conditions on the domestic market. In fact, domestic company law in Great Britain—particularly concerning *private* limited companies—proved to be of a less regulatory nature than the company law of many other legal orders. Thus, it is logical to assume that conducting business on the United Kingdom territory in the form of any foreign company would offer less advantages to businessmen.[144] However, this is not the case for a company transferring its residence from one country to another for purposes not (solely) inspired by company law issues (for example, the interest of sovereign states to counter tax income yield: see below).

---

[142] There is a striking contrast between the vast amount of academic publications in many other countries and the relative scarceness of literature in England on this subject; apart from the fact that in common law countries the rule of precedent (including dissenting opinions) plays an important instructive role, this is probably indicative of the fact that the topic is far less controversial in the United Kingdom.

[143] Clarke (1991) 161.

[144] It is evident that especially those legal orders which connect rigid local company law rules to the liberal 'incorporation' theory are likely to be confronted with abuses: cf. the Dutch experience (see II 1, above). But even in the absence of such rigid domestic company legislation (see below), 'disqualified' directors still can be expected to escape into foreign companies. Cf. however Rajak (1999) 114, with an overview of duties imposed upon companies (Sections 691–703 Companies Act), registered outside the UK but either having a branch, or even their management and control centre in the UK.

Landmark cases

The following quotation clearly reflects the traditional attitude of hospi-
tality towards foreign companies conducting business in England:[145]
'Upon the trial, Lord Chancellor King told me he made the plaintiff give in
evidence the proper instruments whereby by the law of Holland they were
effectually created a corporation there. And after hearing the objections
made by the counsel, he directed the jury to find for the plaintiffs; who
accordingly did, and gave them £13,720 damages.'[146] A critical observation should be added here, for the crucial element of this decision, liberal
as it may be, lies in the admission of the corporation in proceedings before
an English Court (i.e. the *ius standi in iudicio*), rather than in a commitment
to the 'incorporation' theory.[147] When it comes to determining the real
basis of the 'incorporation' theory, current doctrine considers other decisions, such as *Baroness Wenlock v River Dee Co.*[148] and *Lazard Bros. v Midland
Bank*[149] to be landmark cases.[150] A clear-cut standard with respect to foreign entities was asserted by Lord Hanworth MR in *C.L. Dreyfus v
Commissioners of Inland Revenue, L.L. Dreyfus v Commissioners of Inland
Revenue*, in which he stated: 'Now we have upon the facts (. . .) a clear finding that there was an entity apart from these partners constituted by
French law, and we have to recognise that entity so established, and treat
the body so set up as having had attributed to it the status which ought to
be recognised over here. (. . .) We must respect the foreign entity so established because it is not a mere matter of the *lex fori*; it is a matter of the status which an entity brings over here with it.'[151] Later on, this liberal
attitude also appeared in the wording of the Companies Act 1948:[152]
according to section 406, the existence of foreign ('overseas') companies
should be regarded as self-evident, for it did not even explicitly mention

---

[145] *Henriques v Dutch West India Co.* (1728) LD Raym. 1532.

[146] Lord Raymond, quoted by Foote (1882) 473.

[147] Again, one needs to know whether 'recognition' should be understood in a broad or a
narrow sense, i.e. including the acceptance of the *lex societatis*, or merely recognition as an
'entity', but without necessarily applying foreign company law. (See also ch 2 II 2, above, and
observations on the ambiguous character of the *Moguntia* case in Dutch conflict of laws, II 1,
above).

[148] (1883) Ch D 675: 'What you have to do is to find out what the statutory creature is and
what it is meant to do; and to find out what this statutory creature is you must look at the
statutes only, because there, and there only, is found the definition of this new creature'
(Bowen LJ).

[149] (1933) AC 279, 289.

[150] None the less, Dicey/Morris (2000) 1105, support the view that the *West India* case is an
illustration of 'rule 153': the existence or dissolution of a foreign company, duly incorporated
or dissolved under the foreign law is indeed recognized in England.

[151] *C.L. Dreyfus v Commissioners of Inland Revenue, L.L. Dreyfus v Commissioners of Inland
Revenue* (1929) TC 560.

[152] At present, the Act of 1985.

any conditions for the recognition of foreign companies.[153] The image arising from everyday practice is one of courts hardly dealing with questions of recognition either, '. . . and there is also a lack of direct authority on the meaning and effects of recognition of foreign-incorporated companies.'[154]

Restrictions to the incorporation principle: public international law

On the other hand, businessmen establishing a company should not delude themselves into believing that recognition cannot be refused; several dicta support the conclusion that all foreign-incorporated companies are recognized on the basis of the classic conflict of laws principle of comity. But if we look at *public* international law, there is no obligation to recognize a foreign company. Scrutton LJ made the following observation on this principle in *Banque Internationale de Commerce de Petrograd v Goukassov*: 'in the case of artificial persons, the existence of such a person depends on the law of the country under whose law it is incorporated, recognised in other countries by international comity, though its incorporation is not in accordance with their law.'[155]

Despite the liberal attitude of the English legal order towards foreign companies, courts seem to show some reluctance when confronted with associations of persons which are conferred with legal personality under the law of incorporation, despite a lack of express statutory incorporation or anything corresponding to it. However, the status of such associations is usually recognized under English law as well.[156] According to Drucker, English courts first examine as a question of fact the nature of the precise status of a foreign legal entity under the system of law under which that entity was formed, then it will examine whether company law or the law governing partnerships, as defined by English law, should apply to the entity by analogy.[157] Thus, as a reminder, English law, by regarding foreign associations as 'legal entities' or possibly even companies, takes a fundamentally different position to the law of real seat countries, by treating foreign companies as if they were partnerships.[158]

As a logical consequence of the 'incorporation' theory, it is correct to assume that an amalgamation of a foreign entity in compliance with the law of incorporation is also to be recognized. It should be noted that

---

[153] cf. Drucker (1968) 42; and Vaughan Lowe (1988) 164.

[154] Drucker (1968) 42.   [155] [1923] 2 KB 682, 691.

[156] *Von Hellfeld v Rechnitzer and Mayer Freres & Co.* [1914] Ch 748; *Skyline Associates v Small* (1974) 50 DLR (3d) 217.

[157] Drucker (1968) 29.

[158] cf. III 3, below (Germany). It should be borne in mind, however, that recognition of foreign associations of persons, even if the entity turns out not to be registered anywhere, does not put aside personal liabilities of the partners under the law of 'incorporation' either.

although learned writers each place emphasis on different cases,[159] they unanimously conclude that the principle of incorporation is undoubtedly accepted under English law. However, due to section 691(1)(a) of the Companies Act 1985, companies incorporated outside Great Britain which carry on business in Great Britain are obliged to file a copy of their instrument of incorporation with the Registrar of Companies.[160] This requirement, which affords a certain measure of protection to persons dealing with a foreign corporation in England, is to be methodologically qualified as mandatory law, inspired by local legal notions of the ultra vires doctrine.

Domicile, nationality, and residence of the company

The anthropomorphic concept: an issue-by-issue approach

In defining the area where the company is located, most doctrinal concepts are framed in terms of a (human) 'birth'.[161] As a result of this construction, anthropomorphic[162] notions such as 'domicile', 'nationality', and 'residence' need to be explained further; they must be suitable for various company and taxation law purposes. Furthermore, the common law notion of conflict of laws leads to the well known issue-by-issue approach, for '. . . each of the [connecting factors] calls for separate treatment, since the country whose law governs the various matters concerning a corporation varies with the character of the questions requiring a decision'.[163]

As stated in the first part of this book, the 'incorporation' theory should be seen in a broader context, namely the freedom to choose the 'proper law of the company' offered to those planning to establish a company. In most cases, when designating the type of entity to be created in the articles of association, some reference will be made, at least implicitly, to a specific

---

[159] cf. *General Steam Navigation Company v Guillou* (1843), 11 M&W 877 and the above-mentioned *Dreyfus* case, both cited by Drucker (1968) 28: the first case was about a company formed in France by royal ordinance, the second concerned a *société en nom collectif*, also formed in France.

[160] North/Fawcett (1999) 289 et seq.

[161] Drucker (1968) 31; Dicey/Morris (2000) 1101 et seq.; North/Fawcett (1999) 171; and Rajak (1999) 123. Clarke (1991) 162, quotes an observation by the Scottish Lord Carmont in *Carse v Coppen* 1951 SC 233, 243 et seq.: 'A company's domicile is created by its registration: it is so to say born in Scotland and however widespread its activities and contact with other systems in the days of its vigour, to Scotland it must come to be laid to rest when its days are done, and according to Scots law, should its affairs be wound up.'

[162] Clarke (1991) 162.

[163] cf. North/Fawcett twelfth edition (1992) 171. Thus, the method followed here (ascertaining the proper law first, and designating of its scope afterwards) may seem somewhat academic. However, as the reader may notice, in everyday practice a number of issues are lumped together and governed by the proper law of the company, i.e. the law under which the company is incorporated.

national law.[164] According to common law, the notions of 'domicile' and 'nationality' must be considered to be similar;[165] they stand for the law under which the company is incorporated.[166] Confusion may be caused by the fact that, despite the existing freedom to choose the *lex societatis*, we are not talking about the domicile of choice, but the domicile of origin. Again, the metaphor is used: 'Every person, natural and artificial, acquires at birth a domicile of origin by operation of law. In the case of the legitimate natural person it is the domicile of his father; in the case of the juristic person it is the country in which it is born, i.e. in which it is incorporated.'[167] This domicile of origin[168] is assumed to adhere to the corporation throughout its existence: there is no way to alter the domicile of origin. Of course, this notion of a company's domicile only applies to the entity, not to its organs or members.

Singularity of domicile

The analogy between a natural person's and a company's birth thus having been established, a company is consequently precluded from having more than one domicile. As Farwell LJ stated: '. . . I think that the expression "domicile" as used by [Lord St. Leonards] in *Carron Iron Co. v Maclaren* is a little unfortunate, for he speaks of a foreign corporation having two domiciles whereas in truth it is not possible for one person to have more than one domicile'.[169] Logic must lead to the conclusion that under

---

[164] There are, however, exceptions to the rule. Some systems of law (e.g. the Netherlands, articles 26 et seq. of the Second book of the Civil Code, concerning the *vereniging met beperkte rechtsbevoegdheid*) still consider entities that are not registered as legal persons, even in the total absence of articles of association. The legal personality of such entities depends on substantial criteria (a specific group of persons who appear to be associated and organized to some degree, presenting themselves as an organized entity to the outside world).

[165] cf. *inter alia Janson v Driefontein Consolidated Mines Ltd.* [1902], AC 484, and comments thereto by North/Fawcett (1999) 175 et seq.: '. . . the test of nationality of a corporation according to English law is the country of its incorporation, but according to most continental laws [it is] the country where the central management exists.' Cf. Dicey/Morris (2000) 1101 et seq.

[166] *Gasque v Inland Revenue Commissioners* [1940] 2 KB 80; *National Trust Co. v Ebro Irrigation & Power Ltd.* (1954) DLR 326.

[167] North/Fawcett (1999) 175. According to Dicey/Morris (2000) 1102 et seq.: '. . . applicable only to human beings; but states ocasionally and infelicitously attribute a domicile to corporations.'

[168] A corporation is domiciled where it is incorporated, cf. recently *A-G v Jewish Colonisation Association* [1990] 2 QB 556.

[169] *Saccharin Corp. Ltd. v Chemische Fabrik von Heyden* [1911] 2 KB 516, 527, i.e. except for situations when a company, incorporated under a foreign system of law, permitting the voluntary change of domicile, on the condition that this change also accords with the law of the new domicile: *Carl Zeiss Stiftung v Rayner & Keeler Ltd. No. 3* [1970] Ch. 506, 544. Cf. Dicey/Morris (2000) 1102: 'a corporation incorporated in two countries or more may be recognised as so incorporated, if, under the law of each such country, this situation is recognised as having come about. Accordingly, an English court should recognise such a corporation as having a domicile in each of those countries by virtue of being incorporated there.'

existing law splitting the proper law of the company is not possible either.[170] Neither can a company's domicile be altered 'as a result of its own volition'.[171] It goes without saying that the notion of what precisely constitutes the 'domicile' of the company is of decisive importance when it comes to analysing 'internal' company affairs.[172]

Dual residence

However, things are different when the company's 'residence'[173] is at stake. In the past, a number of disputes predominantly involved the associated issue of taxation law motives,[174] while company law matters were not contested. Some of these cases even show us a glimpse of what was still to come in a European setting.[175] In the past it was held, for example in *Cesena Sulphur Co. v Nicholson*, that a company is regarded by the law as 'resident' in the country where the centre of control exists, i.e. where the seat and management power of the company are located.[176] The facts in *Cesena Company* were as follows. Cesena was incorporated in England under the Companies Act 1862 for the purpose of taking over and working sulphur mines at Cesena in Italy. The practical business and administration were concentrated in Italy. Furthermore, none of the products were ever exported to England and the majority of shareholders were Italian residents. However, an English board of directors controlled the 'sale, order, and management' of the company's mining functions, the mode of disposal thereof, and the general business of the company. Meetings of shareholders were also to be held in London. The outcome was that the company's *main* residence was held to be in England; accordingly, the company was held liable to pay income tax on the whole of its profits, wherever these profits had been earned. It is noteworthy that doctrine considers the place of incorporation as 'only one' of the evidentiary facts to be

---

[170] Drucker (1968) 30. Common law systems seem to be divided on this subject: whereas American state law allows companies to possess more than one domicile, under English law a company incorporated in a single country may only have one domicile.

[171] Dicey/Morris (2000) 1102, referring to *Gasque v Inland Revenue Commissioners* [1940] 2 KB 80, 84. This principle also influences the transfer of the company's registered office: see II 2, below.

[172] cf. II 2 above on the company's status in general, in relationship with II 2 below, various issues fall within the material scope of the proper law of the company. Besides, it forms the basis for international jurisdiction: s 42 of the Civil Jurisdiction and Judgments Act 1982, as amended by the Civil Jurisdiction and Judgments Act 1991.

[173] The expression 'actual seat of the company' is also frequently employed. Drucker (1968) 35, and comments in Part 1 above.

[174] cf. Dicey/Morris (2000) 1103: 'The residence of a corporation is important in determining its liability to United Kingdom taxation.'

[175] cf. ECJ *Daily Mail* [1988] ECR 5483, and ch 2 IV 2 above. From an English perspective, see Bentley (1991) 195 et seq.; and Drury (1999) 354 et seq.

[176] *Cesena Sulphur Co. v Nicholson* (1876) Ex D 428, approved in *i.a. San Paulo (Brazilian Rail Co. Ltd. v Carter* [1896] AC 31; *Goerz v Bell* [1904] 2 KB 136; and *American Thread Co. v Joyce* (1913) 108 LT 353. Cf. North/Fawcett (1999) 172.

considered in the course of ascertaining where the control resides.[177] The words 'only one of the evidentiary facts' appear to reflect the relatively minor importance of the factor of incorporation, since it is possible to emphasize that the fact of incorporation has nothing at all to do with the actual central control of the company (cf. Part 1, above).

By using extensive teleological interpretation—or should one say: the homeward trend approach?—a similar outcome to that of the *Cesena* case can be found in a less obvious case. In *De Beers Consolidated Mines Ltd. v Howe*[178] it was held that, notwithstanding the incorporation of the company in South Africa (instead of England[179]) and the fact that the directors met in both Africa and London, control of the company's affairs was considered to be in the hands of the London board. As a result, the profits, although entirely obtained from the mining and sale of diamonds in South Africa, were deemed liable to English income tax. Again, when comparing legal persons to their natural counterparts, Lord Loreburn made the following observation: 'We ought therefore to see where it really keeps houses and does business (. . .) the real business is carried on where the central management and control actually abide.' Not surprisingly, the determination of exactly what constitutes the company's 'residence' depends upon where it is actually controlled,[180] not where it ought to be controlled. This determination consistently meets tax law objectives, because any other method of reasoning would encourage businessmen to circumvent tax law. The element of 'central control', which forms the yardstick of the definition of 'residence', also precludes companies from having more than one residence at the same time.

The *Swedish* case,[181] however, leaves room for some doubts. The main goal of this company, incorporated in England in 1870, was to construct and control a railway in Sweden. The company had its registered office in London. In 1900 the articles of association were amended, in order to resituate the management and control centre in Sweden, shareholders' and directors' meetings subsequently being held in Stockholm. But a regular

---

[177] *Cesena Sulphur Co. v Nicholson* n 176 above 171. Slightly different, Dicey/Morris (2000) 1103, stating that neither the place of incorporation, nor the country in which central management and control ought to be exercised is necessarily the place of residence of a corporation. Reference is made to *Unit Construction Co. Ltd. v Bullock* [1960] AC 351, and *Re Little Olympian Each Ways Ltd.* [1995] WLR 560.

[178] *De Beers Consolidated Mines v Howe* [1906] AC 455, designated the *locus classicus* case by Drucker (1968) 35.

[179] One should bear in mind the importance of incorporation as a factor in the determination of the 'residence' of the company (see above).

[180] *Re Little Olympian Each Ways Ltd.* [1995] 1 WLR 560, referred to by North/Fawcett (1999) 174.

[181] *Swedish Central Rail Co. Ltd. v Thompson* [1925] AC 459 at 508. Usually this case is compared with the *Egyptian* case, *Egyptian Delta Land and Investment Co. v Todd* [1929] AC 1. Cf. North/Fawcett (1999) 173 et seq.

committee meeting for the purpose of dealing with share transfers, drafting, and sealing share certificates and signing cheques on the London banking account was established in London. The company secretary also resided in London, and it was there that annual accounts were made up and audited. The House of Lords held that the company *was resident in both England and Sweden*.

At first sight, it might appear that the fundamental principle of an indivisible, single management and control centre had been overruled. Learned writers, however, tend to minimalize the importance of the *Swedish* case: in their view, the *Swedish* case and other decisions can be reconciled because if the company's control is equally divided between two or more countries so as to preclude the possibility of identifying a single place of central control, then the company must be regarded as resident in each country in which a substantial degree of control is in fact exercised.[182] Dicey/Morris emphasize that Parliament may 'of course' provide for a legislative solution to the problem of dual residence in particular cases: an example was section 84 of the Finance Act 1984,[183] dealing with taxation of controlled foreign companies.[184] In this respect, the re-enactment of the Income and Corporation Taxes Act 1988, to be read in conjunction with the Finance Act 1988, seems provocative: companies incorporated in the United Kingdom are for taxation purposes now regarded as being resident in the United Kingdom as well, even if the central management and control is situated elsewhere (remember the *Daily Mail* case). The residence of companies incorporated abroad will, however, continue to be determined for taxation purposes by reference to the place where central management and control is exercised.[185] Thus, only companies with a single residence bear the risk of double taxation. Of course, the question arises, whether the outcome in *De Beers Consolidated Mines v Howe* was appropriate in the light

---

[182] ibid. 174 et seq. Another attempt to combine the best of both worlds was quoted by Dicey/Morris (2000) 1103 et seq.: 'Central management' should by no means be equated with 'the power of final arbitrament'. The former possibly being divisible, the latter should necessarily be situated in one place. As a factor distinguishing between the two notions however, this vision is hard to sustain. The risk of casuistry lurks at every corner here. Dicey/Morris also considered the distinction to be 'unsound'.

[183] Repealed by the Finance Act 1988: a company incorporated in the UK is regarded as resident there for taxation purposes, even if the centre of management and control is situated somewhere else: s 66 of the 1988 Act. The residence of a company incorporated abroad, however, will for taxation purposes continue to be determined by reference to the place where central management and control is exercised.

[184] cf. the previous edition of Dicey/Morris, (1987) 1132.

[185] Dicey/Morris (2000) 1103. Cf. Clarke (1991) 167, who refers to the fact that 'by Section 66 and Schedule 7 of the Finance Act 1988, a company incorporated in the United Kingdom is now regarded, with some exceptions, as a resident there for taxation purposes, *even if the central management and control is elsewhere*. The residence of a company incorporated abroad will, however, for tax purposes continue to be determined by reference to the place where its central management and control is exercised' (emphasis added). Cf. UK tax law related to ECJ *Daily Mail*: see ch 2 IV 2, above.

of the facts. It should be noted once again that the principal weakness of the 'real seat' theory lies in the complex nature of ascertaining a company's residence, for single companies and groups of companies alike.[186] The issue of the company's residence is purely factual and therefore to be determined by 'the scrutiny of the course of business and trading of the company'.[187]

Scope of the applicable law

Civil law versus *common law approach*

From a civil law point of view, the proper law of the company must first be ascertained, and then the precise scope of the proper law of the company must be defined. At least theoretically speaking, common law operates the other way round: a company may indeed be connected with a particular legal order, but this ultimately depends on the subject matter of the litigation. Each question dealt with calls for an independent analysis, 'since the law whose country governs the various matters concerning a corporation varies with the character of the questions requiring a decision'.[188]

In practice, however, there is of course considerable similarity between civil law (e.g. the Netherlands and Switzerland) and common law countries (e.g. England) which adhere to the 'incorporation' theory. Basically, the system of law applicable to the company is that under which the company was incorporated, unless mandatory law measures impose themselves.[189]

Capacity and constitution

In so far as exceptions to the main rule are not rooted in mandatory laws, discrepancies between common law and civil law conflict of laws methodology traditionally arise when matters of capacity and internal management are at stake. Disputes concerning capacity are often to be decided by synthesizing the proper law (more particularly, the constitution) of the company and the proper law of the contract: whereas the capacity of a corporation to enter into any legal transaction is governed both by the constitution of the corporation and by the law of the country which governs the transaction in question, all matters concerning the corporation's constitution are governed by the law of the place of incorporation.[190] From a con-

---

[186] This is easy to explain: whereas the 'incorporation' theory stands for freedom to choose the applicable law, the 'real seat' doctrine in fact does no more than determine an objective proper law test, which ultimately leads to weighing all the connecting factors involved. (Cf. ch 2 I 3, above.)

[187] Drucker (1968) 35.   [188] North/Fawcett (1999) 171.

[189] See the following section.

[190] Thus, 'rule 154' more or less summarizes the conflict of laws rule concerning capacity: Dicey/Morris (2000) 1109 et seq. References there to the following cases: capacity: *Risdon Iron*

tinental point of view, the first part of this 'rule' apparently does nothing more than to refer indirectly to the proper law of the company. In the common law conception, however, the *ultra vires* doctrine considerably limits the scope of the *lex societatis*.[191] Since the corporation is only able to exist by virtue of its constitution, acts done on its behalf can be undertaken only to the extent that they do not exceed its provisions.

Contractual matters

Capacity may be limited by the law of the country governing the transaction concluded between the company and third parties. In a number of cases this will turn out to be the proper law of the contract. To a certain extent, however, there is an asymmetrical effect: a foreign corporation carrying out business activities in England, authorized by its constitution, for example to acquire immovables, may be subject to restrictions prescribed by the proper law of the contract;[192] on the other hand, the ultra vires principle prescribes that if a company would have greater capacity under the *lex situs* than under its own incorporation statute, the latter will prevail. As a consequence of its self-denying scope provision, the 1980 Rome Contracts Convention, as implemented in the 1990 Contracts (Applicable Law) Act,[193] does not apply to 'questions governed by the law of companies and other bodies corporate or unincorporate . . . (etc.)'[194] As a consequence, common law rules designating the proper law of the contract are likely to reappear on the scene. However, 'acts or preliminary contracts whose sole purpose it is to create obligations between interested parties (promoters) with a view to forming a company are not covered by the exclusion'.[195] It must be recalled that the law on this subject will be more or less comparable in other states bound by that Convention.[196]

---

and Locomotive Works v Furness [1906] 1 KB 49, 56–7; *J.H. Reyner (Mincing Lane) Ltd. v Department of Trade and Industry* [1990] 2 AC 418; *Arab Bank plc v Mercantile Holdings Ltd.* [1994] Ch. 71; *Merrill Lynch Capital Services Ltd. v Municipality of Piraeus* [1997] CLC 1214; *Sierra Leone Telecommunications Co. Ltd. v Barclays Bank plc* [1998] 2 All ER 821—legislation: Foreign Corporations Act 1991, s 1, and Companies Act 1985, ss 36, 36A, 36C;—constitution: *General Steam Navigation Co. v Guillou* (1843) 11 M&W 877; *Banco de Bilbao v Sancha and Rey* [1938] 2 KB 176 (CA).

[191] cf. the concluding remark in II 2, above.

[192] Dicey/Morris (2000) 1111, mention the former Mortmain Acts, which prohibited foreign companies from holding land in England, even if the *lex domicilii* (the law of incorporation) authorized the company to possess immovables. However, it is doubtful whether this is to be considered as a species of mandatory law, rather than as an 'issue of transaction'.

[193] Entered in force for Great Britain on 1 April 1991.

[194] cf. the exclusion in Art. 1(2)(e) of the Rome Contracts Convention.

[195] Giuliano-Lagarde *Report on the 1980 Rome Contracts Convention*, 12 et seq. Cf. North/Fawcett (1999) 549.

[196] See II 1, above (Dutch law). At the moment, however, the contracting states do not seem to be very eager to attribute (binding) interpretative authority to the European Court of Justice. There are two compromissory protocols from 19 December 1988 (EC Documents

Internal company affairs: jurisdiction, applicable law

According to article 16(2) of both the 1968 Brussels Convention and the Lugano Convention, 'in proceedings which have as their object the validity of the constitution, the nullity or the dissolution of companies or other legal persons or associations of natural or legal persons, or the decisions of their organs' the courts of the contracting state in which the company or legal person has its seat have exclusive jurisdiction.[197] When a company has its seat in a contracting state other than the United Kingdom, no court in any part of the United Kingdom will have jurisdiction to determine any of the matters referred to in article 16(2), many of which concern the internal affairs of a company.[198] The provisions of the Companies Act 1985 may nevertheless apply to foreign companies even where those companies have no presence in the United Kingdom. Whether any particular provision of the 1985 Act so applies depends on the construction of the relevant provision.[199]

Internal company affairs fall entirely within the scope of the law of incorporation. This hard and fast rule is explained by the fact that English courts do not wish to intervene in domestic issues between members and organs of foreign companies.[200] Notwithstanding the fact that hardly any authority for this rule can be found in court decisions, doctrine considers this rule to be sound and clear, and the reference to any other legal system can even be regarded as 'absurd'.[201] Disputes arising from discretionary powers,[202] the extent of an individual member's liability for the debts or engagements of the corporation,[203] the validity of the appointment of directors,[204] the validity of a transfer of assets or liabilities by universal

1989, nr. L. 48, p. 1), whereby the ECJ can be conferred with uniform jurisdictional powers, provided that the Second Protocol, fundamentally establishing the basis for such a uniform jurisdiction, had been ratified by the then twelve member states; the First Protocol establishing interpretative jurisdiction by the ECJ should be ratified by seven of the RCC Contracting States.

[197] Dicey/Morris (2000) 1114.

[198] ibid. referring to *Newtherapeutics Ltd. v Katz* [1991] Ch. 226; *Gruppo Torras SA v Sheikh Fahad Mohammed Al Sabah* [1996] 1 Lloyd's Rep. 7 (CA).

[199] Dicey/Morris (2000) 1115, referring to *Arab Bank plc v Merchantile Holdings Ltd.* [1994] Ch. 71, and to ss 212 and 216 of the 1985 Act. These provisions enable public companies to require information as to the identity of persons interested in the shares of the company and to impose restrictions on such shares in the event of failure to provide such information. These provisions may be invoked against a foreign company which does not carry on business in the United Kingdom and has no other presence there if that company holds shares in an English company either directly or through a nominee.

[200] *Sudlow v Dutch Rhenish Ry.* (1855) 21 Beav.; *Re Schintz* [1926] Ch. 710 (CA) and other cases, quoted by Dicey/Morris (2000) 1112.

[201] ibid.   [202] *Pergamon Press Ltd. v Maxwell* [1970] 1 WLR 1167.

[203] *Risdon Iron and Locomotive Works v Furness* [1906] 1 KB 49 (CA); *Johnson Matthey and Wallace Ltd. v Ahmad Alloush* (1985), 135 NLJ 1012 (CA).

[204] *Sierra Leone Telecommunications Co. Ltd. v Barclays Bank plc* [1998] 2 All ER 821.

succession on amalgation with another corporation[205] are all covered by the *lex societatis*. A 'contract' of membership amounts to an implied choice of law.[206]

Mandatory local law provisions

Registration and disclosure requirements

In contrast with the 'incorporation' theory, the danger of abuse of domestic law provisions is countered effectively under the 'real seat' doctrine. It should be recalled once again, however, that unlike the situation in the Netherlands,[207] fears for evasion of substantive company law by foreign companies mainly conducting business on domestic territory were felt far less in the United Kingdom. As a consequence, infringements of the incorporation principle can be found particularly in the sphere of the 'birth' and 'death' of the company.[208]

Under section 691(1)(a) of the Companies Act 1985[209] companies incorporated outside Great Britain having established a place of business in Great Britain are obliged to file a copy of their instrument of incorporation with the Registrar of Companies. Later changes must likewise be registered (section 692). Those companies must also comply with provisions concerning the registration of business names (s 693) and provide for the acceptance of procedural notices served on them at an address in the United Kingdom (s 694).

Provisions concerning disclosure of information in prospectuses which, by law, must accompany invitations made in the United Kingdom to subscribe for corporate securities, also apply to companies incorporated 'abroad' (ss 72–9). Any failure to comply with these requirements is a criminal offence (s 78). According to sections 700–3, overseas companies (i.e. incorporated abroad but having an established place of business in the United Kingdom) are also obliged to furnish accounts to the British authorities.[210] Bearing in mind that English law is relatively lenient when

---

[205] *National Bank of Greece and Athens SA v Metliss* [1958] AC 509; *Steel Authority of India Ltd. v Hind Metals Inc.* [1984] 1 Lloyd's Rep. 405, 407; *The Kommunar (No. 2)* [1997] 1 Lloyd's Rep. 8; *Global Container Lines Ltd. v Bonyad Shipping Co.* [1999] 1 Lloyd's Rep. 287.

[206] *Brown, Gow, Wilson v Beleggingssociëteit NV* (1961) DLR (2d) 673, 694–5.

[207] See II 1, above.

[208] cf. parallels between 'birth' and 'death' of natural and legal persons: II 2, above (England) and III 2, below (France). Obviously, the urge to neutralize the preferred proper law of the company in its functioning is felt less for the 'going concern' period inbetween.

[209] The following 'catalogue' was partly inspired by Vaughan Lowe (1988) 163 et seq.

[210] Albeit the fact that (i) the English and the Dutch environmental contexts are entirely different (see II 2, above) and (ii) the concept pursued by the English legislator emphasizes penal sanctions, rather than the personal liability of company directors, there are at least some parallels between the British legislation and the Dutch experience as regards pro-forma foreign companies; see II 1, above, and the comparative analysis of this problem by Drury (1998).

it comes to setting up a company, at least from a continental perspective, it seems justifiable to ask what benefit remains in conducting business in England under a foreign *lex societatis*, if any. It has been supposed that the attraction stems mainly from the fact that directors who have been disqualified for reasons of earlier misconduct or wrongful trading, might prefer a foreign *lex societatis*.[211]

Dissolution and winding-up: the jurisdiction of English courts

Mandatory law provisions also have an impact on a company's dissolution and winding up. Problems may occur when, for example, a company has its central place of business inside or outside the UK, and/or where it is registered inside or outside the United Kingdom. Another problem is that of unregistered companies, or branches, that are still a 'going concern' in the United Kingdom, for example when a foreign parent company has been dissolved under the law of incorporation. Basically, English courts have jurisdiction to wind up any company registered in England, whether the company is solvent or insolvent,[212] as well as any unregistered company if there is a sufficient connection between the company and England and if there are persons who would benefit from the making of a winding-up order, provided that the company is insolvent or, if solvent, does not have its seat in a contracting state to either the 1968 Brussels Convention or the Lugano Convention.[213] For any unregistered company whose central management and control is excercised in England, but which is incorporated in another Brussels or Lugano contracting state and which state regards the company as having its seat in that state, courts of that state will also have jurisdiction and the English courts must decline jurisdiction if the courts of that state are first seized.[214]

None the less, the jurisdiction to wind up a company registered in England is a matter of discretion.[215] Furthermore, pursuant to the mandatory-law based sections 665–74 of the Companies Act 1985, British courts have a broad competence to wind up foreign[216] companies, even those

---

[211] This was put forward as a hypothetical incentive by S. Goulding at a conference workshop at Maastricht, April 1995. 'The European Private Company?', eds. H.J. De Kluiver/W. Van Gerven, Antwerpen/Apeldoorn 1995. It was admitted, though, that any answer must be highly speculative, no case-law being traceable on this subject.

[212] Dicey/Morris (2000) 1116 et seq., *inter alia* referring to the Insolvency Act 1986, ss 221(1), (5), and 225, and case-law. Cf. *Re Mid East Trading Ltd.* [1997] 3 All ER 481, affirmed without reference to this point at [1998] 1 All ER 577 (CA); *Re Howard Buildings Inc.* [1998] BCC 549; *Re Latrefers Inc.* [1999] BCLC 271.

[213] Dicey/Morris (2000) 1117. Not surprisingly, s 43, subss (1)(a), (2)(a), and (3)(a) of the Civil Jurisdiction and Judgments Act 1982 attribute jurisdiction to English Courts to wind up any company registered in England, irrespective of whether the company is solvent or insolvent. Cf. Dicey/Morris (2000) 1116.

[214] ibid.   [215] ibid. 1118, referring to *Re Harrods (Buenois Aires) Ltd.* [1992] Ch. 72.

[216] cf. however the restrictions to this rule by the Brussels and Lugano Conventions, above.

companies which have in the past conducted business exclusively in the United Kingdom.[217] The court may order the company to be wound up if the company has been dissolved or ceased to carry on business, or is carrying on business for the sole purpose of winding up its affairs. The same principle applies to companies that are unable to pay their debts. The court may even order such a company to be wound up for the sole reason that it is just and equitable that the company be wound up.[218] The company need not have (had) an established place of business in the United Kingdom. It is sufficient that the company conducted business there once.[219] Besides, an English court can accept jurisdiction if the law of the country of incorporation has 'curiously outmoded process involving the intervention of a jury', or when the place of incorporation is inappropriate if the company does not do business there.[220] *Re Titan International Inc.*[221] may be considered a borderline case: the Secretary of State presented a petition against a company incorporated in Connecticut seeking the winding up of the company in the public interest because the company was operating an illegal money circulation scheme. It appeared that the operation of the scheme in England was controlled by a company incorporated in Wyoming and that the Connecticut company was a mere offshore investment vehicle for the scheme, that company receiving part of the proceeds of funds collected in England. The latter company had no assets in England, effected no transactions in England, had no directors resident in England, and played no part in the promotion or operation of the scheme in England. The Court of Appeal held that granting a winding-up order would constitute an impermissible and unjustified extension of the jurisdiction of the English court. The Court of Appeal further pointed out that where a sufficient connection with the jurisdiction was shown to exist, the requirement that there must also be a reasonable possibility that a winding-up order would benefit

---

[217] These long-armed jurisdiction rules, allowing British courts to wind up domestic and 'foreign' (i.e. registered outside the UK) companies alike, are given far more attention in English law than in other 'incorporation' countries. For example, Dutch law in this respect sticks to the principle that jurisdiction over the dissolution and winding up of (solvent as well as insolvent) foreign companies should be left to the system of law under which the company was incorporated. Only *vis major* permits Dutch courts to wind up foreign companies: cf. District Court of The Hague 9 March 1933, *NJ* 1933, p. 1662 (cf. *in extenso* Vlas, *Rechtspersonen* (1993) 113 et seq.). Perhaps British rules on jurisdiction in this field more or less reflect a countervailing attitude towards what is called a 'rescue culture', which is considered more important in other continental legal orders.

[218] Dicey/Morris (2000) 1120, with further reference.

[219] To be proved by showing the existence of assets or the presence of persons in the UK claiming to be creditors of the company: *Banque de Marchands de Moscou v Kimbersly* [1951], Ch. 112; *Re Azoff v Don Commercial Bank* [1954], Ch. 315.

[220] Dicey/Morris (2000) 1123, referring to inter alia *Re A Company (No. 00359 of 1987)* [1988] Ch. 210, 226–7; and *Re A Company (No. 003102 of 1991) ex p Nyckeln Finance Co. Ltd.* [1991] BCLC 539, 541.

[221] [1998] 1 BCLC 102 (CA).

those applying for it became, in the context of a public interest petition, a requirement that the public interest would be promoted by the making of a winding-up order.[222]

Prior to the entry into force of the Companies Act 1985, this 'wide jurisdiction'[223] of British courts was already established by Megarry, J in *Re Compania Merabello San Nicholas SA*:

(1) There is no need to establish that the company ever had a place of business here. (2) There is no need to establish that the company ever carried on business here, unless perhaps the petition is based upon the company carrying on or having carried on business. (3) A proper connection with the jurisdiction must be established by sufficient evidence to show (a) that the company has some asset or assets within the jurisdiction, and (b) that there are one or more persons concerned in the proper distribution of the assets over whom jurisdiction is exercisable. (4) It suffices if the assets of the company within the jurisdiction are of any nature; they need not be 'commercial' assets, or assets which indicate that the company formerly carried on business here. (5) The assets need not be assets which will be distributable to creditors by the liquidator in the winding up: it suffices if by the making up of the winding-up order they will be of benefit to a creditor or creditors in some other way. (6) If it is shown that there is no reasonable possibility of benefit accruing to creditors from making the winding-up order, the jurisdiction is excluded.[224]

As a complement, the jurisdictional borderline was created in 1988, when it was held that for an English court to have jurisdiction to wind up a foreign company it was not necessary to show that the company had assets within the jurisdiction. A basis for jurisdiction could be found in the cumulative grounds that (i) the company had sufficient connection with the jurisdiction, (ii) that there was no other jurisdiction in which it would be more appropriate to wind up the company, and (iii) that there was a reasonable possibility of benefit accruing to the creditors from the making of a winding-up order.[225] It might as well be concluded that this judgment therefore represents a species of the well-known *forum [non] conveniens* doctrine.[226] Under the conditions formulated in *Re A Company*, however, a positive clash between English courts and foreign courts adhering to the 'real seat' theory is to be expected, now that the courts of both the legal orders involved show themselves willing to decide on the dispute before them.

---

[222] Dicey/Morris (2000) 1122.   [223] Vaughan Lowe (1988) 164.
[224] (1973) Ch. 75 (91).
[225] In *Re A Company* [1988] Ch. 210, commented on by Dicey/Morris (2000) 1121. This decision was alleged to be consistent with the aforementioned case of *Re Compania Merabello*, since in both cases the relevant assets would fall into the hands of the petitioner if the company was wound up.
[226] cf. comment by Dicey/Morris (2000) 1120.

Jurisdiction: the Insolvency Act 1986

At first sight, it may seem paradoxical that the Insolvency Act 1986 curtails the jurisdiction of English courts in interlocal company law relationships. Sections 221(1) and 441(2), which should be read in conjunction with sections 225 and 221(1) and (3), restrict English courts from winding up any company registered in Scotland, or Northern Ireland (except when such companies have carried on business in Great Britain and have ceased to carry on such business), or any unregistered company having a principal place of business situated in Scotland or in Northern Ireland, but not having a principal place of business situated in England.[227] Instead, by virtue of section 426 of the Insolvency Act 1986, English courts will be obliged to assist other United Kingdom courts in relation to insolvency law. According to section 426(5) of the Act, the winding-up rules of either the requesting country or England may eventually apply, having regard to the rules of private international law.

In spite of the far-reaching scope of the jurisdiction rules in the Companies Act 1985, a problem which remains unsolved is that of British courts being confronted with the branch of a foreign parent company, the latter being considered 'dissolved' at the moment of the Court order according to the system of law under which it was incorporated; this is known as a 'limping legal relationship'. In other words, how should the debts of, or due to, the branch be handled, when the dissolution of the foreign parent company is considered irreversible and it no longer has *locus standi* in a court? Such a branch has been described as 'a submerged wreck, floating on the ocean of commerce'.[228] Consequently, assets of such a branch are neither capable of distribution by a liquidator among creditors nor liable in respect even of transactions with effect in England, even though the agent, acting on behalf on the non-existent branch, would without doubt be personally liable. An answer to the elusiveness of 'floating' (branches of) companies in court was found by a wide interpretation of section 221(5) of the Insolvency Act 1986, concerning the winding up of *unregistered* companies. Whereas the expression 'unregistered company' does not refer to foreign companies explicitly, it is nevertheless understood that such companies may be wound up under the provisions of this Act. The precise wording of the Act—an unregistered company may be wound up if it 'is dissolved'—has been construed equivalent to '*has been* dissolved'.[229] In fact, the orgins of this provision can be traced back to

[227] ibid. 1128 et seq., with further reference.

[228] *Re Russian Bank for Foreign Trade* [1993] Ch. 745 at 764.

[229] Dicey/Morris (2000) 1123 et seq. Cf. the previous edition, (1987) 1141, using similar phrases: '. . . general words (. . .) cover all cases (. . .) however it be construed'. Prior to the 1986 Act: *Re Family Endowment Society* (1870) Ch. App. 118 at 136. In order to invoke section 221(5) there must have been neither a branch in England, nor business carried on within the

discussions on section 91 of the Companies Act 1928, which was 'presumably introduced to deal with the Russian companies which had been dissolved by the Soviets after the 1917 revolution'.[230] Where a company incorporated outside the United Kingdom has been dissolved, its English assets vest in the Crown *bona vacantia*. In such a case the requirement that there must be assets upon which the order can operate is met by treating the Crown's title as a defeasible one which is defeated by the making of the order, whereupon the property revests in the revived corporation.[231]

Dissolution and winding up of companies by an English court: effects

The effects of a company's winding up ordered by an English court (including matters of procedure and substance), are basically subject to English law.[232] This rule is not modified where there is a simultaneous liquidation under the law of the place of incorporation, even though the English winding up is then expressed to be to those proceedings abroad.[233] Not precluded, however, is reference to the law of the place of incorporation, for it may be necessary by virtue of the Insolvency Act 1986 to ascertain whether a shareholder is liable as a contributory under section 226(1), or to ascertain the persons entitled under section 154 to the surplus assets on completion of the liquidation.[234] Reference will also be made to foreign systems of law to discover whether debts alleged to be due either to or from the company are valid under their respective proper laws. The winding up of a company under the Insolvency Act 1986 leads to the property of the company being placed in a trust for the period of the winding up for the benefit of interested parties.[235]

(Simultaneous) company liquidation abroad: effects

The liquidator must take into his custody or under his control all the property and things to which the company is or appears to be entitled (section 144(1) Insolvency Act 1986). However, without authorization (by means of

jurisdiction: cf. *Banque des Marchands de Moscou v Kimbersly* [1951] Ch. 112 (1950) 2 All ER; *Re Compania Merabello San Nicholas SA* [1973] Ch. 75 [1972] 3 All ER 448. It is immaterial whether the interested persons are 'English' or 'foreign', cf. *Re Azoff v Don Commercial Bank* [1954] Ch. 315; [1954] 1 All ER 947.

[230] Dicey/Morris (2000) 1124. Thus, the 1928 version of the Act was given retroactive effect.

[231] ibid. 1124.

[232] ibid. 1132 and 1134, *inter alia* referring to *Re English, Scottish and Australian Chartered Bank* [1893] 3 Ch. 385, 394 (CA); *Re Suidair International Airways Ltd.* (1951) Ch. 165, 173; *Re Sefel Geographical Ltd.* (1988) 54 DLR (4th) 117.

[233] Dicey/Morris (2000) 1135, referring to several cases, cf. *Felixstowe Dock and Railway Co. v US Lines Inc.* [1989] QB 360; *Re Bank of Credit and Commerce International SA (No. 2)* [1992] BCLC 579, 581.

[234] *Re Banque des Marchands de Moscou* [1958] Ch. 182.

[235] Dicey/Morris (2000) 1132, referring to *Re Oriental Inland Steam Co.* (1874) LR 9 Ch. App. 557.

a direction from the court) he is not allowed to operate beyond the English border: this means that unless the court decides otherwise the inquiry should not cover assets outside England,[236] nor should a list of non-English creditors be settled.[237] Arguably, these provisions are convenient in the case of a company incorporated outside England which is being wound up at the place of its incorporation.[238] The liquidation is a liquidation of the company, and not merely of its English affairs. Accordingly, assets collected by the liquidator may be applied in satisfaction of foreign as well as English liabilities.[239] Section 130(2) of the Insolvency Act 1986, which provides that when a winding-up order has been made no action or proceeding against the company or its property is to be commenced or continued without leave of the court, does not apply to proceedings in courts outside the United Kingdom.[240] However, inherent to the discretionary power of the court to restrain foreign proceedings, creditors may be restrained from commencing or continuing proceedings against a company in simultaneous foreign proceedings.[241] In other words, the self-denying character which in the case of foreign proceedings in general was given to section 130(2) (cf. the *Vocalion* case referred to earlier) is not to be understood as an absolute rule leaving no room for exemptions. The Insolvency Act 1986 does not contain explicit provisions for the invalidity of execution elsewhere either. Once again freedom to execute is limited, since an unsecured creditor who levies execution on effects situated outside Great Britain after the commencement of the winding up may, if he is subject to the jurisdiction of the court, be compelled to surrender the fruits of his execution for the general benefit of the creditors.[242]

In the case of a foreign winding-up order, the authority of a liquidator appointed under the law of the place of incorporation is recognized in England. Logic prescribes that the law of the place of incorporation must decide who is entitled to act on behalf of the company.[243] It must be noted that '(t)he effect of a foreign winding-up order in England has seldom been before the Courts.'[244] Of course, the comity principle[245] would not be

---

[236] Dicey/Morris (2000) 1132 et seq., referring to *Re Hibernian Merchants Ltd.* [1958] Ch. 76; *Re Bank of Credit and Commercial International SA* [1994] WLR 708 (CA).
[237] ibid.   [238] Dicey/Morris (2000) 1133.
[239] ibid.   [240] *Re Vocalion Foreign Ltd.* (1932), Ch. 196.
[241] Dicey/Morris (2000) 1133 et seq., referring *inter alia* to *Re North Carolina Estate Co.* (1889) 5 TLR 328; *Re Vocalion (Foreign) Ltd.* [1932] 2 Ch. 196; *Mitchell v Carter* [1997] 1 BCLC 673; *Hughes v Hannover Rückversicherungs-Aktiengesellschaft* [1997] 1 BCLC 497 (CA).
[242] *Re Oriental Inland Steam Co.* (1874) LR 9 Ch. App. 557.
[243] Dicey/Morris (2000) 1141, referring *inter alia* to *Banco de Bilbao v Sancha and Rey* (1938) 2 KB 176 (CA); *Bank of Ethiopia v National Bank of Egypt and Liguori* [1937] Ch. 513, 524; *Felixstowe Dock and Railway Co. v US Lines Inc.* [1989] QB 360, 374–375.
[244] ibid.
[245] The ultimate implication of *do ut des* reasoning might as well be that '(i)t would be contrary to principle and inconsistent with comity if the Courts of this country were to refuse to

of great help to those wanting to invoke such recognition, since it is not likely that the liquidator's authority would extend beyond the country where the company was incorporated,[246] unless there is no likelihood of a liquidation in the country of incorporation. Section 426(11) of the Insolvency Act 1986 provides an exception to the rule: if the foreign court of the relevant country or territory mentioned within this provision appoints the liquidator, that court may on behalf of that liquidator request the assistance of an English court in rendering effective the authority of the liquidator to act in England.

One final remark: no doubt, winding up an extinct company is 'bound to disturb the logician'.[247] In spite of the fact that this 'doctrine of pretence of revivification'[248] cannot be qualified as theoretically sound, it is noteworthy that it was introduced a few decades later at European level, namely in section 3 ('Nullity of the Company') of the first EC Company Law Directive.[249]

British companies: control of foreign participants

Up to this point, the extended application of compulsory legal provisions to foreign companies conducting business on the territory of the United Kingdom has been dealt with. Foreign 'participants' in British companies may also be subject to compulsory legal provisions by the Companies Act 1985.[250] Pursuant to sections 198–220 ('discovery of the beneficial ownership of shares') any person holding more than 5 per cent of the shares in a British public company is obliged to notify the company of that shareholding. The Department of Trade and Industry also has the power, under sections 442–52 of the Act, to investigate the ownership of shares in British companies.

---

recognise a jurisdiction which *mutatis mutandis* they claim for themselves', Hudson LJ in *Travers v Holly* [1953] P 246, 257.

[246] The same principle applies the other way around in the case of a company's liquidation in the country of incorporation. English courts, in exercising their jurisdiction to make an order, are concerned to ensure that the liquidator should not go beyond dealing with the company's English affairs without special direction; *Re Commercial Bank of South Australia* (1866) 33 Ch.D. 174, 178. Cf. the *Re Vocalion* case (n 241, above).

[247] F.A. Mann, [1952] MLR 497.   [248] cf. North/Fawcett (1992) 902.

[249] First Council Directive of 9 March 1968. It should be kept in mind that, as similar as this may seem to the practical approach, the provisions of the EC Directive were elaborated primarily to regulate transactions between a non-existent company and third parties in 'one-dimensional', i.e. purely domestic situations.

[250] Vaughan Lowe (1988) 165, emphasizes the concern in the City of London caused by secret buying of shares in the Consolidated Gold Fields Company in 1979. As a legal source he mentions Scottish case-law, quoting P. Neale, 'The United Kingdom Experience', in: *Extraterritorial Application of Law and Responses Thereto* (ed. C.J. Olmstead (1984): 'an example of extra-territorial application of laws for in that case the foreign owners of shares were being struck at by the freezing and temporary destruction (as it were) of property rights which existed in this country.'

Furthermore, mandatory law provisions are also found in the Industry Act 1975: sections 11–18 empower the Secretary of State to restrict changes in the control of manufacturing undertakings. Pursuant to section 13, he is entitled to make 'prohibition orders', prohibiting changes of control and steps which would amount to, or lead to, changes in control. It should not be overlooked that section 18 contains a territorial scope rule:

(1) Nothing in a prohibition order shall have effect so as to apply to any person in relation to his conduct outside the United Kingdom unless he is (a) a citizen of the United Kingdom and Colonies, or (b) a body corporate incorporated in the United Kingdom, or (c) a person carrying on business in the United Kingdom either alone or in partnership with one or more persons, but in a case falling within subsection (a), (b), or (c) above, any such order may extend to acts or omissions outside the United Kingdom. (2) For the purposes of this Part of this Act a body corporate shall be deemed not to be resident in the United Kingdom if it is not incorporated in the United Kingdom.

Fraud: the Mareva doctrine

Some of the requirements that offer a degree of protection to persons entering into transactions with a foreign corporation in England are methodologically to be qualified as mandatory law, inspired by the nature of the local *ultra vires* doctrine.[251]

Although English law does not directly and compulsorily regulate foreign companies conducting business on British territory, those companies should not to be used as 'a cloak for fraud'.[252] The *Mareva* doctrine,[253] coupled with the procedure known as 'lifting the corporate veil', forced the Court of Appeal to ignore a network of foreign companies and trusts employed improperly to conceal the defendant's beneficial interests in English assets. A disposal of shares in these foreign companies can be subject to restraints imposed by the court, to prevent the transfer of assets out of the jurisdiction, pending the conclusion of litigation in the United Kingdom.[254]

Seat transfers

The quintessence of the 'incorporation' theory is that, contrary to the 'real seat' theory, the 'domicile' and the 'residence'[255] of the company do not necessarily coincide. The general assumption under the incorporation principle is that a cross-border transfer of the company's management and

---

[251] cf. North/Fawcett (1992) 1134.   [252] Vaughan Lowe (1988) 166.
[253] *Mareva Company Naviera SA v International Bulk Carriers SA* (1975) 2 Lloyds Rep. 509, [1980] 1 All ER 213 (CA).
[254] *X Bank Ltd. and Others v G. Times* (London) 13 April 1985, 26 (CA).
[255] See above.

business control centre after the incorporation of the company is permitted. Not surprisingly, England and the Netherlands, both adhering to the 'incorporation' theory, show a comparably lenient attitude towards emigrating or immigrating company seat transfers, whether of the company's 'domicile' or its 'residence'. In future, however, the laws of both countries may be affected by the Fourteenth Directive on the Transfer of the Registered Office or the *De Facto* Head Office of a Company from One Member State to Another.[256]

Transfer of 'residence': tax law purposes

Cross-border transfers of a company's 'residence' (resituating the centre of management and business control) are hardly ever inspired by the intention to circumvent company law regimes. They are usually motivated by taxation policies. In spite of its enormous impact on European cross-border company relationships, the famous ECJ *Daily Mail* judgment was not even remotely linked to company law matters. The preliminary proceedings 'merely' concentrated on the risk of evasion of British tax law that would result from transferring the company's residence. This fear of tax law evasion arising from a 'freedom of *departure*'—which in preliminary proceedings before the European Court of Justice was claimed by the Daily Mail company but denied by the Treasury of the United Kingdom under the EC Treaty—is no longer likely to affect future departures of English companies, since the Finance Act 1988 appears to have effectively blocked the road.[257] Companies incorporated in the United Kingdom are now regarded for taxation purposes as resident in the UK as well, even if their central management and control is situated elsewhere. For tax purposes, the residence of companies incorporated abroad will, however, continue to be determined by the place where central management and control is exercised.

Transfer of 'domicile'

Things are different if a company's domicile is transferred beyond national borders. Under English law, the status of both individuals and corporations is governed by the law of their place of 'domicile'.[258] Sometimes a parallel is established between the 'birth' of a natural person and the 'birth' (i.e. formation) of a company. Due to this legal allegory a company, notwithstanding its own characteristics, cannot change its

---

[256] Doc. XV/6002/97-EN of 20 April 1997. Cf. ch 6 III 2 below and—notably—the consequences thereof for English law; cf. Rajak (1999) 114 et seq.

[257] See above.

[258] A distinction should clearly be made between a company's domicile and that of its members. Company members are governed by the law concerning domicile and residence in their own capacity as natural (or legal) persons: Dicey/Morris (2000) 1103.

domicile voluntarily: 'in the case of the juristic person it is the country in which it is incorporated. If it is a corporation, a transfer can only be pulled through by virtue of the law by which it was incorporated'. But a corporation has the peculiarity that it can have only one domicile[259] and 'this domicile cannot be changed. It cannot be converted into a domicile of choice'.[260] This principle of 'intransferability'[261] has, however, been slightly mitigated with the help of different measures than those used in the Netherlands. Unlike the Dutch approach of permitting 'controlled' domiciliary transfers by means of forerunning Acts of Parliament of both the legal systems involved (i.e. those of the countries of 'emigration' and 'immigration'),[262] English law enables the cross-border transfer of a company's domicile with the help of local law perceptions. Although a company cannot change its 'domicile of birth' voluntarily, the law of domicile may refer the particular issue to another system of law, provided that its internal rules do not oppose such a procedure.[263] Seen from a more general methodological conflict of laws angle, this mechanism closely resembles the instrument of *renvoi* (first or second degree), to be taken either directly from conflict of law provisions or from substantial local law provisions containing a conflicts clause.[264]

---

[259] *Saccharin Corp. Ltd. v Chemische Fabrik von Heyden* [1911] 2 KB 516, 527 (CA); *Jacobson v New York Haven and Hartford Ry.* 347 US 909 (1953) and cases cited there.

[260] Dicey/Morris (2000) 1102 et seq.; North/Fawcett (1999) 175. Legal authority was provided by *Gasque v IRC* [1940] 2 KB 80 and *Kuenigl v Donnersmarck* [1955] QB 515 at 535. Cf. Drury (1999) 358.

[261] Rajak (1999) 111 et seq., asserts that the 1985 British Companies Act requires a formation certificate and articles of association, pursuant to which the company is registered in England, Scotland, or Wales. Although subsequent transfers of the registered office are neither explicitly allowed nor prohibited in articles 2(1) sub (b) and (2), there is authority that even interregionally (e.g. from Scotland to Wales) such transfers are prohibited, cf. P. Davies, L. Gowers *Principles of Modern Company Law*, 6th edn. 1997, s 14. Even a purely *domestic* transfer of the registered office (e.g. from London to Liverpool) presupposes that several formal and material requirements are satisfied (for the precise procedure, see Gower/Davies). This also has consequences for a *cross-border* transfer of the company: see ch 6 II 3, below.

[262] See above.

[263] *Carl Zeiss Stiftung v Rayner and Keeler Ltd. (No. 3)* [1970] Ch. 506 at 544.

[264] Without any doubt, some systems of law adhering to the incorporation doctrine authorize companies either to have their domicile in a state other than where it was incorporated, and/or to alter their domicile (cf. observations in ch 2 I 1, above, notably the classification of the different species of the 'incorporation' theory that are known at present). According to English law, however, a company has its domicile in the state where it was incorporated. A company incorporated in a country may have only one domicile: *Saccharin Corp. Ltd. v Chemische Fabrik von Heyden* (1911) 2 KB 516, 527 (CA). There is no authority to the effect that multi-state corporation is possible: *Jacobson v New York Haven and Hartford Ry.* 347 US 909 (1953) and cases cited there.

3. SWITZERLAND

Historical development

1987 Federal Code on Private International Law: main features

Present-day Swiss private international law is regulated by the 1987 Federal Code on Private International Law.[265] For a number of reasons, this piece of legislation rivals most contemporary conflict of law codes in Europe. First, Switzerland holds a special position in that there are four official languages: as a result, the reader may well be confronted with diverging views as between 'German', 'French', and 'Italian' courts and academic writers alike.[266] Secondly, the 1987 Code contains over 200 provisions:[267] skimming through the chapters, one gets the impression of the well known South American *Codigo Bustamante*, which was elaborated at the beginning of last century. Nearly the complete range of private law relationships is covered by this Swiss legislative project.

However, it should be noted that, as far as company law is concerned, the mere entry into force of the Code did not generate satisfactory legal certainty and predictability. In order to achieve order out of chaos, a short overview of the pre-codification era is necessary. Thereafter, the interaction between the Swiss Federal legislator and the *Bundesgericht* (Swiss Federal Court) is analysed.

Pre-codification confusion

Ambiguity featured in pre-codified Swiss private international law with regard to foreign companies. Instead of offering clear guidelines, the

---

[265] Bill of 18 December 1987, BBl. 1988 I, p. 5. For an authorized text edition, cf. Bucher (ed.) (1997) and Walter/Jametti Greiner, loose-leaf edn Bern. The code entered into force on 1 January 1989. Simultaneously, cantonal civil procedural law was codified by the Federal Code, cf. *Botschaft zum Bundesgesetz über das Internationale Privatrecht*, BBl. 1983, I, 263 and 265. Attempts to codify private international law date back to 1971. For detailed information, cf. *inter alia* Dutoit (1997) XIX et seq., containing a *Bibliographie Générale'* on the Code; Ebenroth/Messer (1989) 49 et seq., esp. regarding the quotation by Schönenberger/Gauch, *Schweizerisches Zivilgesetzbuch mit Obligationenrecht, Textausgabe* 37 edn. Zürich (1988) and others; and *IPRG-Kommentar* (1993) 1 et seq.

[266] French, Italian, German, and Romansh are the official languages of Switzerland. Thanks to the unique position of Switzerland, an authorized quadrilingual (French, Italian, German, and surprisingly, English) text version of the 1987 Code on Private International Law is available. The *couleur locale* of Swiss legal sources is therefore occasionally given attention. In the following, the leading English text version is that referred to by Dutoit (1997).

[267] The vast number of provisions is explained by the fact that each chapter (General Provisions, Natural Persons, Marriage, Affiliation, etc.) contains a plenary trilogy of rules concerning jurisdiction, applicable law, and recognition and enforcement of foreign judgments.

Bundesgericht, although not on purpose, had generated uncertainty.[268] Although there was good reason to assume that the 'incorporation' theory had indeed been adopted, it remained unclear whether the *Gesellschaftssitz* (seat of the company) was to be understood as its *Satzungssitz* (i.e. the place where the company had its registration office, in conformity with article 56 of the Swiss ZGB) or its *Gründungsrecht* (the proper law of the company, i.e. the system of law according to which the company was incorporated).[269] Frequently, the two seats will coincide, but this is not necessarily so.[270] As in the Netherlands,[271] uncertainty arose from the use of double standards. In Switzerland the notion of what precisely was meant by the 'seat' of the company led to uncertainty, whereas unpredictability in the Netherlands stemmed from differing opinions about the expression 'recognition' (accepting the foreign proper law of the company, or merely recognizing the foreign entity as a bearer of rights and duties, i.e. the *ius standi in iudicio*, yet without accepting the foreign *lex societatis*).[272] However, Swiss scholars agreed on the acceptance of the incorporation doctrine.[273] They only seem to disagree on the suitability of the varying methods used to combat the abuse of foreign companies.[274]

1982 Federal Court: acceptance of Fiktionsvorbehalt

From the early 1980s, Swiss private international law was troubled by the debate about whether the 'incorporation' theory was restricted by a general *Fiktionsvorbehalt* for pro-forma foreign companies. Not surprisingly,

---

[268] See. Honsell/Vogt/Schnyder (1996) 1140: for a long period, the Swiss Supreme Court took a hesitant position. For an overview see Vischer/von Planta (1982) 61 et seq.; P. Reymond (1989) 143 et seq.; and Ebenroth/Messer (1989) 56 et seq.

[269] cf. Ebenroth/Messer (1989) 57. BGE 91 II 117.125; 79 II 87.90; 15, 570, 579; 76 I 150, 159; 95 II 442.448; 108 II 398.402. Cf. also *Obergericht* Zürich *SJZ* 1986 245. One could say that the final outcome of whether the company's incorporation seat should be considered as merely fictitious was decisive. For an overview of *'jurisprudence antérieure à la LDIP'* (pre-codification case-law) see Dutoit (1997) 440 et seq.

[270] See ch 2 I 1, above. [271] See II 1, above. [272] See II 1, above.

[273] According to Honsell/Vogt/Schnyder (1996) 1141, and Ebenroth/Messer (1989) 57 (n. 40), hardly any supporters of the 'real seat' theory were known. In their opinion, this theory was only favoured by Siegwart. A vast majority of writers subscribed to the countervailing recognition theory (e.g. Vischer, Meier-Boeschenstein, De Chedid, Niederer, Forstmoser-Hayoz, Weiss, etc.). Cf. also Vischer/von Planta (1982) 13.2; R. Moser (1967) 692 et seq.; and Perrin (1969). The last, however, insists upon maintaining the reservation of the 'fiction' clause (explained below). Honsell/Vogt/Schnyder (1996) 1143, emphasize that Swiss law clearly shifted away from this concept.

[274] For an overview of devices available under the 1987 Code, and comments thereto, see *IPRG-Kommentar* (1993) 1349 et seq. and Honsell/Vogt/Schnyder (1996) 1143 et seq.: (i) the non-codified fiction clause; (ii) general provisions flowing from the first chapter of the Code, e.g. art. 17 (*ordre public*); (iii) mandatory law resulting from art. 18 in conjunction with arts. 156–9. Without reservation, the authors reject (iv) the application of art. 15 (exception clause: a closer relationship to another system of law) since it is essential to the 'incorporation' theory that no close relationship between the proper law of the company and the legal order where the company is active is required.

the Swiss Code on Private International Law is rooted in case-law and doctrine: the impression arising from the field of company law during this period is one of a (spontaneous?) interaction between the Federal Parliament and the *Bundesgericht* (Swiss Federal Court) on one hand, and academic writers[275] on the other.

In 1982 the *Bundesgericht* held that, although a *Stiftung* had been properly incorporated under the law of Liechtenstein for no other purpose than to 'frauder la loi du Siège Réel', Liechtenstein law on corporations was to be disregarded (i.e. the law of Liechtenstein was to be replaced by the—Swiss—law of the country where the *Anstalt* had its central management) since the legal person was deemed to have only a 'fictitiously' foreign nature.[276] At that time, this exception to the rule of the 'incorporation' theory was deemed commensurate with both the Draft Federal Code on Private International Law and earlier case-law of the *Bundesgericht*. But not all Swiss writers shared this view.[277]

1987 Private International Law Code: abrogation of Fiktionsvorbehalt?

On 1 January 1989 the General Private International Law Code entered into force. Article 154 contains the following provision on companies:

Companies shall be governed by the law of the state in which they are organized if they satisfy the publication or registration requirements of that law or, if there are no such requirements, if they are organized according to the law of that state (subs. 1). A company which fails to meet these conditions shall be governed by the law of the state in which it is in fact managed (subs. 2).

Exceptions to the 'incorporation' theory are contained in articles 156–9 (see below). A literal reading of these provisions no longer seems to justify the use of open-ended escape clauses, such as the above cited *Fiktionsvorbehalt* (fiction clause).[278] Consequently, the general assumption was that doubts had been relegated to the past. Nevertheless, attempts were made to let 'the Phoenix rise from its ashes again':[279] some observed that, since the 1982 judgment of the *Bundesgericht* was exclusively based on the (then still draft) Code, it would be only logical to assume that, in spite of the literal wording of the Code, the general escape clause of *fraude à la loi*

---

[275] cf. the abovementioned writings, and *Bundesgesetz über das Internationale Privatrecht* 1980.

[276] BG 7–10–1982, BGE 108 II, 398 et seq. For comments on the *réserve du siège fictif*, see Klein (1989) 368.

[277] cf. F. Vischer, *SchwJbIntR* (1984) 337 et seq.; and Heini (1992) 405. Cf. further *IPRG-Kommentar* (1993) 1343 et seq.

[278] cf. Klein (1988) 93: the doctrine concerning 'fictitious' foreign companies obviously disappeared from the literal wording of the Code.

[279] This phrase was used by Heini (1992) 405.

had not (explicitly) been abandoned.[280] However, the *Bundesgericht* declined this view with regard to a 'limited company' registered in Panama, the shares of which were held by a *Stiftung* in Liechtenstein, whose beneficary was a natural person domiciled in Lebanon.[281] The Geneva lower court still asserted that, in these circumstances, the legal construction had to be considered as an evasion of the prescription of article 235 of the Swiss ZGB, and therefore declared the *Unterhalts-Familienstiftung* to be illegal as a *fraude à la loi*.[282] The *Bundesgericht* over-ruled this decision, observing that the Code does not contain an explicit *fraus legis* exemption clause. Once the requirements of article 154(1) of the Code have been satisfied, it follows from the system of the Code that only the *Überlagerung* rules, enshrined in the provisions of articles 156–9,[283] offer exceptions to the principle of incorporation.[284] The law of incorporation is only superseded by the law of the country where the company's real seat is situated if the conditions of article 154(2) are fulfilled. Obviously, in the observation of the *Bundesgericht*, the Swiss legislator must have intended to safeguard the company's existence whenever possible,[285] even if this may have (undesirable) consequences. Thus, a 're-entry' through the back door created by the 'fiction clause' was not likely to be targeted by the Swiss legislator.

'Incorporation' theory: investment policies

Although Switzerland is not a member of the European Union, it never-theless appears to be more liberal in granting freedom of establishment to foreign companies than most 'European' (to be more precise: EC) coun-tries.[286] As in the Netherlands, arguments in favour of this generous

[280] Notably French-speaking authors like Perrin (1989) advocated maintaining the '*réserve de la fraude à la loi*'. For an overview see Dutoit (1997) 441, *inter alia* quoting others. Supporters of the *fraude à la loi* exception believe that this device is of general application, open to use in the areas of conflict of laws as well as substantive law. Others (notably German-speaking authors like Heini and Vischer) believe that the Swiss legislator has balanced all interests, whereafter without any reservation the 'incorporation' theory was preferred.

[281] *Chilon Valeurs Inc. v Financial Construction Company Inc.* BG 17 Dec. 1991, BGE II 7, 494 et seq.

[282] Heini (1992) 405, ironically observes that it was not surprising that a French-speaking Court was willing to save the *Fiktionsvorbehalt* (fiction clause). Cf. also *IPRG-Kommentar* (1993) 1345 et seq.

[283] The *Bundesgericht* explicitly rejected the view that any room was left for the application of general provisions like art. 15 (*fraus legis*) or art. 18 (*ordre public*).

[284] Most of these rules envisage creditor protection, e.g. art. 159: 'If the business of a com-pany formed under foreign law is conducted in or from Switzerland, the liability of the per-sons acting on behalf of the company shall be governed by Swiss law'; see II 3, above.

[285] However, to quote Klein (1989) 368, it would have been preferable '*im Interesse des Verkehrs, auf einfache Weise Klarheit [zu] schaffen* (to make things clear in the interest of every-one)'.

[286] Conversely, as we will see, EC member states have been condemned for applying the 'real seat' doctrine to corporations duly established in other EC member states, whilst on the

attitude seem to be predominantly based on economics.[287] If one takes into account the disadvantageous geographical position of Switzerland ('lack of natural resources'[288]) and its institutional isolation (for political reasons EC membership is not (yet?[289]) expected in the near future[290]), foreign investors bringing prospering markets and a rise in employment would be welcome. A liberal financial market (*freier Finanzplatz*) combined with the 'incorporation' theory (the latter from a point of reciprocity is expected to lead also to the recognition of Swiss compamies having their residence abroad[291]) should maintain the attractiveness of the Swiss market as a *Standort* for foreign investors.[292]

Scope of the Applicable law

Basis: chapter 10 of the 1987 Federal Code on Private International Law

Both Swiss substantive company law and chapter 10 of the Private International Law Code are deemed to be of a 'classical and liberal' nature.[293] However, and this is important to note, the drafters explicitly refrained from claiming to regulate the plurality of all the interests

---

basis of bilateral Conventions concluded with *non*-EC states the 'incorporation' theory is applied to companies from these countries, even though their real seat is on the territory of an EC member state. See below on 'discriminatory' application of recognition theories.

[287] Legal certainty and predictability also play an important role. Dutoit (1997) 441, observes that the 'incorporation' theory is favourable to the company's creditors, now that '*la société une fois créée continue à exister juridiquement en dehors de l'Etat où elle est incorporée*'. Cf. Ebenroth/Messer (1989) 59.

[288] ibid. 60. Cf. the jubilation expressed by J.A. Reymond (1989) 297, stressing the '. . . avantages bien connus (. . .) centre de l'Europe (. . .) réputation et discrétion de ses instituts bancaires, sa stabilité politique et monétaire (. . .) sans compter la présence d'une population, c'est-à-dire, d'une clientèle potentielle jouissant d'une niveau de vie élevée.'

[289] cf. however the vast explorations (1246 pages) under the auspices of Cottier/Knopse (1998) concerning '*Der Beitritt der Schweiz zur Europäischen Union, Brennpunkte und Auswirkungen: l'Adhésion de la Suisse à l'Union Européenne, Enjeux et conséquences*'. Note that on 3 February 1999 the Swiss government released the Integrationsbericht (http://www.europea.admin.ch/d/intindex-int.htm), weighing all the (dis)advantages of 4 possible integration policies: (i) full accession to the EU; (ii) participation in a second European Economic Area; (iii) approach to the EU via bilateral sectoral agreements; (iv) '*Alleingang*', i.e. nonparticipation in the European integration process.

[290] The emphasis is laid on the accessibility of Swiss society, cf. Ebenroth/Messer (1989) 51: 'Integrationsprozeß' 'Europafähigkeit'. Yet Switzerland should not be considered isolated, since it is 'a quadrilingual central European country and important international political and economic centre where over 15 per cent of the population is foreign' Samuel (1988) 681.

[291] Note that this argument was also put forward in the Netherlands as well: see II 1, above.

[292] Ebenroth/Messer (1989) 60. Cf. also 'Botschaft zum Bundesgesetz über das internationale Privatrecht', BBl 1983 I 440 et seq.

[293] Honsell/Vogt/Schnyder (1996) 1119; and *IPRG-Kommentar* (1993) 1316.

involved.[294] Chapter 10 cannot be analysed without taking into account article 21 (chapter 1).[295] This general provision briefly defines some elementary notions. According to subsection (1) '(f)or companies, the registered office is equivalent to domicile'. This notion is further clarified by subsection (2): 'A company's registered office is deemed to be located at the place designated in the by-laws or the articles of association. Failing such a designation, a company's registered office is located in the place where the company is in fact managed.'[296] Furthermore, subsection (3) states that a company's place of business 'is located in the state in which the company has its registered office or branch'. This subsection authorizes Swiss courts to accept jurisdiction when the *lex societatis* does not clearly follow from the facts.[297] In fact, article 21 was shaped in conformity with the substantive law provision of article 56 ZGB (Swiss Civil Law Code).[298] Like most incorporation countries, the registered office is primarily decisive in defining the company's domicile.[299]

[294] ibid.: '*Kaum Berücksichtigung fanden (. . .) unternehmensrechtliche Aspekte, welche zum Zweck haben, die Gesamtheit an einer Gesellschaft beteiligten pluralistischen Interessen rechtlich zusammenzufassen.*' In those days, conflict of laws was still deemed to be capable of regulating the 'multi-party interests' underlying cross-border company relationships properly. Cf. ch 2 IV 2, above, and the plea for an integrated approach of EC law and private international law, ch 3 above, and VI 1, below.

[295] Formerly (in the draft Code) subs. (2) of Art. 21 still completed art. 150 as subsection (3).

[296] Dutoit (1997) 68, observes that when a registration office is fictitious ('*fraude à la loi*'), the company's real seat in any other country shall be taken into account, 'notamment pour la reconnaissance d'une faillite étrangère, conformément à l'article 166'. This provision reads as follows:

'(1) A foreign bankruptcy decree rendered in the state of the debtor's domicile shall be recognised in Switzerland on application of the trustee in bankruptcy or of a creditor: (a) if the decision is enforceable in the state where it was rendered; (b) if there is no ground to deny recognition within the meaning of article 27 (*ordre public suisse*); and (c) if reciprocity is accorded in the state where the decision was rendered.

(2) If the debtor has a branch in Switzerland, the procedure provided for in art. 50(1) of the Federal Act on Debt Collection and Banktruptcy may be followed until such time as the schedule of debts within the meaning of Art. 172 of this Act becomes final.'

[297] Dutoit (1997) 68, referring to art. 151 of the Code (jurisdiction principle in company matters, see below).

[298] While debating the law concerning *personnes morales* (legal persons), francophone sources of Swiss doctrine (cf. the quadrilingual approach, above) are inclined to take the law on nationality, in combination with the law on aliens, as a starting point. In doing so, notably French-speaking Swiss authors like P. Reymond (1989) 143, take the view that the Federal Act of 25 June 1891 on *droit civil des citoyens établis ou en séjour* does not refer to companies at all. He advocates extending the notions of art. 21 of the (*lex specialis*) Federal Code on Private International Law to national substantive law rules. In contrast with the francophone approach, 'German' authors observe that '*der Begriff der Nationalität einer juristischen Person ist für das IPR ohne Bedeutung* (as regards conflict of laws, the concept of nationality is of no relevance to legal persons)', *IPRG-Kommentar* (1993) 1315.

[299] cf. Dutoit (1997) 68: '*En précisant que "pour les sociétés le siège vaut domicile", l'article 21 (. . .) confirme (. . .) que le siège a, en matière des sociétés, la même fonction de rattachement que le domicile pour personnes physiques, à ceci près toutefois que, pour la détermination du droit applicable, le recours à la théorie de l'incorporation relègue le siège effectif de la société au deuxième rang comme circonstance de rattachement (cf. art. 154).*' Ebenroth/Messer (1989) 71 and Nobel (1987) 179 et seq. (with regard to the earlier draft version).

Scope: legal persons and other organizations

A catalogue of sixteen provisions is listed in chapter 10. It commences with a definition of a group of entities.[300] In spite of the somewhat misleading heading of chapter 10—'*Gesellschaftsrecht*' (company law)—article 150(1) provides that: '(f)or the purposes of this Act, a company means any organized grouping of persons and any organized economic unit'.[301] However, according to subsection (2) of this provision, '(c)ontracts akin to partnerships but not creating an organization are governed by the provisions of this Act relating to the law applicable to contracts (articles 116 et seq.)'.[302] The precise degree of 'organization' required by article 150(1)[303] has nothing to do with the legal form (with or without legal personality) of the company.[304] Whilst at present groups of companies are not recognized by Swiss company law,[305] one can say that article 150(1) at least leaves the door open for future developments.[306]

[300] Honsell/Vogt/Schnyder (1996) 1120, however, state that it makes no sense to regulate *Konzernrecht* (i.e. company groups): as these groups normally operate from several sovereign states, any national conflict rule would fail to cover the group as a whole. Cf. *IPRG-Kommentar* (1993) 1317, referring to the Draft for a European 9th Company Law Directive, which is however not expected soon.

[301] Art. 150 is subject to autonomous qualification based on the *lex fori*: Honsell/Vogt/Schnyder (1996) 1121. Dutoit (1997) 432, observes that for the purposes of the Code, the concept was defined '*de façon large, afin d'éviter des problèmes de qualification*'. Honsell/Vogt/ Schnyder (1996) 1119, speak of '*organisierte Personenzusammenschlüsse*' and '*organisierte Vermögens-einheiten*'. As a consequence of this widened scope, the range of *formations juridiques* recognized by Swiss law, regardless of whether they are to be considered as a legal person, are outnumbered by the Federal Code, cf. Ebenroth/Messer (1989) 66; and Klein (1989) 364: 'Anstaltungen, Stiftungen (Anlagen)', as well as the English forms of trusts. Cf. *IPRG-Kommentar* (1993) 1321.

[302] ibid. 1326 et seq. Dutoit (1997) 433, asserts that in order to be acknowledged as a 'company', it is not enough for partnerships to prove that they co-operate: they can only escape art. 150(2) by demonstrating a degree of external organization. Cf. Ebenroth/Messer (1989) 68: simple partnerships and *Treuhand* (trust) are considered to fall within subsection 2. They even take the view that, since entities of this kind are not 'organized' (subs. 1), subs. 2 adds nothing to Art. 150 at all.

[303] Klein (1989) 360 et seq., stresses that it follows from the terminology, that whether these associations are given legal personality by their national legislators depends more or less on opportunistic considerations. The English club, the German *studentische Korporation*, the Swiss *Idealverein*, none of them actually legal persons, still fall within the reach of chapter 10 of the Code. Crucial for the application of chapter 10 is some level of organization. If no such organization can be found, the chapter on contracts must be applied. In the view of Klein, this is a rather arbitrary and unsatisfying touchstone ('*rein faktisches Unterscheidungsmerkmal*'). In the same vein, see Ebenroth/Messer (1989) 67; and P. Reymond (1989) 159, the latter even speaking of 'rebaptising' the former notion of *droit des sociétés* as '*droit de l'entreprise*' (i.e. substituting the more general notion of the law of enterprises for that of company law).

[304] Had legal rather than factual elements been decisive, this would have led to a qualification *lege causae*; instead, it is for the *lex fori* to decide whether, according to the circumstances, the level of organization justifies the application of art. 150: see Nobel (1987) 179 and 182 (on the earlier draft version). Having determined the proper law of the company on the basis of art. 150, it is exclusively for the *lex causae* to grant the entity legal personality, or not.

[305] cf. BGE 108–1b–37, 448; and Klein (1988) 85 et seq.

[306] It is conceivable that Swiss Courts will in future have to deal with German *Konzernrecht* (company groups).

The main jurisdiction rule: article 151

In conformity with other chapters contained in the Code, the conflict rules designating the applicable system of law are preceded by jurisdiction rules.[307] As regards cross-border company relationships in particular, there are three jurisdiction rules. Article 151 has been given unilateral effect: '(1) (i)n the event of disputes pertaining to company law, Swiss courts at the company's registered office have jurisdiction to entertain actions against the company, its members, or persons liable under company law.'[308] Swiss courts have jurisdiction over all disputes arising from company law relationships, irrespective of whether actions are brought against the company, company members, or those who appear to be in charge of the company's management.[309] Generally speaking, Swiss courts ought to deny jurisdiction by virtue of article 151(1) if the registered office is situated abroad. They are, however, permitted to accept jurisdiction when such a company conducts activities on Swiss territory.[310] The jurisdiction rule of article 151 was given a wider scope in subsection (2):

Swiss courts at the domicile or, failing a domicile, at the habitual residence of the defendant also have jurisdiction to entertain actions against a member of a company or a person liable under company law.[311] (3) Notwithstanding a choice of forum,[312] Swiss courts at the place of a public issue [i.e. in their district] also have

---

[307] See II 3, above on the threefold concept of the Federal Code: (i) jurisdiction; (ii) applicable law; and (iii) recognition and enforcement of foreign judgments.

[308] Honsell/Vogt/Schnyder (1996) 1128 et seq., 1227 et seq., are unhappy about the relatively narrow basis of art. 165 (recognition of foreign judgments in matters of company law), compared to the generous jurisdiction rule of art. 151. Dutoit (1997) 435, however, observes that this rule at least complies with art. 53(1) of the (Parallel) Lugano Convention on Jurisdiction and Enforcement of Judgments in Civil and Commercial Matters of 16 September 1988.

[309] i.e. Swiss courts have jurisdiction if the company is registered in Switzerland: *IPRG-Kommentar* (1993) 1330.

[310] Dutoit (1997) 435, distinguishes the following situations: (i) the *succursale* (branch or agency) of such a foreign company may establish the competence of a Swiss court (art. 160); (ii) likewise, Swiss courts may accept jurisdiction with regard to an *établissement secondaire* (i.e. subsidiary); (iii) in the absence of such a *succursale* or *établissement secondaire* one must simply conclude that the foreign registered office is not to be regarded as fictitious, as a consequence of which Swiss courts will have to deny jurisdiction; and (iv) this is different when the *administration de fait* is carried out in Switzerland: despite case-law of the Federal *Bundesgericht* (see below), this must be considered as *fraude à la loi*. In Dutoit's view, Swiss courts should therefore be given international competence.

[311] Again, this appears to be compatible with the Lugano Convention, now that this Convention preserves its exclusive jurisdiction rule of art. 16.2 solely for matters of validity, nullity, or dissolution of the company, or the decisions of their organs: *IPRG-Kommentar* (1993) 1130. It is by no means prohibited to submit other matters such as *actions en responsabilité* (liability matters) to an alternative conflict rule: Dutoit (1997) 435.

[312] Though not explicitly referring to how such a prorogation has been agreed upon (bylaws or articles of association, perhaps?) this provision strongly reminds us of the ECJ case of *Powell Duffryn*: see above, ch 2 IV 2.

jurisdiction when the action is brought to establish liability for an issue of equity and debt securities.[313]

The latter provision prevents plaintiffs from using the tool of qualification as an escape device. For instance, qualifying the matters mentioned in sub-section 3 as tort might also lead to the application of a proper law of the tort rather than that of the 'place of public issuance' prescribed by subsection 3.[314]

Special jurisdiction rules: articles 152 and 153

Special jurisdiction rules are contained in the articles 152 and 153. Article 152 reads as follows:

The following courts have jurisdiction to entertain actions against a person liable under article 159 or against the foreign company for which such person is acting: (a) Swiss courts at the domicile or, failing a domicile, at the habitual residence of the defendant; or (b) Swiss courts at the place where the company is actually managed.

This provision thus corresponds with the conflict rule in article 159 concerning liability of a foreign company and the law applicable thereto.[315] Article 152(a) does not infringe upon the Lugano Convention, as that provision simply *'complète le compétence internationale prévue à l'article 2 de la Convention.'* Article 152(b), however, must be set aside if the defendant appears to be either a company having its registered office in one of the Lugano Contracting States, or if persons domiciled in a Lugano Contracting State act on behalf of the company.[316]

Article 153 more or less reflects the *forum rei sitae* principle. It reads as follows:

---

[313] *IPRG-Kommentar* (1993) 1332.

[314] Apart from that, any prorogation clause establishing the competence of another court is prohibited: Honsell/Vogt/Schnyder (1996) 1132. Of course, the mandatory jurisdiction provision of art. 151(3) favours uniform and equal treatment if the plaintiffs reside in different countries. Here, I refer to earlier observations on multi-party relationships and the common interest of the non-proliferation of jurisdiction, in ch 2 IV 2 (concerning the repercussions of the ECJ *Powell Duffryn* judgment on cross-border company relationships), above.

[315] *IPRG-Kommentar* (1993) 1335, stressing *inter alia* that Swiss courts also have competence when the defendant appears to be a mere *'Hilfsperson'* or *'faktische Organ'* (i.e. others than company members, e.g. men of straw). This provision must be seen as a safeguard against the abuse of foreign companies by businessmen residing in Switzerland, in that it authorizes Swiss courts to give effect to *'la responsabilité que peut encourir une société étrangère en Suisse pour les activités qu'elle y exerce'*: Dutoit (1997) 437. Contrary to art. 151, *'les organes de fait et les auxiliaires'* (i.e. other than the company's *organs or members*) are envisaged by art. 152. Neither does this provision apply to the company as such. The category mentioned in art. 152(b) is important if the acting persons do not have residence in Switzerland.

[316] Dutoit (1997) 438. In such situations the Lugano jurisdiction rules of arts. 2, 5, and 17 prevail over art. 152 of the Swiss Code.

Measures intended to protect the property in Switzerland of companies having their registered office in a foreign country are within the jurisdiction of the Swiss judicial or administrative authorities at the place where the property to be protected is located.[317]

The provisions of articles 3 (*forum necessitatis*) and 4 (*forum arresti*) apply as a last resort.[318]

Applicable law: single proper law governing company relationships

As a consequence of the three-stage concept elaborated by the drafters of the Code (jurisdiction, applicable law, recognition and enforcement of foreign judgments), the incorporation principle itself is not referred to until article 154. The Swiss legislator deemed it important not to disturb the unity and coherence of company law; separate proper law determinations for internal and external company relationships were to be avoided.[319]

Article 154 reads as follows:

(1) Companies are governed by the law of the State under whose law they are organized, if they fulfil the publicity or registration requirements provided by such law or, where such requirements do not exist, if they are organized under the law of such state. (2) A company which does not fulfil these requirements is governed by the law of the state in which it is actually managed.[320]

It should be emphasized, that article 154 considers the *Rechtsfähigkeit* (capacity) of foreign companies to be a mere matter of fact, resulting from the *lex societatis*; in other words, this provision does not establish the legal personality of a company.[321] Reports underscore that publicity requirements only relate to the formation issue; they do not apply to bordering issues.[322] The use of subsection 2 might be frustrated when it comes to

---

[317] This provision was introduced by the Conseil National in order to implement provisional measures envisaged by art. 10 of the Code: Dutoit (1997) 438. Any nationalization and/or confiscation measure taken by foreign authorities can thus be countered effectively. Cf. also *IPRG-Kommentar* (1993) 1338; and Honsell/Vogt/Schnyder (1996) 1137: art. 10 is compatible with art. 24 (provisional measures) of the Lugano Convention.

[318] cf. *IPRG-Kommentar* (1993) 30 et seq.

[319] Schnyder (1990) 133. To that end, party autonomy should not extend to splitting the proper law of the company for internal and external company matters either: *IPRG-Kommentar* (1993) 1328.

[320] ibid. 1346 et seq. Honsell/Vogt/Schnyder (1996) 1133, however, observe that the 'incorporation' theory has indisputably been given preference over the 'real seat' theory: the fundamental principle—*favor recognitionis* (i.e. avoiding non-recognition of the company, whenever possible) follows from the fact that the Swiss legislator opted for a subsidiary application of this rule. In everyday practice, the rule is likely to apply to partnerships. In the view of Klein (1989) 366, it is noteworthy that the Swiss Federal Code on Private International Law, in preferring the 'incorporation' theory, shifts away from recent law reforms in neighbouring countries (Austria and Germany).

[321] Ebenroth/Messer (1989) 73; and Nobel (1987) 179 (with regard to the earlier draft version).

[322] cf. Ebenroth/Messer (1989) 74. This is explained by the fact that such requirements would otherwise provoke (undesirable) changes in the proper law of the company.

ascertaining the proper law of a trust: whereas the formation of an English trust does not require any publicity,[323] support could be given to the assumption that freedom of choice exists in the case of formation of an 'express private trust'.[324] However, article 154 was not meant to introduce this idea: there is Swiss authority that in this case the applicable law must be taken either from the place of formation or from a more closely related system of law (article 15 of the Swiss Federal Code).[325]

Scope of the proper law of the company

The domain of the proper law of the company *'doit être conçu de façon aussi large que possible'*.[326] Altogether, article 155 embraces nine issues:

Subject to articles 156 to 161,[327] the law applicable to a company governs in particular: (a) the legal nature of the company; (b) its formation and winding-up;[328] (c) its capacity to have and exercise rights and obligations; (d) its name or trade name; (e) its organization; (f) internal relations, including the relationship between the company and its members;[329] (g) liability for the violation of company law provisions;[330] (h) liability for the company's debts; and (i) the authority of persons acting on behalf of the company, in accordance with its organization.[331]

Claims arising from public issues

Subsequently, various matters were explicitly excluded from the reach of the proper law of the company (articles 156–9). These exceptions to the *lex*

Ultimately, this would even affect the 'incorporation' theory. Examples of bordering issues can be taken from the First EC Law Council Directive on Company Law of 9 March 1968, 68/151 EEC, OJ nr. L 65/8, *inter alia* containing measures on compulsory disclosure by capital companies.

[323] The 'charitable trust' is an exception to the rule.

[324] cf. art. 7 of the 1.7.1985 Hague Convention applicable to trusts and their recognition.

[325] Klein (1989) 366.

[326] Dutoit (1997) 443. This quotation once again clearly expresses that splitting the proper law should be avoided whenever possible: *IPRG-Kommentar* (1993) 1352. It must be emphasized that art. 155 also encompasses partnerships.

[327] cf. art. 151. Obviously, art. 162 was overlooked: Ebenroth/Messer (1989) 77, n 121.

[328] Pre-incorporation contracts, concluded with the intention to establish a company, are governed by the proper law of the contract and are therefore excluded from the material scope of this provision: *IPRG-Kommentar* (1993) 1353. Doubts have been expressed as to the matter of nationalization and confiscation measures (see above) taken by foreign authorities: no such measure can effect properties located on Swiss territory. For further information: Dutoit (1997) 443 et seq.

[329] Internal relationships between trustee and beneficiary may, in special situations, be subordinated to Swiss law whenever Swiss interests are involved; escape clauses are offered by art. 99 (immovable property situated in Switzerland) and arts. 52 et seq. and 90 et seq. dealing with matrimonial property and estates.

[330] This subs. clearly borders art. 159 (liability of persons acting in name of a foreign company).

[331] This catalogue is non-exhaustive: Honsell/Vogt/Schnyder (1996) 1146.

societatis only play a role if the interests of third parties outweigh the interests of the company and its organs.[332]

According to article 156, '(c)laims arising out of public issues of equity and debt securities by means of prospectuses, offering memoranda, or similar notices are governed either by the law applicable to the company or the law of the state where the issue takes place'.[333] It remains to be seen, however, whether this *Prospekthaftung* is restricted to liabilities under company law in a strict sense, or whether liabilities from, for example, contract or tort law are also included.[334] At first sight, both the system of the Code (article 156 belongs to the chapter on company law) and article 151, concerning international jurisdiction, seem to justify a restrictive interpretation. However, it is arguable that the question whether disputes about liability qualify as matters of company law, contract, or tort is in fact a matter of pure coincidence. Besides, due to a restrictive interpretation, shareholders abroad could find themselves in a disadvantageous position if a company has its registered office in Switzerland.[335]

Protection of name or trade

Article 157 reads:

(1) The protection of the name or trade name of companies registered in the Swiss Commercial Register against infringements taking place in Switzerland is governed by Swiss law. (2) Failing a registration in the Swiss Commercial Register, the protection of the name or trade is governed by the law applicable to unfair competition (article 136) or to infringements of personal rights (articles 132, 133, and 139).

A distinction must be drawn between article 155(d)—the name or style of the company are governed by the *lex societatis*—and the unilaterally formulated, territorially self-limiting provision of article 157, concerning the protection against infringements in Switzerland on the name and the style of the company.

Unlike other provisions contained in the Code, no uncertainties as to the functional scope of article 157 arise: it is clear from the wording that, of all possible qualifications (company law, contract law, tort law), protection

---

[332] cf. Schnyder (1990) 133, stressing the need to safeguard the consistency of internal and external company relationships (see above).

[333] This provision thus introduces several options for the plaintiff: *IPRG-Kommentar* (1993) 1360 et seq. According to Honsell/Vogt/Schnyder (1996) 1155 et seq., this provision clearly envisages protection, as well as equal treatment of domestic and foreign investors. Art. 156 is an *allseitige Kollisionsnorm* (i.e. a neutral, reciprocal conflict rule): Swiss law and any other system of law may apply.

[334] Ebenroth/Messer (1989) 78. Honsell/Vogt/Schnyder (1996) 1156, state that contractual claims fall outside the scope of this provision. The same type of problem can be noticed with respect to art. 159: see below.

[335] ibid.

cannot be found by invoking company law.[336] The second subsection of this provision was given a slightly wider territorial scope.[337] None the less, foreign and Swiss companies enjoy the same level of protection under article 157.[338] Special protection of the company's creditors is also needed in the event of the company's dissolution or emigration transfer.[339]

Company representation: third party protection

Important restrictions of the incorporation doctrine emerge from the provisions of articles 158 and 159. Article 158 cannot be considered as a traditional conflict of law provision. The substantive law rule which it contains directly protects justified interests of third parties:

A company may not avail itself of limitations to the authority of a body or representative which are unknown in the law of the state in which the other party has its place of business or habitual residence, unless the other party was or should have been aware of these restrictions.[340]

From a present-day perspective, several interests are at stake here. In everyday practice, it is for courts to operate at the crossroads of (internal) company law, (external) contract matters,[341] and—in EC member states— European company law directives.[342] It depends on the circumstances of the case, however, whether the substantive law-orientated notion of good

---

[336] Swiss law on unfair competition (art. 3.2 UWG), the law concerning the protection of a name or style (arts. 28 et seq. ZGB) or tort law (art. 41 OR) will have to be invoked by the plaintiff.

[337] This approach was disapproved by Ebenroth/Messer (1989) 81. See further Nobel (1987) 179 (on the earlier draft version). On the other hand, it seems strange to restrict the material scope of subs 2 to competition law or the law concerning rights *in personam*.

[338] For more information see Honsell/Vogt/Schnyder (1996) 1163–73. Dutoit (1997) 448, criticizes the Swiss legislator and courts for not taking into consideration the Convention on the Protection of Industrial Property of Paris of 12 March 1883, granting international protection of commercial names of companies residing in contracting states, i.e. not merely to companies registered in Switzerland. A company which is not registered in Switzerland must invoke article 157(2), provided that such a company *'a fait usage en Suisse de cet nom ou de sa raison sociale ou si ce dernier a acquis en Suisse une certaine notoriété.'* However, as far as this condition is concerned, the Swiss Federal Court is rather lenient.

[339] See II 3, above.

[340] cf. Moser (1980) 283 et seq., F. Vischer (1960) 49, 59 et seq.; Ebenroth/ Messer (1989) 83 et seq.; and *IPRG-Kommentar* (1993) 1371 et seq.

[341] Art. 158 more or less copies art. 36 (protection against incapacity of *natural* persons) of the Swiss Private International Law Code: see Honsell/Vogt/Schnyder (1996) 1175 et seq. There is however a difference between the provisions: for the application of art. 158, it is irrelevant where the transaction between the company and its counterpart is concluded (cf. art. 36: '. . . if he or she was capable under the *law of the state where the transaction was made'*). The generally accepted principle of the protection of third parties unaware of incapacity or restrictions to representation powers of their contractual counterpart was codified at an earlier stage (e.g. art. 11 of the European Convention applicable to International Contractual Obligations, of 19 June 1980, Rome 1980).

[342] Although Switzerland is not an EC member state, the drafters did apparently look at this source of law (see below).

faith as provided for in article 158 should ultimately override principles of company law (article 155, see above) and the law on agency (article 126: the applicable law is that of the state in which the agent has its place of business). Article 158, which was elaborated by way of analogy with article 36 (protection against the incapacity of natural persons) was predominantly inspired by the unfortunate consequences flowing from the English *ultra vires doctrine*,[343] restricting the company's 'capacity' (the organs lack power to bind the company, unless the articles of association explicitly authorize them to do so). The 'incorporation' theory, known for its judicial and economic liberalism, would thus be thwarted.[344]

Some incidental remarks should be made here. First, restrictions on binding the company resulting from this doctrine must be qualified as matters of capacity, rather than as problems of representation of the company.[345] Secondly, company law has not been entirely set aside: if the other party was or could have been aware of the restrictions, the provisions of article 155 (c) and (i) apply. If, on the contrary, the third party was not aware of the restrictions, the company is likely to be bound anyway, despite the fact that its organ lacked representation powers.[346] Since article 158 is bilaterally formulated, foreign counterparts of Swiss companies may also invoke this provision.[347]

Article 159 forms another important restriction to the incorporation principle in order to protect company creditors: 'When the operations of a company created under foreign law are carried out in or from Switzerland, the liability of the persons acting in the name of the company is governed by Swiss law'.[348]

Branches of foreign companies

Article 160 governs branches of foreign companies engaged in business in Switzerland:

(1) A company having its registered office in a foreign country may have a branch in Switzerland. Such branch is governed by Swiss law. (2) Swiss law governs the authority to act on behalf of such branch. At least one of the persons authorized to represent the branch must be domiciled in Switzerland and be registered in the

---

[343] cf. *IPRG-Kommentar* (1993) 1371; and Dutoit (1997) 449. Honsell/Vogt/Schnyder (1996) 1175, underscore that art. 158 has a broad material scope, in that it applies to (i) both restrictions to company representation and restrictions emanating from the *ultra vires* doctrine, and (ii) company representation by company organs, as well as by other persons ('*Prokuristen und wohl auch faktische Organe*').

[344] However, the *ultra vires* doctrine was intrinsically neutralized by European law, namely the 1st Company Law Directive of 1968.

[345] Ebenroth/Messer (1989) 84–5.

[346] Honsell/Vogt/Schnyder (1996) 1177, observe that the company is entitled to *Ersatz* indemnification claims, to be paid by the organ or functionary who acted in the name and on behalf of the company.

[347] Dutoit (1997) 450.   [348] See the following section for more detail.

Commercial Register. (3) The Federal Council determines the implementing rules concerning the mandatory registration in the Commercial Register.

One can hardly speak here of a traditional conflict of law approach; like the representation issue, article 160 is an example of a substantive law rule. One would expect such a provision to appear in legislation on aliens. The question whether there is such a branch must be answered by Swiss law.[349] The assumption is that, as to the notion of what precisely constitutes a 'branch', the observations of the Swiss Federal Court (BG) must be relied upon:

La notion juridique de la succursale vise toute établissement commercial, qui, dans la dépendance d'une entreprise principale dont il fait juridiquement partie, exerce d'une façon durable, dans des locaux séparés, une activité similaire, en jouissant d'une certaine autonomie dans le monde économique et celui des affaires; l'établissement est autonome lorsqu'il pourrait, sans modifications profondes, être exploité de manière indépendante; il n'est pas nécessaire que la succursale puisse accomplir toutes les activités de l'établissement principal; il suffit que l'entrprise locale, grâce à son personnel spécialisé et à son organisation propre, soit à même, sans grande modification, d'exercer d'une façon indépendante son activité d'agence locale; il s'agit d'une autonomie dans relations externes, qui s'apprécie de cas en cas d'après l'ensemble des circonstances, quelle que soit la subordination ou la centralisation interne.[350]

Once a foreign company conducts business in Switzerland through a Swiss local branch, subsection 2 places an important restriction upon the *lex societatis*.[351] Compared to article 158, which must be read in conjunction

---

[349] cf. *IPRG-Kommentar* (1993) 1382 et seq. Dutoit (1997) 454, underscores that art. 160 should by no means be considered as an autonomous conflict rule designating a 'proper law of a *branch*': once it is clear that an entity operates as a branch, several Swiss law requirements (e.g. registration, and other procedural measures) must be complied with (cf. registration and disclosure requirements under English law, see II 2, above): nothing more and nothing less. Ebenroth/Messer (1989) 94, add that even if the 'branch' conducts business only in Switzerland, it is still considered as a branch under art. 21, subs. 3 of the Federal Act on Private International Law. Cf. in this respect the ECJ case of *Centros* (above, ch 2 IV 2) and the 'European' context, above.

[350] BGE 108-II 124: 'The legal notion of a branch implies a commercial place of business being legally subordinate to and forming part of a parent body, whilst the branch which has the appearance of permanency exercises similar activities separate from those exercised by the parent body and with a certain degree of autonomy in business relationships; due to its autonomous position, the branch can be exploited independently without any radical modifications; there is no need that all activities normally undertaken by the parent body be accomplishable by the branch as well; it suffices when, due to specialist employees and a proper organization, the local branch is able to exercise independently as a "local agent"; it is about an autonomous position with regard to external relationships, to be judged as each case arises under the concrete circumstances, regardless of the degree of subordination to the parent body or internal centralization' (author's translation). Note that the decision of the Swiss BG strongly ressembles the definition formulated by the European Court of Justice in Case 33/78 *Somafer—Saar Ferngas*. Cf. Honsell/Vogt/Schnyder (1996) 1190.

[351] For detail see Honsell/Vogt/Schnyder (1996) 1191–6. Cf. from the EC law perspective the ECJ case of *Centros*, ch 2 IV 2, above.

with articles 154 and 155(c) and (i),[352] article 160(2) goes even further: as for representation matters, the *lex societatis*, instead of being corrected in order to protect the justified expectations of local businessmen, is substituted by Swiss law without any reservation. It does not follow from the wording of the text, however, that a branch is to be governed by its own (Swiss) proper law for all matters regarding company law, i.e. not only those mentioned in subsections (2) and (3).[353] The literal wording of article 160 reflects ambiguity: subsection (1) clearly states that, without prejudice, 'the branch shall be governed by Swiss law'; but why then was this principle repeated in subsections (2) and (3) for particular issues such as representation and registration?[354] Moreover, it is doubtful that the Swiss legislator wished internal company relationships also to be governed by Swiss law.[355]

Recognition and enforcement of foreign judgments

As regards the scope of the applicable system of law, one could say that chapter 10 concludes with article 165:[356]

Foreign decisions concerning claims under company law shall be recognized in Switzerland: (a) If they were rendered or recognized in the state in which the company has its registered office and the defendant was not domiciled in Switzerland; or (b) if they were rendered in the state of domicile or at the place of habitual residence of the defendant. (2) Foreign decisions concerning claims relating to the public issuance of equity and debt instruments by means of a prospectus, circular, or similar publications shall be recognized in Switzerland if they were rendered in the state in which the issuance of the equity or debt instruments was made and the defendant was not domiciled in Switzerland.

In a way, article 165 is considered as a *contrepartie* of article 151,[357] which establishes international competence for company law matters. At first glance, one might get the impression that article 165, which derogates from the more general recognition principle of article 149, is given a

---

[352] See above.

[353] Klein (1989) 375 et seq. Does art. 160 bring about an entire *Spaltung* for *Zweigniederlassungen* (i.e. a separate proper law formula for branches) or does it merely promote the interest of *Verkehrsschutz*, to be achieved by protecting the justified expectations in business relationships with regard to some issues, while upholding the proper law that governs the parent body? As regards this *Verkehrsschutz* (protection of third parties), again see the ECJ *Centros* case: ch 2 IV 2 above.

[354] Bearing in mind art. 155(c) and (i), this cannot be explained by the fact that these matters fall outside the scope of the *lex societatis* anyhow, so one cannot speak of a legislative redundancy.

[355] Ebenroth/Messer (1989) 95, take the view that apart from some Swiss protective law provisions, the foreign *lex societatis* remains applicable to branches.

[356] The subsequent provisions of articles 161–4 concerning cross-border seat transfers are analysed below.

[357] Dutoit (1997) 463.

bilateral scope. A closer look reveals that the Swiss attitude towards foreign decisions heavily depends on whether vital Swiss interests are involved. In fact, subsection 1(b) pays homage to the well known *actor sequitur forum rei* principle (decisions rendered in the country where the defendant is domiciled will be recognized). Subsection 1(a) creates yet another possibility for recognizing judgments rendered outside Switzerland, but this possibility will be thwarted if the defendant was domiciled in Switzerland.[358] The same train of thought characterizes article 165(2).

Freedom of incorporation: abuses and remedies

Legal basis from which to fight abuses

The incorporation doctrine demonstrates that it is hard to combine the best of both (legal) worlds: fostering economic growth by granting businessmen freedom to make use of foreign forms of capital companies encompasses the danger of circumvention of (mandatory) domestic legal provisions by both foreign and home investors.[359] It is obvious that the fear of evasion of Swiss law inspired those willing to combat flagrant abuses of a foreign *lex societatis* to search for escape devices in any direction.[360] The general formula enshrined in article 15 of the Federal Code (a closer relationship to another system of law) is excluded from the start, however, since subsection 2 of this provision explicitly restricts its application to the *objective* proper law determination. The general assumption was that applying the well known 'give-it-up formula' to situations in which a choice of foreign (company) law was made would harm the interest of predictability too much.[361] Nor should the doctrine of *fraus legis* be subject to the general principle of *ordre public* (article 17): the former device may indeed be capable of fighting the abuse of foreign substantive law for no other purpose than to evade home law provisions,[362] but the Swiss

---

[358] Dutoit (1997) 464, underlines that art. 59 of the Swiss Federal Constitution of 29 May 1874 prohibits the recognition of foreign judgments of legal orders on whose territory the company has its registered office, although the defendant is domiciled in Switzerland. He bemoans the unfortunate character of that constitutional provision, now that international competence concerning company law matters, as attributed to Swiss courts by art. 151 of the Private International Law Code, is much broader than the 'recognizability' of foreign judgments. Thus, there is a *'manque de réciprocité'*.

[359] This struggle is made manifest by the amount of literature over the past decades in, for example, the Netherlands and Switzerland.

[360] Dutoit (1997) 451, speaks of the *'résultats facheux pour les tiers'* (detrimental effects for third parties) that flow from the 'incorporation' theory.

[361] cf. Ebenroth/Messer (1989) 74.

[362] The essential task of reserving *ordre public* is to combat foreign substantive law that is considered manifestly incompatible with fundamental principles of the forum. J.A. Reymond (1989) 300, takes the view that recourse to *'fraude à la loi'* and *'nullité'* remains possible under the Code. If not, it would be far too easy for *'citoyens Suisse'* to evade mandatory

legislator obviously refused[363] to transplant this substantive law-based doctrine[364] to the Federal Code on Private International Law.

Conflict of laws or substantive law remedies?

As we have seen, the foreign *lex societatis* is mainly subject to restrictions formulated in articles 156–62 of the Code.[365] Meanwhile, the antagonists of abuse may not trespass beyond the demarcation line of article 159, which reads: 'When the operations of a company created under foreign law are carried out in or from Switzerland, the liability of the persons acting in the name of the company is governed by Swiss law'. This provision was meant to favour the Swiss domestic market by introducing a *Wahlrecht des Gläubigers* (i.e. an option granted to company creditors).[366] Remarkably, an earlier draft provision aimed at boosting the principle of 'piercing the corporate veil' contained a *substantive* law rule, rendering all organs of the company (i.e. not only managing directors) personally and jointly liable where a company, having met the publicity requirements and conducting business in either Switzerland or any other country and having its home base in Switzerland, presents itself to third parties as a Swiss company. Rigid rules like these were not common to pre-codified Swiss company law either.[367] Today's version of article 159 shows signs of a compromise. Only those persons acting on behalf of the company are affected and the radical substantive law rule was substituted by a unilateral conflict rule.[368] Neither is it any longer necessary to prove that the actors present the company as a Swiss company.[369]

home law provisions. Mark the parallels in both Dutch and Swiss law between liberality and fighting abuse.

[363] There is, however, some doubt as to whether the 'taciturnity' of the Swiss legislator is to be understood as a 'qualified' taciturnity or not: Ebenroth/Messer (1989) 75.

[364] This doctrine is established in art. 2 of the Swiss Civil Code.

[365] It must be noted that arts. 156 and 158 are of a bilateral character, while arts. 157 and 159 are of a unilateral character. Of course, it could be argued that the provisions of arts. 157 and 159 do not restrict the scope of the (foreign) proper law of the company, now that they are not part of the *lex societatis*. Furthermore, J.A. Reymond (1989) 298, emphasizes that without the jurisdiction provision of art. 152, art. 159 would lose its meaning.

[366] *IPRG-Kommentar* (1993) 1374. Cf. the quotations in Schnyder (1990) 134. For detail see Ghandchi (1991); Kneller (1995); von Overbeck (1995); J.A. Reymond (1989) and P. Reymond (1989); and Honsell/Vogt/Schnyder (1996) 1178 et seq.

[367] For detail see Honsell/Vogt/Schnyder (1996) 1178 et seq.; and Wick (1996). Ebenroth/Messer (1989) 86, even speak of excessive legislative measures leading to a '*Super-Durchgriff*', a radical form of the 'piercing the veil' principle, for pro-forma foreign companies, inspired by the notorious Chiasso affair; see Nobel (1987) 188 (considering the earlier draft version) and Heini (1992) 405 et seq. For a comparative analysis of 'tramp' or 'pseudo-foreign' companies (in the USA, the Netherlands, and Switzerland) see also Drury, (1998) 165 et seq. (see ch 2 I II and IV, above).

[368] J.A. Reymond (1989) 298, qualifies art. 159 as a species of the *renvoi* principle.

[369] Ebenroth/Messer (1989) 87, however, quote the *Botschaft*, 263 and 445, according to which this *Anschein* (i.e. pretend presentation as a 'Swiss' company to the outside world) still forms the point of departure. In a comparable sense Dutoit (1997) 451.

Article 159: fundamental flaws

Although the current version of article 159 may seem sound and clear at first sight, lots of problems have been overlooked.[370] Some of them are mentioned here. It has been criticized for bringing about a curious dichotomy: whereas powers of the company's organs remain subject to the proper law of the company, any violation envisaged by article 159 is immediately subordinated to Swiss law.[371] Furthermore, Klein emphasizes that courts might still be concerned by its ill-defined character.[372] Which kind(s) of liability is (are) meant here: company law *strictu sensu* or further-reaching issues, such as tort or contract?[373] Does it relate to external liability only, or are internal relationships also covered by this provision?[374] Which duties under which proper law are conferred upon precisely whom[375] in the company?[376] Are all types of 'associations' mentioned in article 155 subject to article 159 or should there be separate treatment?[377] Does article 159 apply to groups of companies as well? All of these questions seem reasonable: but so far no conclusive answers have been given.[378] Schnyder believes that article 159 should be interpreted in

[370] Honsell/Vogt/Schnyder (1996) 1187, regret that art. 159, instead of ending problems, provokes them.

[371] Dutoit (1997) 452.

[372] Klein (1989) 371. Nobel (1987) 189 (considering the earlier draft version), even expressed the fear that art. 159 would form the ultimate *Streitsubstanz* (tug of war).

[373] Ebenroth/Messer (1989) 87 et seq., argue that claims arising from company, contract, and tort law do not fall within the reach of art. 159 at all, as the latter provision is exempted from the main rule of art. 155(g), the 'liability arising from the violation of company law'. On the other hand, they do not see why other conflict provisions of the Code should be excluded. Similarly, J.A. Reymond (1989) 302: the claimant should then invoke the provisions of the ninth chapter of the Code.

[374] Ebenroth/Messer (1989) 87, stress that claims rising from internal company disputes (e.g. claims against the company on behalf of shareholders, directors etc.) are also covered by the provision of art. 159. In this respect the scope of art. 159, compared to the draft provision, was widened. This opinion is shared by J.A. Reymond (1989) 303 et seq., but he reminds us that art. 159 should be read in conjunction with the jurisdiction rule of art. 152, of which interpretation by the drafters (e.g. the report) remained obscure and '*mystérieux*'.

[375] Contrary to explicit text provisions, J.A. Reymond (1989) 302, holds that except for 'contrôleurs aux comptes' (accountants and auditors) all persons in charge of the company's management, whether directly or indirectly, are covered by art. 159.

[376] Should duties be determined by the (foreign) *lex societatis* or by Swiss law? Nobel (1987) meets this problem hesitantly; Ebenroth/Messer (1989) 91, believe that the complete set of rules of the proper law of the company should be replaced here neither by Swiss law, nor by a mixture of provisions taken from both systems of law. It does not seem adequate to apply Swiss law provisions to legal forms unknown in Swiss law (English trust or Liechtenstein *Anstalt*) either, since this would only cause the well known conflicting methodological problem of adaptation.

[377] According to the wording of art. 159 only 'companies' are affected: Nobel (1987) 179, 189. There is, however, authority pointing in another direction, cf. the *Botschaft*, 263 and 445: the Swiss legislator had the *Anstalt* under the law of Liechtenstein in mind. Moreover, excluding other 'entities' in advance would take away the efficacy of art. 159.

[378] Schnyder (1990) 135.

'transaktionsbezogen', i.e. on the basis of the circumstances of each case.[379] Nevertheless, article 159 as such does not enable the piercing of the corporate veil: in fact it does nothing more than replace a single element of the foreign proper law of the company with Swiss law.[380] It is doubtful, whether the final outcome is similar to piercing the corporate veil.[381] A balance between welcoming 'honnetês gens' ('genuine businessmen') and deterring 'escrocs' ('villains') was the underlying goal, but there is undeniably some ambiguity in the fact that article 159 does not seem to provide the tools necessary to combat the—relatively seldom—abuses, which after all were the target of its intellectual authors.[382]

The Swiss approach versus *the Dutch experience*

There is clearly a close resemblance between Swiss and Dutch law: apart from the fact that the Netherlands recently codified conflict of laws regarding companies, both Swiss and Dutch law basically remain faithful to the principle of incorporation; as a matter of fact, both legal systems require the foreign company to be formed properly, otherwise the law of the *siège réel* (i.e. in most cases the *lex fori*) will apply. Moreover, once the nature of the foreign company is assessed, the exceptions to the basic rule do not lead to the wholesale substitution of the law of incorporation by the law of the state on whose territory the company has its real seat. The scope of the former is simply adjusted to allow for some concrete mandatory law provisions that originate from the latter. Finally, the total abandonment of the law of incorporation with the help of the *fraus legis* doctrine, which is not recognized in the Netherlands, has apparently been excluded from article 154 of the Swiss Code by the *Bundesgericht*.[383]

Howeve, a closer look at both legal systems also reveals some remarkable differences. In the first place, restrictions on the law of incorporation emanating from articles 156–9 of the Swiss Code are neutrally drafted bilateral conflict of law rules,[384] whereas the Dutch solution to the

---

[379] ibid. 134.

[380] Ebenroth/Messer (1989) 92, express the fear that introducing the complement of Swiss liability law might threaten the interest of congruent decisions to be achieved by applying a single 'proper law' (i.e. the foreign *lex societatis*). Cf. comments above on the concept of a single proper law governing cross-border company relationships, as it was preferred by the drafters of the Code: see II 3.

[381] Klein (1989) 380, is optimistic. Contrary to many writers, he argues that the provisions of arts. 17 and 18 (see above) can also be invoked. Only P. Reymond shares this view. Schnyder (1990) 135 warns against too much optimism among company creditors: Swiss law could be less generous than other legal systems. J.A. Reymond (1989) 301, is pessimistic as well: '*presque jamais*' (hardly ever) is personal and joint liability of those binding the company foreseen under Swiss law.

[382] ibid. 299, in combination with J.A. Reymond's final conclusion at p. 303.

[383] The wording of the text was already clear on this subject, see above.

[384] Of course, the Swiss conflict of law rules might end up ultimately in the application of Swiss law, but another law could apply as well.

problem of abuse by foreign companies was sought in applying Dutch substantive company law rules directly to those companies considered to be 'pro-forma foreign'.[385] And there is another dissimilarity: contrary to Swiss law, once the proper incorporation of the foreign company has been ascertained, a company which a Dutch court considers to be pro-forma foreign is obliged to pass another test. This test comes very close to the notion of the 'siège fictif' which, prior to the decision of the *Bundesgericht* in 1991, was used by Swiss lower courts. A positive response to this test may lead to a result whereby, instead of excluding the law of incorporation entirely, a number of Dutch substantive company law rules apply mandatorily. In everyday practice, though, the penalties imposed on those in charge of the company's management are not likely to differ much under the two legal systems. However, foreign investors will never be sure in advance which law(s) apply. The merits of legal certainty and predictability, resulting from abandoning the *fraus legis* test in Swiss law, are disregarded, it seems. Finally, another striking contrast lies in the contrasting development of the two systems of law: unlike the Dutch attitude, which used to be well known for its liberalism, but which now tends to be more restricted, Swiss law, at least apparently, demonstrates the reverse attitude to incoming foreign companies.

Seat transfers

'Normal' immigration seat transfers

As has been pointed out repeatedly,[386] those systems of law that adhere to the 'incorporation' theory do not raise fundamental objections[387] to the transfer of a company's central management and control office. Transfers of the registered office, on the other hand, cause complications. As regards the latter category, the Swiss legislator distinguishes between 'normal' seat transfers and those transfers necessitated by emergency situations.[388]

---

[385] This need not surprise: whereas it is exclusively for the legal order of the Netherlands to decide whether or not its 'generosity' has been abused, it is exclusively for other legal orders to decide whether they think their laws have also been abused. Once again, the attitude of the Dutch legislator reflects the willingness to take foreign mandatory laws into account as well (cf. art. 7.1 of the 1980 Rome Contracts Convention).

[386] cf. from the 'horizontal' comparative angle, above ch 2 I 4, and this chapter II 1 and II 2.

[387] *IPRG-Kommentar* (1993) 1389. Herewith, in particular, private international law biased objections are meant; but of course other kinds of objections (e.g. concerning taxation law) may interfere with such transfers (see ch 2 IV 2, above).

[388] The procedure more or less resembles the approach pursued by the Dutch legislator. Honsell/Vogt/Schnyder (1996) 1196, even consider *'Mobilitätsgedanken'* to be a major premise of Swiss private international law. In their view, company mobility is advantageous to companies for reasons of, for example, '. . . *Firmenpriorität, Markenpriorität, Steuerfolgen,* etc.'

As regards 'normal' cross-border company seat transfers,[389] the Swiss Federal Code on Private International Law clearly distinguishes between 'immigration' and 'emigration' transfers, governed respectively by articles 161 and 163.[390] Both provisions essentially allow such transfers, provided that certain obligations are satisfied.[391] These provisions clearly do not cover 'transfers' to or from Switzerland after a company's liquidation and reincorporation. Neither did the Swiss legislator envisage the transfer of a company's registered office from one third country to another while its central management office was situated in Switzerland.

Article 161 reads:

(1) A foreign company may, if the foreign law governing it so allows, submit to Swiss law without going through a winding up and a new formation. Such a company must fulfil the requirements set forth by foreign law and must be able to adjust to one of the types of organization provided by Swiss law. (2) The Federal Council may permit a change of legal status, even where the requirements set forth by the foreign law are not fulfilled, particularly if significant Swiss interests are at stake.[392]

It is important to note that article 161 is not strictly of a conflict of laws nature; rather is it considered to be a substantive law provision.[393] This provision cannot be applied to a company's *Um-Inkorporation* (seat transfer) from one third country to another, without the legal order of Switzerland being involved. Remarkably, the situation of a cross-border transfer involving two third countries was totally ignored,[394] although Swiss jurisdiction may have justified interests, namely when companies planning to transfer their registered office have their real head office in Switzerland.[395] Article 161(2) enables Swiss authorities to counter '*politische und wirtschaftliche Krisenzeiten*' effectively.[396]

[389] In the more precise words of Dutoit (1997) 456, the provisions of arts. 161–4 envisage the 'transfert d'une *société*—et non pas à proprement parler du *siège*.'

[390] These provisions impose a uniform treatment on all associations mentioned in art. 150. Before the Code entered into force, such transfers were regulated by substantive law provisions for public capital companies, cf. Ebenroth/Messer (1989) 98, on the (former) art. 14 OR.

[391] There may be legal obstacles to a transfer of the registered office of trust companies, cf. Klein (1989) 376. One should think of mandatory provisions in Swiss family law or the law having regard to immovable property.

[392] It is highly intriguing to note that the final subs. of art. 161 '*ouvre une brèche dans ce système*' in that it paves the way to cross-border company transfers with no goal other than '*d'éviter une confiscation immanente*' (to avoid confiscation measures): Dutoit (1997) 456. Cf. also Ebenroth/Messer, n 390 above, and comments by Honsell/Vogt/Schnyder (1996) on '*Steuerfolgen*'(tax consequences).

[393] ibid. 1201.   [394] cf. Ebenroth/Messer (1989), 97; and *IPRG-Kommentar* (1993) 1390.

[395] Honsell/Vogt/Schnyder (1996) 1201. The *Bundesrat* (Federal Council) took the view that a properly functioning bilateral conflict of law rule can only be elaborated at the level of international treaties. It is also interesting that in this respect certain parallels can be drawn between Swiss and Dutch private international law: see II 1, above.

[396] *IPRG-Kommentar* (1993) 1395; and Honsell/Vogt/Schnyder (1996) 1204. Art. 161(2) appears to concur with the policies pursued by legal orders which adhere to the 'incorporation'

Article 162 fixes the precise moment of the completion of immigration seat transfers. An incoming company:

that is required under Swiss law to register in the Commercial Register is governed by Swiss law, as soon as its intent to be governed by Swiss law appears clearly, it has a sufficient connection with Switzerland, and it has adjusted to one of the types of organization of Swiss law. (3) Before it is permitted to register, a company other than a partnership is required to prove that its share capital is covered by assets in accordance with Swiss law, by producing an audit report issued by an office authorized to do so by the Federal Council.

This 'intertemporal' law-based provision thus corresponds with the newly drafted article 50 of the *Ordonnance sur le registre du commerce* of 7 June 1937, as amended by a Bill of Parliament of 15 November 1989.[397] It has been questioned whether and to what extent company managers must prove that the incoming company has a 'sufficient connection' with Switzerland. Although such proof *'ne doit pas être entendue au sens formel'*, it does not follow from merely expressing a wish to be submitted to Swiss law.[398] It must be shown that 'share capital is covered by assets in accordance with Swiss law'.[399] The previous method of preventive control was mitigated by the current legislation. The re-established Swiss legal person should at least comply with the *numerus clausus* of available company forms under Swiss law.[400] A transfer permit by the Federal Council is no longer compulsory, but it may authorize a submission to Swiss law if the requirements fixed by foreign law are not met (article 161(2)). This provision is rather peculiar, if one considers that the principle of reciprocity was disregarded here. Moreover, the Swiss attitude may well be considered as provocative and encroaching upon the principle of state sovereignty: foreign authorities having a justified interest could be tempted to enact retorsion measures against Switzerland.[401]

'Normal' emigration transfers

Article 163 not only deals with 'normal' cross-border company transfers, but also regulates company departures:

theory: attracting foreign investors, increasing employment rates, etc. Note that the Swiss legislative approach may ultimately result in a twofold identity of the company: continuing identity under the law of the country of departure; and a new identity under the law of the immigration country. In that respect, the outcome closely resembles that of the 'Lamot doctrine': see above, ch 2 II 1, and below, ch 6 III 1.

[397] Dutoit (1997) 459. Cf. also Honsell/Vogt/Schnyder (1996) 1205 et seq.

[398] Dutoit (1997) 458, for further information.

[399] Art. 162(3). In the words of Dutoit (1997) 458, *'(l)a couverture peut consister, par exemple, en réserves visibles ou être garantie par paiement auprès d'une banque de dépôt cantonale'*.

[400] cf. Schnyder (1987) 136, n 15.

[401] It is unlikely that confiscation measures taken by foreign authorities will pass unnoticed. In this sense, Ebenroth/Messer (1989) 99.

(1) A Swiss company may submit to a foreign law without going through a winding up and new formation, by proving: a. that it fulfils the requirements set forth by Swiss law; b. that it continues to exist under foreign law; and c. that it has issued a public notice to its creditors requiring them to state their claims and informing them of the planned change in legal status. (2) The above does not affect the provisions relating to interim measures of protection in the event of international conflicts within the meaning of Article 61 of the Federal Act on the National Economic Supply of October 8, 1982.

This set of safeguards is required, irrespective of whether the transferring company is subject to registration requirements.[402] As regards the first of those requirements both federal and cantonal law provisions must be satisfied.[403]

'Emergency' transfers

Emergency situations call for a *sui generis* approach, in that they may force Swiss companies to temporarily transfer their registered office to another legal order. Such *Krisenzeiten* (times of hardship) inspired the Swiss Federal legislator to enact the Bill of Parliament of 12 April 1957, subsequently amended by a Bill of 24 February 1982.[404] By virtue of this *lex specialis*, the requirements for resituating a registered office are considerably relaxed. Of course, such transfers depend ultimately upon the willingness of third countries to admit such transfers. However, it is generally thought that, from the point of view of reciprocity, the liberal attitude of the Swiss with regard to foreign companies will be met benevolently by the authorities of potential immigration countries.

Special protection of the company's creditors is needed when the company is about to be dissolved. Article 164 provides:

(1) A foreign company registered in the Commercial Register in Switzerland may be deregistered only if the petitioner presents *prima facie* evidence that the creditors have been satisfied or that their rights are secured or that the creditors agree to the deregistration. (2) Collection proceedings may be initiated in Switzerland until the creditors have been satisfied or their rights have been secured.[405]

---

[402] cf. *IPRG-Kommentar* (1993) 1402 et seq., and Dutoit (1997) 460, referring to other authors.

[403] Honsell/Vogt/Schnyder (1996) 1213, *i.a.* refer to the two-third majority decision, representing an absolute majority of the nominated company capital, provided that the articles of association do not prohibit cross-border seat transfers.

[404] See Vischer/von Planta (1982) 15.3; and for further legislative details Honsell/Vogt/Schnyder (1996) 1215; and Ebenroth/Messer (1989) 61 and 98.

[405] For a detailed description of the procedure, see Honsell/Vogt/Schnyder (1996) 1215 et seq. They state that this provision merely establishes procedural safeguards for the benefit of the company's creditors; it is not about the liquidation of the company's assets and the (un)secured character of the claims of company's creditors. Although, contrary to art. 164, a cross-border company seat transfer does not entail the company's dissolution, there are certain parallels when it comes to 'informing' company creditors.

Prima facie evidence means that it is not demanded that all creditors have been satisfied, for the reason that those creditors not reached by the *'appel public'* are not deprived of their rights. The importance of the second sub-section follows from the fact that, unlike for their registered counterparts, a *'contrôle de l'état du règlement de dettes (. . .) à l'occasion de la radiation au registre du commerce'* (an inspection of the company's debts in the event of the company's deregistration) is impossible for unregistered companies.[406]

III. 'REAL SEAT' COUNTRIES

1. GERMANY

The codification gap: 'Sitztheorie'

EGBGB 1900: the capacity of natural and legal persons

The predecessor of the current German EGBGB[407] dates back to the year 1900. The earlier version contained a small number of conflict of law provisions. Although a conflict rule concerning the status of foreign legal persons was missing, the courts never hesitated to apply article 7 to companies by analogous reasoning. According to article 7, the capacity of natural persons was to be governed by their national law. Like their natural counterparts, legal persons were also endowed with *Staatsangehörigkeit* (nationality).[408] It was then just one step further for German courts to control companies engaged in business on German territory: companies having their *Geschäftssitz* (business centre) on German territory were deemed to have German *Personalstatut* (nationality) and were therefore subject to German company law.[409]

EGBGB 1986: the absence of a written conflict rule

The first attempts to realize a thorough reform of the 1900 EGBGB were undertaken in the mid-1970s. About a decade later, the new EGBGB entered into force.[410] Despite the fact that the current version of the EGBGB contains a vast set of conflict of law provisions, a written conflict

---

[406] Dutoit (1997) 461.

[407] *Einführungsgesetz zum Bürgerlichen Gesetzbuch*, the preliminary title of the German Civil Code, which contains conflict of law provisions.

[408] cf. ancient judicature: RG 1927, RGZ 117, p. 215, referred to by Sandrock (1989) 506: US corporation governed by its *Heimatrecht* (its own national law). This was the law of Delaware, now that the company had its *Sitz* (seat) in that state.

[409] ibid.

[410] *Gesetz zur Neuregelung des Internationalen Privatrechts* of 25 July 1986, (in force 1 September 1986).

rule governing cross-border company relationships is still missing.[411] Although the German legislator refrained from prescribing either the *Gründungstheorie* ('incorporation' theory), or the *Sitztheorie* ('real seat' theory), German courts firmly apply the latter theory.[412] German writers have not expressed doubts on this subject.[413] The 'incorporation' theory, though perhaps appreciated for its predictability and legal certainty, is reputed to be *'einseitig gesellschaftsfreundlich'* (too much in favour of those who run the company).[414] Party autonomy is highly controversial in this area of the law. On the other hand, the abundance of academic writing over the past few decades demonstrates that in the eye of many company law observers and European law-oriented observers alike, the relentless notion of the *Sitztheorie* no longer meets the requirements of today's business world.[415]

The concept of nationality

Before examining what exactly constitutes the *Sitztheorie*, two preliminary observations must be made. There can be no misunderstanding that,

[411] Art. 37(2) of the EGBGB explicitly excludes company law matters from the material scope of arts. 27 et seq., because at that time EC law was expected to fill that gap fairly soon. Germany had already ratified the EC Treaty of 29 February 1968 on the mutual recognition of companies: BGbl. 1972 II, p. 369. Other countries were expected to ratify this Treaty as well. Cf. *Münchener Kommentar* (1998), on art. 37; and Kropholler (1997) 487. Cf. Wagner (1999) 210, dealing with the entry into force on 1 June 1999 of the revised EGBGB: the reform envisages conflict of law rules only for non-contractual obligations and real rights.

[412] In the words of von Bar (1991) 450: *'So eindeutig und konstant hat sich die deutsche Rechtsprechung zu ihr (. . .) immer wieder bekannt'*. His assertion is illustrated by number of court decisions. In his view, rhetorical questions whether the *Sitztheorie* is indeed settled in Germany are completely redundant. In the same vein e.g. Ebenroth (1988) 22. Should the *'ausländische Kapitalgesellschaft & Co KG'* (i.e. a German partnership in which a foreign company is participating as a partner) be endowed with special status? Cf. the famous *Landshuter Druckhaus Ltd.* case, adjudicated by the BayOLG on 31 March 1986: *NJW* 1986, p. 3029, 18 September 1986, *RIW* 1987, p. 52; and *inter alia* Ebenroth (1988) 24; Ebenroth/Auer (1990) 139; and Großfeld/Strotmann (1990) 298. Exceptions to the rule have, however, been laid down in bilateral treaties, see the following section.

[413] ibid.: '. . . Beifall des überwiegenden Schrifttums . . .' A catalogue of protagonists of the *Sitztheorie* is also rendered by Ebenroth (1988) 22, n 55. Kegel/Schurig (2000) 504. For the opposite approach (i.e. in support of the 'incorporation' theory), see below.

[414] Firsching (1995) 254, disapproves of the abuse of the *Briefkastenfirma* (post box office). See also Kropholler (1997) 487 et seq. The general feeling is that a company cannot be compared to the institution of (obligations arising from) contract. von Bar (1991) 448, expresses the view that in this area of law party autonomy is barred by fundamental restrictions: any legal person planning to act in the place of a natural person, taking over his, as well as other natural persons' responsibilities, needs the approval and co-operation of state authorities.

[415] Roth (1995) 29, speaks of an 'intensive academic debate'. In the words of Firsching (1995) 254: *'Über die Anknüpfung der Rechtsbeziehungen einer juristischen Person herrscht Streit.'* Section III 1, below focuses on the divided camps, namely (a) those who, in the words of Roth, 'side with the "incorporation" theory', and (b) those who do not fundamentally reject the 'real seat' doctrine, but instead criticize disadvantageous treatment on the basis of the 'real seat' theory of companies duly formed in another EC country, whereas, due to bilateral treaties between Germany and non-EC countries, companies established elsewhere enjoy favourable treatment which is based on the 'incorporation' theory.

contrary to private international law notions in, for example, France,[416] the search for (construed) parallels between natural and legal persons is considered highly inappropriate.[417] Nor is it possible to transplant onto companies the concept of *'gewöhnlicher oder schlichter Aufenthalt'*, a notion comparable to that of a natural person's domicile of choice or factual residence.[418] Furthermore, confusion must be avoided in defining the term 'recognition of foreign companies'. This expression may be used either in a broad sense, meaning that the company is recognized as such (i.e. its internal and external affairs being governed by foreign law), or in a more narrow sense, meaning simply that the foreign company is endowed with legal personality (cf. article 293—formerly article 220—of the EC Treaty). In 'modern German conflict of laws there is no room for any special treatment of the legal capacity of the company: the general conflicts rule governs this issue. If the conflicts rule leads us to a foreign legal order, it is this legal order only which determines whether the company has capacity to act and, if so, under what conditions. Recognition of a foreign company is therefore nothing else than the application of the German conflicts rule plus the company law of a foreign legal system.'[419]

'Sitztheorie': underlying policies

The decisive connecting factor of the German conflict rule on cross-border company relationships is undeniably the real seat of the company.[420] This uncodified[421] conflict rule, which has repeatedly been cited by the German

---

[416] See III 2, below.

[417] Explicitly: Firsching (1995) 254; and Kegel/Schurig (2000) 501: *'Die juristische Person hat kein Heimatrecht.'*

[418] Kegel/Schwig (2000) 502.

[419] Roth (1995) 30. Cf. Kropholler (1997) 489, with regard to BGH 11.7.1957, BGHZ 25, 134: *'eines besonderen Aktes der "Anerkennung" bedarf es hierfür nicht* (a specific recognition deed or certificate is not required).'

[420] It must be remarked, however, that this *Sitz* presumably coincides with the country where *'die Gesellschaft erkennbar organisiert ist'* (i.e. where the organization of the company presents itself to the outside world). In this sense OLG München 6 May 1986, *NJW* 1986, p. 2197. This is illustrated by Kropholler (1997) 491: a company presenting itself as 'Ltd.' at least *presumably* has its real seat in the UK. von Bar (1991) 449, n 58, expresses doubt as to which indicators could be used to sustain this presumption.

[421] Although today's version of the German EGBGB (General Code on Private International Law) still has no conflict rule regarding legal persons, it is reasonable to assume that the German legislator (implicitly) sustains the *siège réel* as the decisive conflict rule. Cf. von Bar (1991) 450; and Roth (1995) 35, mentioning *inter alia*: the German ratification Act accompanying the EC Convention of 29 February 1968, BGBl. 1972 II, p. 369, as companies having their *tatsächlicher Sitz* (real seat) outside the Community are excluded from the application of the Convention (art. 2.1): apparently, this connection factor should be retained in so far as the Convention—had it been in force—would not have been applicable. The same must be concluded from the wording of art. 13 e II S 3 nr. 4 and 13g V and VI from the *Handelsgesetzbuch* (Commercial Code), and, last but not least, from the draft proposal concerning the transformation of companies, whose scope is restricted to companies having their seat in Germany (art. 1.1).

Supreme Court,[422] was constantly followed by lower courts.[423] The underlying policy of the *Sitztheorie* reminds us of the classical Savignian approach (*Sitz des Rechtsverhältnisses*, i.e. most significant relationship), thrown together with substantive law-oriented policies: the *siège réel* is considered to be the law of the legal order which is predominantly affected by the activities of the company. This enables the authorities of the legal order in question to control the company effectively and to protect the company's creditors. Unlike the 'incorporation' theory, there is no need to invoke the general exemption clause of article 6 EGBGB (*ordre publ- lic*), nor is there any need to combat the phantom of pro-forma foreign corporations.[424] By way of *arrêt de règlement*, the Bavarian Supreme Court, more or less ironically, observed that the state on whose territory the company's *Sitz* is situated has no reason to assume that its interest in the implementation of its regulatory policies will coincide with the interests of the founders or members of the company.[425] Regulatory policies that are of fundamental importance—at least in the German tradition—are matters of company capitalization and worker co-determination. It is worth mentioning here that, unlike the 1995 Italian Code on Private International Law, German law clings to the basic principle of reciprocity, in that the *Sitztheorie* applies equally to foreign companies with headquarters in Germany, and to companies incorporated under German law having their real seat abroad.[426]

Sitz: *definition*

Like many other systems of law adhering to the 'real seat' doctrine, German law considers the management and control office (*Verwaltungs- sitz*[427]) to be the real seat of the company. Although finding the company's real seat sometimes may appear to be less feasible than the formal criterion of the 'incorporation' theory,[428] it is believed that this best serves the

---

[422] cf. BGH 11 July 957, BGHZ 25, 134, 144; BGH 30 January 1970, BGHZ 53, 181, 183; BGH 5 November 1980, BGHZ 78, 318, 334; BGH 21 March 1986, BGHZ 97, 269, 271.

[423] A number of lower Court decisions, including comments, are summed up by Kegel/Schurig (2000) 504, and by von Bar (1991) 450.

[424] In the view of von Bar (1991) 455, it is remarkable, however, that once a company has been classified as 'foreign' (i.e. having its headquarters in another country) it will be treated with '*bemerkenswerte Gelassenheit*' (equanimity) by German courts with regard to *inter alia* the absence of minimum capital requirements (cf. BayOLG *DNotZ* 1986, p. 174).

[425] Roth (1995) 31, on BayOLG 7.5.1992, *ZIP* 1992, p. 842, *IPRax* 1992, p. 389 (commented on by H. Kronke in *JZ* 1993, p. 372). Cf. also III 1, below (cross-border seat transfers).

[426] cf. explicitly Ebenroth/Eyles (1989) 9. There are, however, two significant exceptions to the rule, namely when (i) a German company has its real seat abroad, this may be admitted by the law of the state on the territory of which its real seat is situated, and (ii) pursuant to a bilateral Treaty concluded between Germany and another legal order, a foreign company may occasionally rely on the 'incorporation' theory (see below).

[427] von Bar (1991) 451.

[428] Closely related to this problem is that of a company established and incorporated under a foreign system of law, but *presenting* itself to the outside world as a *German*

interests of creditors of the company. Nevertheless, the decisive element in the search for a company's real seat is not the country where the *weisungsgebundenen Betriebsstätten* (i.e. the (main) production plant(s), subordinated to instructions given elsewhere[429]) are situated, but the country where the '*tatsächlicher Sitz der Hauptverwaltung* (the real management and control office)' resides.[430] Problems are not likely to occur if both management and control office and production plants are situated in the same country. Nor can companies be expected to have several headquarters.[431] A company which is duly formed in accordance with a foreign system of law, with headquarters situated in Germany, is considered to be a *nichtexistente Rechtsperson* (a non-existent legal person). German law applies, but it is for the court to decide whether such a 'company' shall be regarded as a species of the German partnership (*BGB-Gesellschaft* or *Offene Handelsgesellschaft*), whose partners are jointly liable for debts of the partnership, or whether AG or GmbH pre-incorporation rules are to be applied by analogy.[432] This is in no way meant to be understood as piercing the corporate veil of *foreign* companies; it is merely a matter of *Rechtsformzwang gegenüber einer Inlandgesellschaft wegen Rechtsformverfehlung* (a legal penalty imposed upon a *domestic* company for not having complied

---

Aktiengesellschaft. With the help of analogous reasoning, these *Scheininlandsgesellschaften*—i.e. pro-forma *domestic* (not foreign) companies—are treated on the same footing as foreign companies which have management and control offices on German territory. Cf. LG Stuttgart 31 June 1989, commented on by G. Fischer (1991) 100: English company, presenting itself as German 'Luxor Management AG' (in name plate, writings etc.) with head office in Stuttgart. The Court, analogously applying art. 179 of the German Civil Code, held that the company's representative was personally liable for the 'AG's' debts.

[429] cf. BayOLG 18 July 1985, *IPRax* 1986, p. 145 (commented on by B. Großfeld). Cf. the transcription rendered by Kegel/Schurig (2000) 504: '*Sitz der juristischen Person ist der Sitz ihrer Hauptverwaltung. (. . .) Hier handelt das "Haupt", das die Tätigkeit der "Glieder" bestimmt. Hier spielt sich das gesellschaftliche Leben ab (Vorstands- und Aufsichtsratssitzungen, Hauptversammlungen) und hier wird ein großer Teil der Verträge mit Dritten geshlossen.*'

[430] BGH 11 July 1957, BGHZ 25, 134; BGH 17 October 1968, BGHZ 51, 27; BGH 30 January 1970, BGHZ 53, 181; BGH 5 November 1980, BGHZ 78, 318; BGH 21 March 1986, BGHZ 97, 269; cf. also more recent lower Court decisions: OLG Frankfurt 24 April 1990, *NJW* 1990, p. 2204; OLG Saarbrücken, decision of 21 April 1989, *NJW* 1990, p. 647. Further information (court decisions and literature) in Ebenroth (1988) 22 et seq.

[431] See von Bar (1991) 451 et seq.: '*Jede Gesellschaft, d.h. auch eine Tochtergesellschaft oder eine Konzernobergesellschaft* (Holding), *hat ihren eigenen Verwaltungssitz; keine hat zwei.*' Consequently, the concept of a single *Sitz* prevents the proper law of the company from being split. In this respect, the *Sitztheorie* closely resembles the 'incorporation' theory. Cf. however the *double* residence of companies under English law (see II 2, above).

[432] LG Marburg 27 August 1992, *NJW-RR* 1993, p. 222; Kammergericht 13 June 1989, *NJW* 1989, p. 3100. LG Aurich, 11 July 1967, IPRspr. 1968–69, nr. 14, with regard to a Liechtenstein *Anstalt* having its management and control office and production plant in Germany. Cf. Kegel/Schurig (2000) 503: '*wenn Sitz und Satzung auseinanderlegen ist meist etwas faul.*' Cf. also Sonnenberger/Großerichter (1999) 726; and Schmidt (1999) 24 et seq. In his opinion, Swiss courts are very '*großzügig*' (generous) towards Liechtenstein legal persons having their real seat on Swiss territory (cf. II 3, Switzerland, above).

with legal requirements),[433] If the 'headquarters' is taken as the decisive indicator, this carries the risk German substantive company law might be circumvented by those in charge of the company. Creative reasoning by courts, however, prevents businessmen from setting up a company in Liechtenstein and appointing there a fictitious management board which receives instructions from Germany. This was illustrated by the notorious case of a Liechtenstein AG, registered in Vaduz (capital city of Liechtenstein), of which the main production plants (*Produktionsstätten*) were situated on German territory, but the management and control office were in Liechtenstein.[434] The German Supreme Court nevertheless held that the *Hauptverwaltung* (central management office) must be defined as *'der Tätigkeitsort der Geschäftsführung und der dazu berufenen Vertretungs- organe, also der Ort, wo die grundlegenden Entscheidungen der Unternehmens- leitung effektiv in laufende Geschäftsführungsakte umgesetzt werden* (the place where the management office and the organs representing the company are engaged in business is the place where fundamental decisions of the management and control office are taken and *effectively carried out'*). The foregoing cases demonstrate that several interests of the German legal order are at stake when production plants are situated on German soil.

There seems to be no good reason to abstain from mitigating the rigid consequences of the *Sitz* doctrine when no vital German interests are at stake. A *Rück- oder Weiterverweisung* (first or second degree *renvoi*) is acknowledged under German private international law when the legal order of the (incorporation) country where the company has its real seat welcomes the company.[435] This is likely to be the case when a *non- German*[436] company decides to move its headquarters from one third country (first degree *renvoi*) to another.[437]

Interzonal conflict rules

One issue which is strongly influenced by the *couleur locale* of post-war German company law is that of the 'Rest-' and 'Spaltgesellschaften'. The

---

[433] Schmidt (1999) 25 (emphasis added).   [434] BGH 21 March 1986, BGHZ 97, 269.
[435] cf. OLG Frankfurt 24 April 1990, *RIW* 1990, p. 583.
[436] cf. however III 1 below, on the transfer of *German* companies: the escape device of *renvoi* is inoperable, because the principle that the company should be wound up if a German company decides to transfer its headquarters does not emanate from the field of conflict of laws, but from substantive company law.
[437] e.g. OLG Stuttgart 18 March 1974, *NJW* 1974, p. 1627 (legal orders involved: Canada and Liberia); OLG Frankfurt 24 April 1990, *NJW* 1990, p. 2204, *IPRax* 1991, p. 403. In this case a company with headquarters in Geneva (Switzerland) had been formed in accordance with the law of Panama. Swiss law recognized this company. German authorities also respected the existence of the company. OLG Hamburg *RIW* 1988, p. 816: company incorporated under the law of England, having headquarters in Switzerland; recognition of the company before German courts, taken into account that Swiss private international law rules (adhering to the 'incorporation' theory) refer to English law.

aftermath of World War II led to changes in the geopolitical landscape of central Europe. Germany was divided into two separate territories, and was confronted with the need to settle private law disputes between subjects of the Federal Republic of Germany and the German Democratic Republic. German courts and academic writers were urged to elaborate conflict rules of an *interzonales/interlokales* (interzonal/interlocal) character as a new species of interregional law. Notably company law relationships were heavily complicated by the clash between capitalist and socialist economic legal concepts. In particular expropriation measures taken by the authorities of the former German Democratic Republic disturbed company relationships. However, the principle of territoriality prevented these expropriation measures from having extraterritorial effect in the Federal Republic of Germany.[438] Henceforth, expropriated companies that were partially resident on the territory of West Germany (i.e. also having property there) continued to exist and became known as *Spalt-* or *Restgesellschaften* (split companies).[439] A *Spaltgesellschaft* results from expropriation measures taken by public authorities of another state. If the expropriation measure does not involve the dissolution and winding up of the company, the two companies would exist separately in the future. If, on the contrary, the company's dissolution is ordered by the authorities, the basic rule that a company's continuing existence is governed by its *Personalstatut* (proper law of the company) is ignored: subsequently, the company will continue to exist in the form of a *Restgesellschaft* beyond the frontiers of the expropriating state. Both *Spalt-* and *Restgesellschaften* are submitted to a *Statutenwechsel* (a change in the proper law): notwithstanding the fact, that it would be theoretically sound to consider a *Spaltgesellschaft*, although not affected by the public interference, as existing in accordance with the law of that state, it would be curious and ineffective not to apply the law of the state where the remaining part of the company resides.[440] It should be remarked that the *Sitz* of the continuing company must be explicitly re-established.[441] After the reunification of Germany), the *Spalt-* and *Restgesellschaften* merged into *Vollgesellschaften*.[442]

---

[438] This principle applies *a fortiori* when no compensation measures are taken by the expropriating authority: Kropholler (1997) 496 et seq.

[439] Firsching (1995) 257 et seq. This was illustrated *inter alia* by the famous *Carl Zeiss Jena Stiftung* case BGH 18 February 1957, BGHZ 23, 333; BGH 29 November 1965, AWD 1966, p. 102.

[440] cf. BGH 31 October 1962, WM 1963, p. 81.

[441] BGH 6 October 1960, BGHZ 33, 195 (203); BGH 20 September 1962, BGHZ 38, 36.

[442] See Kropholler (1997) 496 et seq., for further information on academic writings.

Company groups

The sophisticated German concept of *Konzernrecht*, company law concerning groups of legally independent, but economically closely connected companies),[443] brings problems of a special nature. The basic rule is that, regardless of what instructions are given by the parent company, each cross-border company group member is submitted to its own proper law.[444] However, the cross-border *Unternehmensverbindung* (connection) is governed by the system of law of the *hauptbetroffenen Gesellschaft* (the company which is predominantly affected).[445] This remedy cannot be used in the case of a *Gleichordnungskonzern* simply because there is no predominantly affected company.[446] In some cases German courts therefore opted to use a rebuttable presumption: in case of multi-state activities the real seat is assumed to coincide with the seat fixed by the charter.[447]

Restrictions to the Sitztheorie: bilateral conventions

The German–US Friendship Treaty: the 'incorporation' theory

By virtue of article 3(2) of the 1986 EGBGB, international conventions take precedence over national rules of private international law. It may be doubted whether any of these treaties encroaches upon the German recognition practice described above: in this field, interstate agreements mainly facilitate the functioning of 'business partners' (companies) in neighbouring countries by recognizing their status, without, however, explicitly granting them the freedom to choose the *lex societatis*.[448] But, as has been argued by some writers,[449] there is a striking contrast between the main conflict rule—prescribing the *Sitztheorie*—and the '*Freundschafts-*,

---

[443] If a company is subject to central management and supervision it is described as an *Unterordnungskonzern* (art. 18.1 AktG); in the absence of such a central management the expression *Gleichordnungskonzern* (art. 18.2 AktG) is used.

[444] Großfeld (Staudinger Kommentar), arts. 501 et seq.; Kropholler (1997) 491.

[445] In most cases, this is likely to be the subsidiary, cf. Kropholler (1997) 491. For detailed treatment, see Großfeld (n 444 above); and Kronke (1989) 476 et seq. Of course the question whether the proper law of the company or the proper law of the contract applies depends heavily on the (characterization of the) method of co-operation between parent company and subsidiary.

[446] Then, all systems of law involved should be applied simultaneously: Firsching (1995) 259. Any disharmony of competing rules should be neutralized with the help of adaptation as a general private international law tool.

[447] OLG München 6 May 1986, *NJW* 1986, p. 2197; OLG Oldenburg 4 April 1989, *NJW* 1990, p. 1422.

[448] Treaties have been concluded between Germany and (i) the Netherlands, BGBl., Reichsgesetzblatt 1908, p. 65; (ii) France, BGBl. 1957 II, p. 1661; and (iii) Italy, BGBl. 1959 II, p. 949.

[449] Roth (1995) 36; Sonnenberger/Großerichter (1999) 732.

Handels- und Schiffahrtvertrages'.[450] Under article 25(5) of that Treaty, companies that are set up according to the law of one signatory to the Treaty shall be recognized in the territory of the other.[451]

In fact, German writers all seem to agree that, as far as US companies are concerned, this provision is *ipso iure* nothing less than the acceptance of the 'incorporation' theory.[452] Some of them, however, occasionally plead for additional conditions: Ebenroth and others argue that the American status of companies should be recognized only if there is a 'genuine link' with the USA.[453] They take the view that this is a common principle underlying the discipline of public international law. In doing so, they seek parallels between the doctrine of a genuine link with regard to human beings, as developed by the International Court of Justice in the *Nottebohm* case,[454] on one hand, and similar concepts regarding legal persons on the other. Others do not subscribe to this point of view: for example, Bungert and Ebke deny the primacy of these common principles of public international law; they claim that the Friendship Treaty should be considered as a *lex specialis*, not explicitly requiring such a 'genuine link'.[455] Meanwhile, the phenomenon of American companies having headquarters in Germany is not common.

Case law: compatibility of the Sitz *theory and the EC treaty*

Authority on the Friendship Treaty is available only from very scarce court decisions. Recently, a Delaware company whose central manage-

---

[450] Commonly referred to as German–US Friendship Treaty. Concluded 29 October 1954, BGBl. 1956 II, p. 487. Further information (on literature etc.) in von Bar (1991) 456 et seq. A comparable treaty was concluded between Germany and Spain, 23 April 1970, BGBl. 1972 II 1041 (entered into force 26 November 1972). Further references in Großfeld/Jasper (1989) 55.

[451] Provided that (i) the territorial unit forming part of a composite legal system adheres to the 'incorporation' theory, and (ii) seat transfers are not subsequent to a winding-up procedure.

[452] cf. *i.a.* Ebenroth/Bippus (1988); Roth (1995) 36; Ulmer (1996) 100. Von Bar (1991) 456, emphasizes that this Convention is not to be treated on the same footing as the *Niederlassungsvertrag*, the bilateral treaty between Germany and Spain of 23 April 1970: both Germany and Spain apply the 'real seat' theory. As a result, 'Spanish' companies have their *Hauptverwaltungssitz* (central management and control office) in Spain, not in Germany.

[453] For detailed information on this point: Ulmer (1996) 100, nn 1 et seq.

[454] ICJ 55, 4. Mere formal contacts with this state do not suffice. In order to obtain diplomatic protection of a state there must be a genuine link between the state and the natural person. Meanwhile, one should not overlook the ramifications of *Nottebohm* on the debate concerning interdisciplinary co-ordination of EC law and private international law: see ch 6 II 1, below.

[455] Bungert, referred to by Ulmer (1996) 100, n 15. Ebke (1998) 211, is convinced that the controversial bilateral US–German Friendship Treaty by no means adheres to the 'incorporation' theory: it just defines the precise conditions under which a company incorporated in the US shall be recognized. Nor is a position taken on the question whether an incoming company can simply adopt the status of a German company. This view is said to be shared by American doctrine: H. Walker, 'Provisions on Companies in United States Commercial Treaties', [1956] *Am.J of Int. Law* 373.

ment and control office was situated on German territory was deprived of the privileged status to which it would have been entitled under the 'incorporation' theory. The facts were the following: a contract was concluded in America between a New York brokerage company and a representative of the First O Corporation. Contractual payments were not fulfilled by the First O Corporation. This corporation, although allegedly incorporated under the law of Delaware, and allegedly having its *Hauptsitz* (headquarters) in Washington DC, could not be traced in the US by the brokerage company. As a matter of fact, Düsseldorf appeared to be the only place where the First O Corporation still conducted business. Subsequently, the brokerage company commenced actions against its subsidiary, a German company in Düsseldorf. The defendant was registered as the *Geschäftsführer* (manager) of the *Zweigniederlassung* (branch) of the Delaware First O Corporation. In spite of the fact that *in casu* any genuine link with the state of Delaware was absent,[456] the lower Court of Düsseldorf disregarded both the German–US Friendship Treaty and the doctrine of 'genuine link'; instead, the *Sitztheorie* was applied. However, the Düsseldorf Appeal Court held that, notwithstanding the application of the aforementioned German–US Friendship Treaty, the Delaware First O Corporation could not be recognized as a *juristische Person* (legal person) since there was no genuine link between the Delaware company and the US. As a result of the analogous application of legal provisions to the *Handelndenhaftung*—articles 11(2) GmbHG, 41(2) AktG—those acting on behalf of the Delaware company were held personally liable for company debts.[457] All in all, it should be asked whether the contrast with everyday German court practice as it has been observed by Roth is indeed 'striking'. Bearing in mind the judgment of the OLG Düsseldorf, this contrast may be an apparent one. The reasoning of the OLG Düsseldorf in a way resembles the 1998 Dutch Pro-Forma Foreign Companies Act, purporting to combat the abuse of foreign companies in the Netherlands.[458]

It remains unclear whether the Treaty also envisages the cross-border transfer of a company's headquarters.[459] Furthermore, it is highly questionable whether this Treaty, seen from the point of view of EC law, should be set aside as being discriminatory.[460]

---

[456] Apart from the incorporation, and the place where the contract between the New York brokerage company and the Delaware corporation was concluded, there was no evidence that the First O Corporation was 'settled' in one of the US states.

[457] OLG Düsseldorf, 15 December 1994, *IPRax* 1996 100 (commented on by M.J. Ulmer).

[458] In a way only, because here the final conclusion was that the 'corporation' lacked any form of legal personality, whereas in the Dutch approach there is an intermediate solution: pro-forma foreign companies are not denied recognition as such, but they have to comply with additional requirements under the penalty of joint and personal liability of their directors: see II 1, above, and further comments in ch 6 II 1, below.

[459] See below.

[460] cf. the minimum requirements set by the *Daily Mail* case (ch 2 IV 2, above). For a

Scope of the applicable law

Basic principle: the single proper law governing company relationships

It is the proper law of the company which determines when a company 'entsteht, lebt und wieder untergeht' i.e. matters of its formation, functioning, and dissolution.[461] The scope of the *lex societatis* is therefore extended.[462] This is not surprising, considering that the final outcome of the process of ascertaining the proper law of the company is, more or less, checked in advance by the German legal order: as soon as a company is qualified as 'foreign', any threat of the scope of the applicable law being overextended disappears, simply because from the German legal perspective 'foreign' means that the *Sitz* of the company (its real seat, not its incorporation office) appears not to be situated on German territory.[463] Accordingly, matters of legal status[464] and standing,[465] dissolution and liquidation,[466] and personal liability of those acting on behalf of a nonexistent company[467] are all governed by the proper law of the company, provided of course that the company resides outside German borders. ('Foreign' companies incorporated in a third country, having their real seat on German territory are considered to lack capacity. They are treated as partnerships, or companies 'in the course of formation'.[468]) *Zweigniederlassungen* (branches) also lack legal capacity: branches of foreign business undertakings are subject to special legislative provisions.[469]

general opinion on the relationship between German and EC company law, see Blaurock (1998) 460 et seq. This issue is dealt with in Part 1, above.

[461] Kropholler (1997) 495.

[462] In the words used by Kegel/Schurig (2000) 505: '*(D)as Recht des Sitzes beherrscht die juristische Person in voller Breite* (The law of the 'real seat' governs the legal person in all its aspects).'

[463] Provided, however, that both the headquarters and production plant(s) of the company are situated abroad: cf. the Liechtenstein case, above.

[464] cf. BGH *IPRax* 1985 221 et seq.; OLG Hamburg, IPRspr. 1977, nr. 5; BayOLG *DNotZ* 1986 174; OLG München *RIW* 1985 75 (analogy: composite legal system, in particular *interlokales Recht*; status of GDR-*Kombinat*).

[465] Legal capacity basically entails standing as well. The protection of party expectations may, however, result in court orders endowing a company with standing, notwithstanding the fact that this company is no longer considered to have legal capacity under its own *lex societatis*. See BGH *NJW* 1986 2194; BGH *NJW* 1960 1204; OLG Stuttgart IPRspr. 1974, nr. 7. In the words of von Bar (1991) 460, this is to be considered as a form of '*passive Rechtsfähigkeit*'.

[466] BGHZ 25, pp. 134 et seq.

[467] OLG München *DB* 1986 1767; KG *RIW* 1990 496.

[468] OLG Oldenburg 4 April 1989, *NJW* 1990 1422. English private limited company having its real seat in Germany: '*Bei Inlandssitz nicht rechtsfähig*', Kegel/Schurig (2000) 505. Applicability of art. 11 GmbHG. Cf. the decision of OLG Düsseldorf, 15 December 1994, *IPRax* 1996 100, referred to above, and earlier comments on the *Handelndenhaftung* (joint and personal liability of those acting in the name and behalf of the 'company').

[469] They must comply with the requirements formulated in, e.g. art. 13(b) Handelsgesetzbuch (the German Commercial Code) and art. 44 AktG.

Likewise, the internal organization of the company is subject to the *lex societatis*. One may think of, for example, capital requirements, amendment of the articles of association, duties of organs and members of the company, or responsibility for debts of the company in so far as they flow from substantive company law rules.[470]

Transactions of the company with outsiders: third-party protection

Issues such as capacity and representation of the company generate problems of their own kind: entering into business transactions with a 'foreign' company, whose capacity is, however, considerably restricted under its own proper law, may well be hazardous. In particular, companies duly formed under the law of a state belonging to the common law world are subject to the *ultra vires* doctrine. This doctrine enables companies to invoke the nullity of transactions not authorized by the articles of association of the company. The main rule is that the proper law of the company also defines the *Umfang der Rechtsfähigkeit* (the limits of the company's capacity).[471] It remains uncertain, however, whether third parties who enter into transactions with a foreign company and rely on the capacity (or restrictions to representation powers[472]) of this company, enjoy any protection. Some prefer protective measures, as offered by, for example, article 12 EGBGB. Unlike the surrounding conflict of law rules, article 12 is a substantive law-based provision, which directly honours good faith on the part of third parties. The article was inspired by article 11 of the Rome Contracts Convention of 19 June 1980, which reads as follows:

In a contract concluded between two persons who are in the same country, a natural person who would have capacity under the law of that country may invoke his capacity resulting from another law only if the other party to the contract was aware of his incapacity at the time of conclusion of the contract or was not aware thereof as a result of negligence.

Close reading, however, reveals that the German equivalent of this provision can be found in the second EGBGB section, titled: '*Recht der natürlichen Personen und der Rechtsgeschäfte* (the law on *natural* persons and their legal relationships)'. Therefore it can only be applied with the

---

[470] See Kegel/Schurig (2000) 507 for further information on Court decisions and comments thereto. Kropholler (1997) 495; von Bar (1991) 464 et seq. The formal validity of resolutions is occasionally submitted to the *lex societatis* (e.g. BGH *DNotZ* 1981 451. Amendment of articles of association: proper law of the company) and the law of the place where the act was done (e.g. OLG Düsseldorf *DB* 1989 569. Ibid.: *locus regit actum*; BayOLG *NJW* 1978 500. Transfer of shares to German GmbH: *locus regit actum*). For further information on case-law: von Bar (1991) 464.

[471] See von Bar (1991) 461 for further information

[472] There are no problems of qualification here, von Bar (1991) 462: basically, the issue of representation is also governed by the proper law of the company: see BGHZ 32, 256 and 258.

help of analogous reasoning,[473] notwithstanding the fact that at the same time the overall exclusion of company law relationships from the material scope of the German EGBGB is ignored.[474]

Like many other systems of law, German conflict of laws distinguishes the question whether a legal person *de iure* can be a bearer of rights and duties from the question concerning the existence and validity of contracts entered into by this legal person and the manner of performance thereof. Whereas the first question must be solved in accordance with the proper law of the company, the second has to be solved on the basis of the contract (or perhaps even that of tort[475]) conflict rule.

Worker co-determination

To conclude, matters of *Arbeitnehmermitbestimmung* (co-determination of workers) are primarily governed by the *Gesellschaftsstatut* (proper law of the company).[476] Strictly speaking, these legal rules only apply to companies having their real seat on German territory. Neither 'foreign' companies, having their real seat beyond German borders, nor dependent branches of such foreign companies in Germany would be affected by these rules.[477] It has been suggested, however, that these categories fall within the codetermination rules anyway: given the impact of labour law on a society, article 34 EGBGB (formal mandatory law provisions) could well serve as a legal basis for their application.[478]

Recent developments: a change of course?

Sitztheorie: *fundamental criticism*

Recent writings criticize the non-codified *Sitztheorie*: both its intrinsic value and its compatibility with EC law, as it now stands, raise objections.

---

[473] In favour of analogous application of art. 12 EGBGB to mitigate the rigid legal consequences of both the *ultra vires* doctrine and the restriction of representation powers are: Ebenroth (1988) 25; Firsching (1995) 256; von Bar (1991) 461 et seq., *inter alia* quoting others. Cf. Kegel/Schurig (2000) 505, quoting a decision of OLG Nürnberg, *WM* 1985; these writers agree that a third party ought not to be deprived of protection just because he was aware of the fact that the other contracting party was a foreign company. Generally speaking, it is deemed sufficient for domestic contracting parties to search for data in German registers. Non-applicability of the *ultra vires* doctrine in e.g. OLG Düsseldorf *IPRspr.* 1964/65, nr. 21. Kropholler (1997) 495–6, rejected the analogous application of art. 12 EGBGB.

[474] Earlier observations on the scope of the EGBGB should be recalled: see above and n 411 above.

[475] cf. von Bar (1991) 463. While attributing a tort to a company, it is not even relevant to ask whether anyone is to be considered as an 'organ' of the company under the *lex societatis*: this question is covered by the proper law of the tort as well. However, the matter of *Haftungsdurchgriff* (piercing the corporate veil) is submitted to the proper law of the company again, cf. KG *NJW* 1980 1300; BGH *IPRax* 1981 130.

[476] BGH *IPRax* 1983 70.   [477] Kropholler (1997) 492 et seq.

[478] ibid., with further references.

First, the *Sitztheorie* carries theoretical as well as practical flaws. It has been argued that fighting the abuse of the 'incorporation' theory by prohibiting it would turn things upside down: why deduce a fundamental principle from a corrective measure, which after all had no purpose other than to leave this fundamental principle for exceptional situations?[479] Apart from this, the 'incorporation' theory stimulates international business, since it does not provide for the immediate and compulsory dissolution and winding-up of the company if its company headquarters are transferred to another legal order.[480] Moreover, to quote Roth, 'the conflicts rule with its connecting factor "*siège réel*" may seem adequate in those cases where a company is predominantly operating on a national level. It becomes less and less convincing in a world of corporate decision-making spread over more than one state.'[481] Since the 1970s several theories have been elaborated to mitigate the severe consequences of the *Sitztheorie*: both a splitting of the proper law of the company,[482] and an issue-by-issue approach[483] have been suggested. So far, all efforts have been in vain. Perhaps this is because most theories seek to combine the best of both worlds: combining the 'real seat' theory with the 'incorporation' theory, however, leads to a loss of legal coherence. Allegedly, the German business world prefers to avoid complications. As for expatriating companies, no need is felt to circumvent the law of the country where the real seat of the company resides

[479] In this sense, ibid. 494, suggesting a rehabilitation of the 'incorporation' theory. This train of thought concurs with the ideas of Drury, see ch 2 I 2, and II 2 above. Kropholler further advocates the use of the general private international law escape device of mandatory law. This proposal would serve the interests of creditors even better, since the registered office of a company is often far easier to find (cf. the facts in the above-mentioned *First O Corporation* case, OLG Düsseldorf, 15.12.1994, *IPRax* 1996 100).

[480] Großfeld/Jasper (1989) 55, however are not even prepared to waste further thought on the 'incorporation' theory: '*Da die Gründungstheorie freilich schon im Ausgangspunkt abzulehnen ist, muß sie als unzuverlässige Grundlage für weitere Betrachtungen ausscheiden.*'

[481] Roth (1995) 36. These words are clearly illustrated by the decision of OLG Frankfurt of 23 June 1999, commented on by Borges (2000) 167. The facts were as follows. A private limited company had been duly incorporated in England. Three company managers (air pilots), none of them resident in England, managed the company from different countries. There was no company office in England. A post box in Munich was deemed not to be sufficient to prove that the company's management and control office was situated in Germany either. Board meetings took place in several countries. Remarkably, the Court decided to apply the incorporation theory to this company.

[482] See Grasmann (1970). According to his *Differenzierungstheorie*, the 'incorporation' theory would gain a foothold for internal company law matters, whereas the *Sitztheorie* would remain applicable for external matters of company relationships. It has been doubted by many authors, though, whether such a strict distinction between *Innenverhältnisse* and *Außenverhältnisse* is artificial: see Kropholler (1997) 493.

[483] cf. the *Überlagerungstheorie* elaborated by Sandrock (1989) and (1999). In short, the theory prescribes that the formation of the company should be governed by the 'incorporation' theory. This principle should be set aside, however, if those with a vital interest prefer to apply the 'real seat' doctrine. Like many other attempts, this theory has also been denounced for its impractical character: Staudinger-Großfeld, nr. 59, qualify this method as '*Normenmix*.' See ch 2 II 2, above.

simply by choosing another (i.e. German or third country) *lex societatis*. Nor would domestic investors be attracted by a total freedom to opt for another system of law: they would feel that they were no longer *'Herr im eigenen Hause'* and, more importantly, German tax law and public law are considered not to be sufficiently equipped to cope with an invasion of foreign companies.[484]

Perhaps changes are forthcoming after all, since it is highly questionable whether the *Daily Mail* judgment[485] actually implies nearly total freedom for EC members to regulate the matter of recognition of foreign companies, including the issue of seat transfers in the absence of '(future) conventions or legislation'.[486] Although harmonization efforts in company law are in a bind at the moment, some believe that what has already been achieved by ex article 54(3)(g) of the EC Treaty diminishes the justification for the 'real seat' theory.[487] An English company planning to move its headquarters to Germany could be stopped by German authorities invoking the 'general good' justification under ex article 52 of the EC Treaty, whereas an American company, relying on the 1956 German–US Friendship Treaty, would be free to move to Germany without any such restriction.[488] Although this is logical, the *Daily Mail* judgment disrupted the liberal camp: a pessimistic view is that the 'real seat' doctrine now appears to be stronger than ever.[489]

Compatibility of the German approach with the ECJ case of Centros

According to German commentators, the consequences of the case of *Centros*[490] are the following. Even if the *Sitztheorie* has not been officially

---

[484] cf. the contributions of Ebenroth/Einsele (1988). Kropholler (1997) 493, fears that the whole system would thus end up in a chaos.

[485] Case 81/87, *R v H.M Treasury and Commissioners of Inland Revenue, ex p Daily Mail and General Trust* [1988] ECR 5483.

[486] Some writers categorically deny that the German *Sitz* ('real seat') doctrine is incompatible with EC law: Kegel/Schurig (2000) 504. This view was rejected by, for example, Roth (1995) 36–44.

[487] Kropholler (1997) 494.

[488] Although the 'general good' restrictions are 'of no relevance' to American companies, cf. Roth (1995) 42, it should not be overlooked that, on the basis of OLG Düsseldorf, 15 December 1994, *IPRax* 1996 100 (see above), the extra 'genuine link' requirement forms a serious barrier to American companies as well. Since several EC member states are affected by the (in)compatibility of the 'real seat' doctrine with EC law, this matter will be analysed extensively in Part 3, below.

[489] Over a decade ago, Sandrock (1989) 505, n 2, mentioned German proponents of the 'incorporation' theory (e.g. Beitzke, Lauterbach, Drobnig, Mann, and Behrens). In the early 1990s, however, von Bar (1991) 459, stated that then the position of the 'real seat' theory is even stronger than it ever was: *'Die Anknüpfung an den effektiven Verwaltungssitz einer Gesellschaft steht heute gefestigter da als jemals zuvor.'* Cf. the passionate plea in favour of the *Sitztheorie* by Schmidt (1999) 24 et seq.

[490] Case C–212/97 *Centros Ltd. v Erhvervs- og Selskabsstyrelsen*, [1999] ECR 1999 I–1459, CMLR 551. Cf. critical observations above, in ch 2 IV 2.

abandoned by the Court,[491] a company duly established in any other EC member state can no longer be denied *Rechtsfähigkeit* (capacity) by German authorities,[492] nor should registration of (branches of) said companies be refused. For example, the refusal to register a branch of an English *Briefkasten-plc.* (postbox company) by the Bavarian Court of Appeal[493] is considered to be incompatible with EC law. Furthermore, branches of foreign companies must be able to register as *'Eigentümer in das Grundbuch'* (owners of immovable property).[494] The nightmare of foreign companies 'invading' Germany does not seem to be realistic, though. *Centros* does not preclude German courts from taking other kinds of 'measures' (e.g. holding directors of these companies liable for non-compliance with German company law requirements such as capital requirements). In the view of Ulmer, a *'Differenzierung nach Gefährdungspotential'* (a classification of potential risks) should form the basis for further debate.[495] Submitting the *Innenverhältnisse* (i.e. the relationship between the company and its organs) to the chosen foreign proper law of the company would not meet any objection. The law on *Mitbestimmung* (worker co-determination) on the other hand, would allegedly not be affected by *Centros* either.[496] Finally, capital requirements have always been of pre-eminent importance to German company law. In that respect, it is interesting to note that there is an increasing appreciation of other instruments, such as the English concept of wrongful trading, whereas on the other hand doubts concerning *Minimumkapital* are no longer concealed.[497] Apart from that, any *Betrügerei* (fraudulent behaviour) should be counter-attacked by introducing the penalty of personal liability *beim Handeln mittels einer inländischen*

---

[491] cf. Ebke (1999) 656 et seq.; and Ulmer (1999) 662 et seq. Meilicke (1999) and Sedemund/Hausmann (1999) advocate the opposite view. Doubts were expressed by Sonnenberger/Großerichter (1999) 726 et seq. Sandrock (1999) 1341, deduces the following from *Centros*: (i) the application of the traditional German conflict of law theory ('real seat' doctrine) to companies from other EC member states is no longer permitted; (ii) neither can it be applied to companies duly established in a legal order with which Germany has concluded bilateral treaties, on the basis of which the 'incorporation' theory prevails (see above); (iii) however, the 'real seat' theory remains unaffected when companies from other countries are involved. The first category supposedly leaves room for the application of the *Überlagerungstheorie* (see ch 2 II 2, above).

[492] cf. Meilicke (1999) 627.

[493] BayOLG 26 August 1998, *DB* 1998 2318 et seq., commented on by Sedemund/Hausmann (1999) 810.

[494] Meilicke (1999) 627.   [495] Ulmer (1999) 662 et seq.

[496] ibid., 663: *'Eine Nichtanerkennung der Komplementärfähigkeit der ausländischen GmbH aus gründen der Mitbestimmungsumgehung müßte daher aus der Sicht des Centros-Urteils Bestand haben.'* He expresses his sacrosanct belief that any amendments thereto under a foreign proper law of the company would not even pass the German test of *'ordre public'*.

[497] Ulmer (1999) 664: while comparing the company laws of the EC member states on minimum capital requirements (e.g. German GmbH: DM 50,000; Portugal DM 70,000; Austria: approximately DM 30,000; Netherlands: 40,000 Dutch guilders), he considers the differences *'als nicht so gravierend, wie es auf den ersten Blick erscheinen darf'* (less problematical than they first appeared).

Zweigniederlassung unter Schädigung inländischer Gläubiger (in a case of acting on behalf of a branch to the detriment of domestic creditors).[498]
Piercing the corporate veil functions as a last resort; either English law, or
German law concerning *Haftung wegen eindeutiger Unterkapitalisierung* (liability resulting from non-compliance with minimum capital requirements) could serve as a basis for fighting abuses underlying the *Centros*
case.[499] Altogether, it remains to be seen whether the Danish device—a
multiple-purpose trip: combining a holiday in the UK with setting up an
English private limited company—will become popular.[500]

It is noteworthy, that the goals and methods pursued by the Dutch legislator—cf. the 1998 PFFC Act—are comparable to German legislation:
detailed disclosure requirements function as a *hinreichende Warnfunktion*
(warning for company creditors).[501] It must be recalled once again, however, that it is not completely clear what is permitted and what is not
under the EC Treaty. None of the German writings explored explicitly
expressed the view that the EC Treaty fundamentally opposes restrictive
measures; indeed, Ulmer explicitly rejects the idea of incompatibility of
the complete range of the aforementioned German measures with the EC
Treaty.[502] However, on 30 March 1998 the German BGH issued preliminary proceedings in the ECJ to ascertain whether the German *Sitztheorie*
(real seat theory) still complies with the EC Treaty.[502a]

Seat transfers

Change in the applicable law: exceptions

It is understandable that the 'real seat' doctrine prescribes a change in the
proper law governing company relationships whenever a company
moves either its registered office or its management and control centre

---

[498] Ulmer (1999) 664. Legal basis for liability is S. 823.2 BGB (Civil Code), in combination
with the proper (German) law of a tort.

[499] ibid. 665.

[500] ibid. 664. In the aftermath of ECJ *Centros*, Borges (2000), 177, analyses the following ten-
dencies among lower German courts. LG Potsdam, RIW 2000, 145, acknowledges the registration of a branch in Germany of a company duly established in another EC member state
but this court further explicitly observes that the main rule of the *Sitztheorie* remains unaffected. LG München, RIW 2000, 146 et seq., orders that companies duly established in other
EC member states be recognized.

[501] Ulmer (1999) 663, referring to *i.a.* ss 13.2 and 19 Handelsgesetzbuch (Commerce Code),
s 4 GmbHG (Private Company Law Code).

[502] Ulmer (1999) 665. Cf. criticism of the Dutch 1998 PFFC Act: II 1, above.

[502a] Beschluß vom 30. März 2000—VII ZR 370/98, 'Bundesgerichtshof. Mitteilung der
Pressestelle' (i.e. Press report of the Federal Supreme Court, issued on 5 April 2000,
http://www.uni-karslruhe.de/-BGH/entinfo.htm), and on the Appeal Court judgment
(OLG Düsseldorf: decision of 10 September 1998), which ultimately gave rise to the BGH
judgment. See ch 2 IV 2, above.

from one legal order (*Wegzugstaat*) to another (*Zuzugstaat*).[503] To begin with, international treaties must be analysed. Noteworthy here is that the bilateral treaties concluded between Germany and the US as well as with Spain both superseded the 'real seat' theory.[504] In the absence of such a treaty, the laws of both the country of departure and the country of establishment are involved and therefore must approve the *Sitzverlegung* (seat transfer).[505] Under German law solutions largely depend on whether the company plans to transfer its seat into or out of German territory: correspondingly, there are different types of *Statutenwechsel*.

Immigration transfer

If a foreign company migrates to Germany, due to what has been designated by Firsching as the *numerus clausus*[506] of legal persons under German law, a dissolution of the company in Germany is inevitable. In fact, German law as it now stands could well be characterized as *mobilitätsfeindlich* (hostile to cross-border transfers in general): only foreign partnerships moving onto German territory will experience a *de iure* change into the legal form of a German *Offene Handelsgesellschaft*.[507] Incoming companies lose their status as foreign legal persons; managers of these companies can no longer rely on exemption from personal liability.[508] Provisions of German law concerning the *Vorgesellschaft* (pre-incorporation of a GmbH) are only applied analogously when the reinstatement as a German GmbH is already under preparation.[509] However, German courts tend to be more lenient when they face transfers only

---

[503] BGH 21 March 1986, BGHZ 97, 269; OLG Frankfurt 24 April 1990, *NJW* 1990 2204. The expressions *Wegzugstaat* (country of departure) and *Zuzugstaat* (country of re-establishment) are taken from Kropholler (1997) 489 et seq.

[504] cf. comments above.

[505] cf. the abovementioned judgment of OLG Frankfurt from 24 April 1990. Cf. explicit reasoning in OLG Zweibrücken 27 June 1990, *IPRax* 1991 406: even when the following conditions are fulfilled foreign companies may not register in Germany (cf. arts. 36 et seq. and 45 AktG): (i) according to the rules on conflict of laws in Luxembourg, companies may transfer their head office to another country while retaining their identity, and (ii) the structure of the transferring company is in keeping with German law. A *Neugründung* (re-establishment) of the company under German law is inevitable. A plea for a teleological (to be more precise: less restrictive) exploration of German law in the light of the *zukünftige Rechtsfortbildung der Europäischen Gemeinschaft* met fundamental objections from the Court.

[506] Firsching (1995) 256.   [507] von Bar (1991) 453.

[508] cf. BGH DB 1986, p. 2019; OLG Nürnberg *RIW* 1985 494; OLG München *NJW* 1986 2197; OLG Zweibrücken *RIW* 1990 667. According to von Bar (1991) 454, any omission to reinstate the company properly under German law leads to the applicability of German *Sachrecht* (substantive law): the foreign 'company' will be considered as a 'nichtrechtsfähiger Verein', 'Gesellschaft bürgerlichen Rechts', or as an *OHG*, therefore resulting in personal liability of those in charge of the 'company's' management and control: Schmidt (1999) 24 et seq.

[509] cf. KG *NJW* 1989 3100 (private limited company with headquarters in Germany before having completed the formation of a German GmbH); and Bechtel (1998) 349 et seq.

involving third countries.[510] Once again, one of the well known Liechtenstein cases serves as an example: a Liechtenstein *Anstalt* planned to move its headquarters from Vaduz to Germany. The BGH held that a *Neu-Gründung* (reformation) as a *GmbH*, the German equivalent of a private company limited by shares, and registration in Germany were required.[511] Remarkable in the observation of the highest court, however, was that, contrary to earlier case-law, the *Fortbestehen* (continuing existence) of the transferring company can nevertheless be achieved with the help of analogous reasoning: adaptation to German company law can be achieved by using the *Umwandlungsgesetz*, legislation concerning the domestic conversion of one legal person into another type,[512] in conjuntion with articles 362–99 AktG.[513] Of course, this is only allowed when the laws of both the country of departure and the country of establishment are capable of accommodating this procedure.[514] Whatever the final outcome may be, whether an *identitätswährende Sitzverlegung* (a seat transfer not involving a loss of identity) or not, a *Statutenwechsel* (transformation of the foreign company into the German equivalent form of either an AG or a GmbH, including due registration) is compulsory.[515]

Emigration transfer

German law leaves little room for doubt about the reverse situation of companies which, on the basis of a resolution, aim to transfer their seat abroad while maintaining the company's identity. Even if the foreign legal systems, particularly those adhering to the 'incorporation' theory, were prepared to welcome the German legal person, this willingness is preceded by the compulsory *Auflösung* (dissolution and winding up) of the company under German law as soon as a company commences with its

---

[510] OLG Frankfurt 24 April 1990, *NJW* 1990 2204, *IPRax* 1991 403. In this case a company with headquarters in Geneva had been formed in accordance with the law of Panama. Swiss law recognized the incoming company as such. German authorities also respected the existence of the company.

[511] BGH 21 March 1986, BGHZ 97, 296; OLG Nürnberg 7 June 1984, *RIW* 1985 494; OLG München 6 May 1986, *NJW* 1986 2197; OLG Zweibrücken 27 June 1990, *RIW* 1990 667.

[512] Bill of 11 November 1969, BGBl. 12081. Further information provided by Großfeld/ Jasper (1989) 53.

[513] This was suggested by Behrens (1986) 593. Cf. further Großfeld/König (1992) 380 et seq. However, Roth (1995) 34, underlines that the domestic provisions of company law with regard to conversion and re-registration presuppose that it is a domestic company to be transformed. These rules do not apply in situations involving the transformation of *foreign* companies into *German* companies or vice versa. (For a similar discussion, but in an incorporation country, see II 1, above). An overview of academic writings for and against the continuing identity of transferring companies is given by Großfeld/Jasper (1989) 55. For more recent materials, see below.

[514] cf. Kropholler (1997) 490; Behrens (1986) 590; and Großfeld/Jasper (1989) 52.

[515] cf. OLG Nürnberg *IPRax* 1985 342, on the transfer of the headquarters of an English private limited company from England to Germany, commented on by Rehbinder (1985).

departure.[516] If this principle flowed from the conflict rule, this problem could have been easily solved by introducing the general private international law escape device of *renvoi* (article 4(1) EGBGB). This means that the German conflict rule refers to English law including the English conflict of law rules; the English conflict rule, however, following the incorporation principle, would tolerate German companies moving into English territory. This possibility has been rejected, since the compulsory principle that an emigrating German company is subject to dissolution and winding up stems by substantive company law, and not by conflict of laws.[517] This (unwritten) rule, 'either on the basis of a decision taken by the competent organ of the company,[518] or, if such a decision is absent, by law[519] (. . .) is controversial among commentators.'[520] At this point, the attempt to expatriate a German company, and the resulting decision by the Bavarian Provincial Court of Appeal, deserve closer examination.[521] The facts in this landmark case were the following: a German GmbH was registered in the Commercial Register with its seat in Munich. At the notarially authenticated meeting of the company on 13 August 1991, the sole member resolved to amend the relevant clause of its articles of association so as to transfer the company's seat to London, England. The Registrar, however, refused the application for the changes to be entered in the Register on the ground that the change of the company's seat to a foreign country would put an end to its legal capacity under German law, so that an application would have to be made for it to be wound up. The

---

[516] Some authors, e.g. Ebenroth/Eyles (1989) 9, take the view that *Verwaltungssitz* and *Satzungssitz* (management and control office; registered office) do not have to coincide in all situations. Correspondingly, a German company may survive such a transfer of its real seat (however, on the controversial basis of the *renvoi* provision of art. 4 EGBGB read the following lines) provided that those in charge of the company's management have not cut all ties with its home country: a company may avoid dissolution when (a) there is still a production plant in the country where it was incorporated, or (b) in some way the company remains active there. We should realize, though, that this seems to be contradictory, if we take into account that the 'real seat' doctrine takes the *effektiver Verwaltungssitz* (i.e. the *genuine* management and control office) as a decisive factor.

[517] There is authority on this subject, cf. OLG Hamm, 30 April 1997, *EuZW* 1998 31, commented on with further references to court decisions and literature by K. Schmidt (GmbH: transfer of management and control centre from Germany to Luxembourg. Entry in Commerce Register of Luxembourg was explicitly denied by the Court). Cf. recently Schmidt (1999) 22. A dissenting view was taken by some authors, e.g. Ebenroth/Eyles (1989) 9; and Kropholler (1997) 491, n 13, and 474.

[518] cf. Großfeld (*Staudinger Kommentar*) s 579.

[519] BayOLG 7 May 1992, *ZIP* 1992 842 et seq., *IPRax* 1992 389 (comment H. Kronke in *JZ* 1993 372); *contra*, however, OLG Hamburg in an earlier decision of 28 July 1970, *AWD* 1970 518.

[520] Roth (1995) 33 et seq., referring to Großfeld (*Staudinger Kommentar*) ss 565 and 605. The compulsory *Auflösung* of the company was denied by *inter alia* Behrens (1986) 593; and Knobbe-Keuk (1990) 325, 352 et seq.

[521] BayOLG 7 May 1992, *IPRax* 1992 389 (comment by H. Kronke in *JZ* 1993 372), and *CMLR* 1993 801.

objections against this decision were dismissed by the Landgericht (Commercial Chamber) as unfounded by the decision of 5 December 1991. The appeal was also held to be unfounded. In a summarized form, the grounds were the following: the starting point is the ground that, no statutory rules being available on this subject, recourse should be had to case-law and academic writings. The appeal entailed the transfer of both the registration seat, as well as the administrative seat.[522] Even though the Bavarian Provincial Court of Appeal showed it was aware of the negative repercussions and the undesirable consequences of the *Sitztheorie* on the freedom of establishment under the provisions of articles 43 and 48 (formerly articles 52 and 58) of the EC Treaty, it observed that there was 'no reason to abandon the seat theory which has been adopted hitherto',[523] since this theory is still supported by better arguments. Transfers of the actual seat lead to a change in the own law applicable to the company.

If the state from which it departs requires the company to be dissolved, for that reason alone it is impossible for it to change the applicable law while retaining its identity, regardless of whether the adopted state also requires it to be reconstituted.

As a result, any such transfer would be void. The Court even categorically denies exceptions to the rule:

further exposition of this point is unnecessary because, regardless of which view one adopts, the application to transfer the seat must be dismissed in any event. Nor is this result affected by the fact that this is a transfer of the seat of a German private company from one EC state to another.[524]

Comments

The spirit of the judgment of the Bavarian Supreme Court has been regretted: rather than meeting earlier pleas for enabling companies to move freely from one EC member state to another,[525] it can be considered as a

---

[522] *In casu*, the inquiry was about the continuing existence of a German company migrating to an 'incorporation' country (e.g. the Netherlands, England, Switzerland). What about the transfer of the central office to *another 'real seat' country*? Then, the dissolution rule applies *a fortiori*, since it is believed 'that a company cannot exist as such if the relevant German statute no longer applies': Roth (1995) 34.

[523] Broad attention is given to court decisions and doctrine, since the seat theory 'is adopted almost universally by the Courts and predominantly by learned writers'.

[524] This judgment is sustained by many academic writings, cf. Großfeld/Jasper (1989) 56. In their view, predominant interest of the *Sitztheorie* is the *Arbeitnehmermitbestimmung* (worker co-determination). This is said to be the Achilles' heel of the protagonists of the 'incorporation' theory. Cf. also Part 1 of this book, containing further considerations of the Bavarian Court with regard to the level of European institutional law (e.g. preliminary proceedings of ex art. 177 of the EC Treaty and the realtionship to the aforementioned *Daily Mail* case).

[525] This idea was launched by Knobbe-Keuk (1990) 325; Behrens (1991) 97, in particular with an eye on the proposal for a 14th Company Law Directive, (1998) 353. See ch 6 III 2, below.

step backwards. The comment on this case by Kronke[526] reflects uncon-
cealed disappointment: why did the Court adamantly stick to the 'rule of
dissolution' when in the case before it protective measures in favour of
minority shareholders, creditors of the company, etc. could be dealt with
more effectively by maintaining the identity of the transferring company?[527] Why should the free movement of (legal) persons within the EC
be prohibited on the basis of a German conflict rule? After all, the German
Sitztheorie aims at the protection of company creditors: why then should
emigrating companies (and their creditors) be deprived from the *lex societatis* which was explicitly preferred by the company founders?[528] Why
did the Court miss the opportunity to start preliminary proceedings
before the European Court of Justice, taking into account that the famous,
but primarily tax-law orientated *Daily Mail* decision can by no means be
considered as an *acte clair*? Even those who oppose the 'incorporation' theory often take the view that, *'im Hinblick auf Europa'* the 'real seat' doctrine
should be interpreted in a narrower sense.[529]

2. FRANCE

The legal concept of 'nationality': the status of natural and legal persons

'Real seat' versus siège social: *conceptual differences*

The French concept of the *siège social* can be considered as a species of the
'real seat' theory: both domestic and foreign investors are denied the freedom to choose the proper law of the company. Writers do not conceal that
*'(l)e statut des sociétés étrangères en France implique tout d'abord la discrimina-
tion des sociétés reputées étrangères par opposition aux sociétés françaises* (compared to French companies, the foreign status of companies comports their
discrimination in France from the very beginning)'.[530] The premise that
any *puissance des groupements* (collective power) forms a potential (political) threat to French public interests *a fortiori* applies to influential foreign
companies conducting activities on French territory.[531] This is what the
notions of 'real seat' and *'siège social'* have in common.

---

[526] *IPRax* 1992 389 et seq.

[527] cf. in an earlier stage also Großfeld/Jasper (1989) 55, uttering the thought that
Anpassung (adjustment) without loss of identity should be enabled if problems are not to be
expected. Also further references to literature, pp. 55 et seq.

[528] In this sense Behrens (1999) 331.

[529] cf. the comment of Großfeld/Jasper (1989) 62 on the ECJ case of *Daily Mail*.

[530] Batiffol/Lagarde (1993) 329; Mayer (1998) 651: *'spécialement réglementée, soit par des
règles discriminatoires, soit par des lois de police qui viennent perturber le fonctionnement normal de
la société selon la lex societatis'.*

[531] Batiffol/Lagarde (1993) 325. Mayer (1998) 644, considers companies to be the *'agents
essentiels de l'activité économique'*; it cannot be tolerated that founders of a company be free to
choose any *lex societatis* they consider 'convenient'.

In everyday practice, however, these concepts are used in a different manner. Differences between the two concepts are rooted in divergent methodological premises: the traditional *siège réel* approach mainly concerns the process of finding the proper law of the company by examining where its headquarters are situated. However, one of the outstanding features of French law is that conflict of laws and the law on nationality and aliens appear to be intermingled.[532] French texts on *droit international privé* not only contain a thorough chapter on (French) substantive nationality law, they even connect the two fields of law, by subjecting both natural and legal persons to the law on nationality.[533] Pursuant to this integration, the quest for the *siège social* of the company is far from easy. Natural and legal persons alike are said to cling to *la notion de nationalité* throughout their 'lifetime'.[534] It is ultimately a matter of state sovereignty to define who are considered to be subjects of that state.[535]

The 'nationality' of legal persons: the concept of the siège social

It is difficult enough to define the nationality of a natural person: how should one determine a *company's* 'nationality'? To this end, the notion of nationality should be filled in with the help of the concept commonly referred to as the *siège social*. Article 3 of the Bill of 24 July 1966 concerning *sociétés commerciales* (commercial companies) reads as follows: '*Les sociétés dont le siège social est situé en territoire français sont soumises à la loi française* (companies having their *siège social* on French territory are subject to

---

[532] In most countries, private international law specialists tend to disconnect their discipline from the law on nationality and aliens. This is understandable: substantive law notions lead to attributing a certain nationality or citizenship to a person. This device is unilaterally biased, as it follows from the principle of state sovereignty. Making use of a (natural or legal) person's nationality, as one possible factor to be weighed against others in the process of ascertaining the proper law is something quite different. In the course of ascertaining the closest relationship, courts (either from the state that attributed nationality, or from a third state) confronted with the nationality of any person involved in the dispute are free to give (decisive) weight to this factor or not.

[533] In this respect, the abovementioned contributions of German writers (cf. the explorations made by e.g. Pohlman and Veelken) may well serve as an external '*renvoi* among law professors' (this expression was borrowed from A.F. Lowenfeld, *AJCL* 1982 99): Veelken (1992) 187, observes that French private international law is characterized by an '*umfangreicherer Regelungskomplex* (a more sophisticated set of conflict rules)' than many other systems of law. In his view, the conceptual approach of international company law differs from that pursued in France. A '*renvoi* among *French* law professors' sufficiently demonstrates that French academics are also aware of the *couleurs locales* (peculiarities) of their own law system: see below.

[534] Holleaux/Foyer/Geouffre de la Pradelle (1987) 131, argue that '*l'apatridie (est) une anomalie fâcheuse* (statelessness is a regrettable anomaly)'.

[535] According to Audit (1997) 876, '*deux séries de questions*' need to be answered. In his view, the most important thing is to formulate the '*condition des étrangères*'. And it is merely for reasons of convenience that on a more or less secondary stage also the field of '*conflit des lois*' should be taken into account, in order to find out which system of law governs internal and external company relationships.

French law)'.[536] It must be noted that the nationality of natural persons participating in the company (shareholders, managers etc.) is of no relevance here: otherwise, it would be difficult to ascertain the 'nationality' of a company in which the shareholders' meeting can be considered a melting pot.[537] Shareholders of public companies are hard to trace anyway. Besides, a free transfer of shares must not lead to the conclusion that the company's nationality has suddenly changed, whilst its centre of business remains unaltered.[538] French writers agree, that the *siège social* indeed approximates economic reality.[539] Besides, this conflict rule also forms an efficient safeguard in the process of controlling legal persons and discouraging *fraude au droit des sociétés*.[540] It has been suggested, though, that the notion of a company's 'nationality' should be supplemented by analysing the legal interests involved.[541] Such a case-by-case approach would, however, result in a loss of legal certainty and predictability.

The 'nationality' of legal persons: a fundamental weakness

It is necessary to examine whether the all-embracing analogy of natural and legal persons, as they are both subject to nationality law,[542] suits

[536] cf. art. 1837 of the French Civil Code, L. 4 January 1978. In the words of Holleaux/ Foyer/Geouffre de la Pradelle (1987) 136, this provision replicates art. 3 of the 1966 Act. Needless to say, this 'nationality' emanates from the deed of a sovereign state; it can never be chosen freely by those who set up the company: Batiffol/Lagarde (1993) 336, n 11. Otherwise, this species of party autonomy would lead to the implicit acceptance of the 'incorporation' theory.

[537] This problem could be tackled by what is described by Audit (1997) 881, as *'percer le voile social'* (piercing the corporate veil) in the sense that the nationality of the majority of those natural persons who are *in charge of the management* of the company could be seen as a decisive factor. But the nationality of many personnel of (cross-border operating) companies is likely to fluctuate.

[538] Batiffol/Lagarde (1993) 334. Audit (1997) 881, adds that it would not be appropriate for minimum capital requirements to be dictated by the 'nationality' of the majority of shareholders. It would also be inappropriate to sustain the idea that any company built on foreign investments is a 'foreign' company.

[539] F.A. Mann, F. Rigaux, cf. the overview provided for by P. Mayer (1994) 643. He even takes the view that only seemingly *'tout le problème se ramenant à définir le critère de cette nationalité* (the whole problem is concentrated on how to define this criterion of the nationality of the company)'. He proceeds by observing that here the nationality concept is *'rigoureusement inutile'* (completely redundant). Instead, a shortcut seems to be possible: in fact, nothing more should be done than to introduce an element of reciprocity while applying the text of art. 1837 of the French Civil Code, which provides that companies having their *siège social* on French territory are subject to French law. Thus, the outcome would be similar to applying the *siège réel* test.

[540] Audit (1997) 884.

[541] In the case of *Société Mayol Arbona*, the Tribunal des conflits, 23 November 1959, J. 1961, p. 442 (commented on by B. Goldman), held that the nationality of the company *'ne peut être déterminée qu'au regard des dispositions législatives ou réglementaires dont l'application ou non-application à la société intéressée dépend du point de savoir si celle-ci est ou n'est pas française'*. The court thus shifts away from the traditional Savignian proper law method. Surprisingly, it forms an outstanding example of governmental interest analysis.

[542] See III 2, below, on seat transfers. Seen from French perspective, this issue is consequently described as a *'changement de la nationalité'* of the company. At first glance, the legal

198 Chapter 4: 'Incorporation' Countries versus 'Real Seat' Countries

cross-border company relationships.[543] No doubt, subjecting legal persons to the 'nationality' concept serves justifiable interests: it enables French authorities to expand state sovereignty beyond national borders, as diplomatic protection can be attributed to French *personnes morales* operating on foreign territories.[544] One may well ask whether such protection-biased motives belong to the domain of *public*, rather than private international law.[545] Nevertheless, it cannot be denied that the *'qualité construite'*[546] of natural and legal persons both being subject to the law on nationality and alien status carries evident flaws: *'une société n'a ni père, ni mère* (a company has neither father nor mother)'.[547] Nor can there be any expressed *'affection'* to any state. Aside from this, the fact that concepts such as nationality and citizenship can only be attributed to 'persons' unilaterally[548] will provoke an extra degree of legal uncertainty and unpredictability, at least

consequences of the metaphor of a natural or legal person seems to have less legal consequences under English law (cf. comments on the 'birth' and 'death' of a company, II 2 above). But this is explained by the fact that English conflict of laws adheres to the 'incorporation' theory.

[543] cf. Batiffol/Lagarde (1993) 330, raising the rhetorical question *'qu'il soit inexact de parler de nationalité des sociétés.'* Loussouarn/Bourel (1996) 694, n 5, further emphasize that the nationality concept enables Conventions—frequently speaking of *étrangers*—to capture legal 'foreigners' as well.

[544] Some even believe that there is some allegiance between a legal person and the state of which the legal person is considered to be a subject; cf. Audit (1997) 877 et seq. Batiffol/Lagarde (1993) 331, mention international treaties offering privileged treatment to 'citizens' of contracting states.

[545] It is significant that most French academic texts tend to describe the issue of diplomatic protection of commercial undertakings with the help of *public* international law, cf. Batiffol/Lagarde (1993) 331, nn 2–4, *inter alia* citing Caflish, *La Protection des Sociétés Commerciales et des Intérêts Indirects en Droit International Public*, and the *auctor intellectualis* of the French theory on *lois d'application immédiate*. See Francescakis, R. 1970 609, concerning the decision of the International Court of Justice of 5 February 1970 (*Barcelona Traction*), for further information.

[546] Holleaux/Foyer/Geouffre de la Pradelle (1987) 140. Mayer (1998) 651 et seq., dislikes the controversial character of this concept.

[547] ibid. 651, implicitly referring to the *ius sanguinis* principle. In his opinion, trying to connect the concept of nationality to that of companies is 'regrettable'. For a long time, the notion of nationality as an instrument to regulate cross-border company relationships was subject to serious doubts, cf. Niboyet, J. 1928, p. 30 (*'existe-t-il vraiment une nationalité des sociétés?'*); L. Mazeaud, J. 1928, p. 30; G. Hamel, Mél. Gutzwiler 1959, p. 365 (*'Faut-il parler d'une "nationalité" des sociétés commerciales?'*). Cf. however Audit (1997) 878, who appreciated the nationality concept for reasons of *commodité* and facility in everyday language when speaking about e.g. domicile. This view was supported by Holleaux/Foyer/Geouffre de la Pradelle (1987) 133, who tend to prefer the ancient method which was based on the nationality of the company: in spite of its *'qualité construite'*, *'le "siège social" a paru être le meilleur critère'*.

[548] cf. the aforementioned definition in the 1966 Act; Batiffol/Lagarde (1993) 333, emphasize that, as far as the nationality of *sociétés non Françaises* is concerned, the French legislator of course has to remain silent. But, whereas it is totally prohibited for the French legislator to confine natural (and legal) persons to any non-French nationality, it is considered less problematic for French courts, with the help of their own conflict rules, to confine legal entities to some foreign status. This should be done *'à l'aide du critère qui lui paraît le meilleur'*. Cf. Mayer (1998) 644.

when this method is compared to the traditional, bilaterally functioning conflict rule of the *siège réel*. Of course, as will be seen below, a foreign company may be endowed with a fictitious nationality, but again this test turns out to be quite artificial.[549] Moreover, in spite of the construed symmetry between natural and legal persons, none of the French courts are given *exclusive* jurisdiction to decide a company's nationality.[550] Next to this, questions about how to deal with a company that can be considered *plurinationale*, will cause even more complications in the sense that state authorities probably will be less prepared to give up the exclusive right to control their own 'subjects'.[551] Neither is the nationality concept an appropriate tool for localizing groups of companies, each operating in another country.[552] Apart from the preliminary question whether groups of companies can, or should, be endowed with legal personality, it is doubted whether any proper law formula based on considerations of nationality is acceptable. It should be recalled once again that 'nationality', is not an appropriate instrument for determining 'freedom of establishment' for companies in the European Union.[553] Yet, as will be seen, the methodological struggle to avoid logical but undesired consequences that spring from the nationality concept culminated in an amalgamation of the latter with the more commonly used conflicting concept of the 'closest relationship'. Rather than wishing to sacrifice the traditional and fixed concept of a legal person's 'nationality', a combination of this concept with that of the closest relationship was preferred. It even influenced the meaning of the concept of 'recognition' under article 220 (now: article 293) of the EC Treaty,

---

[549] In earlier times, Niboyet was confused by the idea of an increasing 'population' generated simply by endowing legal persons with 'nationality'. He therefore rejected the use of the concept of nationality for legal persons: P. Niboyet, *Revue de droit international privé* 1927 402. Batiffol/Lagarde (1993) 329 fail to see this point. They think that the idea of an increasing 'population' is a fallacy: legal persons do not belong to the population of a country. Being objects, rather than subjects, they merely represent a form of activity undertaken by human beings. Neither can the principle of *ius sanguinis* be applied to non-physical beings: Pillet, *Les personnes morales en droit international privé*, Paris 1914 123, mentioned by *i.a.* Pohlmann, (1988) 44.

[550] cf. Holleaux/Foyer/Geouffre de la Pradelle (1987) 142, quoting the trib. des conf. in the famous *Mayol Arbona* case, 23 November 1959 (see also below): *'il n'existe aucune compétence exclusive du Tribunal de grande instance en matière de "nationalité" des sociétés, et l'action déclaratoire en reconnaissance de nationalité de l'article 129 C. nat. est fermée aux personnes morales'*.

[551] cf. Batiffol/Lagarde (1993) 331 et seq. It must be noted, however, that the underlying problem of unpredictability applies equally to the less circuitous *siège réel* concept. Audit (1997) 879, even rejects the separate treatment of multinationals. Apart from companies established under European law conventions (e.g. SE, EEIG) or more particularly international treaties (Air Afrique), they do not form 'une catégorie particulière'.

[552] Holleaux/Foyer/Geouffre de la Pradelle (1987) 145, assert that in the long run enterprises operating in number of countries will hardly be prepared to conduct business using the form *'d'un simple bureau, agence ou succurcale'*. In their view, it is not satisfactory to apply the factor of the *siège social* to a part of the total enterprise. On the other hand, they do not believe in the *'quasi-existence'* of a proper law governing groups of companies, either.

[553] Detail in ch 2 IV 1, above.

in that it was hampered by the 'minimum' concept (i.e. bearer of rights and duties only, without reference to the independent identification of the *lex societatis*).[554]

Determination of the *siège social*

Bilateralization of the unilateral conflict rule

The 'incorporation' theory left hardly any traces in France,[555] in other words, the primacy of the *siège social* method has never been seriously contested.[556] This concept was supported by both the French courts[557] and French doctrine. Some conflict of law specialists, however, point to the fact that French writers erroneously ignore court decisions, as they tend to take the *siège réel* as the sole factor in the process of ascertaining the proper law of the company.[558] Contrary to post-war writings in, for example, German doctrine, hardly any plea for the 'incorporation' theory can be found in France.[559] In spite of the fact that the theory of the *siège social* meets

---

[554] cf. criticism by Eyles, (1990) 97 et seq., also referred to in ch 2 IV 1, above.

[555] Nowadays, no room is left for *la volonté* of the founders of the company. Cf. Mayer (1998) 647. Loussouarn/Bourel (1996) 697, emphasize that, although the company can be considered as a species of the *contrat social*, freedom to choose the proper law cannot be tolerated. Cf. however from a comparative angle, Pohlmann (1988) 44, mentioning Pillet, Plaisant, and Thaler. Holleaux/Foyer/Geouffre de la Pradelle (1987) 133, mention an exceptional case: at the dawn of the independence of Algeria, French courts occasionally held that companies residing in Algeria must be presumed to remain 'French' companies, for the reason that this would correspond with the 'will' of the company founders. (Cf. also seat transfers, III, 2 below).

[556] Doubts were merely expressed with regard to the question whether the 'incorporation' theory and the theory of the *siège social (réel)* should be treated on an equal footing, or whether the latter should be considered as an adjustment of the former. According to Audit (1997) 882 et seq, the notion may be sustained that, before determining the genuine *siège social*, the founders of a company at least must have had some idea of a certain 'nationality' of the company.

[557] cf. cases over the past few decades: 30 March 1971, *R.* 1971, p. 451 and J. 1972, p. 834 (comment by Y. Loussouarn); Court of Versailles 6 June 1984, GP 1986, p. 1; Ass. plén. Civ. 21 December 1990, D. 1991, p. 305.

[558] According to Mayer (1998) 647, the normal procedure has always been to search for the registered office of the company first, which was to be superseded only if this registered office turned out to be fictitious or, even worse, fraudulent: *'le siège retenue est en principe le siège statutaire. Les arrêts cités comme ayant fait prévaloir le siège réel ont, en fait, constaté, que le siège statutaire était non seulement fictif, mais frauduleux: simple application de la théorie de la fraude à la loi.'* Cf. Paris 21 May 1957, Rev. cr. d.i.p. 1958, p. 128, commented on by Ph. Francescakis. (Cf. further II 3, above: *'fraude à la loi'* as a general exemption clause in Swiss conflict of laws.) However, and this was overlooked by Mayer, the prohibition in French law against choosing the proper law of the company (which after all is the main core of the *siège réel/social* theory) cannot be denied. Moreover, although the registered office may play a role under the 1966 Act (discussed below), it is merely a secondary role, the applicability of which may only be invoked by third parties, not by the company.

[559] Feasibility, liberalism, legal certainty and—hardly ever spoken of by protagonists of the 'incorporation' theory in other countries—the right to diplomatic protection are considered to be the foremost advantages of the 'incorporation' theory. The final *appréciation*,

approval, many learned writers feel discontent about the idea of a *lex societatis* which can only be arrived at deviously:[560] the unilateral activity of endowing legal persons with French nationality is not a feasible instrument for regulating everyday company law practice. Therefore, courts made attempts to neutralize nationality as a puzzling, yet decisive, element in the process of determining a company's *siège social*. This was achieved by introducing the idea that the closest connection of a company with a system of law *presumably* represents the *foreign*[561] nationality of the company: '*La jurisprudence, raisonnant en termes de conflit de lois, a cherché à définir un critère de rattachement bilateral (. . .) indiquant la loi du pays avec lequel la société présente les liens les plus étroits, laquelle sera qualifiée de la loi nationale de la société.*'[562] Whilst making use of bilaterally functioning conflict rules, courts tend to seek the closest relationship first, then this relationship is qualified as the 'national law' of the company.[563] It goes without saying that the *siège social* cannot be dictated by members of the company: in order to prevent the 'incorporation' theory from re-entering through the back door, any fictitious designation[564] of the company's *siège social* should be disregarded. The aforementioned 1966 Act explicitly provides that '*les tiers peuvent se prévaloir du siège statutaire, mais celui-ci ne leur est pas opposable par la société si son siège réel est situé en un autre lieu*'.[565] The

however, leads to a rejection of the 'incorporation' theory: here too, motives are strongly biased by 'French reasoning' in that, apart from the fear of abuse by lenient and permissive company law systems, it is not tolerated that founders of a company be free to circumvent the objective *siège social* test by simply choosing the 'nationality' of the company, cf. Audit (1997) 882.

[560] cf. Batiffol/Lagarde (1993) 330: '*L'objet de la controverse est de savoir si, pour déterminer la* lex societatis, *il faut au préalable rechercher la nationalité de la société ou si la règle de conflit française ne désigne pas plutôt directement la loi du siège social.*' This process of finding the proper law was disapproved of by *inter alia* Levy (1984), S. 66, R. Libchaber, Rev. Soc. 1991, p. 746, and, from a comparative lawyer's point of view, Pohlmann (1988) 158: '*Letztlich ist der Begriff unnötig. (. . .) Macht man die Beantwortung dieser Fragen von der Nationalität einer Gesellschaft abhängig, so legt man einen überflüssigen Zwischenschritt ein.*'

[561] Once again, I refer to what has been said earlier about attributing a nationality to a (natural or legal) person, which ultimately is a matter of state sovereignty. Consequently, *French* authorities cannot endow a (legal) person with a *foreign* citizenship: in finding the proper law of the company by using the 'nationality' concept, they are therefore prevented from going any further than making use of a *presumed* foreign nationality.

[562] cf. Mayer (1998) 643 and 648. Audit (1997) 884, welcomes the idea that the *siège social* has '*le mérite d'exprimer un lien effectif*'.

[563] Batiffol/Lagarde (1993) 333. Cf. C de C Civ. 1., 18 April 1972, R. 1972, p. 672 (*Société Overseas Apeco Ltd.*, commented on by P. Lagarde). Cf. Mayer (1998) 654. The process of determining a company's nationality is however preceded by the inquiry whether the company has been endowed with some 'personalité' elsewhere, cf. Mayer (1998) 644.

[564] cf. Batiffol/Lagarde (1993) 338: '*Il ne suffit pas de déclarer que le siège social fixé à Londres pour que la société soit étrangère si les affaires sociales sont en fait dirigées à Paris, le "bureau" de Londres se bornant à la réexpédition du courrier*'. Occasionally, the expression *siège réel* is used here.

[565] 'Third parties may rely upon the registration office of the company, but the company is not allowed to rely upon the registration office against third parties if the *siège réel* is situated elsewhere': art. 3(2). In earlier case-law this principle was well settled, cf. Paris Court 27

intention underlying this *'théorie d'apparence'* was that creditors of a company incorporated in France should not be taken by surprise by a company claiming that its *siège social* is outside France.

The siège social versus *the 'centre d'exploitation'*

However attractive the adaptation of the *siège social* to the needs of international law may seem at first sight, it proves to be the source of many theoretical and practical complications. Trying to combine the traditional bilateral conflict of law rule (cf. 'closest connection'; 'proper law', etc.) with the control-based notion of nationality carries the risk that companies will be unjustly presumed to have a foreign nationality.[566] But the moment it turns out that the flaws appear to be system-based, why not simply leave the system (i.e. nationality law coupled with *siège social*) and, instead, apply the *lieu d'exploitation* (business centre) as the decisive factor?[567] Remarkably, supporters of this open-ended proper law formula seek to establish parallels between conflict rules applicable to companies (*lieu d'exploitation*) and those applicable to contracts (*lieu d'exécution*, i.e. the place of performance).[568] A clear distinction should be made between the (highly important) *pivot des interêts* and the mere *centre d'activité technique*.[569] Besides, recent case-law of the European Court of Justice sufficiently demonstrates that involving substantive law perceptions as to the contractual, or institutional, basis of company relationships is hazardous.[570] To avoid complications, the French Supreme Court recently[571] decided that the *siège statutaire* and the *siège social* presumably coincide:[572]

March 1907, J. 1907.768; Rennes Court 1 March 1914, Rec. Nantes, 1914, 1.250; Paris Court 31 October 1957, R. 1958.345.

[566] Batiffol/Lagarde (1993) 333, emphasize that it is impossible to burn the candle from both ends: the quest should be for either the closest connected system of law or the control mechanisms. Yet they do not opt for completely rejecting this twofold method.

[567] In fact, the French Cour de Cassation, after admitting the test of the *lieu d'exécution* two centuries ago (cf. C de C 31 May 1848, *D*. 48.1.444) finally preferred the nationality test to determine the *siège social* of a company.

[568] Audit (1997) 884, points to the similarity between the objective proper law test for contracts (*localisation*) and the conflict of law rule elaborated for companies. Likewise, Batiffol/Lagarde (1993) 334, n 4, who further mention Weiss, Lyon-Caen, Renault, Chavegrin, and others.

[569] Loussouarn/Bourel (1996) 697.

[570] cf. ch 2 IV 2 above, on ECJ case C–214/89 *Powell Duffryn v Wolfgang Petereit* [1992] ECR 1755.

[571] In earlier decisions, the highest Court operated in a slightly different manner. Cf. 8 February 1972, *Clunet* 1973, p. 218 (*Shell Berre*) and 10 March 1976, Rev. cr. d.i.p. 1976, p. 658 (*Shell France*): the *siège social* is situated where the company has *'ses établissements principaux, sa direction et son exploitation en France'*; 18 April 1972, Rev. cr. d.i.p. 1972, p. 672 (*Société Overseas Apeco Ltd.*): Swiss company, taking into account the Franco-Swiss Treaty from 1869 and the following facts. Americans and Swiss in charge of management of the company; company formed and registred in Geneva; *siège effectif* also situated in Geneva. Cf. Mayer (1998) 654.

[572] C de C 21 December 1990, Rev cr. d.i.p. 1992, p. 70.

the latter is considered to be situated in the same place as *'la direction supérieure et le contrôle de la société* (. . .) *et non celui où elle a seulement son exploitation et une direction de caractère secondaire* (the decisive factor is where the central—not the secondary—management and control office of the company is situated, *regardless* of where the working plant is concentrated)'.[573] Today most writers believe that this is the only way to achieve a genuine integration of companies in economic markets.

Foreign control and multiple sièges socials

Throughout the past decades, the notion of 'direction supérieure et le contrôle de la société' has been given special attention by French writers. In World War I French authorities were urged to control companies with a fictitious *siège social* in France (i.e. formed in accordance with French law) 'économique et psychologiqément' if the enterprise appeared to be hostile.[574] The public interest in controlling this type of company *'malgré sa nationalité d'apparence'* led to sequestration measures against company properties.[575] But a closer reading reveals, that this has nothing to do with the company's constitution or 'nationality'. Between the wars, courts occasionally showed reluctance to find companies had their *siège social* in France. A famous example is the *Remington Typewriter* judgment. The facts were the following: a French subsidiary of the Remington company (United States of America) sold machinery in France. This subsidiary did not operate autonomously. The Court held that the *centre d'exploitation*, which was situated abroad, should prevail over the *siège social*, which was situated in France, since, due to the *'interposition de personnes'* (management board consisting of foreigners; capital for 16/18 part provided by Americans), this enterprise was in fact nothing more than the emanation of

---

[573] Req. 28 October 1941, GP 1942.1.18 tends to reject the actual place of external business (*'centre d'exploitation extérieure'*) because this test would fail where economic activities are pursued in plants located in several countries. Concurring: Mayer (1998) 654 et seq.: neither the interests of third parties (identification of the company, particularly when there are no publicity requirements), nor the necessary link between the *lex societatis* and the country from which the company normally conducts business should be overcomplicated. The Cour de Cassation's definition of the *siège social* turns out to be a more suitable factor than the *centre d'exploitation*. (Cf. below, however on the exceptional *Remington* case.) Batiffol/Lagarde (1993) 339, n 6, assert that the central management and control office is of greater weight than the place of the shareholders' meeting. Audit (1997) 884 et seq., does not subscribe to this view: he believes that both the *siège social* and the *centre d'exploitation* have their own specific merits.

[574] Mayer (1998) 656 et seq. Batiffol/Lagarde (1993) 339. Cf. also S. 1916.1.148, R. 1916, 244; Audit (1997) 885 et seq., and Holleaux/Foyer/Geouffre de la Pradelle (1987) 136 et seq.

[575] cf. the *'circulaire du garde des sceaux'*, 29 February 1916, J. 1961, R. 1916.366. The sequestration measures hardly ever led to a company's dissolution. This was ordered only where French law was violated. Cf. subsequent measures mentioned by Holleaux/Foyer/Geouffre de la Pradelle (1987) 137.

a foreign society.[576] As a complement, bilateral treaties between France and other countries were concluded in order to control foreign companies.[577]

Since the measures taken during World War I had proven their effectiveness, they were re-assessed by the Cour de Cassation during World War II.[578] Afterwards, in the *CCRMA* case, the French Supreme Court, though on an issue of taxation law, again held that *'en principe la nationalité d'une société se détermine par la situation de son siège social* (the fundamental rule is that the nationality of a company is determined by the location of its *siège social*)'.[579]

Nowadays, the general assumption is that the decisive factor of the *siège social* is retained under French conflict of laws: the process of ascertaining the *lex societatis* should by no means be frustrated by courts autonomously invoking the instrument of control.[580] Notwithstanding the fact that 'these days, nobody fundamentally rejects the control theory',[581] courts are expected to ignore the existence and status of the company only in exceptional circumstances. And, the regular determination of the proper law of the company should only be outweighed by control interests on the basis of precise conditions to be formulated by the legislator rather than by the courts.[582] Companies wishing to avoid doubts as to whether they will be

[576] Req. 12 May 1931, *R.* 1932.129, *S.* 1932.1.57, discussed by *inter alia* Mayer (1998) 656. Likewise Rennes Court 16 June 1930, Clunet 1931, p. 1099 (Singer: subsidiary enterprise in France with no discretionary powers, American parent company. *Centre de décision* was held to be in the US). Batiffol/Lagarde (1993) 340, n 3, however, argue, that *'filiales'* like those in the *Remington* case cannot apply for French nationality. In the minds of many, the Remington decision is equivocal; jumping to conclusions seems hazardous here. See Batiffol/Lagarde (1993); Audit (1997) 885 et seq.; and Mayer (1998) 656 et seq. The latter quotes some other cases, e.g. Req. 24 December 1928, *S.* 1929, p. 121 (La Soie artificielle de Calais: concluding that the company was French, notwithstanding that the parent company resided in England). Holleaux/Foyer/Geouffre de la Pradelle (1987) 145, *inter alia* quoting B. Goldman, 'La nationalité des sociétés dans la C.E.E.', Rev. cr. d.i.p. 1966–9 232, suggest that, as far as groups of companies are concerned, the centre of management and control of the total group could serve as a factor: thus, the *siège social* and the notion of *contrôle* could be linked.

[577] cf. the Polish–French Treaty (6 Feb. 1922); the German–French Treaty (17 August 1927); and the Belgian–French Treaty (29 October 1927).

[578] C de C 21 November 1956, *R.* 1957.38. Batiffol/Lagarde (1993) 342, emphasize that in fact, *'il s'agit surtout en ces matières de viser les individus à travers la sociétés'* (i.e. a species of piercing the corporate veil, if hostile control of the company is concerned).

[579] C de C 30 March 1971, *R.* 1971.451 (commented on by P. Lagarde) and J. 1972.834 (commented on by Y. Loussouarn).

[580] cf. however the aforementioned *Société Overseas Apeco* case: amidst other factors to be weighed, the *nationalité des dirigeants* obviously still plays a significant role.

[581] Loussouarn/Bourel (1996) 695.

[582] Besides, the burden of proof (who is in charge of management?; who actually controls the company?) will be troublesome. The interests of predictability and legal certainty would be sacrificed too much. While comparing the theory of the *siège social* and the 'incorporation' theory with regard to the possibility of controlling the company, Batiffol/Lagarde (1993) 343, underline that the former leaves room for corrections anyhow, the latter being *'plus formaliste'*. This is why they believe that introducing the control element into the regular ascertainment of the *siège social* should be rejected. Moreover, too large a discrepancy between French international company law and common law ('incorporation' theory) should be avoided.

considered to have their *siège social* in France are advised to safeguard their *'couleur locale'* in advance.[583] It would be too legalistic an approach, however, to conclude from the *Société Mayol Arbona* case, that finding the *siège social* is exclusively a matter of concrete (written) rules,[584] in the absence of which no company can ever claim to be a 'French' company.[585] *A fortiori* it would be erroneous to disregard the fact that some cases were about tax law, not company law: by way of teleological reasoning the Conseil d'Etat, while applying the *Société Mayol Arbona* formula, denied tax advantages to a company that claimed to have its *siège social* in Spain, notwithstanding the fact that the management and control office was situated in Spain. The Conseil concluded that, since the *siège social* was situated in France, privileges for Spanish subjects pursuant to the 1862 French–Spanish tax treaty[586] could not be claimed by the company. A company may thus have different *sièges socials* for different (tax- or company-law oriented) purposes. This is not surprising, since the treasury will be concerned to avoid the danger of losing company tax income. It goes without saying that tax-law oriented interpretations of the *siège social* of a company do not necessarily apply to company law matters.[587] Further, it is clear that a multi-dimensional *siège social*, to be defined case-by-case and related to the interests at stake, is puzzling.[588]

Mandatory local law provisions

Companies having their *siège social* on French territory have to comply with several mandatory substantive (company) law provisions and *formalités* prescribed by French law. The registration of such a company

[583] In everyday practice, uncertainty is reduced by the articles of association of the company: on a regular basis, mention is made of the precise number of French members of the management and/or supervisory board. Cf. the Act of 7 April 1902, on the merchant navy; the Act of 16 October 1919, on *'concessions d'énergie hydraulique'* (hydraulic energy concessions); the Act of 3 January 1967, on *'la francisation des navires'* (navigation under French flag). Capital proportions, however, are only seldom precise (cf. the Acts of 1 August 1986 and 30 September 1986, concerning *le régime de presse* and . . . *liberté de communication*). This is understandable in the light of the above (transfer of shares is a more or less dynamic process; the *Remington* case etc.).

[584] Tribunal des conflits 23 November 1959, *R*. 1960.180, *D*. 1960.223 (administrative proceeding): *'que la nationalité des sociétés (. . .) ne peut être déterminée qu'au regard des dispositions législatives ou réglementaires dont l'application ou le non-application à la société intéressée dépend du point de savoir si celle-ci est ou n'est pas française* (the nationality of a company can only be ascertained by taking into consideration legal provisions or other regulations to which the interested company is or is not subject in order to ascertain whether the company is a French company or not)'.

[585] Otherwise, whenever company documents were silent on this matter Courts would have to enter a process which can be characterized as *'divinatoire'* (divinatory): Batiffol/Lagarde (1993) 345.

[586] Conseil d'Etat 22 January 1960, *R*. 1960.335 and, more recently, 16 October 1992, *JCP* 1992. IV.3017.

[587] cf. the *Daily Mail* judgment, ch 2 IV 2, above.

beyond French borders is not permitted under French law, even when the system of law of the country of registration is identical to French law; the company must still be registered in France.[589] This requirement is said to prevent 'French' companies (i.e. companies 'intégrées dans la sphère économique française') from seeking shelter abroad. As regards the inverse situation, companies having their *siège social* outside France, yet claiming to be registered in France in order to obtain '*la personnalité morale*', are subject to the following rule. Although article 1837 of the French Code Civil remains silent on companies not having their *siège social* in France, it is commonly accepted that it implicitly follows from the *décret* of 30 May 1984 that registration in France is not possible for companies, unless the formation of these companies is completed by their registration elsewhere. However, the 'registration' referred to in the 1984 *décret*[590] has nothing to do with the notion of registration under the 1966 Act, which 'gives birth' to the company. Finally, how should companies having both *siège social* and registered office outside France be dealt with? A restrictive interpretation of the French perception of the *siège social* test would have considerable repercussions on investors: both foreign and French companies having their business centre outside French borders would suffer from the overall denunciation of '*le système anglo-américain de l'incorporation*'.[591] As far as the first category is concerned (companies incorporated under a foreign system of law), due to the bilateral effect given to the unilateral provision of article 1837 of the French Code Civil,[592] all companies must be formed in conformity with the law of the country where the company has its *siège social*. This element of reciprocity may, however, seem excessive if the company resides in a country adhering to the 'incorporation' theory.[593] Like it or not, it is only normal for investors to search for a

---

[588] Batiffol/Lagarde (1993) take the view, that except for express provisions to be promulgated by the French legislator (e.g. in the field of tax law), the factor of the *siège social* should be decisive in each issue, irrespective of the specific interests at stake. The *Mayol Arbona* case, however, ('. . . *législatives ou réglementaires*') seems to reflect another view: see above. Mayer (1998) 654, speaks of the '*méthode impressioniste*' of the French Cour de Cassation, in defining the *siège social* case-by-case.

[589] Mayer (1998) 649.

[590] ibid.: 'immatriculation secondaire, au fins de publicité'. He underlines that there are no Court decisions declaring registration null and void for the sole reason that the company being registered in France would have a fictitious seat (*fraude à la loi*). Cf. the link with *Centros*, dealt with in ch 2 IV 2, above.

[591] Batiffol/Lagarde (1993) 336. They then emphasize that even Swiss law contains a number of exceptions to the main rule of the 'incorporation' theory enshrined in art. 154 of the Swiss Federal Code on Private International Law (see IV 2, above).

[592] cf. Mayer (1998) 643.

[593] ibid. 649, arguing that it would hardly make sense to declare companies having their management and control centre in an incorporation country null and void, simply because they are incorporated elsewhere: '*Si la Grande-Bretagne accepte qu'une société, qui a en Grande-Bretagne son siège et la majeure partie de ses activités, soit incorporée aux Etats-Unis, il paraîtrait peu réaliste que la France considère la société comme nulle.*'

system of law which does not reject *'l'autonomie de la volonté'*, the possibility of choosing the *lex societatis*. In fact, this is what the general private international law tool of forum-shopping, effected with the help of the instrument of *renvoi*, is about.[594] With regard to the second category (companies duly formed in accordance with French law), it could be argued that these companies are ultimately also precluded from having their *siège social* outside France. Since it follows from most versions of the 'incorporation' theory that foreign companies may only be recognized if they are duly formed and considered to exist under the law of the country where they are incorporated, incorporation countries would implicitly be proscribed from recognizing French companies having their management and control office on their territory. Like many systems of law adhering to the theory of the *siège social (réel)*, there is an exception to this rigid rule: provided that no legitimate French interests are at stake, i.e. when both the country where the company resides and the country where the company is incorporated are third countries, a second-degree *renvoi* from the state where the company has its *siège social* to the incorporation country is acknowledged by French law. This is likely to occur where other systems of law adhering to the 'incorporation' theory are willing to accept the foreign (i.e. French) 'nationality'[595] of the company.[596]

Scope of the applicable law

Applicability of the 'loi nationale'

Most French writers pay only scarce attention to what is called the *'domaine de la loi applicable'* (i.e. the scope of the applicable law). The brief treatment of this subject can be partly explained by briefly recalling the main features of French methodology in conflict of laws with regard to companies. As a matter of fact, the emphasis is laid more on the *'loi nationale'* of natural and legal persons. The aloofness towards 'foreign' legal persons engaged in business in France, coupled with the policy of enlarging the scope of the *'loi nationale'* of the company whenever

---

[594] The example of a company incorporated in the United States of America, having its administration centre in Great Britain was taken from Trib. com. Paris, 19 October 1982 (*Banque Ottomane*). Cf. Paris 3 October 1984, Rev. cr. d.i.p. 1985, p. 526, and *Clunet* 1986, p. 156 (commented on by B. Goldman).

[595] To be understood as the *siège social (réel)* of the company.

[596] Paris Court 19 March 1965, R. 1967, p. 85. Remedies like these are not in contrast with those pursued in other 'real seat' countries: whereas foreign companies on the internal market of Germany or Italy find themselves confronted with the 'real seat' doctrine, at least Italian companies are explicitly allowed to 'emigrate': see III 3, below. Doubts have, however, been expressed about whether a German company can also survive such a 'cross-border excursion': III 1, above.

possible,[597] may at first sight be confusing. It must be kept in mind, though, that as far as legal persons are concerned, this *'loi nationale'* by no means necessarily coincides with what, in legal systems adhering to the 'incorporation' theory, is generally known as the registered office.[598] Meanwhile, it could easily be forgotten that the *loi nationale* of legal persons has nothing to do with the 'origins'[599] of the company. Instead, the *loi nationale* of a company can only be determined with the help of the intermediate doctrine of the *siège social*.[600] It should be noted that the outcome of the process of ascertaining this *siège social* is rigorously 'checked' in advance by control policies: from the moment a company's 'nationality' is considered to be 'foreign', any fear that the scope of the applicable law will be over-extended loses its relevance (cf. other systems of law prescribing the *siège réel* theory) simply because the *siège social* of the 'foreign' company appears not to be situated on French territory.[601] As a result, there is no need to apply 'French' instead of 'foreign' law.[602]

Thus, the *'exercice de leurs droits par les sociétés reconnues* (exercise of powers by recognized companies)'[603]—for example, formation conditions,[604] capital requirements,[605] legal objects,[606] the legal relationship between the company and its shareholders,[607] and the functioning of company organs alike—are all subject to the *loi nationale* of the company.

---

[597] cf. Batiffol/Lagarde (1993) 356 et seq.: *'La loi nationale de la société détermine ses conditions de constitution, de fonctionnement et dissolution.'* Cf. Mayer (1998) 650: *'La jurisprudence le comprend (le siège social) de façon extrêmement large* (courts significantly widened the material scope of the law of the *siège social*, i.e. the proper law of the company)'.

[598] It may happen, though, that the two coincide, cf. earlier remarks on the method of rebuttable presumptions, as prescribed by the French Supreme Court. If not, the *siège social* prevails.

[599] Erroneously, one would be inclined to think that the 'national' law of the company is the system of law according to which the company is duly established. In French doctrine, there is no such metaphor for what is called the 'birth' of natural and legal persons in the conflict of laws of Great Britain (cf. II 2, above).

[600] i.e. the centre of management and control of the company, see above.

[601] cf. formerly Paris 13 June 1872, S. 72.2, p. 96 and Paris 14 December 1903, D.P. 1904.2, p. 172.

[602] In this respect, the expression used by Loussouarn/Bourel (1996) 698 et seq., is less confusing: instead of the common formula *'domaine de la loi nationale'*, it reads *'(d)omaine d'application de la loi du siège social'*.

[603] cf. in more detail the following subsection; Batiffol/Lagarde (1993) 356 et seq. Mayer (1998) 651, mentions the *'activité des sociétés étrangères en France'*.

[604] Req. 6 July 1914, J. 1916, p. 1296. Cf. Mayer (1994) 656.

[605] e.g. for the subscription of capital, Paris 22 February 1912, J. Trib. Com. 1913, p. 303, and, concerning the formal validity of types of shares, Trib. Com. 13 February 1967, R. 1968, p. 52.

[606] Crim. 18 June 1909, S. 1912, 1, p. 425.

[607] cf. Civ. 17 October 1972, Rev. Soc. 1974, p. 127, R. 1973, p. 520: *'. . . les conditions dans lesquelles s'acquiert, se conserve ou se perd la qualité d'actionnaire'*.

Company representation: protection of third parties

The representation of the company by its organs is a more complicated subject. Essentially, the (foreign) proper law of the company equally applies to problems of representation. However, third parties may under certain conditions claim protection against a company invoking restrictions to the representation powers, when (a) the contract with the company was concluded '*à l'étranger*' (i.e. in a country other than that of the applicable law: e.g. a contract between a French seller, resident in France, and a buying company having its *siège social* in Germany); (b) the restrictions cannot be found in any legislative provision, but stem from the articles of association of the company; and (c) the third party was unaware of the existence of any such restrictions at the conclusion of the transaction.[608]

While conducting business activities, companies must be considered as existing according to their own *lex societatis*. A company may be considered non-existent or dissolved by the law of incorporation.[609] A company in the course of dissolution and winding up is considered to be a '*société de fait*' in France.[610] To maintain the image of the company as a 'subject' of a sovereign state, rather than an institution created by private law, it could be argued that (for example, in case of revolutions) the dissolution of a company also entails a loss of 'nationality' under French law.[611]

---

[608] Com. 21 December 1987, *JCP* 88.II 21113, Rev. Soc. 1988, p. 398. This solution was inspired by the traditional substantive law provision in private international law concerning the capacity of natural persons entering into a contract with third parties not being aware of the incapacity (cf. art. 11 of the Rome Contracts Convention of 19 June 1980, a provision borrowed from the famous C de C *Lizardi* case, which dates back to 1861). The French Supreme Court, however, refused to apply the *Lizardi* rule in the case of a French company entering into obligations with third parties outside France: Com. 8 November 1988, Rev. cr. d.i.p. 1989, p. 371. It should further be noticed that EC law (First Company Law Directive of 9 March 1968, art. 2(1)(d) JO. ECJ (Case 32/74 *Friedrich Haaga GmbH*) contains strict formal (publication) requirements in respect of restrictions on the power to represent a company.

[609] A company will cease to exist upon dissolution ordered by, for example, resolutions; French tribunals were confronted with '*sociétés russes*', being dissolved after '*les décrets soviétiques*'. Although the courts did not object to such dissolutions, with the help of the *ordre public* escape device, they refused to acknowledge expropriation measures that did not indemnify the company's shareholders (Req. 5 March 1928, D.P. 1928.1.81). Cf. Trib. com. Seine 29 June 1932, GP 1932.2.517: winding up of the company after dissolution, while respecting the interests of others. Jurisdiction was accepted because properties of the dissolved company were situated in France: Trib. com. Seine 21 January 1935, J. 1935, 134. However, liquidators are not competent to decide about company assets situated abroad: Paris 19 July 1943, GP 1944, Suppl. 82. Neither may an individual shareholder act on behalf of the (organs of) the dissolved company: Trib. com. Seine 9 February 1956, R. 1956, p. 647. Cf. the German *Rest-* and *Spaltgesellschaften*, III 1, above.

[610] Bordeaux 2 January 1928, J. 1929, p. 115; Trib. com. Seine 23 January 1934, R. 1934, p. 782; Paris 15 June 1937, J. 1937, p. 812.

[611] In this sense Batiffol/Lagarde (1993) 356. Cf. the opening lines of this section.

The status and exercise of powers by foreign companies in France

The status of foreign companies: recognition 'de plein droit'

Dealings with cross-border company relationships usually proceed as follows. First, it must be examined whether a company is to be considered as a French or foreign 'subject' (i.e. a company having its *siège social* in or outside of France). Once a company is qualified as foreign, its status in France (*'Condition des sociétés étrangères en France'*) must be defined precisely. Should such a foreign company be conferred with 'legal capacity' by the French authorities? A preliminary question should be answered here: are foreign entities capable of exercising legal powers beyond their national borders?[612] If so, will they be submitted to special mandatory law provisions or not?

Like many other systems of law, French company law for a long time considered the legal person as a fictitious being. Later on, this notion evolved. 'Personnes morales' are an everyday occurrence; they simply exist. Accordingly, the recognition of legal persons is no longer a matter of explicit concessions granted by public authorities to individual legal persons. Instead, they should be recognized *'de plein droit'* (i.e. 'just like that'). This evolution is important because, contrary to notions of 'vested rights' in private international law, concessions like any other *'service public'*, as a 'creation' of bodies by public authorities, usually do not reach beyond national borders.[613] Once legal persons are considered as a 'reality' resulting from private law, then why continue to refuse the recognition of their foreign counterparts, provided that they are duly established under foreign law?

On the other hand, there may be exceptions to this rule. Although legal personality may be denied in the interest of (French) state protection, it would be better to recognize the foreign entity, with either restrictions on the exercise of powers, or a requirement of authorization under penalty of sanctions arising under criminal law.[614] Notably, when economic activities are pursued (cf. companies as defendants in court proceedings), any denial of legal personality would lead to complications comparable to those concerning the legal status of the *'morts civils'* before 1854. This is why foreign companies will rarely be denied legal personality (i.e. granted

---

[612] cf. the terminology used by Batiffol/Lagarde (1993) 350 et seq., and Audit (1997) 893 et seq.: *'Aptitude des entités reconnues à la jouissance des droits'* (aptitude of foreign companies to excercise powers)'.

[613] Batiffol/Lagarde (1993) 351.

[614] Batiffol/Lagarde (1993) 351. This concept was followed by, for example, the Act concerning *'compagnies d'assurances étrangères'* (foreign insurance companies) of 15 February 1917, which was modified in 1989.

recognition as a bearer of rights and duties).[615] Prior to the implementation of the 12th EC Company Law Directive, not even single-member companies were denied recognition.[616] Even when the company is not endowed with legal personality under the law of incorporation, French courts have a discretionary power to accept a company's legal personality or not.[617]

Although in the past[618] article 37 of the French Commercial Code required explicit administrative authorization as a condition for *sociétés anonymes* (public companies) acquiring legal personality, courts tended to recognize these foreign public companies '*de plein droit*'. In doing so they ignored the administrative policy of extending the application of this provision to foreign companies as well. After a short period of uncertainty[619] this liberal policy was firmly re-established by the French legislature in 1857.[620] Notably, Belgian public companies were allowed to '*exercer tous leurs droits et d'ester en justice*' (article 1). In addition, article 2 of the Act provides that after a *décret impérial* is promulgated by the *Conseil d'Etat*, capital companies from other countries may benefit from equal treatment. This enabled the *Conseil d'Etat* to investigate the 'checks and balances' in various systems of law. Although the Act itself was never abolished, it is considered redundant nowadays, since as a result of international treaties[621] concluded between France and several countries, and the generosity of the *Conseil d'Etat* in granting this privilege to non-Belgian foreign capital companies, everyday practice closely resembles the recognition '*de plein droit*'. Furthermore, the effects of the Acts were neutralized by the courts: neither does the Act apply to a *SARL* (i.e. the French equivalent form of a private company)[622] nor can it be invoked by those who find themselves in a favourable position under the Act against other companies.[623] Finally, the

---

[615] See Audit (1997) 891.

[616] Prior to the 12th EC Company Law Directive having regard to single-member companies, such companies were not permitted under French law. Cf. Civ. 17 June 1958, R. 1958, p. 704.

[617] Civ. 14 May 1969, JCP 1969.IV, p. 167 (Circus of Budapest, not having legal personality under Hungarian law).

[618] i.e. at the beginning of the 19th century.

[619] This was caused by a Belgian Supreme Court decision of 8 Feb. 1849, as a result of which the French *SA* (i.e. the equivalent of a public company limited by shares) no longer enjoyed the right to be considered as a legal person in Belgium. The impression in both France and Belgium was that this 'accident historique'—in this sense Audit (1997) 891—had to be repaired by legislation. Cf. Mayer (1998) 660.

[620] Art. 1 lists the beneficiaries: '*les sociétés anonymes et les autres associations commerciales, industrielles ou financières qui sont soumises à l'autorisation du gouvernement belge et qui l'ont obtenu*'. However, it is not applicable to '*sociétés de personnes*' (partnerships).

[621] To a certain extent, this is due to the most-favoured-nation clause, cf. *i.a.* the French–German Treaty of 27 October 1956, R. 1959.541. Cf. in the same sense, Audit (1997) 891.

[622] Rouen 8 July 1981, R. 1982, p. 81 (commented on by P. Mayer).

[623] Com. 12 December 1989, R. 1991, p. 667 (commented on by G. Khairallah).

Cour de Cassation held that under article 6 of the European Convention on Human Rights, the principle of due process requires that any person, natural *or legal, 'quelle que soit sa nationalité, pouvait agir en justice en France pour la protection des biens et des intérêts'.*[624] In summary, the previously existing practice of conducting advance control (i.e. the supervisory task of the *Conseil d'Etat*) has now become obsolete.

Exercise of powers: formal requirements

Although the mere recognition of foreign companies is not a serious obstacle, it does not automatically encompass the right for foreign companies to exercise powers on French territory as if they were French companies: *'la reconnaissance de la personne morale n'emporte pas* ipso facto *le droit d'exercer une activité permanente; ce droit peut toujours être réglementé par l'Etat d'accueil'.*[625] It is at least certain that the exercise of legal powers by foreign companies should be conceived in a very broad sense:

La terme 'activité' . . . comprend non seulement l'installation en France d'un établissement permanent, mais toute activité ocasionelle (conclusion d'un contrat), et même le simple fait de saisir un tribunal français, serait-ce à l'occasion d'un contrat conclu à l'étranger. (The expression 'activity' . . . not only includes a permanent establishment in France, but also comprises any occasional activity, for example conclusion of contracts or bringing actions before a French court with regard to contracts concluded elsewhere).[626]

Once again the equal treatment of natural and legal persons could serve as a starting point for restricting the exercise of powers by them.[627] These restrictions should, however, be explored against the background of ascertaining the *siège social* of the company. The *règles discriminatoires* thus function more or less *indirectement*. Like natural persons, foreign companies are not allowed to fulfil public services.[628] Furthermore, the *lois de police* expressing vital French public interests probably interfere with the exercise of powers that stem from the proper law of the company.[629] The *directeur responsable* of any foreign enterprise conducting activities in France in the fields of commerce, industry or *artisanat* (craft industry)

---

[624] C de C Civ. 1st. 25 June 1991, *R.* 1991, p. 667 (*Extraco Anstalt*).

[625] Audit (1997) 894. This phrase is a reminder of above comments on the 'minimum' and 'maximum' concepts of recognition of foreign companies: see ch 2 III 1. Cf. also art. 4 of the Draft Treaty of the Hague Conference on the Mutual Recognition of the Legal Personality of Companies, which project was ultimately a complete failure (see ch 2 III 1, above).

[626] Mayer (1998) 659.

[627] cf. above, III 1, and Mayer (1998) 661: *'Pour le reste, l'étude des personnes morales rejoint celle des personnes physiques'.*

[628] Batiffol/Lagarde (1993) 355, however stress that, if not explicitly provided otherwise, they are allowed to 'assimilate'.

[629] In the words of Mayer (1998) 650: *'La lex societatis est parfois écartée par des lois de police. Mais celles-ci concernent essentiellement l'activité de la société dans les pays autres que celui dont la loi est applicable.'*

should possess a *carte de commerçant étranger;*[630] the special *décret* of 30 October 1935 concerning the protection of transaction partners must also be obeyed.[631]

Exercise of powers: further requirements

Apart from formal requirements, other demands must also be complied with. More generally, *les investissements directs réalisés en France* by *sociétés étrangères ou sous contrôle étranger* must comply with an authorization by the Ministry of Trade. However, investments may be made without this consent if the natural company 'managers' reside in an EC member state.[632] Foreign companies planning to prepare *l'émission de titres* (public issuance) in France also need to comply with authorization from the Ministry of Trade.[633] There are substantive law-based requirements as well: cross-border mergers are subject to substantive law requirements under both legal orders involved.[634] Transnational company take-overs (public offers) are considered to be governed by the law of the country where the stock exchange resides. Apart from these *lois de police*, it is commonly accepted that acts conducted on behalf of the company underlie proper law formulas having regard to contracts or torts. It may also happen that, for the solution of specific problems, several private international law rules need to be applied simultaneously (for example, employees collectively participating in the company, leading to the application of the proper law of both company law relations and employment contracts).[635] There are no impediments to foreign companies suing debtors in court

---

[630] Art. 5 of the *décret* of 2 February 1939 (amended by *décret* of 27 October 1969).

[631] Any 'first' establishment in France, be it a *'succursale, agence, ou tout autre établissement'*, must apply for *'immatriculation au registre du commerce'*, cf. also Mayer (1998) 661 et seq. If there is no secondary establishment in France the articles of association of the company need to be registered at the Tribunal de Commerce in Paris: *décret* of 30 May 1984, amended by *décret* of 16 June 1992, art. 55. *Mandataires des sociétés et collectivités étrangères* who are planning to issue a debenture-loan must be resident in France. Cf. Audit (1997) 894 et seq.

[632] *Décret* of 22 December 1989. Loussouarn/Bourel (1996) 703 et seq., however, render a non-exhaustive list of these *lois d'application immediate*, mainly affecting vital economic interests, cf. the *législation hétérogène* of the *décrets* of 19 October 1919 (*concession d'énergie hydraulique*), 21 April 1920 (*concession de mines*), 12 November 1938 (*sociétés concessionaires de services public*) etc.

[633] *Décret* no. 89.154 of 9 March 1989. If the company has no *'agence, succursale'* etc. in France, it must, prior to the issuance of any capital, deposit two copies of the *statuts* (i.e. articles of association) at the *greffe du Tribunal de commerce de Paris* (art. 57 of the *décret* of 30 May 1984, concerning the register of commerce).

[634] It is acknowledged by Batiffol/Lagarde (1993) 358, and Audit (1997) 896, though, that this is a solution for better or for worse. This topic is dealt with more in detail in the following subsection.

[635] These 'exceptions' have nothing to do with the controversy between 'incorporation' theory and the theory of *siège social (réel)*, nor do they flow from the notion of *lois de police* (mandatory rules), as they follow from the more general private international law device of primary qualification (or characterization): each falls within its own proper law formula concerning contract, tort, etc.

proceedings in France; the same principle applies to contracts concluded by foreign companies with business partners in France e.g. to acquire immovable property *'tant qu'elle* [the company] *ne s'installe pas en France'*.[636]

Seat transfers

Change in 'nationality'; change in the applicable law

To date, French private international law has retained the nationality concept as an intermediate tool for ascertaining the *siège social* (proper law) of a company. Legal persons are said to cling to *la notion de nationalité* throughout their 'lifetime' as if they were natural persons.[637] As for cross-border seat transfers, French texts consequently observe that, *'tout changement de siège social ou tout changement de souveraineté du territoire sur lequel il est fixé, emporte un changement de nationalité de la société'* (any transfer of a company's *siège social*, or any change concerning territorially fixed sovereignty[638] involves the alteration of the company's nationality as well).[639] Cross-border transfers can give rise to changes in domicile, nationality, and the applicable law of the company.[640] Contrary to systems of law that adhere to the 'incorporation' theory, *siège réel (social)* countries consider transfers of both the registered office and the actual residence, due to either *la volonté des associés*, or interventions of state authorities, to be *une opération risquée*.[641] Changes in the company's 'nationality' are not in themselves considered to cause insurmountable problems: the validity of the transfer is not thereby affected.[642] (Once again, it must be noted that most systems of law do not take the 'nationality' of a company to be a decisive factor.) Changes in the applicable law are, however, considered to be more delicate: the company's constitution and its articles of association must conform with to the law of the company's new 'seat'. Ultimately, it depends on the law of both the systems of law involved whether or not the

---

[636] Mayer (1998) 659.   [637] See III 2, above.

[638] cf. Audit (1997) 887, and the historical picture of territorial changes after World War I (Alsace), and problems of state succession, in particular with regard to the *Etats d'Afrique noire*. Cf. also Mayer (1998) 666.

[639] Batiffol/Lagarde (1993) 345. From a practical point of view, this comparison between natural and legal persons may be valid, but it may well be asked whether this assertion is theoretically sound: it follows from neither civil law nor common law systems of law that moving from one country to another by natural persons *eo ipso* leads to changes in their domicile of origin or nationality.

[640] Mayer (1998) 663.   [641] ibid.

[642] Mayer (ibid.) takes the view that the country of departure is no longer interested in 'reigning' over its former subject; according to domestic rules of private international law, the 'immigration' country will have to decide autonomously whether the company is to be considered as its own 'subject' or as a foreign company. The decision taken by company leaders to transfer the company is a serious one, to be approved by a qualified majority or even unanimity of the 'associated' persons.

company should be considered as the same company as before.[643] It is only reasonable that, in order to carry out such transfers, legal requirements set out by all the systems of law involved must be complied with.[644] Periods during which neither of the systems of law involved is applicable should be avoided whenever possible: this could be achieved by applying the originally applicable company law regime until the operation has been completed.[645]

Immigration transfers

How then must the foregoing be interpreted in practice? Apart from case-law, particularly referring to the independence process for Algeria,[646] one will find that French legal sources remain silent with regard to the transfer of a (foreign) company's *siège social* from another country to France.[647] For reasons of financial strength, the French Treasury Department took a rigid position, tolerating *any* transfer of a company's *siège social* from a third country to France.[648] But of course, the proper way to deal with this type of transfer is to find out whether the company's dissolution is compulsorily prescribed by the law of the country of departure, followed by reconstitution in accordance with the law of the country where the company is re-established.[649]

Emigration transfers

Conversely, articles 31 and 60 of the 1966 Act contain general provisions on the transfer of a company's *siège social* from France to another country: such transfers may only be take place after a unanimous shareholders'

---

[643] Mayer (1998) 664, n 54. He emphasizes that, to that end, although systems of law differ considerably, both should envisage the same type of *groupement*.

[644] ibid.: '*Sur le principe de la licéité de l'operation, l'accord des deux lois est nécessaire*'.

[645] ibid.

[646] Holleaux/Foyer/Geouffre de la Pradelle (1987) 153, mention the case Civ. I 30 March 1971 (*CCRMA*): whereas in normal situations a seat transfer entails a change of 'nationality' of the company, CCRMA, a French company with its centre of management and control in Algeria, *remained* French after having transferred its seat from the new-born state of Algeria to France. Loussouarn/Bourel (1996) 700, however, add that most of these specific kinds of transfers were accompanied by conventions between France and the new-born North African states.

[647] Mayer (1998) 664 et seq. Cf. below, however, for attempts to create legal tools: Batiffol/Lagarde (1993).

[648] Rép. min. R. 1972.511. Like the 'incorporation' theory (see ch 2, II 1 and II 3, above), this appears to be a law and economics-orientated device to stimulate economic growth and raise employment.

[649] Batiffol/Lagarde (1993) 345, and Mayer (1998) 664. Remarkably, the Supreme Court of Belgium in its judgment of 12 November 1965, Rev. cr. d.i.p. 1976, p. 506 (*Soc. Lamot Ltd.*), held that the *personnalité* of a company transferring its seat from England to Belgium would be maintained on condition that some requirements (notably adaptations to Belgian law) were fulfilled. From an EC law perspective, this *Lamot* doctrine, including comments thereto, is considered further in ch 6 III 1, below.

decision. Article 154 of that Act provides additional requirements for a transfer of the *siège social* of, in particular, a *société anonyme* (the French equivalent of a public company limited by shares) from France to another country: such a transfer needs authorization from the shareholders (however, this decision does not need to be unanimous), and on condition that such transfer is completed in accordance with an agreement between France and the 'immigration' country. In the absence of any such convention it seems possible to enable the company transfer *'par accord unanime des associés'*.[650] The precise text of the 1966 Act excludes two categories from the scope of the Act: first, legal persons other than capital companies planning to leave France; secondly, all forms of foreign companies planning to transfer their *siège social* to France. It has been argued, though, that for both categories it seems highly inadequate to block the road to cross-border transfers in advance for the sole reason that they were not explicitly envisaged by legislation.[651]

Moreover, how can a company's continuing identity be safeguarded: in other words how is a company's dissolution and winding up to be avoided?[652] To that end, the idea was launched to adopt the legal consequences of a provision elaborated for purely *domestic* transformation procedures (i.e. the conversion of one legal person into another type). Article 5 of the 1966 Act states that *'(l)a transformation régulière d'une société n'entraine pas la création d'une personne morale nouvelle* (the transformation of a company which is performed legally does not entail the formation of another legal person)'.[653] There is, however, no explicit authority to the effect that in cross-border transfers the company's legal status remains unaffected.[654] Of course, if the intention to combat the flight of capital from France to other countries[655] had not been of such great importance,

---

[650] In this sense, Mayer (1998) 663.

[651] According to Batiffol/Lagarde (1993) 347, transfers like these should only be blocked if there are legal problems that cannot be overcome. To underline the possibility of 'immigration' transfers they quote the *Lamot* judgment of the Belgian Supreme Court of 12 November 1965, R. 1967.506, allowing an English company to transfer its *siège social* to Belgium, provided that the company's articles of association comply with Belgian law. In this respect, there is no permissive case-law in France.

[652] It is commonly accepted that such a transfer does not always entail the dissolution of the company. Cf. Loussouarn/Bourel (1996) 699; Batiffol/Lagarde (1993) s 94; and Mayer (1998) 663 et seq.

[653] cf. Mayer (1998) 664, n 53, referring to the Belgian *Lamot* doctrine, and 665, n 58 (dealt with in ch 6 III, below).

[654] Although a teleological, extensive interpretation of art. 5 was suggested by Batiffol/Lagarde (1993) 346, n 1, this was explicitly prohibited by the explanatory report on this provision (rép. min.), JCP 1970.IV.279. This is not surprising: the outcome of the question at stake—continuing identity of the company or not?—depends ultimately on the generosity of the law of the 'immigration' country.

[655] Once again, the doom of the *Daily Mail* case (see ch 2 IV 2, below) inspires academics to express their fears. Mayer (1998) 663, is clear on this matter: he is convinced that, as a result of too lenient laws, member states will suffer considerably from decreasing tax revenue: *'(i)l*

the transfer of a company's *siège social* abroad would probably not have been met with countervailing measures by French authorities. Once a company is recognized in an 'incorporation' country, *'le problème ne peut venir que de l'Etat de l'origine* (problems left can only be attributed to the law of the country where the company was incorporated)'.[656] Perhaps legal reasoning is of less weight here than economic reasons. (In this respect, it is worth re-emphasizing that—again for reasons of financial strength—the French Treasury took a rigid position: any transfer of a company's *siège social* from a third country to France is recognized. Again, this is predominantly inspired by revenue interests.[657])

Creditor protection

In order to protect creditors of the company, it was held that the objective of foreign law provisions was to ensure that the identity of a legal person transferring its *siège social* from the country of origin to France will be respected in France.[658] It has been questioned whether it would be preferable to accept seat transfers if neither the country of departure nor the country of re-establishment raise any objections to such transfers.[659] Of course, subsequent steps to be taken are (i) to inquire under which conditions such transfers are allowed, and (ii) how to proceed if the country of re-establishment lacks equivalent forms of legal persons.

3. ITALY

The ambiguity of policies underlying conflict rules: restricted reciprocity

1865–1942: equal treatment of natural and legal persons

A brief historical survey of Italian private international law on foreign companies shows that three periods can be distinguished.[660] The first

---

se traduit, en effet, par la fuite de capitaux à l'étranger, et par la disparition d'une source de revenues fiscaux. Par ailleurs, la décision de transporter le domicile d'un pays dans un autre est grave, et seule une majorité qualifiée, voire l'unanimité des associés peut l'imposer.' Needless to say, such a transfer is likely to be highly profitable to the country of re-establishment. See further Batiffol/Lagarde (1993) 347; Loussouarn/Bourel (1996) 700.

[656] Batiffol/Lagarde (1993) 347.

[657] cf. the inverse situation (above): company claiming privileges granted to Spanish subjects by the 1862 French–Spanish tax treaty, denied by Court since the *siège social* was considered to be situated in France.

[658] C de C 3 June 1969, R. 1971.743, with regard to a *fondation*, commented on by D. Holleaux.

[659] Batiffol/Lagarde (1993) 346, n 1. See also above.

[660] For access to Italian legal sources, this work pays tribute to earlier comparative research, cf. Rahm (1990) and Ebenroth/Kaiser (1992). The (historical) framework of this section was predominantly based on their findings. More recent developments (i.e. since 1992) have been added by the author.

period, from the second half of the 19th century to 1942, featured extensive interpretation of scarce legislative provisions. The Italian experience resembles the French, as courts and doctrine had to find their way by enlarging the material scope of legal provisions which had originally been elaborated for natural persons. Thus, a legal basis for the treatment of foreign companies was found by analogously applying article 3 of the Codice Civile of 1865: this provision established the principle of equal treatment of strangers (*natural* persons) in Italy. However, since the *trattamento* (treatment) of foreign *legal* persons is preceded by the question of how *riconoscimento* (recognition) must be treated,[661] recourse was had to analogous reasoning as well. Article 6 of the preliminary title of the 1865 Civil Code submitted the status and capacity of persons to the law of their nationality (*nazionalità*).[662] According to the 4th paragraph of article 230 of the 1882 Codicio Commerco (Commercial Code) companies duly formed in a foreign country having both their *sede* (seat) and *l'oggetto principale dell'impresa* (main centre of business activities) in Italy were nevertheless considered to be Italian 'subjects'.[663] To acquire this status, these companies had to meet the requirements formulated under the *lex fori*; *inter alia* their re-establishment under Italian law was inescapable.[664] However, with the help of extensive teleological legal reasoning, it had become everyday practice to recognize foreign companies, an *autorizzazione governativa*[665] (state authorization) no longer being required.[666]

[661] In the words of the famous conflict of laws scholar, P. Mancini, the exercise of powers by a company *ipso iure* presupposes that such a company exists, in: Castagnola, *Introduzioneal commento del nuovo codice di commercio Italiano*; primo libro; fonti et motivi, Torino 1883 632. Later, this perception became known as *autocollegamento*, see below.

[662] Corte d'app. Roma, Foro It. 1932 I, p. 1173, affirmed by the Corte Cass. 29 April 1933, Riv. dir. int. 1934, p. 106: any foreign company recognized by its own legal order retains this status in Italy as well. Such a company is not subject to an explicit deed of recognition by Italian authorities. Cf. the conclusion drawn by Rahm (1990) 30: contrary to the foregoing era, during which powers explicitly had to be attributed to foreign companies, the recognition of said companies flowed directly from the foreign legal order without the mediation of Italian law.

[663] According to Rahm (1990) 27, in those days too, Italian writers showed awareness of the fact that ignoring foreign companies rather then recognizing them would not make sense; the catalogue of duties contained in art. 230 would thus become completely redundant. Meanwhile (ibid. 34), the objective of the 4th subs of this provision, endowing foreign companies with Italian 'nationality', was to combat the *maschera stranieri* (foreign mask) of (proforma?) foreign companies.

[664] Branches were excluded from the *lex fori*; the foreign *lex causae* remained applicable to them.

[665] The Bills of 6 June 1853 and 26 November 1870 were not the foundation for the abolishment of the Royal Assent. The willingness to tolerate foreign legal persons was, more or less, inspired by the desire to attract foreign investors after the unification of the Italian federal states had been accomplished in 1861. More detail in Rahm (1990) 6 et seq. and 21 et seq.

[666] Corte Cass. Giur. It. 1932, I, p. 162. Rahm (1990) 38, however, notices that both the court (cf. Corte Cass., Foro It. 1977 I, p. 2158) and writers occasionally insist on the use of the ancient notion of *riconoscimento*. In his opinion, this is due to (i) tradition, (ii) the absence of a clear conflict rule, and (iii) the aforementioned Recognition Bill of 1860, adhered to by the

1942–1995: reconciliation of legal and economical interests

The second era, from 1942 to 1995, did not introduce any fundamental changes. In the aftermath of World War II, it was generally felt that two opposing interests had to be reconciled: Italy should be transformed from an agricultural society into an industrialized one, yet without being at the mercy of foreign investors.[667] In spite of the fact that a new *Codice Civile* (including a reform of the *disposizioni preliminari*) was concluded in 1942,[668] it still did not bring about legal certainty as to which provisions applied. This was mainly due to the fact that a single, decisive conflict rule had not been elaborated.[669] Most writers tended to read articles 16 and 17 of the *disposizioni preliminari* in conjunction with articles 2505 and 2509[670] of the Italian Civil Code.[671] The fundamental principle of equal treatment of foreign persons laid down in article 16(1) was explicitly extended to *persone giuridiche* (legal persons) in the second subsection.[672] The premise of reciprocity contained in article 16(1) did not, however, extend to the *recognition* of foreign companies, this matter, as has been noted above, allegedly being presupposed by article 16 already.[673] Doctrine deemed article 16 to be of a mere regulatory character with regard to aliens, rather than a suitable instrument to ascertain the proper law of the company.[674] Many took the view that article 17 of the preliminary title should be applied analogously, according to which the status, legal capacity, and standing of *persons and families* were governed by the law of the state of which they are a subject. After all, nationality as the outstanding connecting factor was heralded by the founding father of Italian conflict of laws doctrine, Mancini. But, as was concluded earlier from the French experience,[675] the core concept of establishing parallels between natural and legal persons carries

Commerce Code of 1882. Contemporary leading Italian scholars have no doubt that in the course of ascertaining the proper law of the company, the recognition issue no longer plays an independent role.

[667] *Mutatis mutandis*, some decades later this dilemma was to reappear at Community law level: see ch 2 IV, above.

[668] Together with the first book of the remodelled Civil Code, the *disposizioni sull'applicazione della legge in generale* were given effect earlier, namely on 1 July 1938.

[669] Rahm (1990) 41, n 18.

[670] These provisions replaced the former arts. 230–2 of the Commercial Code.

[671] For the precise translation into English of these former law provisions see M. Beltramo/G. Longo/J.H. Merryman, *The Italian Civil Code*, 1969, New York.

[672] For more detailed information, Broggini (1996) 68 et seq. and Ballarino (1996) 341, the latter expressing the view that this reciprocity principle was accepted '*faute de mieux*'.

[673] In this sense e.g. Corte Cass., Riv.dir.int.priv.proc. 1986, p. 353; Corte Cass. Riv. dir.int.priv.proc. 1980, p. 362.

[674] Santa Maria (1996) 46, adds that once art. 16 is seen as an instrument to recognize any 'foreigner', the use of public policy to combat abuses is excluded. Others share this view, cf. those mentioned by Rahm (1990) 45, n 27.

[675] cf. the French concept of *nationalité des personnes morales*, III 2, above.

major intrinsic flaws.[676] Apart from grammatical objections,[677] it was doubtful whether the nationality concept was suitable for regulating international company law relationships in every aspect. A company has neither 'father' nor 'mother', nor can there be any expressed 'affinity' to a state. In addition, courts of one legal order are by no means permitted to endow a company with the 'nationality' or 'citizenship' of a third state. This one-sided process provokes an unacceptable degree of legal uncertainty and unpredictability. Furthermore, questions such as how to localize cross-border operating companies cause even greater difficulties in that state authorities will probably be less prepared to give up the exclusive right to control their subjects. Neither does the nationality concept provide an answer to the question how to localize groups of companies,[678] each of which operates separately in various legal orders. Even if all group members should be governed by a single proper law of the company, it is highly questionable whether this traditional nationality concept should form the basis of the *lex societatis*. Finally, it was asked whether or not Mancini's ideas were developed with the intention of encouraging the feeling of togetherness of the population of a newly born unitary state. At that time, the notion of 'nationality' could not be simply transplanted to the newly elaborated concept of a 'legal' person.[679] Although perhaps not perfect, ascertaining the location of a company's management and control centre seemed less complicated. Those who were in favour of the nationality principle therefore took a contrasting position:[680] rather than applying article 17 analogously, the unilaterally formulated provisions of articles 2505 and 2509 of the Civil Code[681] should be bilateralized. According to article 2505, companies established abroad were subject to Italian law, including provisions concerning the formation, in so far as their *sede dell'amministrazione ovvero l'ogetto principale dell'impresa* (centre of management or centre of main business activities) was in Italy: a *società straniere* would thus be compulsorily converted into a *società nazionalizzate*.[682] However, article 2509 disregarded the reciprocity principle, providing that companies established in Italy *remained subject to Italian law*, even when their *oggetto della loro attività* (main centre of business activities)

---

[676] cf. Azzolini (1993) 900, and Ballarino (1996) 341, for further information.

[677] See Rahm (1990) 46: art. 17 speaks of 'delle persone', but not all co-operative entities (e.g. partnerships) are *persona* (legal persons). In a comparable sense, Santa Maria (1996) 46.

[678] See Ballarino (1996) 348 et seq.   [679] See Rahm (1990) 49.

[680] Rahm (ibid. 51) notices a loss of popularity of the nationality concept in modern Italian doctrine: in his opinion, the 'nationality' of a company is to be seen as the outcome of the process of finding the proper law, rather than as the point of departure.

[681] See Azzolini (1993) 906 et seq. According to Santa Maria (1970) 44, those provisions originate from the old provisions of art. 230 of the 1882 Codice Commercio (see above). This view provoked criticism, because that provision dates from an era in which legal persons were still regarded as 'fictitious', cf. Rahm (1990) 55.

[682] Rahm (1990) 61.

was concentrated abroad.[683] But then again, the provisions of articles 2505 and 2509 remained silent over the preliminary issue of the existence and legal capacity of the company as a (legal) person. This problem was settled by the device of *autocollegamento* the assumption that referring to the foreign *lex societatis ipso iure* implies a recognition of the foreign company.[684]

For a considerable period it remained uncertain whether articles 2505 and 2509 of the Civil Code should be combined into one single conflict rule, governing all international company relationships, or whether one of these provisions had preference over the other. (Article 2505 refers to the *teoria della sede*, i.e. the 'real seat' doctrine; article 2509 refers to the *teoria dell'incorporazione*, the 'incorporation' theory). If not, each article would cover different types of international company relationships. There is no reason to assume that one of these principles outweighed the other.[685]

The 1995 Private International Law Code: the main features

December 1995 marked the entry into force of the remodelled Private International Law Code, and is taken as the starting point of the third period.[686] A threefold explanation can be given for the need to review Italian conflict of laws: (i) Mancini's ideas on the role of nationality in conflict of laws were considered obsolete; (ii) in 1987 the Supreme Court had held that several conflict of law rules did not conform with the Constitution;[687] and (iii) the drafters faced the task of bringing domestic

---

[683] Provided, however, that the management and control office was located on Italian territory, cf. Rahm (1990) 50, and Ebenroth/Kaiser (1992) 228, referring to further materials. Sonnenberger/Großerichter (1999) 724 n 24, however, advocated their belief that the (non-Italian) system of law under which the company is duly incorporated remains applicable, together with special mandatory law provisions. Reference is made to Benedetelli, in: Bariati, *Le nuovo leggi* 1996. But this would be contradictory to the notion of a single law governing company relationships (cf. Italian doctrine, set out in III 3, below). So far, there is no case-law on this matter.

[684] cf. Mancini, above, and Quadri, referred to by Ebenroth/Kaiser (1992) 228, n 32. They touch upon the tendency demonstrated by Italian Courts to solve the recognition problem by applying art. 16(2) of the preliminary provisions of the Civil Code.

[685] Indeed, support could be found for a theory that art. 2509 should be taken as the point of departure, after which the opening lines of art. 2505 were to be followed by the incorporation statute, cf. Rahm (1990) 61. It is clear, however, that this persuasive approach is over-construed.

[686] Another date could equally be used, namely 8 July 1985, when the expert committee on the reform of private international law (incl. the law on international civil procedure) was installed by the Justice Department, cf. for a historical overview of the *'progetto di legge del 1984 al testo di legge del 31 Maggio 1995 n 218'*, Broggini (1996) 57, 66 et seq.; and De Meo (1996) 46. Cf. Clerici/Mosconi/Pocar (1995); Fumagalli (1993); Davi' (1990); Franceschelli (1995); and Gaja (1994). A draft Code was published in 1989. For the complete text of this draft, including an Official Explanatory Report, see Riv.dir.int 1989 932–85. After some minor alterations, the final text was adopted in 1993: Gazetta Ufficiale no. 128 of 3 June 1995.

[687] Notably, conflict rules concerning family law matters were considered to be discriminatory (cf. the development in Germany under the former EGBGB, III 1, above).

conflict of law provisions into line with international conventions.[688] Successful conflict of law codifications in many other European countries were said to have inspired the Italian legislator.[689] The Code is divided into four chapters.[690] Chapter III on *persone giuridiche* (legal persons) consists solely of article 25.[691] This is divided into three subsections, and reads as follows:

(1) Companies, associations, foundations and other bodies, both public and private, even though not having the characteristics of an association, shall be governed by the law of the State in whose territory their incorporation was completed. Nevertheless, Italian law shall apply if the seat of management is in Italy and if the principal object of the aforesaid bodies is situated in Italy.

(2) The law governing the specific body shall in particular apply to:
    (a) legal status;
    (b) trade or corporate name;
    (c) incorporation, transformation and dissolution;
    (d) capacity;
    (e) establishment, powers and operation modalities of the organs;
    (f) agency;
    (g) acquisition or loss of membership of the company or the association as well as the rights and obligations resulting therefrom;
    (h) liability for obligations undertaken by the body;
    (i) consequences resulting from infringement either of the law or of the memorandum of association;

(3) Any transfer of the registered office to a different state as well as mergers of bodies having seats in different States shall take effect only when performed in accordance with the laws of the aforesaid States.[692]

---

[688] De Meo (1996) 46. Boschiero (1996) 143, summarizes the following grounds: (1) the then existing 'hard and fast' conflict rules lacked flexibility; (2) substantive law notions, such as weaker party protection, were totally absent; (3) conflict of law and international civil procedure lacked coherence; (4) the need to further the coherence between Italian conflict of laws and, notably, the EC Conventions regarding Jurisdiction and Recognition and Enforcement of Foreign Judgments (Brussels, 1968) and the Contracts Convention (Rome, 1980).

[689] Azzolini (1993) 893 et seq., with a comprehensive catalogue of modern conflict of law codifications, e.g. Czechoslovakia (1963), Albania (1964), Portugal (1966), Spain (1974), Hungary (1979), Turkey (1982), Austria (1978), Germany (1986), and Switzerland (1987). The *'eccessivà laconicità'* of the Italian legislator was strongly criticized by many Italian authors (ibid. n 2).

[690] The following order of the chapters corresponds with the four divisions of the Codice Civile.

[691] It has been stressed that it is difficult to capture a great variety of 'entities' in one provision: Azzolini (1993) 895.

[692] This provision is a remake of the draft provision of art. 23 of the draft Code on Private International Law. Furthermore, as one can see, the recently abolished provisions of arts. 2505 and 2509 more or less foreshadowed today's conflict rules. The official text of this provision is contained in the Gazetta Ufficiale no. 128 of 3 June 1995. It reads as follows:
    Art. 25 (*Società ed altri enti*)
    1. *Le società, le associazioni, le fondazioni ed ogni altro ente, pubblico o privato, anche se privo di natura associativa, sono disciplinati dalla legge dello stato nel cui territorio è stato perfezionato il pro*

Legal persons cum annexis

The conflict of law provision of article 25 was predominantly inspired by article 155 of the Swiss Code on Private International Law.[693] It has been given a relatively wide scope, in that it applies to 'Companies, associations, foundations and other bodies, both public and private, *even though not having the characteristics of an association*'.[694] This appears to be in compliance with case-law from the precodification era having regard to *Anstalten* as well as *Treuunternehmen* that were duly established under the law of Liechtenstein. Though occasionally used solely to circumvent Italian law, said foreign 'bodies' were not *ab initio* denied recognition.[695] Neither had single-member companies been denied recognition under the law in the preceding era.[696] The same policy was pursued by the drafters of the new Code. From 1995 onwards, an extended range of legal persons appears to be covered by the scope of article 25. In the meantime, it should not be overlooked that, although the mere 'recognition' of foreign 'bodies'

cedimento di constituzione. Si applica, tuttavia, la legge italiana se la sede dell'amministrazione è situata in Italia, overso se in Italia si trova l'oggetto principale di tali enti.

2. *In particolare sono disciplinati dalla legge regolatrice dell'ente:*
   a) *la natura giuridica;*
   b) *la denominazione o ragione sociale;*
   c) *la constituzione, la transformazione e l'estinzione;*
   d) *la capacità;*
   e) *la formazione, i poteri e le modalità di funzionamento degli organi;*
   f) *la rappresentanza dell'ente;*
   g) *le modalità di acquisto e di perditadella qualità di associato o socio nonchè diritti e gli obblighi inerenti a tale qualità;*
   h) *la responsabilità per le obbligazioni dell'ente;*
   i) *le conseguenze dello violazioni della legge o dell'atto constitutivo.*
3. *I trasferimenti della sede statutaria in altro stato e le fusioni di enti con sede in Stati diversi hanno efficacia soltano se posti in essere conformemente alle leggi di detti Stati interessati.*

[693] Ballarino (1996) 339. For Swiss law I refer to II 3, above.

[694] According to Broggini (1996) 57 et seq., referring to the *auctor intellectualis* Eduardo Vitta, this was necessitated by the fact that '*la terminologia* (of art. 25) *dovrebbe coprire fenomeni della realtà social equipollenti: le società ecc. dovrebbero tutte appartenere alla categoria delle persone giuridiche, come contrapposto alle persone fisice* (the terminology used should be able to cover phenomena of today's social reality: as a pendant of the category of natural persons, the provision of art. 25 should comprise legal persons in all its figures)'.

[695] Azzolini (1993) 897 and, in respect of bilateral treaties concluded between Italy and other countries, 898, n 16. Cf. further Ballarino (1996) 342, and III 3, above. Doubt has been removed. In the words of Broggini (1996) 59: '*La conclusione è ovia:* (. . .) *Anche enti ignoti al sistema giuridicho italiano, come il* Trust *o l'*Anstalt *o la* Treuunternehmen, *sono riconducibili alla disciplina dell'art.* 25 (The conclusion is clear: those entities that are unknown under Italian law—e.g. Trust, *Anstalt* or *Treuunternehmen*—all fall within art. 25)'.

[696] Apart from the fact that there was no reason to deny the existence of foreign single-member companies, Italian law also introduced this company form. Act of 3 March 1993: *Recentemente il decreto legislativo* (. . .) *relativo alle società a responsabilità limitata con un unico socio* (emphasis added) *ha proveduto ad inserire nel diritto societario italiano tale instituto, ponendo il nostro ordinamento alla pari di quelli degli altri paesi europei*': Azzolini (1993) 899 et seq., who brings up the issue of the equivalent of single-member companies in other European legal orders (n. 17); also Broggini (1996) 59.

is not opposed,[697] the second sentence of article 25(1) forms an effective safeguard against abuse by foreign legal persons engaged in business activities on Italian territory.

The issues of the recognition of foreign companies and the law applicable to them are not dealt with separately.[698] The notions of *riconoscimento* and *nazionalità* are apparently no longer relevant.[699] Of significant importance, however, is the relationship between article 25(1) (second sentence) on one hand—'Nevertheless, the Italian law shall apply if the seat of management is in Italy and if the principal object of the aforesaid bodies is situated in Italy'—and EC law on the freedom of establishment for legal persons, on the other. ECJ *Centros*[700] is said to have inspired both the (Italian[701]) Advocate-General La Pergola and the ECJ to acknowledge special mandatory rules promulgated by legislators of EC member states in order to protect company creditors.[702]

Companies on Italian territory: the sede theory

A superficial reading of article 25 may suggest that the 'incorporation' theory prevails.[703] However, the dispute between the proponents of the conflicting theories was decided by the expert committee in favour of the 'real seat' doctrine for several reasons.[704] In the course of ascertaining the foreign law, courts were expected to be troubled by complications, *inter alia* because the search for a foreign proper law of the company is deemed to be hypothetical as long as it remains certain that the alleged *lex societatis* applies. It is worth mentioning here that the draft article 23 originally stated that the management was presumed to reside in the country where the company was incorporated. By making use of this provision, courts would be given a legal basis for applying the 'incorporation' theory where no central management seat could be found.[705] Today, it is clear from the

---

[697] Note, however, that in this context the word 'recognition' is used in a narrow sense (cf. ch 2 I 2, above). In the same sense Ballarino (1996) 352.

[698] Ebenroth/Kaiser (1992) 237 (quoting G. Beitzke, *Juristische Personen im International-privatrecht und Fremdenrecht*, 1938, p. 42) and 239, underline that discussing the proper law of the company presupposes that this company exists. Cf., however, the temporary revival of a separate treatment, explained by the urge to combat unwished consequences flowing from bilateral treaties (see III 3, below).

[699] Capotorti, quoted by Rahm (1990) 125, n 17, states that the nationality can only play a secondary role (*lege lata*).

[700] Case C–212/97, [1999] *CMLR*, 551. See ch 2 IV 2, above.

[701] This was stressed by Sonnenberger/Großerichter (1999) 725.

[702] If applied on the basis of factual circumstances, this device would have a considerable impact on legal certainty and predictability: ibid.

[703] See de Meo (1996) 47, explicitly taking the 'incorporation' theory as a point of departure.

[704] For details, Azzolini (1993) 901 et seq.

[705] cf. Ebenroth/Kaiser (1992) 235, underlining firmly that the 'incorporation' theory was to be applied only as secondary option.

wording of the final sentence of article 25(1) ('Nevertheless . . . Italy') that the applicability of Italian law cannot be frustrated by a fictitious management centre in a foreign legal order, if business activities, are predominantly undertaken in Italy.[706] The expert committee took the view that in such cases a fictitious management centre is *de iure* considered to be situated in Italy.[707] The same principle applies when a company decides to move its headquarters from Italy to any other country while the main business activities remain in Italy.[708] Like their fellow specialists in other 'real seat' countries, Italian writers point to the fact that it is fairly complicated to ascertain a company's real seat, since this criterion *'appartenga all'area fattuale e non all'area giuridico-formale'*.[709]

In spite of the fact that the present-day conflict of law rule in article 25 can be expected to work similarly to the previously existing recognition practice,[710] there are some striking contrasts with the original draft provision of article 23. First, the first sentence of article 23(1) still took the 'real seat' doctrine as the starting point,[711] whereas the final version of article 25(1) fundamentally provides that companies are to be governed by the law of the country where the company is incorporated.[712] Secondly, the rebuttable presumption that the administration office coincides with the incorporation seat was abolished.

Registration and re-incorporation requirements

Once a company has either its *sede dell'amministrazione* (headquarters) or its *oggetto principale* (main centre of business activities) on Italian territory, it must comply with several legal requirements.[713] First, the company has

[706] Ebenroth/Kaiser (1992) 235, mention the case of a company with its real seat in Switzerland, business activities being undertaken in Italy. It must not be overlooked that the other side of the coin might well be that as well as Italian law, a foreign law also applies to the company.

[707] cf. the explanatory report of the expert committee in Riv.dir.int priv.proc. 1989 932 and 955.

[708] See further III 3, below.

[709] Broggini (1996) 61: 'this criterion is of a factual, rather than a formal legal character'. Ibid. 80 et seq., with regard to groups of companies. Cf. Ballarino (1996) 348.

[710] One must, however, heed the fact that case-law explicitly referring to the 1995 Code is still scarce. Furthermore, when compared to its predecessors (i.e. arts. 2505 and 2509 CC), the now applicable art. 25 has been given an extended scope, simply because, except for the final sentence of the first subsection, it has been bilateralized.

[711] The decisive factor of art. 23(1) was the *amministrazione centrale* (central management office).

[712] This difference is of major importance if neither the company's management and control centre, nor its registered office is located on Italian territory. In other words: there is no need for Italy to deprive companies of their 'foreign' status where no vital Italian interests appear to be at stake.

[713] Ballarino (1996) 349 et seq. Only after all requirements have been met is the company considered to be Italian: *'e porta con sé l'ammissione alle attività che la legge italiana riserva ai soggetti nazionali'* (as a consequence of which, said company is permitted to conduct activities as if it were an Italian subject).

to be registered properly in the company register; this registration must be homologated. Thereafter, it must be transformed into an an Italian *società commerciale*. All these requirements must be obeyed under penalty of *'la responsabilità illimitata e solidale per le obbligazioni sociali di coloro che agiscono in nome della società'* (article 2508 of the Civil Code),[714] i.e. joint and several liability for company transactions are imposed on those acting on behalf of the company. As the applicability of the foreign *lex societatis* is not touched upon by article 25(1) *in fine*, this results in a *duplice nazionalita* (double nationality, i.e. two proper laws both govern company relationships).[715] Even after an incoming foreign company has been duly re-established (i.e. re-incorporated) under Italian law without the intention to split, the ultimate consequence might also be that there are two companies.[716]

Sede statutaria—sede dell'amministrazione: definitions

Although the conflict of law rule concerning companies has been rewritten, this does not mean that the hitherto commonly applied decisive factors lost their relevance under the 1995 Code. The definitions of, for example, the *sede dell'amministrazione centrale* (the central management and control office), the *sede statutaria* (the registered office) and the *attività prevalente* (the country where the main business activities are undertaken) survived the private international law reform.[717] To begin with, the *sede dell'amministrazione centrale*, is also commonly referred to as the *sede reale o effetiva*. To be acknowledged as such, a durable and externally apparent *impulsi volitivi* (administration) is essential.[718] Although *de facto* this does not encompass *l'oggetto principale dell'impresa* (the place where the main business activities are conducted), the latter factor also plays a significant

---

[714] Ballarino (1996) 349. To avoid misunderstandings, he emphasizes that *'omissione della formalità'* do not entail nullity of the company, ibid. 353.

[715] Ballarino (1996) 350, observes that in this case both the foreign proper law and the Italian law provisions of arts. 2392 and 2394 may apply to the responsibility of the *'amministratori'* (company directors).

[716] cf. Ballarino (1996) 354, quoting Dicey/Morris, eds. (1987): 'A company incorporated under the Companies Act 1985 cannot be reincorporated elsewhere so as to have more than one domicile. Should companies in such company wish to re-incorporate in France and do so, then, as a matter of English law, two distinct corporations (one French and one English) are created.' The legal construction of a company, which after its transfer finds itself subject to two systems of law, reminds us of the consequences possibly flowing from the Belgian *Lamot* doctrine: II 1, above. See also III 3, below.

[717] The drafters of the new Private International Law Code also considered these notions to be key concepts while elaborating a new conflict rule.

[718] In this sense e.g. Trib. Roma decision of 2 May 1963, Giust Civ., 1964 I 698, with regard to the former provision of art. 2505 CC; Trib. Genova, introducing the notion of the *impulsi volitivi*, Riv.dir.int.priv.proc. 1967, p. 802; Corte Cass., Riv.dir.int.priv.proc. 1975, p. 545. Cf. also Ballarino (1996) 350. From comparative angle, Ebenroth/Kaiser (1992) 238, and Rahm (1990) 65.

role in determining the proper law of the company.[719] The personal status of managers is not relevant.[720] A literal interpretation of the *sede statutaria* would mean that this is the place simply referred to in the incorporation *contract*;[721] the same problem arises when the *luogo constituzione* (place of formation) as contained in article 2509, is examined.[722] It is generally assumed, however, that the incorporation seat is meant, i.e. the law of the state in conformity with which the company is established. Needless to say, the registration of pro-forma foreign companies under a foreign *lex societatis* is very likely to meet objections from those legal orders that adhere to the 'real seat' doctrine. Like its predecessor (article 2505 Civil Code[723]), the present version of article 25 of the Private International Law Code relentlessly submits these companies to Italian law.[724] In other words, a genuine link should exist between the chosen registered office and the country where the company's real seat is situated. Finally, the *attività prevalente* sprung from the notion of the *ogetto principale dell'impressa*, as follows from article 2505 of the Civil Code, and was meant to designate Italian law as the proper law of the company if the business activities were predominantly in Italy.[725]

Opificio, filliale: *definition*

An additional remark must be made here with regard to the concept of the *sede secondaria*, also known as *opificio, filiale*, etc.[726] This is a branch of a foreign company, settled in Italy. Articles 2506–8 of the Civil Code contain substantive law provisions that should be read in conjunction with the conflict rule of article 25 of the Code. In order to acquire the status of a 'branch', a body should form an independent entity, which operates more

---

[719] The Genova Court held that whilst the predecessor of art. 25 (art. 2505) was applied, this factor should retain an autonomous position in the process of ascertaining the proper law of the company: *riv.dir.int.priv.proc.* 1967 802. More below.

[720] e.g. nationality, or domicile, cf. Trib. Roma, Giust. Civ. 1964 I, p. 702. A contrasting view reminds us of the 'control theory' (Part 1, above).

[721] cf. Ebenroth/Kaiser (1992) 238.

[722] cf. Rahm (1990) 68: is it the legal order under whose law the company came into being, or the country where the company is finally registered? In most situations, these places coincide, see ch 2 I 3, above.

[723] This provision spoke of the *luogo di constituzione*, i.e. the country where the company was established. Allegedly, this 'constitution' was understood as the compulsory acquisition of legal capacity under Italian law: Rahm (1990) 68.

[724] There is however authority that '*l'intervento necessario del diritto italiano*' should be applied '*restringendosi*', i.e. in a restrictive manner: Azzolini (1993) 908.

[725] cf. the above cited Trib. Roma decision of 2 May 1963, Giust. Civ., 1964 I 698, and Rahm (1990) 67. Note that at present this factor is no longer considered relevant. Ebenroth/Kaiser (1992), quoting G. Grasmann (1970) 241, take the view that it is an obsolete remnant of ancient Belgian doctrinal influences ('*centre d'exploitation*'). Another opinion is supported by Rahm (1990) 66, quoting a decision of the Genova Court (see above).

[726] cf. further *stabilimento, succursale* or *agenzia*, referred to by Ebenroth/Kaiser (1992) 136, n 150.

or less permanently as the representative[727] of a foreign company.[728] Once acknowledged as a 'branch' the undertaking is obliged to register in compliance with articles 2506 and 2507 of the Civil Code[729] under the penalty of joint and several liability of those acting on behalf of the company (article 2508 Civil Code). This liability does not, however, remove or even restrict the liability of the foreign parent company.

Restrictions to the *sede* theory: bilateral conventions

Bilateral treaties: Switzerland and Germany

As noted above, the concepts of *riconoscimento* (recognition) and *trattamento* (treatment) of foreign companies do not necessarily coincide. Sometimes, recognition of a foreign company is conceived in a narrow sense, meaning that although a foreign company is acknowledged as a bearer of rights and duties, it is subject to Italian law.[730] The word recognition may also be given wider effect, though, meaning that a company is permitted to operate, with its (foreign) substantive company law rules being respected by state authorities.

How far do treaties between Italy and other states derogate from what has been concluded from earlier findings?[731] The general provision of article 2 of the 1995 Private International Law Code states that:

(1) the provisions of this law shall not affect the enforcement of any international convention to which Italy is a party. (2) The interpretation of the aforementioned conventions shall take account of their international character as well as the need for uniform enforcement.

By virtue of bilateral Friendship Treaties, companies duly established under Swiss or German[732] law are recognized as such in Italy, provided that such recognition is not manifestly incompatible with public policy (to be understood here as *ordre public*).[733]

---

[727] Notably in legal proceedings. Other powers of representation (e.g. to conclude contracts for the company, etc.) do not suffice in this respect.

[728] cf. Trib. Roma 24 November 1987, *La Società* 1988 395 ('*una certa autonomina amministrativa*'); Corte Cass. Giust. Civ. 1961, I, p. 650; Corte Cass. 2881/68, Giust. Civ. 1969, I 1736 (concerning permanent representation power). Cf. in detail, Ballarino (1996) 355 et seq.

[729] This provision declares the written requirements for *Società per Azione* (the Italian equivalent of a public limited company) to be equally applicable.

[730] See ch 2 I 2, above.   [731] See III 2, above.

[732] Art. 22 of the Treaty concluded between Italy and Switzerland 27 January 1923, Gazz. Uff. nr. 41 of 2 February 1923, p. 270. This Treaty was also declared applicable to Liechtenstein by an Act of Parliament of 24 December 1928, this declaration however being ordered null and void by the Constitutional Court in its decision of 28 July 1977, nr. 3352. For comments and further references see Azzolini (1993) 897; Ballarino (1996) 343; and from comparative perspective, Ebenroth/Kaiser (1992) 231, n 45. Cf. further art. 33 of the Italian–German Treaty of 21 November 1957.

[733] As well as the bilateral conventions mentioned here, see art. 16 of the 1995 Private International Law Code.

Countervailing capital exportation: the Liechtenstein Anstalt

Italy, although essentially not an incorporation country, and like its neighbour (Switzerland[734]) was troubled by Italian subjects who, having established a Liechtenstein *Anstalt* for the sole purpose of circumventing claims by both the Treasury Department and the creditors of the 'Anstalt', were exporting capital to Liechtenstein.[735] Formerly, Liechtenstein *Anstalts* were welcomed because they attracted foreign investors and brought prosperity to Italy.[736] But a Bill from 1956, which, without any restrictions, granted those investors the right to export profits gained in Italy, inspired *Italians* to export their capital. These developments persuaded the Italian legislator to make covert exports of capital by Italian subjects a criminal offence in 1976. Since then, it is proscribed to create the false image that assets situated or activities carried out in Italy must be attributed to persons not being resident in Italy. It should be emphasized, however, that this legislative initiative did not affect the 1956 Bill. Creative reasoning inspired courts to disregard the recognition of *Anstalts* from the very start: this observation was based on the perception that under article 16(2) of the Civil Code Preliminary Title foreign (legal) persons were granted the same civil rights as Italians, and if possible vice versa as well. If the *Anstalt* was to be considered as *tertium genus*[737] under Italian law, the rights of Italian subjects under that provision would be violated; any recognition claimed by these *Anstalts* could therefore be dismissed.[738] The highest court of Italy, however, pursued another route:[739] by a judgment of 28 July 1977,[740] the Supreme Court for the first time explicitly held that, contrary to the decisions of the lower courts, these *Anstalts* could not fundamentally be denied recognition.[741] A legal basis was found in the preliminary

---

[734] See II 3, above.

[735] Rahm (1990) 86, *inter alia* quoting many Italian authors, speaks of one of the most controversial themes in Italian private international law. Allegedly, it even generates paranoia. Problems arising from the acceptance of the 'incorporation' theory strongly resemble the fight against *formeel buitenlandse vennootschappen* (cf. the 1998 Pro-Forma Foreign Companies Act) under Dutch law (see II 1, above). [736] Rahm (1990) 87.

[737] This expression was used by Santa Maria (1996) 44, adding that these *Anstalts* could be classified neither as partnerships, nor as associations.

[738] cf. Corte d'App. Venezia, Giur. It. 1975 I, 2. p. 835. Cf. further, invoking the *'ordine pubblico internazionale'* of art. 31 CC prel. Trib. Milano, Giur. comm. 1978 II, 122.

[739] The aforementioned method of art. 16(2) was severely criticized, since it revived the ancient recognition theory (II 3, above). Cf. Rahm (1990) 90.

[740] Corte Cass. 28 July 1977, Giust. Civ. 1978, pp. 536 et seq., Foro It. 1977, I 2158 et seq.

[741] cf. Azzolini (1993) 897, and Santa Maria (1996) 46 and 47, quoting an earlier judgment of the Court of Milan, (1975), Giur. comm. 346, supporting this view. The latter emphasizes that private international law is about the recognition of foreign legal institutions, not because they are equivalent to domestic legal persons but because they are different. His view is sustained by the wording of art. 25 of the new Code ('companies . . . and *other bodies*'). So basically, the problem of Liechtenstein *Anstalts* is not different from any other problem which faces private international law specialists.

provision of articles 16 and 22 of the Swiss–Italian Friendship Treaty. Neither could it any longer be maintained that incorporation by a single shareholder or the subsequent loss of plurality of shareholders during the existence of the company must be considered contrary to the public policy of the Italian legal order.[742] The Court, however, continued by declaring that a distinction should be made between the *riconoscimento* (recognition) and the *trattamento* (treatment) of a foreign legal person.[743] Subsequently, the Court applied article 2362 of the Civil Code, which declares in the case of bankruptcy that a person is liable for all *company*[744] debts arising from the period during which this person owned all the shares.[745] Any liability arising from Italian law is considered supplementary, in the sense, that it does not take away liabilities envisaged by the home legal system of the foreign company.[746] There is no doubt that article 25 of the Private International Law Code, covering foreign private bodies in the widest sense (see above) would currently apply; however, in the light of the foregoing it is not clear whether the Liechtenstein *lex societatis*, even when its application results from a (bilateral) convention, can still be thwarted by the escape devices of either *ordre public* (article 16 of the 1995 Code), or mandatory law provisions (article 17);[747] it is conceivable that mandatory law may lead to setting aside (parts of) the proper law of the company, since vital interests of both the Italian state and the company's creditors are at stake.

---

[742] Later confirmed by judgments of the Italian Supreme Courts, cf. Corte Cass., Foro It. 1977 I, p. 2158; ibid., Foro It., 1980 I, p. 1303; Ibid., Riv.dir.int.priv.proc. 1986, p. 353, ibid., Foro It. 1986 I, p. 744. Cf. also Santa Maria (1996) 45, quoting lower court decisions, opposing the orientation of the Supreme Court.

[743] This approach was also advocated by Luzatto, quoted by Rahm (1990) 39, n 11.

[744] The courts declared, *inter alia*, that when compared to the Italian public company limited by shares, it would not make sense for a Liechtenstein *Anstalt* be privileged.

[745] There are interesting parallels between the Italian and the Dutch remedies against abuse by foreign legal persons; under s 5 of the Dutch 1998 CLC Act, however, it is irrelevant whether all shares are in the hands of one person.

[746] Santa Maria (1996) 47.

[747] e.g. art. 2362 of the Civil Code. Santa Maria (1996) 47, stresses that unlimited liability can even be seen as a general principle, applicable to those acting in the name of a foreign entity. The penalty may also be that the company is considered as a *società non riconosciuta*: Rahm (1990) 41. Ebenroth/Kaiser (1992) 254, mention the decision of the Corte d'app. Milano of 16 December 1986, Foro Pad. 1988 I, 31, ordering the nullity of the (foreign) company. Cf. also a judgment of the Courts of Padua, Riv.dir.int.priv.proc. 1975, p. 545. Under the exhaustive list of nullity grounds contained in art. 12 of the 1st EC Company Law Directive, it remains to be seen, however, how much room now remains to conclude that the company is null and void.

Scope of the applicable law

The basic principle: a single proper law governing company relationships

Little attention is paid to the precise *ambito di applicazione* (scope) of the law.[748] Subsection 2 of article 25 of the 1995 Private International Law Code (see p. 222 above) sets out the issues to which the law shall apply. Apparently, this catalogue of issues is not meant to be exhaustive ('shall apply *in particular* to. . .')

Italian courts and academics share the view that it makes no sense to split the proper law of the company without good reason: once the *legge nazionale* (proper law of the company) is ascertained, that system of law governs status, legal capacity, internal organization, including transformation matters, and the dissolution and winding up of the company.[749] It is conceivable that legal orders adhering to the 'real seat' theory see no good reason to split the proper law of the company in favour of other systems of law.[750] As in other legal orders, company representation, although initially subject to the proper law of the company, can also be subject to the law of the country where a contract between the company and a third party is concluded, in order to protect legitimate third party expectations (e.g. where a third party is unaware of restrictions on the powers of representation emanating from the *lex societatis*).[751]

Exceptions: the proper law of the contract

The proper law of the contract might however take preference over the *lex societatis* in respect of transactions entered into by those planning to establish a company in the near future.[752]

---

[748] cf. Ballarino (1996) 361 et seq, and Broggini (1996) 63 et seq.

[749] Ballarino (1996) 361 et seq.: no complications arise *'sinché la società ha uno statuto exclusivamente straniero* (if a company is of an entirely foreign nature)'. The applicability of Italian mandatory law may, however, be imposed by art. 25(1) *in fine* JO art. 17 of the 1995 Code. Vice versa, the proper law of the company is set aside by the *lex fori* when the liquidation of the company follows from any intervening power of a foreign legal order: observation made by Broggini (1996) 63 et seq. Cf. Corte Cass., Foro It. 1986 I, pp. 744 et seq. From the comparative angle, Rahm (1990) 124.

[750] The Italian legislator embraced the concept of *l'unicità e l'universalita*, resulting in the application of one proper law of the company whenever possible, Broggini (1996) 63. In a comparable sense, see III 2 above, on French law. Sonnenberger/Großerichter (1999) 724, n 24, advocated another view. They believe that pursuant to art. 25 the (non-Italian) system of law under which the company is incorporated remains applicable to companies having their real seat on Italian territory, together with special mandatory law provisions. Reference is made to Benedetelli, in: Bariati, *Le nuovo leggi* 1996.

[751] Ballarino (1996) 365.

[752] ibid. 363. Cf. Azzolini (1993) 921: the Rome Convention on the Law Applicable to Contractual Obligations of 19 June 1980 is likely to apply to contractual aspects (see below).

Seat transfers

Change in the applicable law

Any *trasferimento di sede* (cross-border seat transfer) involves several legal orders: such transfers have to comply with the laws of both the state of departure and the state of re-establishment. However, this obligation does not arise from European law; one may say that only the margins are touched upon by European law as it now stands.[753] To date, national systems of (private international) law have not provided satisfactory tools either. This is why, throughout Europe, academics[754] have tried to find a way out of this legal vacuum by advocating the analogous application of national legislation, intended to regulate purely domestic transformations of one legal person (or partnership) into another, to cross-border transfers.[755]

Undeniably, article 25(3) of the 1995 Private International Law Code explicitly refers to cross-border company seat transfers (and mergers). But it does not reach beyond the obligation that '(a)ny transfer of the registration office to a different State as well as mergers of bodies having seats in different States shall take effect only *when performed in pursuance of the laws of the aforesaid States.*' This blank can only be filled in with the help of a retrospective analysis of former legal provisions, combined with the preparatory works of the expert committee in this field.[756] It has always been generally assumed that making radical changes was not the intention of the drafters of the 1995 Code.[757] Until 1995, articles 2505 and 2509, to be read in conjunction with article 2498 of the Italian Civil Code, were taken

---

[753] These margins are considered in more detail in ch 6 II 1, below. The following observation made by Santa Maria (1996) 51 is highly intriguing, not to say provocative: instead of prescribing rules of private international law, art. 58 (now art. 48) of the EC Treaty is said to presuppose that, in all cases, the law regulating companies has already been determined by the usual mechanisms of private international law.

[754] cf. German law, III 1, above.

[755] A more substantive law approach was envisaged by the *Lamot* doctrine in Belgium. For more detailed comments, see ch 6 III, below.

[756] cf. with regard to art. 2498 of the Italian Civil Code, Ballarino (1985) 401, and Azzolini (1993) 915 (with further reference). The latter observed: '*Tale articolo, in realtà, prevede i casi di trasformazione di società in nome collettivo o in accomandita semplice in società di capitali. Tuttavia è possibile ritenere che esso sia applicabile (almeno in via analogica) non solo ai casi in cui una società di capitali si trasformi in una società di persone, ma anche quando si tratti di persone giuridiche sottoposte ad un diritto straniero che modificano la loro struttura conformandosi alla tipologia e alla normativa italiana.*' This statement is followed by a detailed description of how such cross-border transfers should properly be carried out in everyday practice. For example, the appropriate way to meet *qualsiasi persona giuridica stranieri* (company forms that appear to be quasi-foreign), the transformation of an incoming partnership '*non è una società commerciale*' (is not a commercial body), which appears to be unknown under Italian law; formal requirements, etc., pp. 915 et seq. On a supranational level, efforts are being made to regulate cross-border transfers with the help of bilateral rules: see ch 6 III 2, above.

[757] See Azzolini (1993) 912 et seq.

as a basis to govern cross-border transfers of companies. As above,[758] several modes of cross-border transfers must be examined.

Immigration transfer

During the 'pre-Code era' (i.e. before 1995), it clearly followed from the wording of article 2505 of the Civil Code that foreign companies had no option other than to re-establish under Italian law.[759] An additional complication—at least for a number of foreign company types—was that substantive Italian company law required a notary deed to be registered by the notary public within thirty days of its issue.[760] The Italian legislator removed this obstacle by ordering that for foreign companies this period only begins when *the company moves into Italian territory*.[761] There is a change in the proper law of the company after this procedure has been complied with.[762] Any attempt to circumvent this procedure was deemed to be *contra legem*, and therefore to lead to a *disconoscimento* (i.e. denial of recognition) of the company. There is therefore no legal capacity,[763] and this ultimately results in joint and personal liability of those in charge of the management of the 'company' pursuant to article 2331 of the Civil Code.

Emigration transfer

As for the departure of Italian companies, there is a lively debate about whether a departing company is subject to compulsory dissolution and winding up.[764] Under Italian law, it would be bold to assert that a departing company is always submitted to compulsory dissolution and winding up. Some decades ago, the Torino Court of Appeal ordered that a

[758] cf. II 1–3, III 1–2, above.

[759] Ballarino (1996) 354 and 358 quotes Dicey/Morris: 'A company incorporated under the Companies Act 1985 cannot be reincorporated elsewhere so as to have more than one domicile. Should companies in such company wish to re-incorporate in France and do so, then, as a matter of English law, two distinct corporations (one French and one English) are created.'

[760] See Azzolini (1993) 916. This registration of the company forms an essential part of the company's constitution: art. 2331 CC.

[761] Bill of Parliament of 21 March 1980 (emphasis added). See for further information Azzolini (n 760 above); Broggini (1996) 63; and Rahm (1990) 71.

[762] cf. Trib. Roma, Giust. Civ. 1964 I, p. 698. Likewise, parallels were sought between this approach and the absence of representative power, cf. Corte d'App Venezia, Giur. int. 1975 I, p. 835.

[763] This legal consequence may of course harm the interests of creditors of the 'company': it has been suggested, though, that the non-existence or even nullity of foreign 'companies' not (yet) having complied with the transformation requirements should be avoided by treating them as *società irregulare*, rather than as *società di fatto*: cf. Azzolini (*supra*) and Rahm (1990) 75 et seq. Another remedy was to order the 'nullity *ex nunc*', cf. Trib. Milano, Riv.dir.int. priv.proc. 1979, pp. 125 et seq.

[764] This is so in Italy as well as in other 'real seat' countries. Cf. the German approach, III 1, above, dissolution and winding up of departing company based on conflict of laws—if so, can this be overcome with the help of *renvoi*?—or by substantive company law?

company be wound up after a decision of the management board to change the proper law in the course of a transfer of the company.[765] This judgment did not, however, meet total approval from Italian doctrine.[766] Companies planning to leave Italy[767] were subject to the conflict rule of article 2509 of the Civil Code. Several situations need to be examined, though. Article 2509 created the impression that companies established in Italy remained subject to Italian law, even when their main centre of business activities was concentrated abroad. Apparently, a number of writers assume that transferring a company's registered office did not bring about any change in the proper law of the company.[768] Contrary to the law of most 'real seat' countries, however, a company was permitted to transfer either its *sede dell'amministrazione* (centre of management) *or* its *ogetto principale dell'impressa* (centre of business activities) to another state, without the consequence of being dissolved and wound up.[769] If *both* connecting factors were transferred from Italy to another legal order, the outcome depended on whether the departing company had originally been established in Italy (article 2509), or elsewhere (article 2505). In both situations, the legal order of Italy is clearly involved. The assumption is that in the former case there is no change in the proper law.[770] In the latter case, one

---

[765] Corte d'App. Torino, Riv.dir.int.priv.proc. 1958, p. 607.

[766] Like their German counterparts, Italian writers differ on this point: Azzolini (1993) 918 et seq. (for further information), refers to *'la prassi italiana (. . .) in passato'* (the former Italian law practice). Allegedly, any cross-border seat transfer entailed the company's compulsory dissolution and winding up. At present, however, this view is opposed by many who believe that a company may survive such a transfer, provided that *'le legislazioni dei due Stati interessati consentano una simile possibilità* (such a transfer is allowed by the laws of both interested legal orders).' Authority can be taken from e.g. Appeal Court of Milano 7 May 1974, Giur Comm. 1975 II, pp. 832 et seq., *'per il quale le società italiane possono trasferisi all'estero mantenendo il loro carattere italiano* (an Italian company moving abroad while maintaining its Italian identity).' A position inbetween is taken by Ballarino (1996) 359: pursuant to art. 2437, an Italian company leaving Italy will have to respect that members resign from the company. A company 'welcomed' abroad must retain its real seat in Italy (art. 25.1 of the 1995 Code, cf. also below). Neither is an incoming company always subject to a loss of its identity (cf. above).

[767] From a comparative point of view, it is striking that Italian authors commonly speak of *trasferimento della sede sociale* (transfer of a company's social seat), yet without clearly distinguishing the *sede statutaria* (registered office) from the *sede effetiva o reale* (real seat). See the analysis of Italian law sources by Rahm (1990) 80.

[768] See Azzolini (1993) 918, and, from a comparative angle, Rahm (1990) 80, mentioning other sources. It is clear that those who prefer the 'incorporation' theory do not subscribe to this point of view.

[769] See Rahm (1990) 82.

[770] Ballarino (1996) 359, asserts that *'(u)na società italiana puó trasferire la propria sede all'estero, comme si evince dall'art. 2437 CC* (an Italian company may, pursuant to art. 2437 of the Italian Civil Code, transfer its seat abroad)'. According to art. 25(1) of the 1995 Private International Law Code, such a company is not subject to compulsory dissolution and winding up, provided, however, *'che conservi la sede effetiva in Italia* (that the real seat remains on Italian territory)'. Prior to the entry into force of the 1995 Code, Rahm (1990) 84, was reluctant to draw rigid conclusions, since arts. 2505 and 2509 were based on several competing factors, none of which was given more weight.

can at least say that it does not make sense to assume that a company planning to leave Italy would be prevented from returning to its 'home' country.

The character of article 25(3)

Article 25(3) is perfectly balanced, in that it also covers situations of cross-border seat transfers from one third country to another. Ultimately, it is for the state *'di arrivo'*, on whose territory the company is re-established, to decide whether the company retains its identity and under which conditions.[771]

In the light of the foregoing, it is surprising that the 1995 Private International Law Code confines itself to *one* single conflict rule on both cross-border transfers *and* mergers. Subsection 3 of article 25 reads:

(3) Any transfer of the registered office to a different State or merger of bodies having seats in different states shall take effect only when performed in pursuance of the laws of the aforesaid states.[772]

Capturing two very complicated procedures in one breath, this conflict rule is of misleading simplicity for more than one reason. In the first place, it merely envisages the transfer of the *sede statutaria* (registered office), not of the management and control office;[773] in the second place, it is misguided to believe that multi-party relationships such as cross-border company mergers or transfers can be carried out with the help of just one sweeping statement.[774] In the meantime, previous Italian legal practice has probably survived the new Code. After all, courts are not in a position to disobey a procedure which would have been followed anyway, namely to take into account the laws of both legal orders involved.[775]

---

[771] Ballarino (1996) 359.

[772] This provision is the successor of art. 23 of the draft Code on Private International Law. Furthermore, as one can see, the abolished provisions of arts. 2505 and 2509 already bore the signature of today's conflict rules. For information: Daniele (1995) 1242 et seq.; Franceschelli (1995) 42 et seq.; Ballarino (1996) 339; and Broggini (1996) 71 et seq.

[773] ibid. 61: '*Si tenga presente che il n 1* (i.e. subs. 1 of art. 25, SR) *parla di sede dell'amministrazione e non di sede statutaria, come il n 3.*' See also ibid. 358. Once again, from a comparative point of view, it is striking that Italian authors commonly speak of *trasferimento della sede sociale* (transfer of a company's social seat), yet without clearly distinguishing the *sede statutaria* (registered office) from the *sede effetiva o reale* (real seat), cf. the analysis of Italian law sources by Rahm (1990) 80.

[774] According to Azzolini (1993) 896 et seq., Art. 25(3) should be seen as a species of the general private international law device of mandatory law: '*l'art. 25 considera (. . .) sia la questione relativa ai casi di applicazione "necessaria" del diritto materiale italiano, sia la regolamentazione delle ipotesi di trasferimento della sede statutaria in altro Stato e di fusione di enti con sede in Stati diversi.*' It remains to be seen whether legislative 'one-liners' that find their origin in national conflict of law codes should be considered as a mere *Programmsatz* (one-liner), rather than as a suitable instrument to carry out complicated procedures such as cross-border company mergers or seat transfers: see ch 6 III 1, below.

[775] Even the Rome Convention on the Law Applicable to Contractual Obligations of 19 June 1980 might be relevant: although company law matters were explicitly excluded from

While concentrating on the transfer issue, it must be kept in mind that the Italian conflict rule is ambiguous: whereas Italian companies having their real seat abroad enjoy generous treatment (article 25(1), first sentence), foreign companies having their real seat on Italian territory are subject to the 'real seat' theory (second sentence). Consequently, only those companies which decide to move into Italy are subject to a change in the proper law of the company,[776] re-establishment of the company and registration under Italian law being required.

However, a transfer from Italy to any other legal order also reveals restricted reciprocity: at least under Italian law, such a company is not subject to compulsory winding up and liquidation procedures.[777] Contrary to draft article 23, it is no longer explicitly required that after its departure the company's predominant activities continue to take place in Italy.[778]

its scope (art. 1), there is no reason to assume that it does not apply to contractual aspects of cross-border seat transfers or mergers. Cf. in this sense Azzolini (1993) 921 and Ballarino (1996) 363.

[776] From a comparative point of view, Ebenroth/Kaiser (1992) 247, advocate the view that recognition by Italian authorities of an immigrating German company on the basis of art. 33 of the German–Italian Friendship Treaty would be precluded by the fact that under German law such a company would be compelled to wind up and liquidate. However, this view is not shared by many others. Cf., among others, Roth (referred to in III 1, above).

[777] cf. Azzolini (1993) 919 et seq.; and Rahm (1990) 81. Of course, it also depends on the law of the country where the emigrating company is re-established (real seat or incorporation country), whether there are additional legal requirements.

[778] This result can still be overruled by the principle laid down in both the draft provision of art. 23 and the final version of art. 25(3), namely that Italian law only remains applicable on condition that this is 'in accordance with the laws' of the states involved. Cf. the expert committee, rev.dir.int.priv.proc. 1989, p. 959 and the views expressed by Azzolini (above). Another position is taken by Ballarino (1996) 359: any transfer abroad of an Italian company entails the dissolution of this company (art. 2437 CC), unless, on the basis of art. 25(1) of the 1995 Private International Law Code, the company *'conservi la sede effetiva in Italia'* (that the real seat remains on Italian territory).

5

Provisional Conclusions

I. COMPARATIVE APPROACH: THE ENVIRONMENTAL CONTEXT OF THE LEGAL ORDERS INVOLVED

Part 1 of this book ended by asking how it is possible to explain the para-doxical situation of a progressively developing Single Market, despite which authorities of EC member states adamantly either stick to the 'real seat' theory, or, even worse, take a step backwards by limiting the liberal concept of the 'incorporation' theory. In order to develop an answer, the law of six legal orders (all of which, except Switzerland, are EC member states) three adherents of the 'incorporation' theory, the others applying the 'real seat' theory, have been analysed. With an eye to the common interest of cross-border company mobility in Europe, the prevailing question is, of course, whether something can be learnt from the existing disparities between 'incorporation' and 'real seat' countries.

In comparing legal orders, private international law specialists face a complicated task: although comparing the relevant legal orders may be useful, and from point of view of furthering the Single Market necessary, it is an illusion to think that the *tertium comparationis* is indeed comparable. To establish that the environmental (e.g. legal, socio-economic, cultural, historical) context of an 'incorporation' country, for example the Netherlands, differs fundamentally from that of another EC member state adhering to the 'real seat' doctrine is axiomatic and does not bring us any further. Attempting to explain different legal attitudes towards foreign companies is like trying to square the circle: satisfactory explanations can only be found by unveiling the underlying legal and other (e.g. economic) national policies of the legal orders involved.

II. COMPARATIVE APPROACH: 'VERTICAL' *VERSUS* 'HORIZONTAL' TREATMENT

The need not to bear in mind the intrinsic environmental context of each legal order involved in the comparison also explains why a 'vertical' (i.e. country-by-country), rather than 'horizontal' (issue-by-issue) treatment of those legal orders is preferred. First, a coherent picture of the evolution of a legal order over a particular period of time must be sketched. One could not interpret significant dissimilarities between the legal orders if one were unaware of the environmental background. One experience resulting from the 'vertical' approach is striking, and may therefore be taken as a starting point: considering that (i) the eternal controversy between the 'incorporation' theory and the 'real seat' theory clearly dates back to the pre-EC law era, and (ii) hardly any EC member states have radically[1] changed their attitude towards foreign companies since then, it is logical to assume that differing historical and environmental backgrounds still play some role today.

III. 'INCORPORATION' COUNTRIES: HISTORICAL AND SOCIO-ECONOMIC CONTEXT

The costs and benefits to society determine a legal order's policies. It is reasonable to assume that company law policies, in particular, are predominantly, although perhaps not exclusively, economically biased. As regards the attitude of a sovereign state towards foreign legal persons, the balance of costs and benefits of the legal orders compared shifts from country to country.

Currently, three of the legal orders examined here pay homage to the 'incorporation' theory, although for quite different reasons. The Netherlands and Switzerland both preferred the 'incorporation' theory as a tool to further industrial development. Both were clearly in favour of this liberal concept in the post-war era. The Netherlands pursued the following policies: (i) attracting foreign investors in order to stimulate the transformation from an agricultural economy into an industrialized one, and (ii) while applying the 'incorporation' theory, it was hoped that on the basis of reciprocity Dutch companies would meet the same benevolence abroad. *Mutatis mutandis*, the same policies were endorsed by Swiss

---

[1] Although the Netherlands did impose restrictions on the 'incorporation' theory (ch 4 II 1, above) one cannot say that the adjustments emanating from the Pro-Forma Foreign Companies Act 1998 resulted in a radical change in attitude towards foreign legal persons.

authorities; apart from that, Switzerland—not (yet) being a Member State of the EC[2]—had other good reasons to attract foreign investors. England has endorsed the 'incorporation' theory for centuries. As regards the recognition of foreign *private*[3] limited companies, this need not be surprising. Why should businessmen (either foreign or domestic) settling on English territory be troubled by using the—relatively over-regulated—foreign equivalent of an English private company limited by shares?[4] In this respect it is noteworthy that both the Netherlands and Switzerland are more frequently troubled by purely domestic enterprises setting up a proforma foreign private company in order to circumvent stricter domestic company law regimes. This explains why, for example, the Netherlands seems to have taken a step backwards by limiting the liberal concept of the 'incorporation' theory.[5] Other types of remedies against the abuse of, for example, Liechtenstein *Anstalts* inhibit Swiss law, it seems.[6] It should of course be kept in mind that any single-issue approach would distort the overall image of what cross-border company relationships are all about: regardless of which recognition theory each legal order adheres to, apart from company law interests they also have apparent interests in tax law, social security law, etc.[7]

IV. 'REAL SEAT' COUNTRIES: HISTORICAL AND SOCIO-ECONOMIC CONTEXT

Germany and France both adhere to the 'real seat' doctrine. In Germany, the applicability of the *Sitztheorie*, although not codified, is beyond doubt. Its underlying policy reflects the classical Savignian approach (*Sitz des Rechtsverhältnisses*, i.e. most significant relationship), thrown together with substantive law-oriented policies. The law of the legal order which is predominantly affected by the activities of the company is deemed to be that of the state where the company's *Sitz* is located. This enables the authorities of the legal order concerned to control the company efficiently, as well as to safeguard the protection of the company's creditors and other interested parties. Unlike the 'incorporation' theory, there is no need to invoke

---

[2] cf. recent developments, ch 4 II 3, above.

[3] Although for types of *public* company the situation is quite different (see ch 6 I 2, below, on the European Company Law Harmonization Programme), there seems to be no good reason to prefer foreign equivalent company forms either, knowing that e.g. the worker codetermination regime is quite different from that in England.

[4] Criminal convictions of company directors might be a reason: ch 4 II 2, above.

[5] cf. the 1998 Pro-Forma Foreign Companies Act, ch 4 II 1, above.

[6] cf. ch 4 II 3, above, in particular with regard to the *Fiktionsvorbehalt* and general private international law exemptions such as *ordre public*.

[7] cf. Part 1, above.

the general exemption clause of article 6 EGBGB (*ordre public*), nor to combat the phantom of pro-forma foreign corporations. The regulatory policies that are of fundamental importance—at least in the German tradition—are matters such as company capitalization and worker co-determination. These days, however, the unrestricted application of the *Sitztheorie* in its severest form has been criticized. Compromises between safeguarding the aforementioned domestic policies and the need to comply with EC law are being sought.[8]

Remarkably, no such criticism of the basic concept of the *siège réel* theory is uttered in France, which also represents the 'non-codification' group. This concept, which is still generally endorsed today, is only criticized with regard to the difficulty of determining a company's 'nationality' in everyday practice.[9]

Compared to other 'real seat' countries, Italy takes an intermediate position. In December 1995, a remodelled Private International Law Code entered into force. The reasons for reviewing the Italian conflict of laws were threefold: (i) Mancini's ideas on the role of nationality in conflict of laws were considered obsolete; (ii) in 1987 the Supreme Court held that several conflict of law rules did not conform with the Constitution; and (iii) the drafters faced the task of bringing domestic conflict of law provisions into line with international conventions. Chapter III of the Code, on *persone giuridiche* (legal persons) consists of one sole article, article 25, which is divided into three subsections. It is remarkable that, whereas the *teoria della sede* governs companies residing on Italian territory, the 'incorporation' theory is applied to companies duly formed in Italy but resident abroad. Thus, departing companies are—at least from the Italian legislator's point of view—not subject to the threat of being dissolved and wound up (cf. German law), although to the detriment of irreciprocity.

Rather than trying to bridge the gap between the two opposing recognition concepts, legal orders thus focused their attention on *national* policies, such as the stimulation of economic growth by attracting foreign investors, or imposing national company law on both domestic and foreign investors. They still do so today. But, as will be seen, the current progressive stage which the Single Market has reached places a duty upon these member states to abstain from imposing disproportionate measures which would hinder companies planning to migrate from one EC member state to another.

---

[8] See below.   [9] See below.

V. THE 'NATIONALITY' OF NATURAL AND LEGAL PERSONS

In both 'incorporation' and 'real seat' countries, analogies are sought between natural and legal 'foreigners'. Ancient concepts, of the 'birth' and 'death' of natural and legal persons alike, are inadequate devices to ascertain the proper law of the company. Any construed analogy between human and legal beings carries fundamental and practical flaws. From a common law, as well as an 'incorporation' point of view, the anthropomorphic concept is troublesome: it does not cohere well with the (singular or dual) 'domicile' and 'residence' of a company.[10]

Neither is there a convincing consistency between the French civil law concept of *nationalité des personnes morales* and the traditional *siège réel*: the intermingling of the concepts of the conflict of laws and the law on nationality and aliens cannot conceal fundamental weaknesses.[11] No doubt this concept serves justified interests: it enables French authorities to expand state sovereignty beyond national borders, as diplomatic protection can be extended to French *personnes morales* operating on foreign territory. On the other hand, it can be said that motives like these belong to the domain of *public*, rather than private international law. The unilateral character of the 'nationality' concept causes even more problems: for example, French authorities can never endow a company with German nationality. Neither is the concept of 'nationality' suitable for regulating multinational companies, let alone groups of companies. Last but not least, natural and legal persons—both more or less to be considered as 'nationals' of EC member states—cannot be treated on precisely the same footing under the provisions concerning freedom of establishment of the EC Treaty.

VI. SCOPE OF THE APPLICABLE LAW

The continuing controversy between 'incorporation' and 'real seat' theorists hardly affects the scope of the proper law of the company. There is a *communis opinio* that once the proper law of the company is ascertained with the help of one or both theories, the applicable system of law should be applied whenever possible. In this respect, the common law seems to prescribe that each 'issue' should be dealt with by its own proper law: in everyday practice the law under which a company is incorporated usually applies to all matters of formation, organization, dissolution, and winding up. In this respect, Chapter 10 of the 1987 Swiss Private International Law

---

[10] cf. ch 4 II 2, above.   [11] cf. ch 4 III 2, above.

Code, article 25 of the 1995 Italian Code on Private International Law, and section 3 of the Dutch 1998 CLC Act all clearly express that any catalogue of issues governed by the *lex societatis* is non-exhaustive. For more than one reason this is understandable: (i) submitting separate issues to several (alternative or cumulative) systems of law would disrupt the internal coherence;[12] (ii) furthermore, both recognition theories are more or less 'forechecked' already, in the sense that the permissive 'incorporation' theory allows company managers to choose the *lex societatis*, whereas the authorities in 'real seat' countries are no longer concerned as soon as they consider a company to have its 'real' seat abroad. In other words, the dispute is about the recognition principle, not about the scope of the applicable law.

What the 'incorporation' theory and 'real seat' theory have in common is that they may frustrate courts seeking to solve borderline cases. In this sense, it is remarkable that, for example, the topic of third-party protection related to company representation is often decided in accordance with an exemption commonly used to solve problems of natural persons lacking capacity: the application of the substantive-law oriented device of good faith prevails over the conflict of law rule applicable to matters of capacity or representation of the company. Moreover, this device is used in both civil and common law countries. The same can be said about other borderline issues: occasionally, the proper law of a contract or tort, or even the *locus regit actum* principle, overrides the proper law of the company. To conclude, worker co-determination, notably in Germany, is considered to be a matter of local mandatory law, rather than a matter subject to the classical Savignian conflict of law rules.

VII. CROSS-BORDER COMPANY MOBILITY: SEAT TRANSFERS

As stated above, the progressive stage of the Single Market now places a duty upon these member states to abstain from introducing disproportionate measures which would hinder companies planning to migrate from one EC member state to another. A distinction must be made between the transfer of a company's registered office and its real head office. Whereas the former type of transfer is highly problematic in both 'incorporation' and 'real seat' countries, the latter type only meets problems if one or both of the legal orders involved is a 'real seat' country. Several types of problem arise.

---

[12] cf. comments about the intermediary concepts of *Differenzierung* and *Überlagerung*, ch 2 II 1, above.

The expatriation of a company duly etablished under the law of a 'real seat' country, to begin with, might also result in the company's compulsory dissolution and winding up. Even if the country of re-establishment does not oppose the incoming transfer, such a transfer can still be frustrated by the fact that such a departure is prohibited by the substantive company law rules of that country.[13]

There is yet another problem. EC member states are reproached for impinging upon EC law by applying the hostile 'real seat' theory to companies duly established in other EC member states, whereas at the same time the more welcoming 'incorporation' theory is applied to companies from third countries on the basis of bilateral treaties. A growing chorus of critics is responding to this phenomenon in Germany. Both doctrinal[14] and legislative[15] attempts to overcome the lack of cross-border company mobility in Europe have all proved unsuccessful. This is understandable: versatile supranational instruments are needed to accommodate cross-border company transfers, whilst all vital interests (i.e. the continuing existence of the company, internal and external company interests, etc.) are safeguarded.

---

[13] cf. the instrument of *renvoi*, discussed in ch 4 III 1, above. However, Italian law is an exception to the rule, as the real seat is firmly applied to incoming companies, whereas Italian companies are free to leave their domestic country while retaining their identity: see above, ch 4 III.

[14] cf. suggestions to expand the functional scope of national substantive company law provisions on the transformation of one type of legal person into another.

[15] cf. what has been said about the mere *Programmsatz* (i.e. one-liner) character underlying art. 25(3) of the 1995 Italian Code on Private International Law, ch 4 III 3 above. A more sophisticated set of rules, which could also be a source of inspiration for the EC legislator, is that of the 1978 Swiss Private International Law Code: see ch 4 II 3, above.

Part 3

Future Outlooks: An Integrated Law Approach

Generally speaking, the amount of literature published in the legal orders here considered more or less reflects the struggle to balance all competing legitimate interests. As may be concluded from the state of art of EC law and private international law disciplines, it is not surprising that in every-day practice these interests often appear not to be in concert with each other. Rather than trying to find an all-embracing formula for the recognition problem from scratch, specialists from both disciplines should commit themselves to phasing out existing disparities between all areas of the law, step by step. This is why the time has come to integrate EC law with private international law.

6

The Treaty of Amsterdam: Synthesis of EC Law and Private International Law

I. EC LAW RECONSIDERED

1. INTRODUCTION

Put bluntly, there is no tangible freedom of establishment for legal persons under EC law as it now stands.[1] The ECJ even observed that article 52 of the EC Treaty (i.e. before the entry into force of the Treaty of Amsterdam) 'does not attempt to solve *any* of the problems that the co-existence of these two theories (the 'incorporation' theory and the 'real seat' theory) might create, but the Community has managed to live with this situation from the outset.'[2] A short reminder first:[3] for a considerable period of time, the drafters of the EC Treaty were not at all troubled by the constant 'trench war' between the 'incorporation' and the 'real seat' theorists: this is explained, first, by the fact that at the beginning of the EC era all

---

[1] See Case 81/87 *R v. HM Treasury and Commissioners of Inland Revenue, ex parte Daily Mail and General Trust PLC* [1988] ECR 5483, and the provisional conclusions drawn from this case (ch 2 IV 2, above).

[2] Richards (1991) 2. In the same sense Roth (1991) 647: since the ECJ seems to put up with the fact that the EC Treaty does not apply to the recognition of companies, even the mere *Einflußnahmne auf das Internationale Gesellschaftsrecht der Mitgliedstaaten* (ability to influence international company law of the member states) is relinquished as well. Ebke (1998) 209, ironically observes that the law of the member states concerning cross-border company relationships may safely be regarded as *'niederlassungsfreiheitresistent'* (i.e. resistant to the freedom of establishment).

[3] See the introductory lines of ch 4 I, above.

member states still adhered to the 'real seat' theory,[4] and secondly, because the accomplishment of a Single Market was then still a long way ahead. Now that the transitional period has expired, the problem of the status of 'foreign' companies, or more precisely: companies duly established in other EC member states, can no longer be ignored.[5] We must realize that the recognition problem has become even more urgent, now that the 'intense relationship between the company and the socio-economic sphere of the state of its central office is a good enough reason to exclude party autonomy (the 'incorporation' theory) and to opt for a mandatory connecting factor.'[6]

Whereas EC law has shown itself not to be capable (yet) of reconciling the co-existing recognition theories that originate from the discipline of private international law, the converse also applies: neither have private international law specialists managed to promote the free movement of legal persons in the EC, notably because the 'real seat' theory was predominantly inspired by notions of nationality, state sovereignty, and control policies[7] rather than by the attempt to accomplish a single market by abolishing national borders. Even more, it is only due to the absence of EC company law directives that national control policies flourish today as they do.[8]

It may be true that, from a retrospective view, articles 52 and 58 (explicitly or implicitly) neither imposed nor prohibited any of the existing recognition theories, but this does not mean that member states have full discretionary power to interpret the aforementioned provisions as they wish. It is not simply a matter of all or nothing. This leaves us with the question of how to define the precise margins of those provisions within the total framework of the EC Treaty after the entry into force of the Treaty of Amsterdam on 1 May 1999, and with an eye to future developments. To this end, the following matters are next considered: first, the legal situation after the entry into force of the Treaties of Maastricht and (notably)

---

[4] The Netherlands did not explicitly opt for the 'incorporation' theory until the law on the enforcement of the Hague Treaty of 1 June 1956 on the Mutual Recognition of the Legal Personality of Foreign Companies came into force (The Treaty itself never reached this status: ch 2 III 1 and ch 4 II 1, above. Other legal orders adhering to the 'incorporation' theory (e.g. the United Kingdom and the Republic of Ireland) did not join the EC until 1973.

[5] In the words of Knobbe-Keuk (1990) 332, we cannot simply ignore the *Daily Mail* judgment. The least we should do is try to interpret it in as *'gemeinschaftsverträglich'* a way as possible. Drury (1999) 360, on the other hand, observes that the merit of *Daily Mail* lies in the fact that it 'proved to be the catalyst for reform proposals'.

[6] Roth (1995) 41.

[7] cf. Sandrock (1989) 508; and, *inter alia* quoting Josephus Jitta with regard to the 'harmless' character of nationality, Vlas (1982) 30 and 38 et seq.

[8] Like no other part of private law, EC company law appeared to resist the tremendous harmonization efforts: Ebke (1998) 196 et seq. Behrens (1996) 833, even speaks of *'Krisensymptome in der Gesellschaftsrechtsangleichung* (a crisis in the company law harmonization process)'. Cf. I 2, below.

Amsterdam; secondly, some premises are formulated for the purpose of further investigation. These premises encompass a brief résumé of the operative margins of company law for national authorities under articles 43, 44, and 48, as well as 293 (previously articles 52, 54, 58 and 220) of the EC Treaty. Thirdly, functional and methodological disparities between EC law and private international law are explored. On the basis of these findings, it is considered whether a dialogue between the two areas of law would be of practicable benefit. Only then is it possible to shape legal instruments in order to further company cross-border mobility in the territory of the EC.

2. Premises for further investigation

The Treaty of Maastricht

Of course, the continuing process of EC law developments is not merely a matter of amending the literal text of primary or secondary EC law.[9] On the other hand, it is necessary to establish whether the Maastricht Treaty and its Amsterdam successor provide for substantial changes? Article B of the Maastricht Treaty[10] can be taken as a starting point for further exploration. According to this provision:

The Union shall set itself the following objectives: *to promote economic and social progress* which is balanced and sustainable, in particular through the creation of an *area without internal frontiers,* through the strengthening of economic and social cohesion and through the establishment of economic and monetary union, ultimately including a single currency in accordance with the provisions of this Treaty.[11]

Correspondingly, undertakings should be encouraged to transnationalize by extending their business activities to other member states.[12] This strategy is rooted in economic theories which emphasize the so-called comparative economic advantage: business undertakings are expected to maximize the allocation of their means of production. They will continuously weigh all relevant production factors against each other (e.g. capital, know-how, socio-economic infrastructure, taxation levels, consumer

---

[9] See again ch 2 IV 1, above. Notably Eyles (1990) 84, underscored that, although the wording of arts. 52 and 58 of the Rome Treaty had not been amended for about four decades, these provisions can only be properly interpreted against the background of a rapidly developing Single Market.

[10] Signed on 7 Feb. 1992, OJ 1992 C 191. A consolidated version of the EC Treaty is published in OJ 1992 C 224.

[11] Emphases added.

[12] cf. the Preamble to Directive 94/45 of 22 September 1994, concerning the European Works Council, OJ 1994 L 254, 64, quoted by Wouters (1996/97) 2.

markets, governmental investment policies, etc.).[13] Ultimately, all these factors will culminate in an accountable decision on where to concentrate business activities and where to generate benefits. A retrospective view shows that from the beginning of the EC era, attempts were made to bring article 52 into line with these theories.[14] Granting undertakings the freedom of establishment in order to enhance economic prosperity is therefore of crucial importance.[15] To realize this goal, both entry and exit barriers should be removed.[16] From this perspective, the interpretation of 'establishment' is influenced predominantly by *economic* inducements.

But this retrospective view also demonstrates a discrepancy between this ambitious, economically biased phraseology and the deficiency of legal instruments to accomplish this goal. Lip-service is paid to 'cross-border establishment, concentration and co-operation of companies',[17] while the elaboration of adequate legal devices is falling behind. At the beginning of the twenty-first century, it has to be admitted that, from a *legal* point of view, no substantial progress has been made. Most member states perceive national company and labour law institutions to be more important than the aforementioned (uncontested) economic interests resulting from the freedom of establishment for legal persons under articles 52 and 58 of the EC Treaty. As a result of this, the 'real seat' theory still stands firm today. Proof of this can even be found in secondary EC law sources: both article 12 of the European Economic Interest Group

---

[13] cf. ch 1 I above, on cross-border company mobility in general. Wouters (1996/97) 3, n 15, provides detailed information about the economic theory of notably D. Ricardo. Note that this perception of economizing benefits had been used in an earlier stage on a national level: notably small, non-industrialized countries attempted to attract foreign investors by welcoming foreign companies. This strategy was pursued by both the Netherlands (ch 4 II 1 above) and Switzerland, the latter being a non-EC country (ch 4 II 3 above). Italy took a slightly different position: although also favouring industrialization, the Italian authorities were not prepared to be entirely at the mercy of foreign investors. This resulted in a *sui generis* approach, described in ch 4 III 3, above.

[14] Wouters (1996/97) 3 (n. 16) et seq., *inter alia* quoting one of the founding fathers of the EC, Spaak in 1956: *'il est de l'intérêt commun que les industries qui exigent beaucoup de main-d'oeuvre, se développent principalement là où la main-d'oeuvre est abundante, celles qui reposent sur les matières premières pondereuses, à proximité des lieux de production ou de livraison de ces matières, celles qui comportent de lourds investissements, dans les pays où les capitaux sont plus abondants et les charges financières moins élévées. (. . .) La libre circulation progressivement établie pour ces facteurs de production tend en outre à faciliter cette égalisation, qui, loin d'être une condition préalable du fonctionnement du marché commun, en est au contraire une conséquence.'* Cf. ch 2 IV 2, above, on the synthesis between this theory and Sandrock's *Überlagerungstheorie*.

[15] Wouters (1996/97) 4, presenting the 'economic teleological' views of Troberg, Bleckmann, and others, and adding the common interest of spreading knowledge, rationalizing economic structures, enhancing competition, creating employment, accomplishing political integration, etc.

[16] This reminds us of the 'freedom of *departure*', requested by the *Daily Mail* company (see ch 2 IV 2, above).

[17] cf. the Preamble to Directive 94/45 of 22 September 1994, concerning the European Works Council, OJ 1994 L 254, 64, quoted by Wouters (1996/97) 2.

Regulation and article 5 of the draft proposal for a European Company 'carry at least the smell of the (real, SR) seat theory'.[18] In other words, 'the *siège réel* philosophy has crept into secondary Community law'.[19] National authorities showed no eagerness to give additional momentum to the freedom of establishment under Maastricht either.[20]

The Treaty of Amsterdam

The pillar change: Article 65 of the EC Treaty

Until this point the Maastricht Treaty has been focused on. However, its successor, the Treaty of Amsterdam,[21] contains no drastic changes with regard to company mobility. The new Title IV (articles 61 to 69, concerning the 'progressive establishment of an area of freedom'[22]) did not result in any explicit provision substantially affecting the free movement of *legal* persons. In the (near?) future, however, the so-called pillar change,[23] as a result of which the area of private international law is no longer the *exclusive* domain of the national member states, might provoke profound changes in the area of company law as well. Article 61(c) (previously article 73i(c)) of Title IV should be read in conjunction with article 65 (previously article 73 m). The latter provision[24] mentions 'measures in the field

---

[18] Roth (1991) 629 and (1995), p, 40. According to art. 12 of the EEIG Regulation, the registered office (which is decisive for the applicable national law) must be either the place of central administration of the group or the place of the central adminstration of its members. Art. 5 of the draft Regulation for the Societas Europea requires that the SE's registered office and the company's central adminstration coincide. Cf. Vlas (1999) 61 et seq. and III 2, below on the influence of the EEIG and SE legislation on the draft proposal for the transfer of a company's management and control centre.

[19] Roth (1991). Clearly opposing these feelings of disapointment, Großfeld/König (1992) 435: these writers express contentment with the *Daily Mail* judgment. Cf. for further details concerning the transfer of an EEIG's 'seat', III 2, below.

[20] A rather rigid position was taken by, for example: the **German** OLG Hamm 30 April 1997, *EuZW* 1998 31: the case was about a German GmbH, planning to transfer its management and control centre from Germany to Luxembourg. The German Court deemed this company to be (still) subject to compulslory dissolution and winding up under German law. No need was felt to reiterate preliminary proceedings under the Maastricht Treaty. Cf. ch 2 IV 2, above (comments on *Daily Mail*); ch 4 III 1, above (seat transfers under German law); and ch 6 II 2 below (comments to the Proposal for a 14th EC Company Law Directive). **Danish** authorities, refusing the registration of a branch of a company duly established in another member state, for the sole reason that the foreign company did not conduct any economic activities in the country of its formation. Cf. ECJ *Centros*, ch 2 IV 2, above.

[21] The Treaty of Amsterdam was signed on 2 October 1997. It entered into force on 1 May 1999. It amends the Treaty on the European Union and the three Community Treaties. For the consolidated text see Blackstone's *EC Legislation* 1998–9 (9th edn.), 1998 520 et seq. and the 'Editor's Note', explicitly referring to OJ C340, 10–11–1997, pp. 173–308.

[22] Langrish (1998) 7, who was quoting the unconsolidated text version (arts. 73i–q).

[23] *Säulenwechsel; troisième pilier; Derde Pijler.*

[24] cf. the total framework of the Treaty. Pursuant to art. 3(1), '(f)or the purposes set out in article 2, the activities of the Community shall include, as provided in this Treaty and in

of judicial co-operation in civil matters having cross-border implications', to be adopted only *'in so far as necessary for the proper functioning of the Internal Market.'*[25] According to article 65(a), these measures shall *inter alia* include, 'the system for cross-border service of judicial and extrajudicial documents', and 'the recognition and enforcement of decisions in civil and commercial cases'. Pursuant to article 65(b), these measures shall also include *'promoting the compatibility of the rules applicable in the member states concerning the conflict of laws and jurisdiction'*.[26] This provision is striking. It is highly intriguing to speculate about forthcoming interpretations,[27] as to the question whether either the subsidiarity principle or the principle of compatibility of national conflict of law provisions with EC law will prevail.[28] Kohler expresses uncertainty: the *'communautarisation de la coopération judiciaire, en matière civile, est, sur le plan institutionnel, hésitante et incomplète et, sur le plan matériel, de portée incertaine'*.[29] It is uncontestable that in the long run company law developments will be affected by this matter of competence. For the moment, however, we must concentrate on the *ius constituum*, rather than the *ius consituendum*.

An integrated approach to EC law and private international law

As set out above, the fundamental pillar change did not result in revolutionary changes in EC law on the recognition and status of foreign legal persons.[30] Admittedly, the objectives of the Amsterdam Treaty were 'rel-

---

accordance with the timetable set out therein: (. . .) (d) measures concerning the entry and movement of persons as provided for in Title IV.'

[25] Emphasis added.

[26] Emphasis added. Cf. Langrish (1998) 8; and Jayme (1997) 236.

[27] Pursuant to art. 68 (*ex* art. 73p), art. 234 (*ex* art. 177) of the Treaty applies equally to art. 65. For detail see Israel (2000) 81.

[28] cf. Jayme (1997) 236; and Sandrock (1999) 1345. According to Barents (1997) 129, art. 293 (*ex* art. 220) is thus given extra weight. From a retrospective view, Basedow (1997) 609, regrets the legal basis for not being *tragfähig* (capable of accomplishing the goals set earlier). Besides, he is sceptical about the newly created basis: he would have preferred the use of the already existing art. 95 (*ex* art. 100A), in the awareness of the fact that (i) majority decisions can still be taken by the Council, and (ii) European Parliament then has a say in the matter as well. The least we can say now is that the newly drafted provisions are enshrined in the Title 'free movement of persons': this means that a proper functioning of the Single Market could influence conflict of laws as regards the free movement of, for example, companies, workers, etc. His overall conclusion is that, although we can no longer maintain the cliché that conflict of laws with regard to family law is excluded from EC law, no real progress has been made.

[29] Kohler (1999) 8, *inter alia* pointing to the special position of the United Kingdom, Ireland, and Denmark (cf. art. 69 of the Treaty). Cf. Lagarde/von Hoffmann (1996).

[30] This explains why broad treatment of the Treaty of Amsterdam would fall outside the scope of this book. For a survey on the most important topics, I refer to e.g. Barents (1997); Labayle (1997) 105 et seq.; Basedow (1997) 609; Ehlermann (1998) 246 et seq.; Langrish (1998) 3 et seq.; Shaw (1998) 63 et seq.; and Kohler (1999) 4 et seq., for further information, and recent editions of texts on EC law.

atively modest'.[31] Neither did the ECJ *Centros* judgment[32]—which after all was decided on the brink of a new era—fundamentally disrupt the conflict of laws practice of the member states.[33] As a consequence, a neutral observer faces the paradoxical situation of a Treaty whose liberalism only seems impressive at first glance.[34] Critical observers wake up to the fact that answers to problems arising from international company law can no longer be obtained by simply exploring ECJ case-law and doctrinal comments on the EC Treaty. Although useful in the context of creating favourable investment conditions, ready-made answers cannot be expected from a law- and economics-oriented approach either. Matters of international company law have become far too complicated to be solved exclusively within the framework of either EC law or private international law. These areas of the law can no longer be disentangled.[35] The ultimate challenge is to find adequate answers to the problems set out in the first and second part of this book. Today more than ever, Community law and private international law specialists need to start a dialogue in order to bring EC law and conflict of laws into line with each other.

The EC Treaty: articles 43, 48, and 293

The ECJ cases of Daily Mail *and* Centros *reconsidered*

Subsequent to the ECJ *Daily Mail* judgment,[36] the legal landscape can be sketched as follows. (i) EC law does not now impose the 'incorporation' theory upon member states; (ii) neither is the 'real seat' theory prohibited under the EC Treaty; (iii) the status of foreign companies does not fall within the scope of the EC Treaty anyway and must be 'dealt with by future conventions or legislation'.[37] The Treaty in fact only grants certain

---

[31] Langrish (1998) 18, quoting the Reflection Group Report: 'The Heads of State or Government have identified the need to make institutional reforms as a central issue of the Conference in order to improve the efficiency, democracy and transparency of the Union. In that spirit, we have tried to identify the improvements needed to bring the Union up to date and to prepare it for the next enlargement. We consider that the Conference should focus on necessary changes, without embarking on a complete revision of the Treaty.'

[32] Case C–212/97, ECR 1999 I–1459, (1999) *CMLR* 551. See ch 2 IV 2, above.

[33] See ch 2 IV 2, above.

[34] Even more, today's tendency is that even in incorporation countries (cf. the Netherlands, and, from a third-country perspective, Switzerland: ch 4 II 1 and II 3, above) loud pleas to combat fraudulent behaviour by introducing restrictive national measures are also heard.

[35] cf. Kohler (1999) 4, who condemns the absence of coherence between EC law and private international law, despite the fact that EC specialists are increasingly occupied with either unification of conflict of law rules in general, or with flanking legislative measures (concerning e.g. detachment of employees, insurance and consumer contracts, etc.).

[36] For an analysis of ECJ *Daily Mail* and its consequences, see ch 2 IV 2, above.

[37] ECJ *Daily Mail*, cons. 23: ch 2 IV 2 above.

rights to *secondary* establishments.[38] Whilst attempts to reformulate the freedom of intra-community company mobility have not yet borne fruit, borderlines beyond which member states and EC authorities ought not operate should continue to be respected after the Amsterdam Treaty.[39]

Has the EC landscape undergone fundamental changes since the *Centros* judgment?[40] Various views were attributed to the ECJ. To a considerable extent, these views were based on speculative reasoning. Like the ECJ case of *Segers*, writers seem to be confused, as the facts underlying *Centros* were centred in two 'incorporation' countries, the United Kingdom and Denmark. On the other hand, *Daily Mail* demonstrated that obiter dicta,[41] rather than contributing to legal certainty, create uncertainty, simply because they are not suited to deal with a problem *'erschöpfend'* (in detail).[42] It is crucial for the proper functioning of the Single Market that neither foreign companies nor their secondary establishments are withheld the freedom of establishment. Quite another question is, of course, whether these primary or secondary establishments are submitted to restrictive legislative measures of EC member states, and, if so, to what extent these measures are allowed under the EC Treaty.

Articles 43 and 48 (previously articles 52 and 58): amount of freedom offered to companies from (non-) EC member states

It has been argued that subsequent to, or even perhaps due to, the *Daily Mail* judgment, the EC Treaty endows companies with a considerable amount of freedom. This is partially due to the wording of article 48 (previously article 58). This provision requires a company to have its registered office, central administration, *or* principal place of business within the territory of the Community (emphasis added). It has been indicated that in fact these notions were more or less borrowed from private international law:[43] the first two notions correspond with the 'incorporation' theory or the 'real seat' theory, and the third notion reflects the additional factor which is contained in article 25 of the 1995 Private International Law

[38] Ebke (1998) 208. As to the precise meaning of 'subsidiaries', 'branches', and 'agencies', see ch 2 IV 1 and 2, above.

[39] In the following, it depends on the context whether reference is made to 'articles 52, 58, 220', etc. (the former EC Treaty provisions), or to 'articles 43, 48, 293', etc. (consolidated text version after the entry into force of the Treaty of Amsterdam; cf. Blackstone's *EC Legislation* 1998–9 (9th edn.), 1998 520 et seq. and the 'Editor's Note', explicitly referring to OJ C340, 10–11–1997, pp. 173–308).

[40] For an analysis of *Centros* and its consequences, see ch 2 IV 2, above.

[41] cf. *Daily Mail*, cons. 23: '(i)t must therefore be held that the Treaty regards the differences in national legislation concerning the required connecting factor and the question whether—and if so how—the registered office or real head office of a company incorporated under national law may be transferred from one member state to another as problems which are not resolved by the rules concerning the right of establishment but must be dealt with by future legislation or conventions'.

[42] Ebke (1999) 661.   [43] See ch 2 I 1, above.

Code of Italy.[44] The issue, however, is what precisely is meant here by the word 'or'. The *Daily Mail* judgment is clear on the following issues: those who plan to establish a business undertaking in an EC member state are not permitted (i) simply to transfer a company's 'real seat' from one member state to another;[45] nor are they free (ii) to choose any (foreign) *lex societatis*. But it would be erroneous to conclude that the word 'or' should therefore be replaced by the word 'and'.[46] Instead, the word 'or' expresses nothing more than[47] that it is essentially for the member states—not for those in charge of the company—to decide which of the two recognition theories is applicable.[48] Apart from that, the word 'or' allegedly allows companies to have their registered office only (i.e. not their 'real seat') in the territory of an EC member state, for the sole purpose of becoming the beneficiary of the freedom of establishment. Not surprisingly, this generosity has met disapproval, because fraudulent behaviour would be promoted.[49] This problem is directly linked to the problem discussed earlier of 'natural' foreigners, who appear to be 'in control' of fraud committed by the company. At present, hardly any of the explored legal orders place decisive weight on the 'nationality' of a legal person as if it were a natural person, in order to ascertain the proper law of the company.[50] Neither is the 'control theory' generally accepted: except for situations of war, a company should not be deprived of its rights for the sole reason that the nationality of the (majority) of managers or shareholders appears to be 'foreign'. This feeling is commonly shared by European law, as well as private international law, specialists.[51] Today, it is considered to be of major concern that it is a common interest of a prospering market that foreign

[44] For analysis, see ch 4 III 3, above. The principal place of business will usually, but not in all situations, coincide with the management and control office.

[45] On the other hand one might as well say that *Daily Mail* 'doesn't *deny* that companies have a right (. . .) to *physically* transfer their central headquarters. A simple prohibition to move the central office away or to move it into the state would certainly infringe Article 52 juncto 58 EC', Roth (1995) 37.

[46] cf. Wouters (1996/97) 147, for further information.

[47] However, not in its severest consequences, as we will see below.

[48] Ebenroth/Eyles (1988) 13, underline that it only appears to make no difference, which of the factors mentioned links a company to a legal order.

[49] cf. ch 2 IV 2, above (on *Centros*). This fear had already been expressed at the dawn of the EC era (i.e. the mid-fifties): Wouters (1996/97) 149, *inter alia* quoting Loussouarn and Everling.

[50] In this respect, France takes an isolated position: see ch 4 III 2, above.

[51] cf. however, the former joint initiative of Italy and France, to provide art. 58 with an additional subs. by virtue of which freedom of establishment could be refused to companies *'soumises à une influence prépondérante exercée par des ressortissants d'un Etat tiers ou des capitaux étrangers à la Communauté* (companies subject to either the predominant influence of persons domiciled in a non-EC state or foreign capital suppliers)'. Ultimately, however, this concept was rejected: Wouters (1996/97) 127.

investors should not be excluded from access to that market.[52] The disadvantages of sweeping statements banning all investors from third countries would outweigh the benefit of saving the market from malefactors. However, the general concern put forward in France, namely that companies from third countries would thus be given the opportunity to enter the European market too easily (cf. the above mentioned 'post box companies', i.e. companies having only their registered office in EC territory) was removed by including in article 52 of the EC Treaty an extra requirement, namely that agencies, branches, and subsidiaries be 'established in the territory of any member state'. According to the General Programme, these agencies, branches, and subsidiaries may only be established in the territory of an EC member state by companies or firms formed in accordance with the law of a member state (including overseas territories) and having their registered office, central administration, or principal place of business within the territory of the EC or an overseas territory of a member state. If, on the contrary, they only have their registered office on EC territory (including overseas territories), their activities should have genuine and continuous ties with the economy of a member state (including their overseas territories).[53] On top of this, companies which only have their registered office in the territory of an EC member state are *de facto* excluded from primary establishment, the possibility of transfers of the registered office being tolerated by both 'incorporation' and 'real seat' theory only in exceptional circumstances.[54]

Article 293

In addition to the above concerns, it is highly uncertain how far article 293 (previously article 220) of the EC Treaty can still serve as a feasible instrument to regulate the company recognition problem. With regard to the former provision of article 220, it has been observed that it

requires the classic negotiation of a convention, with all the Member States signing and subsequently ratifying the instrument. On the accession of new Member States it is difficult to include such conventions in the 'acquis communautaire': renegotiation may be required. Further, it is difficult to secure the position of the European Court of Justice in respect of interpretation and application of the convention as

---

[52] Besides, it would be a hazardous task to formulate criteria and provide control mechanisms for situations in everyday practice, cf. comments above (ch 4 III 2) on French law on capital fluctuations, anonymity of holders of bearer shares, etc.

[53] These ties, however, may not be made dependent on the nationality of managers, organs, or capital suppliers. For detailed information: Wouters (1996/97) 150 et seq.

[54] cf. the expatriation of NV Indonesische Aardoliemaatschappij from the Netherlands to the Republic of Indonesia, ch 4 II 1: both the country of departure and the country of new residence should authorize this type of transfer by *ad hoc* legislation. Cf. however art. 4 of the Dutch 1998 CLC Act, ch 4 2 1, above.

part of Community law. For all these reasons attempts to rely on this Article have not borne fruit.[55]

Besides, attempts to build bridges in this area under the pre-Amsterdam era were based on article 54 of the EC Treaty, rather than on article 220, as will be seen.[56]

'Recognition' *versus* the harmonization programme

Primary and secondary EC Law: the remaining competence of national authorities

Although no hard and fast rules can be deduced from primary or secondary Community law concerning the recognition of foreign companies, it would be incorrect to conclude that EC law does not impose any restrictions upon the member states. Prior to the *Daily Mail* judgment, efforts had already been made to define the borderline with regard to discretionary margins under the EC Treaty, beyond which authorities of the member states ought not operate. For example, the Dutch *Raad van State* (State Council), considering the then draft legislation in the Netherlands concerning the abuse of *formeel buitenlandse rechtspersonen* (pro-forma foreign companies)[57] was inspired by the philosophy expressed in 1981 by the Dutch scholar Timmermans: taking the desirability to harmonize company law as a point of departure, the co-ordination of national legislation no longer allows for an unrestricted application of national company law.[58] Instead, national company law is expected to be gradually substituted by harmonized law until ultimately this dynamic process culminates in the acceptance of the 'incorporation' theory throughout Europe. However, a dissenting view was taken by Wouters, among others:[59] although the freedom of establishment of companies is of paramount concern under EC law, it may not be concluded from the progressive stage of harmonization measures that the *de iure* adoption of the 'incorporation' theory is near. He argues that such a dynamic approach would hardly be conceivable. This is demonstrated by the fact that for some issues (e.g. capital requirements: 2nd EC Company Law Directive; account and auditing: 4th and 7th EC Company Law Directives) the law of the 'incorporation' country would apply, while the law of the 'real seat' country would remain applicable to non-harmonized matters. This method would give

---

[55] Richards (1991) 5. Cf. the 1968 EC Draft Treaty on the Mutual Recognition of Companies (ch 2 IV 1, above) that ended up in complete failure. Cf. also Clarke (1991) 161 et seq.

[56] Ch 6 III 2, below.

[57] More detail in ch 4 II 1, above. The compatibility of this legislative project with EC law is discussed in II 1, below.

[58] Diephuis/Timmermans (1981) 49.

[59] cf. the contribution of Wilmowsky (1992), and II 1, below.

rise to yet further complications, bearing in mind that (i) the 4th EC Company Law Directive offers options, rather than hard and fast rules; and (ii) the (non) exhaustive character of EC Company Law Directives is by no means clarified yet.[60] In this respect, the suggestion made by Timmermans was criticized for being based on the false premise that article 58 (now article 48) of the EC Treaty inflicts the 'incorporation' theory upon member states.[61]

EC company law harmonization programme: inventory

It is necessary to define the reach of the harmonization programme established on the basis of article 44(2)(g) (previously article 54(3)(g)). To that end, existing draft legislative measures are summed up briefly. The following Directives have become law:[62]

—First Directive on co-ordination of company law on disclosure, validity of obligations entered into by a company, and nullity of public and private limited companies;[63]
—Second Directive on co-ordination of company law on capital of companies;[64]
—Directive 92/101 amending the Second Directive on company law;[65]
—Third Directive on the co-ordination of company law on mergers of public limited liability companies;[66]
—Sixth Directive on the co-ordination of company law on the division of public limited liability companies;[67]
—Fourth Directive on the co-ordination of company law on the annual accounts of certain types of companies;[68]
—Seventh Directive on the co-ordination of company law on consolidated accounts;[69]
—Two Directives of 8 November 1990 amending the 4th and 7th Directive on consolidated accounts as concerns the exemptions for small and

---

[60] Wouters (1996/97) 615. With regard to the character of EC company law directives (exhaustive or minimum level of protection, still leaving discretionary powers to member states?), cf. ECJ C–83/91 (*Meilicke*) and C–42/95 (*Siemens*).

[61] Wouters (1996/97). Note that 2 preliminary questions were addressed to the ECJ in 1999 and 2000: cf. ch 4 II 1 and ch 4 III 1, above.

[62] At October 2000. For a more detailed overview of the current progressive stage which EC company law harmonization has reached, see the literature *a quo*: Wiesner (1998) 619 et seq.; Hopt (1998) and (1999); Boucourechliev (1999) 1 et seq.; and Edwards (1999). For an outlook concerning cross-border company law in the 21st century: Lutter (2000).

[63] 9 March 1968 (68/151/EEC), OJ 1968 L 65/8.

[64] 13 December 1976 (77/91 EEC), OJ 1977 L 26/1.

[65] 23 November 1992 (amending Directive 77/91/EEC), OJ 1992 L 347/64.

[66] 9 October 1978 (78/855/EEC), OJ 1978 L 259/36.

[67] 17 December 1982 (82/891/EEC), OJ 1982 L 378/47.

[68] 25 July 1978 (78/660/EEC), OJ 1978 L 222/11.

[69] 13 June 1983 (83/349/EEC), OJ 1983 L 193/1.

medium-sized companies and the publication of accounts in ECUs and as regards the scope of those Directives;[70]
—Eleventh Council Directive on the co-ordination of company law concerning disclosure requirements in respect of branches opened in a Member State by certain types of company governed by the law of another State;[71]
—Twelfth Council Directive on the co-ordination of company law on single-member private limited liability companies;[72]
—EC Regulation on the European Economic Interest Grouping (EEIG);[73]
—Directive on the establishment of a European Works Council;[74]
—Recommendation on the promotion of participation by employed persons in profits and enterprise results;[75]
—Directive on the information to be published in the case of a major holding in a listed company;[76]
—Directive co-ordinating regulations on insider dealing.[77]

The following measures have been proposed:[78]

—Proposal for a Fifth Directive concerning the structure and functioning of organs of public limited companies;[79]
—Proposal for a Tenth Directive concerning cross-border mergers of public limited companies;[80]
—Amended Proposal for a Thirteenth Directive on the co-ordination of company law concerning take-over bids;[81]

[70] 8 November 1990 (90/604/EEC), OJ 1990 L 317/57 and 8 November 1990 (90/605/EEC), OJ 190 L 7/60.
[71] 21 December 1989 (89/666/EEC), OJ 1989 L 395/36.
[72] 21 December 1989 (89/667/EEC), OJ 1989 L 395/40.
[73] 25 July 1985 (2137/885/EEC), OJ 1985 L 199/1.
[74] 22 September 1994 (94/45/EC), OJ 1994 L 254/64.
[75] 27 July 1992 (92/443/EEC), OJ 1992 L 245/53.
[76] 12 December 1988 (88/627/EEC), OJ 1988 L 348/62.
[77] 13 November 1989 (89/592/EEC), OJ 1989 L 334/30.
[78] cf. Hopt (1999) 577, elaborating ideas concerning European company law with an eye on company groups and the Proposal for a Ninth Directive, which after several reanimation attempts has finally been abandoned; and Edwards (1999), ch XIX (overview of miscellaneous draft legislation).
[79] The first initiatives to harmonize this subject-matter date back to 13 December 1972, OJ 1972 C 131 (incl. suppl. 10/72), whereafter several attempts were made to revive this controversial project, cf. the amended proposal of 9 September 1983, OJ 1983 C 240 (incl. suppl. 6/83). In December 1996 the Commission initiated further inquiries (questionnaires were sent to approximately 100 business, academic, and governmental 'representatives') on the basis of which an analysis was made by the Commission in December 1997. A follow-up paper, containing conclusions, was published in April 1998. For recent information: Wiesner (1998) 620; Boucourechliev (1999) 2; and Edwards (1999) 387 et seq.
[80] Submitted by the Commission to the Council on 14 January 1985, COM (84) 727 final, OJ 1985 C 23 11. For descriptions of the current position: Boucourechliev (1999) 5; and Edwards (1999) 391 et seq.
[81] Submitted by the Commission to the Council on 10 November 1997, COM (97), 565 final. Cf. Edwards (1999) 393 et seq.

—Proposal for a Fourteenth Directive on the transfer of the registered office or the *de facto* head office of a company from one member state to another.[82]

Company law harmonization programme: scepticism

The European company law harmonization programme is not considered by all to be an overwhelming success. To some extent, this can be explained by the fact that at the beginning of the harmonization era decisions had to be taken on the basis of unanimity.[83] Also, it is not always clear which fundamental premises, if any, can be deduced from the provisions of articles 43, 44, and 48 of the Treaty (old articles 52, 54, and 58) and the EC company law harmonization programme.[84] Some writers take a more daring position, asking what the use of company law harmonization is, anyway. Several rhetorical questions were raised: should we not take note of the fact that in the USA over fifty company 'types' compete with each other freely? Should the EC legislator perhaps focus its attention only on corrective measures (e.g. protection of weaker parties or capital protection)? Does it make sense to harmonize the company law of so many countries (including the new member states)? What about the subsidiarity principle of article 5 (previously article 3b) of the Treaty, the alleged elusiveness of so many projects that are undertaken by the Commission, the risk of 'petrification' as a result of overstressing the need for company law harmonization, etc.? Why not try an alternative route instead, for example, by shaping *Modellgesetze* such as the American Model Business Corporation Act, or the Uniform Partnership?[85] Why not acknowledge the importance of SMEs (small and medium-sized enterprises) by introducing a 'private european company' as a *sui generis* enterprise form?[86]

No positive momentum was given to expectations, whether 'hopeful or fearful',[87] by the *Daily Mail* judgment: as long as the recognition of com-

---

[82] Doc. XV/6002/97-EN of 20 April 1997. Cf. III 2, below.

[83] cf. Boucourechliev (1999) 1, as regards the former procedures.

[84] ibid., 2 and 4: harmonization *a minimo,* or (cf. the proposals for a 5th and 9th Directive) harmonization in all details? In this respect, she speaks off the fear that perhaps the subsidiarity principle (cf. art. 3b of the Maastricht Treaty) has been violated.

[85] For a kaleidoscope view, cf. Ebke (1998) 197 et seq. (with reference to many authors on both sides of the Atlantic Ocean) and 202 n 35, concerning the 'Europeanization' of company law. Ebke (2000) 204 et seq. advocates the establishment of a European Law Institute, to concentrate on the achievement of models for a genuine European company, rather than focusing on a mix of EC member states' national laws.

[86] cf. the assessments made in ch 1 II, above. Due to the contractually biased *intuitu personae* character of these company types, however, shaping a *sui generis* company form might be an even more complicated task: Boucourechliev (1999) 6.

[87] Wilmowsky (1992) 536. Cf. comments about recent attempts to reanimate the draft proposal for a *Societas Europea* on the basis of the EC Directive concerning the European Workers Council 94/45. Further: Ebke (1998) 197, and ch 2 I IV, above. Hopeful words were, however, uttered by those in charge of a special issue (1–2) of the German *ZGR* 1999, entirely devoted

panies from other EC member states is not covered by EC company law directives, host states seem to be free to apply their substantive company law to any company planning to settle on their territory, even though they are incorporated in another member state. Nevertheless, an incomplete EC company law harmonization programme may directly influence both private international law rules of the member states[88] and further attempts to facilitate cross-border company mobility.[89]

II. EC LAW *VERSUS* PRIVATE INTERNATIONAL LAW: A DIALOGUE[90]

1. FUNCTIONAL DISPARITIES

EC law and private international law: different points of departure

A fruitful dialogue between EC law and private international law presupposes that the functional disparities between both disciplines are brought to the surface. The search for conclusive answers to questions concerning the recognition of foreign companies and, subsequently, their status under the law of the host state is seriously hampered by the fact that EC law and private international law, although they represent fundamentally different worlds, merge into each other.

Unlike EC law, conflict of law rules, provided that they are not harmonized by EC Treaties,[91] or international conventions, to a certain extent,[92] still belong to the domain of national legislators and courts. EC law and conflict of laws also serve intrinsically different goals: whereas the active role of conflict of laws is finished once the proper law of the company is ascertained, EC law perpetually and increasingly influences the substantive (company) law of the member states. It is incontestable that, here, the classical Savignian concept of simply[93] trying to fill in the open-ended

to the Proposal for a Fourteenth Directive on the Transfer of the Registered Office or the *De Facto* Head Office of a Company from One Member State to Another: see III 2, below.

[88] As will be seen—cf. the final considerations of II 1, below—it is striking that, of all legal orders, those that adhere to the European-law oriented 'incorporation' theory, in particular, will run the risk of being reprimanded for having used the instrument of fraud too hastily. Evidence can be found in the *Centros* judgment (see ch 2 IV 2, above). See also II 1, below.

[89] cf. III 2, below, on proposals to regulate cross-border company seat transfers.

[90] The title of this section was inspired by Jayme/Kohler (1995) 343: 'Europäisches Kollisionsrecht 1995. Der Dialog der Quellen'.

[91] cf. comments on the 'third pillar' in the foregoing section.

[92] Not exclusively, however: see comments on art. 65 of the Treaty, I 2, above.

[93] Of course, the multiple tasks of modern private international law specialists are far from easy; conflict rules today hardly ever mirror the old, single goal of ascertaining the system of law to which the legal relationship—geographically speaking—is deemed to be most closely connected. From the early 1970s, social engineering has increasingly influenced private international law thinking.

formula of the 'closest relationship' and the methodology of supranational legal thinking are beyond compare. A practice-orientated reformulation of these theoretical contemplations leads to the following observations. The 'closest connection' which is required under an objective proper law test, and the 'genuine and continuous ties with the economy of a member state (including overseas territories)'[94] within the EC market for EC law purposes, are far from interchangeable concepts. Neither can one properly speak of the 'nationality' of legal persons as if they were human beings. Likewise, the xenophobic notion of foreigners 'controlling' the company has become obsolete.[95] Under EC law, 'nationality' no longer serves the single goal of finding the *lex societatis*; rather, it functions as an instrument to attribute specific rights (notably: the freedom of establishment) to 'EC subjects'. Once companies are regarded as 'community' entities of co-operation, they all share the same basic rights (i.e. access to the single market and rights to conduct economic activities thereon[96]). It has become totally redundant to ask which is the 'original' nationality of these EC subjects.[97]

EC law and private international law: coherence

Although EC law and conflict of laws essentially represent two different worlds, they cannot be isolated from each other. Because article 48 (previously article 58) of the EC Treaty is 'conflictually biased',[98] these worlds organically merge into each other. A satisfactory co-existence needs to be found somehow. However, defining parameters for such an interdisciplinary approach appears to be complicated. While restricting the search for such parameters to the domain of cross-border company relationships, the objective observer will find parallels between private international law-oriented notions such as 'freedom of choice', or 'closest relationship' on one hand, and the EC-law based concept of the 'four freedoms' enshrined in article 43 (previously article 52) of the Treaty on the other.[99] Inasmuch as conflict of law rules have to comply with EC law, it has been observed[100] that the ECJ case of *Dassonville*[101] should be regarded as a touchstone for further debate. In a nutshell, *Dassonville* was about intolerable quantitive restrictions and measures, covering all trading rules

---

[94] cf. I 2, above, and problems related *inter alia* to the freedom of establishment on EC territory of 'agencies, branches and subsidiaries' of companies from third countries.

[95] ibid., and ch 4 III 2, above, on the French concept of the *nationalité des personnes morales*.

[96] Once again, it is important to recall ECJ *Centros*: see ch 2 IV 2, above.

[97] Wouters (1996/97) 126.

[98] cf. Roth (1991) 631: '*Art. 58 (. . .) ist als Norm mit kollisionsrechtlichem Gehalt gedeutet worden*'; also ch 2 IV, above.

[99] Whereas the 'real seat' theory is an example of the objective proper law test, the 'incorporation' theory pays homage to the principle of party autonomy: ch 2 I 3 and 4, above.

[100] Wilmowsky (1998) 3 et seq.

[101] Case 8/74, *Procureur du Roi v Dassonville* [1974] ECR 837.

enacted by member states which are 'capable of hindering, directly or indirectly, actually or potentially, intra-Community trade'. This train of thought is applicable, because the conflict of law provisions enacted by member states must also be considered capable of hindering intra-Community trade. In this respect, it has been suggested that party autonomy (i.e. the 'incorporation' theory?) best meets the interests of a Single Market, and therefore should prevail over an objective proper law test (i.e. the 'real seat' theory?), which is believed to be more likely to result in a 'hindrance'.[102] It has to be acknowledged, however, that the *Dassonville* principle, attractive as it may seem at first sight, is not a suitable instrument for regulating cross-border company relationships in detail. What can be learnt, then, from the *Dassonville* rule for private international law developments concerning the recognition of foreign companies? Perhaps its importance lies in the Court's determination that an objective proper law test to ascertain the *lex societatis* will 'hinder' legal certainty more than a subjective test would.[103] It should not be overlooked, however, that it is easier to apply the principle of party autonomy to, for example, international contracts than to companies, the latter category being said to have a 'multi-party' character, involving multiple (company law, tax law, social security law, etc.) interests.[104] This explains why, even acknowledging the functional disparities that exist between the EC law and private international law disciplines, it is wishful thinking to assume that the war between the 'real seat' and the 'incorporation' theorists is likely to end all by itself as a result of steadily increasing party autonomy.

European private international law: the status quo

As regards the constant conflict between the 'real seat' and 'incorporation' theorists, neither EC law nor private international law specialists have ever been able to create a breakthrough. National conflict of law concepts supporting the 'real seat' doctrine appeared to be resistant to various attempts made to offer companies from other EC member states a wider amount of freedom of establishment. This is both paradoxical and distressing if one takes into consideration that other conflict of law rules contained in EC directives were even simultaneously 'implemented' in European Economic Area countries.[105] However, these ambitions towards the outside world (i.e. non-EU countries), even in the area of conflict of

---

[102] ibid.

[103] cf. the fundamental flaws of the 'real seat' theory, set out in ch 2 I 3, above.

[104] cf. earlier observations in chapter 1 and ch 2 IV 6, above.

[105] For an impression: Lagarde/von Hoffmann (1996); a birdseye view in Jayme/Kohler (1995) 344 et seq., mentioning EC directives in the fields of *inter alia* consumer protection, time-sharing, and the protection of cultural property. Third countries often opt to 'implement' EC legislation in the expectation of joining the European Union in the near future.

laws, cannot conceal that the furtherance of one of the fundamental freedoms under the Treaty seems still to be in a dark alley. Notwithstanding the functional disparities that still exist between the two areas of law, a (perhaps intermediate) *modus vivendi* must be elaborated at the crossroads of EC law and private international law. Formulating answers, if this is possible, presupposes that the two legal areas are brought into line with each other.[106] To that end, it is necessary to start with an analysis of the repercussions of EC law (particularly in respect of the freedom of establishment) on the private international law of the EC member states. A closely related matter is the phenomenon of private international law, being frustrated in its application by a (too) narrow interpretation, or even abuse of EC law for no purpose other than to persevere with the application of the 'real seat' theory and all its consequences.

The impact of EC law on private international law methods

Freedom of establishment: a minimum standard

As regards the influence of EC law, in particular with regard to freedom of establishment, on the private international law of the EC member states, it is necessary to recall a few essential ECJ decisions. It follows from the *Daily Mail* judgment that the member states are not entirely free to do as they wish. Indeed, the Court stressed that 'it should be borne in mind that, unlike natural persons, companies are creatures of the law and, *in the present state of Community law*, creatures of *national* law. They exist only by virtue of the varying national legislation which determines their incorporation and functioning' (cons. 19).[107] Here, the Court concluded that both the differences in national legislation concerning the required determining factor (registered office or centre of management and control) and the question which of these factors can be transferred, and if so how, are problems which are not resolved by Community law, and they therefore need to be dealt with by future legislation or conventions (cons. 23). In the meantime there is, however, the 'underestimated quality'[108] of the Court's observation that the Treaty not only imposes obligations on the host state, but 'also prohibits the Member State of origin from hindering the establishment in another state of one of its nationals or of a company incorporated under its legislation which comes within the definition contained in article 58' (now article 48) of the EC Treaty. As the Commission convincingly observed, the rights guaranteed by articles 52 et seq. (now article 43) would be rendered meaningless if the member state of origin could pro-

---

[106] cf. the provisional conclusions drawn in ch. 3, above.
[107] Emphasis added. See ch 2 IV 2, above, for details.
[108] Wouters (1995) 127.

hibit undertakings from leaving in order to establish themselves in another Member State' (cons. 16).[109]

Convergence between conflict rules and EC law

This minimum standard should be taken as a starting point for further debate as to whether and how Community law approaches legal persons which operate across borders. Recently, Wouters has explored the impact of EC law on the private international law of the member states.[110] He indicates that national conflict of law rules should be interpreted as far as possible in conformity with EC law. Although the *Daily Mail* judgment may not have put an end to the ancient controversy between the recognition theories, this still does not justify the conclusion that member states have full discretion to model their conflict rules as they wish. On the contrary, it has been argued that now more than ever they have a duty to bring national law into compliance with EC law.[111] For example, it would be a violation of the Treaty to withhold recognition from a company duly established in another EC member state for the sole reason that the legal form of the foreign company is not recognized in the law of the host country.[112] Likewise, unrestricted use of the instrument of *ordre public* could amount to an infringement of article 10 (previously article 5) of the EC Treaty.[113] Attempts were made to bridge gaps between EC law and private international law, in that article 10 of the EC Treaty adds an extra

[109] According to Wouters (1995) 127, this is in line with the Court's interpretation of Treaty provisions on free movement of persons and services, as member states are clearly prohibited from impeding the free movements of their own nationals, e.g. by not recognizing professional qualifications acquired in another member state, or by restricting the use of an academic title obtained in another member state, cf. Case 19/92 *Krause v Land Baden-Württemberg* (1993) ECR I–1663.

[110] Wouters (1996/97) 615 et seq.

[111] ibid. 616, *inter alia* quoting K. Zweigert, who had already emphasized in 1966 that '*sich allenfalls aus dem allgemeinen Grundsatz in Artikel 5 EWG-Vertrag eine Pflicht der Richter im EWG-Raum herleiten (läßt), von der ordre public-Klausel mit der Zurückhaltung Gebrauch zu machen, welche die Verbundenheit der Mitgliedstaaten in einem Gemeinsamen Markt nahelegt. Das bedeutet eine "Färbung" des ordre public im Sinne angespannter Respekts vor ausländischen Normierungen (. . .) in den Bereichen des Handelsrechts, Wirtschaftsrechts (. . .), soweit Rechtsnormen eines anderen Mitgliedstaates aus diesen Bereichen über das Kollisionsrechts anzuwenden sind.*'

[112] See Wouters, 618 et seq. on cf. the following cases: Brussels Commercial Court denies recognition of German sole-member GmbH for the reason that such recognition would be contrary to the *ordre public* in private international law, Kh. Brussels 4 Feb. 1938, JT 1939, p. 173. Neither can recognition be refused on the ground of *ordre public* because the foreign company does not comply with the minimum capital standard of the host country, cf. OLG Hamburg, 21 January 1987, *RIW* 1988, p. 816: company incorporated in England, having its management and control office in Switzerland; plaintiff before a German Court. Non-recognition for reasons of *ordre public* as contained in art. 30 EGBGB rejected (Cf. comments above on the narrow and broad concepts of 'recognition', ch 2 I 2).

[113] cf. Advocate-General Reischl in the *Koestler* case, 24 October 1978, Case 15/78 [1978] ECR, 1971.

dimension to the traditional (obsolete?) Savignian concept of private international law.[114]

With an eye to the supremacy of EC law, some even insist on a fundamental revision of private international law methodology.[115] It is then highly ironic that, of all the legal orders, those that adhere to the European law-oriented 'incorporation' theory will run the highest risk of being reprimanded for having used the instrument of fraud too hastily.[116] Notably the Dutch *Wet op de formeel buitenlandse vennootschappen* (1998 Pro-Forma Foreign Companies Act)[117] was subject to criticism: restrictions on the 'incorporation' theory envisaged by sections 3, 4, and 5 of the Act are reproached for being contrary to EC law for more than one reason.[118] To begin with, section 3 obliges pro-forma foreign companies to publish additional information on company documents and instruments. However, to a certain extent, this duty is covered already by the first and second EC Company Law Directives.[119] Furthermore, it could be problematic to

[114] Roth (1995) 38, advocates a general obligation to promote the effectiveness of the freedoms in the sense that national authorities should change their legal infrastructures. Cf. Steindorff (1981) 426 et seq.; Samtleben (1981) 245; Fletcher (1982) 50. The latter introduces the idea that member states should critically review their conflict of law provisions and, if necessary, revise them as to maximize the extent to which conflict rules conform with the principal objectives of the Community.

[115] E. Brödermann (1992) 91.

[116] cf. from German perspective, Sonnenberger/Großerichter (1999) 727 ('*Der liberale Gesetzgeber wird bestraft, der reglementierenden dagegen belohnt*'), and Wilmowsky (1992) 535: as a consequence of the fact that substantive company law goals differ from country to country, '*ein Übergang zur Gründungstheorie, angereichert um Regeln für pseudo-fremde Gesellschaften, in der EG dramatischer Konflikte aufwerfen würde* (a move to the 'incorporation' theory, supplied with rules specially written for pseudo-foreign companies, would cause even more dramatic conflicts').

[117] See ch 4 II 1, above.

[118] The Dutch initiative to supress the abuse of pro-forma foreign companies turned out to be necessary *inter alia* because both the courts and Dutch private international law doctrine deny the concept of *fraude à la loi* (see ch 4 II 1, above and the following considerations). According to the law of another 'incorporation' country, Switzerland, doctrine considers it highly questionable whether, pursuant to the 1989 General Code on Private International Law, this instrument can still be used to fight abuse by legal persons (notably the Liechtenstein *Anstalt*) that are only 'fictitiously' foreign: ch 4 II 3, above. But of course, the Swiss authorities are not troubled by EC law requirements.

[119] For detail see ch 4 II 1, above. Wouters (1996/97) 625, asserts that if such a 'pseudo-foreign' company was formed in another EC member state, the legislative rules complied with in that state will have to be into taken account by the Dutch authorities. In his view, this is a direct consequence of *inter alia* ECJ *Vlassopoulou* C 340/89, ECR [1991], I–2357. Although this case represents the free movement of *natural* persons under art. 52 (now art. 43) of the EC Treaty, it shows a certain impact on *legal* persons as well, in that it prohibits member states from creating barriers by ignoring qualifications and experience (e.g. certificates, degrees etc.) acquired in another member state. (The *Vlassopoulou* case was named after Irene Vlassopoulou, a barrister in Athens, Greece. She applied for admission to the bar of Baden-Württemberg, Germany, but was refused by the Justice Department there, even though she had earned her doctorate in Germany, for the reason that she first had to comply with the requirements under German law, and pass a German law degree (*Staatsexam*). The Court *inter alia* observed that, although as yet there is no harmonized law in this respect, certificates, degrees, etc. earned in other member states must be taken into account.

apply Dutch legislation on capital requirements analogously to these pro-
forma foreign companies if these companies are established in other EC
countries.[120] Finally, the rules on accounts and auditing contained in
Dutch legislation would be contrary to the Eleventh EC Company Law
Directive.[121]

Abuse of the EC law vacuum

In spite of all efforts to integrate the two areas of law involved, the *Daily
Mail* judgment could also have a boomerang effect: both European law
and private international law specialists regret that the free movement of
companies can be frustrated by a (too) narrow interpretation, or even
abuse, of EC law for no other purpose than to save the sacrosanct belief in
domestic company law institutions. Although it may be true that, subsequent to the *Daily Mail* judgment, a European law 'vacuum' needs to be
filled,[122] this is still no justification for applying the 'real seat' theory in its
severest aspect. The mere existence of a company that originates from the
law of another EC member state as an 'entity' (i.e. recognition in a narrow
sense[123]), its legal capacity, its *ius standi in iudicio*, etc. may by no means be
denied on the sole basis that the European Court of Justice submitted the
'right of establishment (for companies) to (. . .) future legislation or
conventions'.[124] Recently, some German writers[125] have raised their
voices aginst the 'extremely impeding'[126] measures towards foreign

---

[120] Wouters (1996/97) mentions the fact that, for example, Belgium and France already
apply the capital protection rules contained in the Second Company Law Directive voluntarily to *private* limited companies. I would say that it is even more problematic to apply the
Dutch legislation referred to, to companies from EC countries that have *not* opted for an analogous application of Directive to their equivalent form of private limited companies.

[121] ibid. 625 and, in more detail, 498. This view is contested by Vlas (2000) 340, who
observes that pursuant to arts. 4(5) and 5(3), art. 4 of the Dutch 1998 PFFC Act does not apply
to a company subject to the law of another EC member state or a state party to the Agreement
on the European Economic Area of 2 May 1992, to which the Second, Fourth, and Seventh
Company Law Directives also apply.

[122] cf. Roth (1991) 631; Rammeloo (1995) 50; and Drury (1999) 354.

[123] cf. ch 2 I 2 and IV 2, above (on ECJ *Centros*).

[124] Cons. 23 of the *Daily Mail* Judgment.

[125] Roth (1995) 29: 'the number of German scholars who side with the "incorporation" theory has grown with the years'. Cf. further e.g. Knobbe-Keuk (1990) 327; and Eyles (1990) 314.
Although arguing forcibly, they still must be regarded as a minority. Cf. 'new developments',
ch 4 III 1 above. Remarkably, French writers hardly participate in this intensive debate.

[126] cf. the translated qualification (*'uiterst belemmerend'*) expressed by Wouters (1996/97)
622. Non-recognition forms a 'highly efficacious' hindrance to companies entering the EC
Market: ibid. 623. This argument concurs with the view expressed by e.g. Ebke (1998) 208: in
so far as they are permitted under the EC Treaty, measures taken by the member state authorities should at least be proportional. For a more general perspective of the relationship
between German and EC company law: Blaurock (1998) 460 et seq.

companies under German law, as a consequence of which hardly any 'freedom' of establishment for these companies remains.

Opinions vary on whether such an approach is discriminatory under the EC Treaty. It is commonly accepted that a distinction must be drawn between recognition as such, and the more complicated problem of a company transferring its seat from one EC member state to another.[127] The recognition of companies duly established under the law of other EC member states may not be totally excluded under the Treaty.[128] It goes without saying that, apart from the company's interests, the interests of creditors of such a 'company' would be seriously prejudiced. Furthermore, unwillingness to recognize the equivalent of *public* limited companies from other EC member states, all of them being subject to equalized capital requirements, certainly would be a violation of the Second EC Company Law Directive. Although, as yet, there is no EC directive on the worker co-determination which is directly linked to the organization of capital companies,[129] fundamental principles of proportionality must be respected. It would be hard to convince public limited companies from other EC states that they should obey domestic co-determination rules of the host country if these rules no longer apply to home companies of an equivalent type.[130] In conclusion: the 'real seat' theory is not excluded; but EC member states should not attempt to apply this recognition in its severest form.

Interdisciplinary co-ordination

Disharmony: favouring US companies; disfavouring EC companies

The functional disparities that divide EC law and private international law have had some peculiar effects. In particular, the German experience shows that there is a striking contrast between the main conflict rule concerning cross-border company relationships—*Sitztheorie*—and the *Freundschafts-, Handels- und Schiffahrtvertrages.*[131] Article 25(5) of this bilat-

---

[127] This legal institution receives separate consideration in III, below.

[128] cf. earlier comments on the potential spin-off from the *Vlassopoulou* doctrine (primarily relevant to the freedom of establishment of *natural* persons) for the freedom of establishment of *legal* persons: above.

[129] See I 2, above.

[130] Wouters (1996/97) 623 et seq., refers to the recent German company law reform (Bill of Parliament of 2 August 1994, BGBl. 1994 I, p. 1961), as a consequence of which small public companies (*kleine Aktiengesellschaften*) with less than 500 employees should no longer compulsorily be represented on the supervisory board (*Aufsichtsrat*). In a comparable sense, Roth (1995) 624.

[131] Commonly referred to as German–US Friendship Treaty, concluded on 29 October 1954, BGBl. 1956 II, p. 487. For further details (literature etc.), see ch 4 III 1, above. See against the background of the facts underlying the recent judgment of OLG Düsseldorf from 10 September 1998, JZ 2000, 203, it is even more striking that companies being incorporated in

eral Treaty provides that companies set up according to the law of one of the partners to the Treaty shall be recognized in the territory of the other partner.[132] In fact, German writers all seem to agree that, as far as US companies are concerned, this provision is *ipso iure* nothing less than acceptance of the 'incorporation' theory. Occasionally, an additional requirement was pleaded for, namely that the American status of companies be recognized under German law only when the American company is 'genuinely linked' with the USA.[133] They take the view that this is a common principle underlying the discipline of *public* international law.[134] It is astonishing that companies from third countries (here: the USA) find themselves placed in a more favourable position than companies which are 'EC subjects'. Some interesting thoughts on this matter were elaborated by Roth: he said that if article 25(5) of the German–US Friendship Treaty also applies where a US-based company transfers its seat to Germany,

we will have to ask whether Germany can rely on the general good justification *vis-à-vis* an English company moving its central office to Germany, when at the same time the general good considerations are of no relevance *vis-à-vis* an American company moving its central office to Germany. The Court of Justice has argued in a number of judgments that the general good has to be pursued in a consistent, and not in a sporadic manner, in order to justify the restrictions of the relevant freedom. I think it is hard to explain why the interest in workers' co-determination and in the protection of creditors is so important as to justify restrictions on the freedom of establishment, when at the same time these interests are not taken care of in the German–US relationship. Only a very restricted interpretation of the German–US Friendship Treaty may help Germany to evade the predicament I have just described.[135]

another EC member state but having their management and control centre on German territory are even considered to lack *Rechtsfähigkeit* (i.e. legal capacity) and *Parteifähigkeit* (i.e. the right to appear in court proceedings). This judgment prompted the BGH (judgment of 30 March 2000) to turn to the ECJ with preliminary qustions (cf. ch 4 III 1 above).

[132] Provided that (i) the territorial unit forming part of a composite legal system adheres to the 'incorporation' theory, and (ii) seat transfers are not preceded by a winding-up procedure.

[133] In this sense, Roth (1995), see below. The conflict rule of the German–US Frienship Treaty—'incorporation' theory combined with the additional requirement ('genuine link' with the system of law under which the company was established)—resembles the proposed attempt to combat the abuse of pro-forma foreign companies in the Netherlands (ch 4 II 1, above) except that the systems of law take opposite points of departure.

[134] In doing so, they seek parallels with the doctrine of genuine link for *natural* persons, developed by the International Court of Justice in the *Nottebohm* case (ICJ 55, 4.). In order to enjoy diplomatic state protection there must be a real and genuine link between the state and the natural person on one hand, and the similar doctrine with regard to legal persons on the other. Mere formal contacts with a state do not suffice. Others disagree: in their opinion, the German–US Friendship Treaty should be considered as a *lex specialis*, not explicitly requiring a 'genuine link'. Again see ch 4 III 1, above.

[135] Roth (1995) 42. Großfeld/König (1992) 433 et seq., took the contrasting view that the preservation of workers' co-determination constitutes a general interest justifying the dissolution of the company when its headquarters are moved from one member state to another, the latter not offering the same level of worker co-determination.

It should also be asked why German legislation on co-determinatition remains applicable to a company of which the *siège réel* has been replaced.[136]

The EC Market and the market for corporate charters: 'Delaware' reconsidered[137]

Drury points to another significant link between private international law and EC law, namely what is referred to as 'the development of a market for corporate charters in listed companies'.[138] By many, this 'market' is held responsible for the 'Delaware syndrome'. The explanation for that is as follows. In the first place, 'states which have rules which are particularly lax or favourable to managers will attract most corporations to the benefit of that state's coffers and the local bar'.[139] But then again:

a civilising jurisprudence should import lifting standards; certainly, there is no justification for permitting them to deteriorate. The absurdity of this race to the bottom, with Delaware in the lead—tolerated and indeed fostered by corporate counsel—should arrest the conscience of the American bar when its current reputation is in low estate.[140]

This train of thought was continued by others who allege that market forces

will discourage managers from seeking incorporation in states with legal rules that permit managers to 'exploit' shareholders. Incorporation in such states would increase the company's vulnerability to takeovers (which threaten managers' jobs), lower managers' compensation and other employment-related benefits, and harm managers' present and future job prospects.[141]

Notwithstanding the fact that other states are also reputed for having relatively mild company law regimes (e.g. Nevada and Wyoming) the advantageous position of Delaware is assumed to be the result of 'comprehensive statutes and case law, experienced judiciary, wealth of precedence and the interests of a state that depends more heavily than its competitors on incorporation revenues.'[142] It should, however, be recalled

---

[136] Roth (1995) 39, insists that any claim arising from *ordre public* be pursued in a consistent manner. In my opinion, however, it must be doubted whether indeed this principle applies, even if thousands of workers are still employed in German undertakings.

[137] See ch 2 II 3, above.

[138] Drury (1998) 184.   [139] ibid. 185.

[140] Cary (1974) 663, cited by Drury (1998) 185.

[141] Bebchuk, whose view, according to Drury (1998) 185, was taken over by Easterbrook, Fischel, Winter, and others: Delaware's dominance is seen to be due to its adoption of rules which are most efficient from the *shareholders'* point of view. In their opinion, the 'race for the bottom' is converted into a 'race for the top'.

[142] Drury (1998) 185 et seq. According to Bebchuk, this is instead a 'race for predictability and stability'. He even advocates an expansion of federal law for areas now still governed by state law. Minimum standards should be elaborated with respect to self-dealing transactions,

that businessmen in Europe notably profit from the 'Delaware effect' in, for example, the Netherlands: when compared to the mass of formation requirements of a Dutch *besloten vennootschap* (the Dutch equivalent of a private limited company)[143] the benefits are clear. The formation of a Delaware corporation (or any other foreign company) can be considered as a rubber-stamping procedure: no declaration of no objection (i.e. an inquiry of the pasts of those who will be in charge of the company's management) from the Justice Department is required; there are no minimum captal requirements; accounts and auditing are not subject to EC directives; and the registration of shareholders is not compulsory. Provided that a legal order adheres to the 'incorporation' theory, it is only logical for 'local' businessmen to incorporate their company under a more lenient foreign law, for the sole purpose of circumventing strict home company law provisions. What have been identified as advantages for the state of Delaware (tax and incorporation revenues etc.) might also be attractive to, for example, Liechtenstein or Gibraltar. There is, however, hardly any need to fear a Delaware syndrome in Europe for several reasons: (i) due to the ECJ case of *Ponente*, annual incorporation fees may not be required from foreign companies having their registered office on the territory of the state of incorporation;[144] and (ii) EC member states are 'not inclined to give anything like "full faith and credit" to companies stemming from such a source'.[145] 'Real seat' countries allegedly should not fear unfair competition, knowing that 'foreign investors cannot enjoy rights greater than those of equivalent domestic corporations; "incorporation" countries on the other hand are by no means to be considered as "powerless" to defend themselves against abuses,[146] as there are several techniques to combat such abuses'.[147] The truth probably lies somewhere in the middle.

---

taking of corporate opportunities, freeze-out mergers, all aspects of takeover bids and proxy contests, and limitations on dividends.

[143] Altogether, it is not surprising that the Delaware effect particularly caught the attention of commentators in those legal orders that (i) adhere to the 'incorporation' theory, whilst at the same time (ii) their domestic company law is strictly regulated. This is the case in the Netherlands. Cf. van den Braak/C.R. Huiskes (1992) 1165; Brood (1989); Debets (1987); and J.A.J. van Velzen, Rapport Delaware Corporations in Nederland, Culemborg 1995. For detailed information, see ch 4 II 1, above. Contrary to developments in the Netherlands, in the United Kingdom—which after all is als an 'incorporation' country—relatively little attention is given to the Delaware effect: the second condition (notably as regards the *private* limited company) appears not to be fulfilled in the company law of the United Kingdom.

[144] Case 71/91 and 178/91 *Ponente Carni Spa* [1993] ECR 1947. See ch 2 I 4, above.

[145] Drury (1998) 187.

[146] cf. ECJ *Centros*, referred to in ch 2 IV 2, above.

[147] Drury (1998) 188. At p. 191, he indicates that even in the UK 'it has long been the case that, despite a very liberal attitude to recognition of foreign companies, certain safeguards have been put in place to protect those who do business with them. The UK has for many years protected its citizens by requiring all "overseas companies" which establish a place of business in Great Britain to register in the Companies Registry in accordance with the provisions of the Companies Acts and to disclose their accounts.' Today, the same information

Harmony: matching EC law with other areas of law

The ECJ judgment in the case of *Powell Duffryn*[148] demonstrates that, occasionally, EC law and private international law are in concert with each other. The facts of *Powell Duffryn* can be summarized as follows: in the course of the compulsory winding up and liquidation of a holding company, incorporated under German law and resident in Germany, the shareholders were ordered by the trustee Petereit[149] to pay up their (registered) shares. The Powell Duffryn company, as a shareholder of the holding company residing in England, contested the competence of the German *Landgericht*, denying it was subject to a jurisdiction clause contained in the articles of association of the German holding. This clause read as follows: 'By subscribing for or acquiring shares or interim certificates the shareholder submits, with regard to all disputes between himself and the company or its organs, to the jurisdiction of the Courts ordinarily competent to entertain suits concerning the company.' The shareholders appeared to be domiciled throughout Europe. Being requested to give preliminary rulings on whether the cited clause complied with the conditions pursuant in article 17[150] of the Brussels Convention on Jurisdiction and Recognition and Enforcement of Judgments in Civil and Commercial Matters, the Court was given the difficult task of balancing EC law interests with private international law interests. (i) Freedom of establishment of companies under the EC Treaty should not be reduced to mere lip-service; (ii) private international law rules from the (EC) Brussels Convention should be adjusted to the needs of everyday legal practice;[151] and last but not least, (iii) how to further transborder business co-operation such as that which gave rise to the *Powell Duffryn* judgment, given the stagnating EC law harmonization programme in the field of company law?[152] It should not be overlooked that, compared with, for example, contract law, company law fundamentally involves 'multi-party' relationships, the litigants perhaps being domiciled throughout Europe.[153] Inconsistent court decisions, resulting from a proliferation of jurisdiction, should therefore

plus other particulars must be provided under the 11th EC Company Law Directive. For US techniques, see ch 2 II 3, above; for legal instruments in the Netherlands and Switzerland, see ch 4 II 1 and II 3, above.

[148] Case 214/89, *Powell Duffryn plc v Wolfgang Petereit* [1992] ECR 1755, see ch 2 IV 2, above.

[149] The trustee was installed by the German Court.

[150] Which governs prorogation of justice (choice of forum).

[151] Considered in II 1, below.

[152] See earlier observations on the vicious circle of companies not being recognized and the stagnating process of harmonization measures in the field of company law, I 2, above.

[153] Polak *CMLR* (1993) 412. In his opinion, 'scattered litigation' will lead to cumbersome proceedings pursuant to arts. 21 and 22 (*lis pendens*—related actions) of the Brussels Convention.

be avoided at all costs. The Court's policy[154] of avoiding a proliferation of closely connected disputes under the Brussels Convention, bearing the risk of them ultimately being decided inconsistently, turned out to be fortunate. Streamlining multi-party relationships by concentrating the settlement of disputes before one single Court—notably the chosen *forum societatis*—favours equal (fair?[155]) treatment of all shareholders, and the danger of inconsistent court decisions is countered effectively.

In spite of the fact that *Powell Duffryn* does not directly affect the EC law framework on the freedom of establishment of (legal) persons, its additional values are clear: (i) a convenient and appropriate jurisdiction framework for multi-party relationships under the Brussels Convention has been created, and (ii) interdisciplinary thinking is encouraged. Like no other case, *Powell Duffryn* reflects the struggle to regulate cross-border company relationships at the crossroads of Community law and company law (including substantive law and conflict of laws) of the EC member states. Seen from both EC law and private international law points of view, pragmatism has thus been given full effect by the *Powell Duffryn* judgment. Henceforth, an increasing number of choice of forum clauses in the articles of association of companies operating in more than one country can be expected.[156] In the absence of such a clause, litigants will be deprived of legal certainty, because the question whether the (registered or real) 'seat' (articles 2 and 16 of the Brussels Convention) of the company is situated on the territory of the state of the seized court depends on the private international law rules of the *lex fori* (article 53 of the Brussels Convention). Furthermore, choice of forum clauses are of no help in complex situations such as seat transfers, tax law-oriented problems, or the co-determination of workers, because these matters usually fall within the competence of the member state on whose territory the company's 'real seat' is situated. Even if we must accept that the antagonism between the existing recognition theories is not likely to end soon, at least conditions should be formulated to maximize companies' opportunities to increase their mobility in EC territory under the law as it now stands.

---

[154] For judgments and comments, see ch 2 IV 2, above.

[155] cf. the worthiness of protection of (individual?) shareholders: ch 2 IV 2, above.

[156] Note that in the *Powell Duffryn* case, the German holding company had both its registered office (incorporation seat) and its management and control centre ('real seat') on German territory. So companies having 'seats' in *different* countries still risk inconsistent Court decisions, resulting from a proliferation of jurisdiction. Cf. however the following section.

The Convention on Jurisdiction and Enforcement of Judgments in Civil and Commercial Matters: reform initiatives

The Accession Treaties: legal basis

The enlargment of the European Union and the necessity of amending the text of the Convention on Jurisdiction and Enforcement of Judgments in Civil and Commercial Matters[157] have so far resulted in three Accession Treaties.[158] Following the accession of Austria, Finland, and Sweden to the European Union, a Fourth Accession Treaty entered into force for some EC member states on 1 December 1998/1 January 1999.[159] Prior to the entry into force of the Treaty of Amsterdam, these Accession Treaties were based on article 220 (now article 293). In future, however, amendments to the Brussels Convention are likely to be based on a Directive, i.e. article 65 (previously article 73m) in conjunction with article 94 (previously article 100) of the EC Treaty.

Reform predraft—January 1998

During the past years, documents have been drafted whose status is not clear. Like their predecessors, the proposals to amend the Brussels Convention reflect the struggle to overcome the ancient controversy between the 'real seat' theory on one hand, and the 'incorporation' theory on the other.

A predraft for a new Accession Treaty to the Brussels Convention first saw the light at the end of January 1998.[160] Rather daringly, its drafters decided to eliminate the detrimental effects that flow from article 53. A substantive law approach was preferred. The domicile of both natural *and legal* persons should no longer be determined with the help of private international law rules of the forum; instead, these notions were decided autonomously by the EC legislator. Furthermore, according to article 2(2), the central management and control office of a company is given equal status with the residence of a natural person under the Convention. Also remarkable is the fact that the draftsmen amended the exclusive jurisdiction rule contained in article 16(2): in proceedings which have as their object 'the validity of the constitution, the nullity or dissolution of companies or other legal persons having their *registration office* in a Contracting State (. . .)', jurisdiction is attributed to the courts of that state. This means

---

[157] Hereinafter referred to as the Brussels Convention.

[158] More detail in ch 2 IV 1, above.

[159] See information provided in Vlas (1999) 136: the Kingdom of the Netherlands, Austria, Sweden, Denmark, and Germany ratified the Fourth Accession Treaty. As a consequence, the parallel Lugano Treaty became irrelevant for litigants from these legal orders.

[160] OJ nr. C 33/21 of 31 Jan. 1998. At that time, this document had the status of a discussion paper.

that according to the proposal some fundamental company law issues are directly distributed to the courts of the contracting state where the company has its registered office, whereas other kinds of disputes must be solved by courts of the country where the company has its 'real seat'. The concept envisaged by the drafters thus resembles the notions of *Überlagerung* and *Differenzierung*.[161] Another consequence of this concept is that any prorogation clause in the articles of association of the company which refers to the company's 'seat' would still leave questions unanswered.[162]

Reform draft—April 1999

On 26 April 1999 yet another document was published.[163] The proposal for the distribution of jurisdiction under article 16(2) was dropped. In conformity with the present version of article 16(2), it is for the courts of the contracting states to determine—with the help of their own conflict of law rules—whether or not a company is established on their territory. Neither are there any spectacular changes to article 53: courts of contracting states remain competent to decide—with the help of their own conflict of law rules—whether a company is resident on the territory of the forum. They thus put decisive weight on (a) the company's registered office, (b) the company's headquarters, or (c) the company's principal place of business (article 53(1)). This is in accordance with article 48 (previously article 58) of the EC Treaty. As explained above, the (sub)category (c) is rooted in Italian private international law.[164]

As regards prorogation clauses (article 17 of the Brussels Convention) in the articles of association of a company, the landmark case was *Powell Duffryn*.[165] It was concluded from that decision that although an increase of choice of forum clauses in the articles of association of cross-border operating companies is to be expected, there is no answer yet to the question how such clauses should be dealt with when the company's management and control office and its registered office are situated in different countries. This controversy has not yet been solved satisfactorily. This means that, at least for the time being, companies having 'seats' in *different* countries are still in danger of mutually inconsistent court decisions from different jurisdictions under article 53 of the Brussels Convention.

---

[161] See ch 2 II 1, above. The latter two concepts are, however, related to the applicable system(s) of law; art. 16 of course regulates the matter of jurisdiction.

[162] How to handle companies *not* having their registered office in a contracting state? The precise reach of art. 16(2) requires an interpretative ruling by the ECJ.

[163] SN 2581/1/99 REV 1, DG H III.

[164] On the notion of *l'ogetto principale dell'impresa*, contained in art. 25 of the 1995 Code on Private International Law, see ch 2 IV 1 and ch 4 III 3, below.

[165] Case 214/89, *Powell Duffryn plc v Wolfgang Petereit* [1992] ECR 1755.

Finally, the draftsmen decided not to codify the points ruled on in *Powell Duffryn*. A new subsection 4 was added to article 17, however, extending the requirement that a prorogation clause must be 'in writing' or 'evidenced in writing' to include any *electronic* and *permanent* registration of the prorogation agreement.[166]

III. INTRA-COMMUNITY COMPANY MOBILITY: CROSS-BORDER SEAT TRANSFERS

1. PREMISES FOR FURTHER INVESTIGATION

Cross-border company mobility: incentives

Perhaps the first thing to ascertain is why a company would want to take the step of moving its head office to another Member State. Modern means of communication would surely facilitate the operation abroad of many things that a company might want to do. For the wary and well advised company this is undoubtedly true, and it can appoint foreign agents and sales representatives, set up branches abroad and even incorporate a subsidiary company to further the corporate design. If it did all of these things from a head office in its country of incorporation there would be no serious conflict of laws problem to consider. However, an unwary company might begin in the way outlined, but get more and more involved in the business run by its foreign extension. Its directors or senior managers could become more and more mobile and increasingly emmeshed in the fascinating process of running the foreign operation, especially if this proved either a resounding commercial success or a potentially serious loss-making concern. They might even begin taking important decisions about the enterprise as a whole engaged in the process of hands-on management abroad. This is where the problems can begin. Once major decisions about the company as a whole are taken regularly in another jurisdiction there is a possibility that the courts in the host state of the foreign operations would decline to recognize the whole company as valid, and possibly treat it as something which did not have corporate personality and in consequence as something which no longer posessed limited liability. If potential losses were the main cause of concern, the last thing the controllers of the company would want to lose is limited liability. Such a company might well want to regularise its position by formally transferring its head office to the seat of its foreign operations. (. . .) The pressures would begin to build from both commercial and possibly from fiscal perspectives for a relocation of its head office to a situation nearer to its principal markets and to local advisers and skilled employees. In both

---

[166] Internet or Intranet? In this respect, the requirement that such a registration must be permanent may cause difficulties. Perhaps, somewhere in the future, company transparency will result in a 'European Company Register', with digital registration of company data files accessible all over Europe.

cases it is unlikely that such companies would be able to move their head office from one jurisdiction to another under the relevant national laws.[167]

Legal premises

Before analysing the technical legislative ins and outs of how precisely cross-border company mobility should be facilitated, the legal premises underlying both EC law and private international law need to be clarified. The facts underlying the *Daily Mail* judgment are a 'true test'[168] of the freedom of establishment for companies in the EC: cross-border company transfers are particularly likely to produce a variety of problems as they involve the legal environments of (at least)[169] two states. Although 'the problem of company migration basically mirrors the antagonism between the *"siège réel* system" and the "incorporation system" '[170], it also comprises EC law, private law (preservation of the interests of creditors, third parties, etc.), tax law, co-determination legislation, etc. Separate treatment of all these matters one after another does not seem to be adequate; instead, cross-border multi-party company relationships require an integrated, *sui generis* approach. Individual member states cannot be expected to square the circle: even if they should be prepared to intensify and combine their efforts, they are simply not equipped to handle all the complications simultaneously and adequately.[171] Henceforth, newer national conflict of law provisions, such as article 25(3) of the 1995 Italian Code on Private International Law, or section 4 of the 1998 Dutch CLC Act, could play a greater role as a kind of *Programmsatz*, i.e. a lawyers' guide to supranational law sources. It is, however, an illusion to think that highly complicated procedures such as cross-border transfers or mergers can be carried out by applying conflicting 'one-liners' such as article 25 of the Italian Code. That provision reads as follows: 'Any *transfer* of the seat to a different state as well as *mergers* of bodies having seats in different States shall take effect only when performed in pursuance of the laws of the aforesaid states.'[172] But, as will be seen, no clear answers can be drawn

---

[167] Drury (1999) 354 et seq. (see also ch 1 I, above).   [168] Roth (1995) 41.

[169] Sometimes more legal orders are involved: cf. the example in ch 4 II 3, above concerning the cross-border transfer of a company's management and control centre from one state to another, its registered office being located in yet another state.

[170] Bellingwout (1995) 79.

[171] An interesting countervailing view was expressed by de Wulf (1999) 321 et seq., based on ECJ *Centros* (see ch 2 IV 2, above): a distinction should be made between the transfer of the company's *headquarters* only to another EC member state, and the cross-border transfer of a company's *activities*; whereas the former situation does not simultaneously constitute *establishment* under the EC Treaty, the latter permits companies to invoke the freedom of establishment, as a result of which even *primary* establishment is granted under the EC Treaty.

[172] Emphasis added. See ch 4 III 3, above. One has to keep in mind, though, earlier comments on the analogous application of national law rules governing purely domestic transformations of one type of legal person into another, in particular art. 2498 of the Italian Civil Code: cf. ch 4 II 3, above. For a comparable approach, cf. the Dutch experience, ch 4 II 1,

either from articles 43 and 48 (previously articles 52 and 58) of the EC Treaty. In other words, there is an infrastructural hiatus, which needs to be filled in by secondary EC legislation, covering all the issues that are mentioned.

The EC Treaty: Articles 43 and 48, seat transfers and national barriers

National law: disproportionate hindrance

The leading *Daily Mail* judgment justifies no other conclusion than that for the moment article 43 (previously article 52) of the EC Treaty:

has no direct effect only insofar as the conflict of law issue is concerned. The Court observes that a company has no right to transfer its central management while 'retaining' its status as a foreign company ruled by foreign law: the *Statutenwechsel* (change in the applicable law) provided for by the *siège réel* theory (as well as by the *incorporation* theory!) cannot be attacked in national Courts.[173]

Corresponding, however, with earlier remarks in respect of the recognition matter,[174] the national laws of EC member states ought not disproportionately to hinder company plans for a cross-border transfer. In other words, 'the substantive law of the member state, dealing with the transfer of the central administration and with its consequences has to stand up to the exigencies of freedom of establishment'.[175] Meanwhile, it should not be overlooked that cross-border transfers of a company's incorporation seat (the *registered* office) are rare; this type of transfer is actually even more puzzling than the transfer of a company's 'real seat' (the *management and control centre*).[176] Consequently, the following text focuses on the transfer of a company's headquarters.[177]

above. From a non-EU perspective, similar provisions apply: note that this feeling was explicitly shared by the Swiss *Bundesrat* (Federal Council), having regard to national conflict of law rules, in particular arts. 161–4 of the Swiss Federal Code on Private International Law: see ch 4 II 3, above.

[173] Roth (1995) 37. Although the conclusion may be drawn from the *Daily Mail* judgment that a *Statutenwechsel* cannot be attacked in national courts, I do not agree with Roth's view that such a change in the applicable law is 'provided for by (. . .) the *"Incorporation"* theory'. The transfer of the management and control centre could not be attacked for *tax* law reasons: this has nothing to do, however, with *company* law. Neither UK, nor Dutch conflict of law rules having regard to companies object to any cross-border transfer of a company's headquarters, as the "Incorporation" theory is adhered to in both legal orders; in other words, in the case of a transfer of the company's *headquarters*, a *Statutenwechsel* is never envisaged by the "Incorporation" theory. This is different when the transfer of a company's *registered office* is at stake (see below).

[174] See the previous section.   [175] Roth (1995) 37 et seq.

[176] cf. also ch 6 I 2, above. Even those legal orders that adhere to the 'incorporation' theory tolerate the cross-border transfer of a company's registered office only in exceptional situations: see ch 4 II 1 (Netherlands) and ch 4 II 3 (Switzerland). Such transfers are likely to be carried out in emergency situations only.

[177] The *Daily Mail* judgment demonstrates that companies are more interested in this kind of transfer.

One (negative) example of how fundamental principles of EC law can be frustrated is the notorious German *Zweibrücken* case.[178] A German Court held that the refusal to recognize a foreign company was not contrary to EC law, since—apart from article 220 (now article 293) and the ECJ *Daily Mail* judgment—the 1968 EC Treaty on the Mutual Recognition of Companies never attained the status of law. Roth considers this to be overt discrimination against foreign companies by German law: whereas domestic companies are at least given the chance to change their legal status from one company type into another without losing their legal personality, such a transformation is not open to foreign companies.[179] Obviously, the Court saw no reason to apply purely domestic transformation provisions by analogy to foreign companies entering German territory, as this 'would go beyond the limits of judge-made law'.[180] This observation met with disapproval: it has been argued that

Member States are under a general obligation to promote effectiveness of the freedoms (article 5 EC[181]) and therefore must change their legal infrastructure in a way that the freedoms are not unnecessarily impinged upon. Member States have to put an end to any form of discrimination whatsoever. (. . .) German Courts should not and cannot rely on the argument concerning the limits of judge-made law to remedy this situation: analogy is a common tool in the repertoire of the Courts.[182]

The German legislator shaped the law in accordance with Community standards, by explicitly extending the newly reformed law of transformation to foreign companies.[183]

Creative reasoning: the Belgian Lamot doctrine

The 1993 KPMG *Report* contains both legal and practical arguments defending the possibility of cross-border seat transfers: (i) in all member states a company can replace its *siège réel* within the jurisdiction without dissolution. It is undesirable that the existence of national borders can prevent a company from transferring its *siège réel* to another EC member state. (ii) As far as the legal arguments are concerned, it has been argued that applying article 58 (article 48 of the Treaty of Amsterdam) a company

---

[178] OLG *Zweibrücken*, 27 June 1990, *IPRax* 1991 406 and KG Berlin 13 June 1989, *NJW* 1989 310. Cf. more recently OLG Düsseldorf 10 September 1998, *JZ* 2000 203, which gave rise to preliminary proceedings initiated by the German BGH on 30 March 2000 (see ch 2 IV 2 above).

[179] Roth (1995) 38.   [180] ibid.

[181] cf. comments on art. 5 (art. 10 since the Amsterdam Treaty) ch 6 I 2, above.

[182] Roth (1995) 38.

[183] ibid., although admitting that, as far as the protection of company creditors is concerned, such a 'transformation' of an English private limited company entering German territory might as well be more burdensome, in the sense that the applicability of the complete set of GmbH rules, protecting the company's creditors, could also be an extremely 'restrictive' measure (p. 43).

should have the right of establishment under article 52 (article 43 of the Treaty of Amsterdam) in the same way as natural persons do.[184]

Whereas German courts failed to address the matter of cross-border company mobility in a constructive manner, neither plausible arguments for the far-reaching restrictions thereto, nor any workable alternative for companies being adduced, the Belgian *Lamot* doctrine appeared to be more in the spirit of EC law. Despite the fact that Belgian private international law unconditionally adheres to the 'real seat' theory,[185] a *modus vivendi* was found to safeguard the interest of company mobility even long before the transitional period expired. The facts in the *Lamot* case[186] were as follows. In the mid-1920s Lamot Breweries, residing in Belgium, planned to attract more capital. To that end, an English company, Lamot Ltd., was established. The registered office was situated in England, but the company's business activities were exclusively conducted in Belgium. The Court observed that there was no circumvention of Belgian law, taking into consideration that Lamot Ltd. had clearly been established to attract foreign capital: the company was listed on the Stock Exchange of London. Furthermore, until 1932 board meetings and shareholders' meetings were also held in London. Early in 1932 the shareholders' meeting took the decision to transfer the head office of Lamot Ltd. to the city of Mechelen in Belgium. The transfer decision was meant to put an end to the burden of double taxation.[187] It was not until 1959 that an individual shareholder, Mr W. Lamot, brought an action against the company. He claimed *inter alia* that Lamot Ltd. had ceased to be a company, because pursuant to article 102 of the Belgian *Vennootschapswet* (Company Act) a company was not allowed to survive for more than thirty years, which period in his view had expired in 1957. The Belgian Supreme Court, like the Court of First Instance and the Court of Appeal, observed that article 197 of the *Vennootschapswet* applied generally to companies having their head office in Belgium, irrespective of whether this head office had been

---

[184] cf. the KPMG *Report*, 14, mentioning Knobbe-Keuk (1990) 325 et seq. This *Report* is considered in the following section. In my view, however, it is an over-simplification: the multiparty character of company relationships, and the considerable impact of cross-border seat transfers on the interests of all actors involved (company shareholders and creditors, employees, tax and social security authorties, etc.) opposes the abstraction that natural and legal persons are to be treated alike under the EC Treaty: see ch 1 II, above.

[185] According to art. 197 of the Belgian *Vennootschapswet* (Company Act), the proper law of the company is the law of the country where the head office of the company resides. This conflict rule is to be applied in a bilateral manner; Belgian courts apply foreign law to a company having its head office abroad. For detailed information with further references: Wouters (1996/97) 632 et seq. Note that this approach (i.e. bilateralization of a single-sided conflict rule) closely resembles the French method: see ch 4 III 2, above.

[186] Cass., 12 November 1956, Pas., 1966, I, p. 336, R.P.S. 1966, p. 136. For detailed comments read Jacob (1993) 879 et seq.; Wouters (1996/97) 632; and Wymeersch (1999) 136 et seq.

[187] Thus, the *Lamot* case represents *avant la lettre* the post-*Daily Mail* predicament, cf. comments by Wouters (1996/97).

located in Belgium from the moment the company had been established, or had been subsequently transferred to Belgium. Both the Court of First Instance and the Court of Appeal, however, rejected Mr Lamot's claim: the period of article 102 was held to be retroactive only to the date of the company's transfer in 1932. Consequently the period of thirty years only started to run in 1932 and had not expired in 1959.[188] The Supreme Court's observation that 'it cannot be concluded from any Belgian legislative provision that solely on the ground that a company has transferred its head office in the way described above, it has ceased to be a legal person under Belgian law' (author's transl.) became famous. The Court saw no reason to deny the company's continuing existence, provided that after the transfer, the requirements of Belgian law (e.g. amendment of the articles of association) were satisfied.

It is remarkable that although the law of Belgium clearly adheres to the 'real seat' theory, transfers from both the UK and the Netherlands now take place on a regular basis as a result of the *Lamot* judgment.[189] However, any cross-border company seat transfer must comply with five preconditions: (i) the absence of *fraus legis*; (ii) all the legal requirements of the emigration country must be obeyed; (iii) the continued existence of the legal person must also be permitted under the law of the emigration country;[190] (iv) the immigration country must not oppose the continued existence of the legal person; and finally (v) the structure of the company should be fundamentally compatible with the law of the immigration country: 'essential' changes in the company structure are not permitted. The Dutch scholar Bellingwout takes the view that a cross-border seat transfer from an 'incorporation' country (the Netherlands) to a 'real seat' country (Belgium), *but not entailing a loss of the company's identity*, is thus facilitated.[191] This means *inter alia* that the management board has to take a decision, and amend the articles of association to adopt the form of a Belgian BVBA.[192]

---

[188] In other words, the maximum period of 30 years had started, not in 1927 (the year in which Lamot Ltd. was *established*) but in 1932, the year of the company's *seat transfer* to Belgium. This has been criticized: see III 2, below.

[189] cf. Bellingwout (1997). For further information Wouters (1996/97) 634.

[190] It is not surprising that Belgium in particular is confronted with company transfers from legal orders that adhere to the 'incorporation' theory: see above.

[191] Bellingwout (1997) 204. It should not be overlooked, however, that the absence of a loss of identity might also result in double 'nationality' of the company (i.e. Dutch *and* Belgian). Bellingwout believes that this is not necessarily incompatible with Dutch law. Note that double nationality can also result from the application of art. 161(2) of the 1987 Swiss Code on Private International Law, ch 4 II 3, above.

[192] For a detailed description of the transfer procedure (e.g. the role of the general meeting, amendment of articles of association, alteration of the name of the Dutch BV into the Belgian equivalent company form of a BVBA, capital nomination in Belgian currency, 'assistance' of a Belgian public notary, etc.) and comments, see Jacob (1993) 879 et seq.; and Wouters (1996/97) 632. From a Dutch perspective: Bellingwout (1997), and ch 4 II 1, above.

The *Lamot* judgment, which after all dates back to the mid-1950s, seems to be more in the spirit of EC law than *Daily Mail*.

2. THE 1993 KPMG REPORT

Fundamental principles

Point of departure: coexistence of the 'real seat' and 'incorporation' theories

The ECJ *Daily Mail* judgment on the freedom of departure for legal persons dates from 1988. Ever since, the advance of one of the fundamental freedoms under the EC Treaty, the freedom of establishment for legal persons, appears to have been into a dark alley. The European Commission has expressed the view that efforts should be made to remove intra-state barriers, but the crucial question was where to make a start. A document containing concrete draft proposals to further cross-border company mobility in the EC was published in 1993.

This document was entitled 'Study of Transfer of the Head Office of a Company from one Member State to Another'. It was written by 'Philip Bentley QC in collaboration with KPMG European Business Centre, Brussels'.[193] The ECJ had explicitly referred to 'future legislation or conventions' for solutions: the KPMG document took up this challenge.[194] Although sadder and wiser after the setbacks in the area of company law (the draft 1968 Treaty on the mutual recognition of companies and harmonization efforts[195]) the drafters refrained from pursuing the over-ambitious goal of resolving the controversy between the existing recognition theories once again.[196] A more modest objective was formulated instead:

Within the framework of the harmonization of company law, based on article 54 of the Treaty of Rome,[197] the Commission plans to investigate which measures would be appropriate in order to facilitate the transfer of the head office of a company from one Member State to another Member State without dissolution of the company in question.

Companies should be provided with legal instruments to transfer their real seat from one member state to another, yet without being dissolved. They should however remain subject to measures taken by member states

---

[193] cf. Drury (1999) 360. I refer to this hereafter as the KPMG document.

[194] Which was long overdue, if one takes into consideration that in 1962 G. Beitzke had already informed the European Commission on the issue of company migration: Bellingwout (1995) 75.

[195] cf. ch 2 IV 1 and ch 6 I 2, above.

[196] This might also turn out to be unrealistic: in the view of Bellingwout (1995) 80, '(t)he existing dissimilarities between national systems of international company law need not form an impediment; from this perspective, the Incorporation system and the *siège réel* system can continue to co-exist'.

[197] Now art. 44.

justified for the protection of the general good. One consequence to be avoided is that the transferred company could find itself subject either to two legal systems[198] or to no legal system at all.

Two draft proposals

Two draft proposals were elaborated: (i) a proposal based on the 'incorporation' theory, allowing the transfer of the company's headquarters without dissolution, yet keeping an eye on the protection of German worker co-determination, and the safeguard of tax neutrality;[199] (ii) another proposal based on the *siège réel* theory, allowing a company to transfer both its registered office and its headquarters without being dissolved. Here too, the interests of workers, shareholders, creditors, debenture holders, and tax authorities should be safeguarded.

Despite detrimental experiences,[200] parallels between natural and legal 'persons' are raised once again. According to the Report:

(i)n everyday practice, a company exercises its right of establishment by opening a branch, a so-called 'secondary' establishment. A natural person does not usually do this because he can only be physically present in one place at a time, so his primary establishment usually follows his residence. Note that when a natural person changes his primary establishment, he does not by this fact alone change his nationality, nor his place of birth, nor does he change his proper law—at least not immediately. Thus, for example, a UK individual who moves his residence to France (. . .) does not change his proper law in matters such as capacity, personal property, matrimonial relations (. . .). *By analogy*, article 58 (now article 48) should be interpreted as saying that a company can move its primary establishment from one Member State to another without changing its proper law. Primary establishment *for this purpose* does not mean the company's place of birth or its state of incorporation, but its *siège réel*.[201]

Having reached the conclusion that intra-community company transfers should be facilitated, the *Report* focuses on problems that need to be tackled. Shareholders' rights are not likely to change under the incorporation

---

[198] This appeared to be one of the possible consequences of the *Lamot* doctrine: see III 1, above.

[199] Reference to these two topics need not surprise. It can safely be assumed that so far the matter of worker co-determination (cf. the Draft Proposal for a 5th Company Law Directive on the Functioning of Organs which was revised over and over again), and the issue of tax neutrality (cf. the *Daily Mail* judgment) both appeared to be insurmountable obstacles.

[200] The national conflict of law concepts of several EC member states were dealt with in Part 2, above.

[201] *Report*, 16 (emphasis added). This concept of drawing parallels between natural and legal persons has met with disapproval, cf. the English (ch 4 II 2, above) and the civil law points of view (ch 2 IV 1, above). The European Court emphasized that 'it should be borne in mind that, unlike natural persons, companies are creatures of the law and, *in the present state of Community law*, creatures of *national* law. They exist only by virtue of the varying national legislation which determines their incorporation and functioning' (cons. 19 of the *Daily Mail* judgment, emphasis added). See ch 6 II 1, above.

statute. Special protective provisions might, however, be needed for transfers to a *siège réel* country: that type of transfer should be approved by the
general meeting in the manner required to change the articles of association.[202] The same principle applies *mutatis mutandis* to the protection of
creditors of the company and employees.[203] The rights of these categories
are preserved unchanged under the 'incorporation' theory, assuming that
there will be no *Statutenwechsel*, so that the proper law of the company will
not undergo changes. Again, this is different under the 'real seat' theory:
an explicit provision is needed not to discontinue legal capacity. Besides,
creditors might be taken by surprise by a legal person who should be sued
before a foreign court.[204]

The EEIG experience

The KPMG *Report* underscores that the transfer of an official registered
office has already been made possible by the Regulation on the European
Economic Interest Grouping (EEIG).[205] On the basis of article 6 of the EEIG
Regulation, an EEIG shall be registered in the state in which it has its official address. It also explicitly governs the transfer of this official address.
By virtue of article 14, the proposal to transfer the official address must be
filed at the registry and published in the national gazette; the publication
of this proposal starts a period of two months during which the competent
authority of a member state may object to the transfer on the grounds of
public interest, in which case the transfer cannot take place. After the expi-
ration of the two months without objections, the transfer may be carried

[202] The *Report*, p. 19, proposes a majority similar to that required under the 10th Company
Law Directive on Cross-Border Mergers, since in practice the effect is comparable. Note that
in such situations even a prorogation clause in the articles of association, making the 'seat' of
the company the decisive factor (*Powell Duffryn*, ch 6 II 1 above) would not help.

[203] Drury (1999) 364, regrets the absence of any substantive provision for them. He argues
that the KPMG *Report* 'lumps them in with unsecured creditors and other third parties and
says that there should in principle be no difference between companies and individual persons in this respect'.

[204] *Report* 19. This would result in inconvenience and additional costs. The writers, however, see no reason to protect *unsecured* company creditors against emigrating debtors, since
this route is open to individuals as well. Apart from this, it is their belief that it is easier to
pursue companies because they have to be registered at a commercial registry which is open
to the public, cf. the Explanatory Memorandum to the 'second proposal', p. 47, below.
Debenture holders, as well as *secured* creditors, however, have legitimate interests; e.g. floating charges over the company's assets should be reregistered: ibid. 20. But this involves the
risk of losing priority over other charges. Rather than being a matter of company law, this
must be seen as a problem of private international law, namely the issue of *res in transitu*,
goods during cross-border transportation, being subjected to changes in the proper law,
affecting rights *in rem*.

[205] *Report* 23. OJ L 199 of 31 July 1985. The proposed Regulation on the European Company
and the 10th Company Law Directive on Cross-Border Mergers is also referred to. Thus 'the
siège réel philosophy (. . .) crept into secondary Community law'; see ch 6 I 2, above.

out by registering the EEIG in the transferee state; the registration in the state of departure can only then be cancelled. Until the cancellation of the old address has been published, third parties can continue to rely on the old address unless they have actual knowledge of the transfer. It should be noted that under the EEIG Regulation considerations of the 'general good'—although undefined—can be grounds for opposing a transfer.[206] Taking into account earlier findings (company transfers produce a great variety of problems, each of a special nature: see ch 3 III 1, above) an exhaustive catalogue of what falls within the scope of 'general good' is not to be expected.[207]

Draft proposals for directives

Before addressing the technical ins and outs of the KPMG proposal, it is necessary to point out the somewhat confusing approach pursued by KPMG. Bellingwout perceives the following inconsistencies:[208] (i) although the KPMG assignment was initially restricted to the transfer of the head office *from and to a* siège réel *system*, this restriction was set aside in the *Report*; (ii) KPMG, thus confronted with a broad range of possible species of seat transfers to be covered,[209] apparently lost its way:[210] erroneously, the problem of company migration was thus reduced to a choice between the incorporation system and the *siège réel* system. Consequently, the assignment was rephrased as follows:

In the light of the foregoing discussion it can be seen that the question of transfer of the 'head office' or '*siège réel*' of a company can be formulated in two different ways: (i) should the theory of the place of incorporation be generalised throughout the Community so that a company can transfer its *siège réel* while retaining a

---

[206] *Report* 25.
[207] The *Report*, 26 et seq., mentions another approach, which was pursued in the 10th Company Law Directive on Cross-Border Mergers. 'General good' issues are:
—national rules on company representation in the company's board of directors;
—protection of employees in accordance with Directive 77/187/EEC;
—Member States shall provide adequate protection for creditors and debenture holders;
—holders of securities other than shares may require that their securities be repurchased;
—certain formalities may be required in order to ensure that the transfer of certain assets, rights and obligations are effective against third parties;
—civil liability of directors of the acquired company and of the expert is to be governed by the law of the Member State governing that company;
—limited number of nullity grounds of the operation, to be laid down clearly.
[208] Bellingwout (1995) 82.
[209] In cross-border transfers, at least two legal orders are always interested: the country of departure and the country of re-establishment. Each of these may be either an 'incorporation' or a 'real seat' country. Third countries may also appear to be involved (e.g. cross-border transfer of a company's management and control centre from one state to another, its registered office being located in a third state).
[210] In this respect, the drafters appear to be in good company, cf. comparable confusion concerning arts. 161 and 163 of the Swiss Code on Private International Law: ch 4 II 3, above.

registered office in the state of Incorporation? (. . .) (ii) Should the theory of *siège réel* be generalised with the proviso that the transfer of the *siège réel* does not entail the dissolution of the company? (. . .) In this way a company would be able to transfer its *siège réel* and change its proper law at the same time.

Indeed it is an understatement to say that a choice in favour of the 'incorporation' theory would be 'a bridge too far' in the present situation.[211] Anyway, the reformulation of the problem in the *Report* led to two different proposals, the first accepting the 'incorporation' theory as the foundation,[212] the second[213] regulating transfers of head offices with a change in the proper law of the company, but retaining legal personality.[214]

The first proposal

Definition

The first proposal concentrates on 'the transfer of the *siège réel* of a company from one EC member state to another without dissolution (while remaining subject to the law of the state of incorporation)'.[215] After some general observations on the institutional legal basis,[216] this proposal con-

---

[211] Bellingwout (1995) 82. Cf. Drury (1999) 361: '(t)he first proposal (. . .) would require the wholesale adoption of the place of incorporation approach. It is this element which dooms the proposal because the real seat jurisdictions are too firmly wedded to their own approach to applicable law and hence to recognition rules to make such a fundamental change acceptable, and the *Report* itself acknowledges this'.

[212] As a result of this approach, 'the head office could be transferred anywhere in the Community, but the company would *continue to be governed by the law of the place of incorporation* (my emphasis) in matters such as validity, nullity, and winding up.' It resembles the concepts of *Differenzierung* and *Überlagerung*, see ch 2 II 1, above. Remarkably, in the view of the *Report*'s authors, this would result in a 'retrograde step for those Member States which apply the theory of *siège réel* without dissolution': *Report* 27. It is, however, questionable whether this is logical: systems of law adhering to the *siège réel* theory hardly ever allow companies to transfer their headquarters without being dissolved and wound up: cf. French law, ch 4 III 2, above. Moreover, if such transfers were allowed under *siège réel* regimes, they could be expected to take place more often.

[213] According to Drury (1999) 360, this proposal 'seemed somewhat more promising'.

[214] The *Report* wishes to avoid two types of problem, namely that of definition and that concerning fictitious transfers, by introducing the presumption that the company's *siège réel* is situated at its official registered address. Third parties, however, should be allowed to show that the *siège réel* is in fact situated in a state other than that of the official registered address. This approach was said to have been borrowed from French and Portuguese law. On the disadvantages of the *siège réel* theory, e.g. the arbitrary system of ascertaining a company's 'real' seat, see ch 2 I 3, above.

[215] Document XV/6002/97-EN of 20 April 1997. The main features of the first and second draft proposals are sketched below.

[216] The general observation reads as follows: 'The Commission would have power to make this proposal pursuant to article 54 EEC, except insofar as the Directive involves a modification of Council Directive 90/434/EEC, OJ L 225 of 20 August 1990, a taxation measure, which would have to be modified pursuant to Article 100 EEC.' Furthermore, the pattern of the 10th Company Law Directive was taken as a point of departure 'to the effect that the existence of article 220 EEC does not prevent the matter being harmonized by directive rather than by multilateral convention'.

tains the text of the draft Directive, as well as an explanatory memorandum.

Main features

Article 1 defines the scope of the draft Directive,[217] and article 2 contains further definitions. The procedure for seat transfers is set out in article 3: the first subsection obliges member states to regulate transfers of a company's 'real seat' out of or into the member state, in accordance with the Directive. A transferring company shall retain its official registered address in the state of incorporation. Member states shall adapt their private international law rules so that, for a company having its 'real seat' and its 'incorporation' seat in the Community, the proper law shall be that of the state in which the official registered address is located and this shall also be the company's seat under the Brussels Convention (article 3(2)). The state of arrival may require the company to register a branch at the place where the *siège réel* is situated. The procedure will be similar to the registration of a branch by a company in another member state (article 3(3)). After a company has transferred its *siège réel*, subsequent transfers are allowed in accordance with the Directive (article 3(4)). No member state shall consider a company to be incorporated or to have been dissolved for the sole reason that its *siège réel* has been transferred to a member state other than that of incorporation.[218] The state of arrival, however, need not apply the Directive in respect of companies which transfer their 'real seat' for no reason other than to circumvent provisions of the state of arrival that would have been applicable if the company had been incorporated there (article 3(5)).[219] Article 4 prescribes that the transfer of the *siège réel* shall require no more than the approval of the organ or organs of the company competent to authorize the transfer within the state of

---

[217] According to the Explanatory Memorandum (further referred to as EM), the draft proposal envisages both public and private limited companies, for there is no reason to exclude either from the freedom of establishment. This provision 'fixes the scope as *the same* as for the Third Company Law Directive' (OJ L 225 of 20 August 1990, concerning mergers), EM 31; although this Directive is only applicable to public companies, the drafters 'see no reason why the forelying draft Directive should not encompass private companies, in which case art. 1 could be extended to refer to companies falling within the scope of the 12th Directive, whether or not such companies indeed had a single member'. Furthermore, art. 1(2) and 1(3) of the proposal 'mirrors the same provisions of the third Directive'.

[218] EM 32: 'In short, both the state of incorporation and the state of arrival are obliged to implement the theory of the law of the place of incorporation and abandon the theory of the law of the *siège réel*. However each state would be free to apply other rules *vis-à-vis* companies coming from third countries.' Experiences from the past demonstrate, however, that reconciliatory concepts attempting to combine the 'incorporation' theory and the 'real seat' theory have failed (cf. academic writings, ch 2 II, and the 1956 and 1968 draft Conventions of the Hague Conference and the EC on the Mutual Recognition of Foreign Companies, ch 2 III 1 and IV 1, above).

[219] This proposal was clearly inspired by the opinion of AG Dermon in the *Daily Mail* case and art. 11(2) of the aforementioned Directive on Mergers, EM 33.

incorporation in accordance with the law of that state.[220] Other authorization requirements are, however, acknowledged where national laws allow the transfer of the *siège réel* to be regulated by the articles of association of the company. The consequences of a seat transfer are dealt with in article 5: the legal personality shall be 'continuous and uninterrupted by the transfer'.[221] This applies in particular to the rights of creditors and employees of the company in accordance with Directive 77/187/EEC.[222] Article 6 contains an amendment to Council Directive 90/434/EEC:[223] the transfer of a company's *siège réel* shall be treated as a transfer of assets within the meaning of subsection (c), and the 'transferring company' shall be the company prior to the transfer of its *siège réel*, and the 'receiving company' shall be the same company after the transfer of its *siège réel*.[224] The final provisions of articles 7 and 8 regulate the implementation of this Directive.

The second proposal

Definition

The second proposal is entitled 'Draft Directive on the transfer of the official registered address of a company from one Member State to another without dissolution (with consequent change of the proper law of the company)'. Although, seen from a procedural perspective, it closely ressembles the first proposal[225] methodologically speaking, it follows a different pattern. Contrary to the first proposal, the transfer of the *siège réel* entails a *consequent* change of the proper law of the company: the transferring company *no longer remains subject* to the *law of the state of incorporation*.

Main features

As in the first proposal, article 1 defines the precise scope of application, and article 2 contains further definitions.[226] According to article 3, the offi-

---

[220] Taking into consideration that there is no change in the proper law of the company, no extra protection measures for shareholders are necessary, unless the company itself requires such measures, EM 33.

[221] Art. 5 'simply states this for the avoidance of doubt', EM 33.

[222] OJ L 61 of 5 March 1977.   [223] OJ L 225 of 20 August 1990.

[224] This provision was also inspired by the *Daily Mail* case, which after all was responsible for considerable restrictions on the freedom of 'departure'. Taking into account that such a departure may give rise to tax charges, these charges may be contrary to the objective of Directive 90/434/EEC on the taxation of cross-border mergers, which should facilitate corporate reorganizations within the Community in a tax-neutral manner. Art. 6 proposes a modification of the aforementioned Directive to assimilate a transfer of the *siège réel* to a transfer of assets which would not be taxable by virtue of art. 9 of said Directive: EM 34.

[225] The legal basis is identical to that of the first proposal, cf. the foregoing section. It also contains the text of the draft Directive and an explanatory memorandum.

[226] So far, the two proposals appear to be quite similar.

cial registered address shall bind the company as to the location of its 'seat'.[227] Consequently, a transfer of this seat results in an alteration of the proper law; the legal personality of the company, however, is not touched upon. Third parties shall be entitled to prove that the company does not in fact maintain its seat as its official registered address.[228] It must be acknowledged, however, that this system is not entirely consistent: it would seem logical only to 'allow an appeal to the head office *in states that adhere to the* siège réel *system'*, as 'in the incorporation system the location of the head office is irrelevant'.[229] Third parties are not members of the company's organs. It is necessary to recall, once again, that this draft proposal has a neutral character: it does not oblige member states to give up the private international law recognition theory to which they adhered before. It only provides a 'mechanism' for transferring the official registered address of the company, leaving both recognition theories intact. The view has been expressed, though, that the method pursued by the proposal slightly influences both the 'incorporation' and the 'real seat' theories:

After all, for the company itself, such a transfer (i.e. of the registered office, SR) will lead to it being governed by the laws of the state of arrival, *regardless of whether the head office is transferred as well*. This is unknown to both the incorporation system and the *siège réel* concept. Thus, it entails an infringement on both national systems.[230]

---

[227] This is considered to function as 'proof of the location of (the company's) seat', EM 42. According to Bellingwout (1995) 83, this is 'an interesting turn': if the head office of the company would have been preferred to fulfil this role, this would have resulted in a loss of legal certainty and predictability, since 'facts can be assessed differently by the various member states'.

[228] In the view of the EM 42, 'this is a question for each Member State's Private International Law. If, for example, a company incorporated in state X which applies the 'real seat' theory, transfers its official registered address to state Y, without however at the same time transferring its centre of management and control, third parties may prove that the proper law of the company is still that of the state of incorporation. In situations like these it would obviously be inappropriate for the management body to claim otherwise.' Bellingwout (1995) 83, concludes from this that basically 'the incorporation system's susceptibility to fraud (. . .) appears to be overcome in this way'.

[229] Bellingwout (1995) 85. Thus, any third-party protection provision would be redundant for a Dutch NV converting into an English plc, irrespective of whether the head office is (still) located in the Netherlands.

[230] ibid. 84: 'immigration of the official registered address of a foreign legal entity in my opinion does not result in the application of Dutch company law; emigration of the registered office is not allowed'. Both assertions may, however, be doubted. As far as *immigration* is concerned: except for e.g. Sweden (after incorporation, the law applicable to the company is that of the country of first registration) most incorporation theorists link the *lex societatis* with the registered office; a company moving its *registered office* into the Netherlands will therefore—although not *automatically*—be obliged to change the proper law of the company as well. *Emigration* transfers, though problematical, are by no means totally excluded, cf. the case on the transfer of the NV Indonesische Aardoliemaatschappij (Wet of 28 October 1959, Stb. 386), and art. 4 of the 1998 CLC Act referred to in ch 4 II 1, above.

Article 4 obliges member states to bring their national law in compliance with the Directive, as regards the transfer of the company's official registered address (article 4(1)). If a company retains a place of business in the member state of departure, it shall register that place as a branch in accordance with the law of that state.[231] Article 5 obliges company managers to draw up draft terms of transfer in writing, *inter alia* specifying (a) the type and official registered address of the company before the transfer and the proposed type and official registered address after transfer;[232] (b) whether, and in what way the company's capital is to be converted into the currency of the state of arrival, and in that event the manner of redesignation of the shares;[233] (c) proposed modifications (if any) to the company's name and statutes to bring them into conformity with non-discriminatory laws of the state of arrival. Article 6 requires publication of the draft terms of transfer in the manner prescribed by the law of the state of departure, at least two months before the date fixed for the general meeting which is to decide thereon.[234] Article 7 regulates the approval of the general meeting. Similar to the Third Company Law Directive, it differs from the first proposal in that it contains an absolute rule a majority of not less than two-thirds of the votes attaching either to the shares or to the subscribed capital represented or the majority required to modify the company's statutes is required. Any derogation from this rule shall be void, unless the laws of the member state provide that a simple majority of the votes shall be sufficient when at least half of the subscribed capital is represented. Moreover, rules governing amendment of the statutes, insofar as they are prescribed by EC member states, shall apply (subs. 1). Article 7(2) distinguishes various classes of shares. Subsection 3 prescribes that the decision

---

[231] 'In other words, the company must be treated in exactly the same way as a company originating in the state of arrival which opens a branch *de novo* in the state of departure', EM 43.

[232] The EM admits that at first sight this may look redundant, now that the Directive only covers one company type. It is of extreme importance though that shareholders remain adequately informed in all situations. Furthermore, if the existing company name is incompatible with non-discriminatory rules of the state of arrival, it will have to be changed, in which case the shareholders should also be informed: 43 et seq.

[233] At present, the state of arrival can (still) legitimately require that the currency of the share capital of the company be the national currency. If the exchange rate used does not produce a round figure, it may be useful for the company to convert its shares into shares representing a fixed percentage of the total share capital, EM 44. Of course, problems related to currency will be considerably reduced when the euro is introduced. Only EC member states that do not join in, and third countries, will be affected by it.

[234] Again, this provision copies art. 6 of the Third Company Law Directive on mergers, except that the period of publication has been extended from one to two months prior to the general meeting (cf. art. 14 EEIG Regulation, and art. 5A of the SE draft Regulation), EM 45. No explicit reasons are given for this change. Perhaps the reason is that, unlike the Third Directive, which is about *national* mergers, this proposal and the EEIG and SE legislation apply to situations of an *international*—and therefore simply more time-consuming—character.

shall cover both the approval of the draft terms of merger and any amendment of the articles of association necessitated by the transfer.[235] Article 8
obliges the management board to draw up a written report on the transfer, including legal and economic grounds.[236] Shareholders shall, on the
basis of article 9, be entitled to inspect documents (i.e. the draft terms
required by article 5 and the management report by article 8) and to
receive copies at the official registered address of the company at least two
months prior to the transfer decision.[237] Article 10 copies article 5 of the
first proposal: the legal personality shall be 'continuous and uninterrupted
by the transfer'. This applies in particular to the rights of creditors[238] and
employees of the company in accordance with Directive 77/187/EEC.[239]
The same principle applies to the protection of secured creditors (article
11),[240] debenture holders (article 12), as well as other security holders (article 13).

Administrative and judicial supervision

Article 14 specifies the administrative or judicial supervision: if there is no
judicial or administrative control of the legality of transfers in member
states, or if this control does not extend to all acts, the minutes of the general meeting which decide on the transfer shall be drawn up and certified
in due legal form (article 14(1)). The competent notary or authority must
check and certify the existence and validity of legal acts and formalities
required of the company (for which such notary or authority is acting) and
of the draft terms of transfer (article 14(2)). Article 15 prescribes how the
registration of the transfer should be carried out:[241] no decision to transfer

---

[235] As in merger situations, shareholders of the acquired company deserve particular protection, as it is their company which moves to another legal order: EM 45.

[236] cf. art. 9 of the Third Company Law Directive. However, no need was felt to require an
expert's report, as prescribed in art. 10 of that Directive because, unlike merger situations,
there is no exchange of assets for shares in another company; in a transfer there is a one-to-
one correspondence between the assets and the shares of the company before and after the
transfer: EM 46.

[237] cf. art. 11 of the Third Company Law Directive: EM 46.

[238] This matter was considered in III 2, above.

[239] OJ L 61 of 5 March 1977. This means *inter alia* that if an employee is dismissed after a
transfer, he can claim continuous service with the same enterprise uninterrupted by the
transfer: EM 47.

[240] According to EM 48, the secured creditor is confronted with problems: the law applicable to any security given by way of charge over the company's assets will change. An example is given of a mortgage over real property, and an example having regard to a registered
general floating charge over all the company's assets. The second example in particular gives
rise to several questions: what if new creditors can register charges over the same assets after
the transfer? The drafters opt for the solution that the secured creditor be given a right to
enforce his charge before the transfer. They express their doubts as to whether publication of
the transfer proposal to 'the whole world' gives sufficient notice to individual secured creditors. As pointed out earlier, this case represents the problem of *res in transitu* in private international law: ch 6 III 2, above.

[241] The procedures for the EEIG and the SE are similar: EM 50.

the official registered address may be taken for two months after publication of the proposal in accordance with article 6. The transfer shall take effect on the date of registration in the state of arrival. There must be evidence in the form described in article 14 that the proposal to transfer the official address has been duly approved by the general meeting (article 15(1)). Likewise, termination of the registration in the state of departure will only be effected when evidence has been produced that the company has been registered with its official registered address in the member state of arrival. Upon such termination all information already recorded in the registry of the state of departure shall be preserved by that registry. The state of departure may close such register only upon proof of dissolution of the company in accordance with the laws of a member state having jurisdiction (article 15(2)). Publication of the company's new official address may be relied upon against third parties. However, third parties may continue to rely on the old official registered address if the termination of registration of the company in the state of departure has not been published, unless the company proves that third parties were aware of the new official address (article 15(3)). The laws of member states may provide that the transfer shall not take effect if, within the two-month period, a competent authority in that member state opposes it, which is only possible on the ground of public interest. Review by a judicial authority must be possible (article 15(4)). Article 16 governs matters of liability and nullity. All such matters are subject to the law of the state of departure in respect of acts or events taking place before the transfer, and to the law of the state of the arrival in respect of such events taking place after the transfer. The effective date of transfer is to be determined in accordance with article 15(3). In determining such matters, member states apply the same rules to the company as they apply to companies incorporated in their own jurisdiction (article 16(1)). Article 16(2) contains exclusive conditions of nullity: (a) nullity must be ordered by a court; (b) transfers may only be nullified if there has been no judicial or administrative supervision of their legality, or if the minutes of the general meeting have not been drawn up and certified in due legal form, or if it is shown that the decision of the general meeting is void or voidable in the state of departure; (c) nullification procedures may not be initiated more than six months after the date on which the transfer becomes effective as against the person alleging nullity, nor if the situation has been rectified; (d) where possible, courts shall grant a company time to rectify defects liable to render a transfer void; (e) a judgment declaring a transfer void shall be published; (f) where the laws of a member state permit a third party to challenge such a judgment, they must do so within six months of publication of the judgment; (g) a judgment declaring a transfer void shall not of itself affect the validity of obligations owed by or in relation to the company in each of the member states which arose before the judgment was published and after the date of registration of the company in the state of arrival.[242] Article 17 resembles article 6 of the first proposal: the transfer of a company's *siège réel* shall be treated as a transfer of assets within the meaning of subsection (c) above, and the 'transferring company' shall be the company prior to the transfer of its *siège réel*, and the 'receiving company' shall be the same company after the transfer of its *siège réel*. Finally, the provisions of articles 18 and 19 regulate the implementation of this Directive.[243]

Critical observations

Harmonization attempts: diverging levels of comparison

While debating the issue of cross-border company mobility, it would be highly tempting to compare legislative initiatives (the KPMG *Report*, national private international law Codes[244]) with relevant case-law from EC member states (in particular the Belgian Supreme Court *Lamot* decision[245]) on one hand, and ECJ case-law (*Daily Mail* judgment) on the other. But a critical observer will consider such an approach as mere self-deceit: first and foremost, it should not be overlooked that nearly three decades separate the *Lamot* judgment and the KPMG *Report*.[246] In the second place, the *Lamot* judgment, though perhaps not entirely 'introspective' (cf. the

---

[242] The provision on nullity was again based on art. 22 of the Third Company Law Directive. The drafters express the view that it is for the organs of the company to ensure that the company is properly transferred, i.e. that the statutes are in conformity with the law of the state of arrival, that the number of directors is at least the minimum required by the law of that state, that the company has not lost more than half its share capital, etc.: EM 50. They see no need for authorities of the state of arrival to verify these matters as a condition precedent to the transfer of the company's official registered address. Instead, it is for those in charge of the company organs to accept the consequences. These consequences must be the same as when a company incorporated in the state of arrival ceases to be duly organized in accordance with the law.

[243] cf. EM 51. The drafters underline that Council Directive 69/335/EEC, OJ L 225 of 20 August 1990 on the taxation of mergers, divisions, transfers of assets, etc., does not apply here: 'if this fiscal barrier is allowed to persist, the possibility of transfer of the official registered address of a company will lose most of its attraction, and companies will set up shell companies and merge with them in order to obtain the tax neutrality organised by Directive 90/434/EEC'. It is therefore proposed that this Directive be amended, although this will require unanimity of all the member states.

[244] For national law-oriented legislative attempts, see ch 4 II (Netherlands and Switzerland) and ch 4 III (Italy), above.

[245] More detail in ch 6 III 1, above.

[246] In the meantime, company law has undergone substantial changes: (i) EC law: accession of new member states, some of them applying the 'incorporation' theory; (ii) EC law: company law harmonization programme; (iii) national law: differing views on capital requirements, workers' co-determination, 'one-tier' or 'two-tier' board, Dutch *structuurregime*, etc. See ch 6 I 1 and 2, above. This also explains why there is good reason for excluding party autonomy from the field of company law: I 1, above. Cf. further III 1, in particular the German *Zweibrücken* judgment and comments thereon.

second and third conditions), predominantly focused on the legal order of Belgium, whereas the KPMG drafters faced the far more complicated task of reconciling the laws of all member states at EC law level.

Company immigration: Lamot *reconsidered*[247]

Let us briefly recall the transfer requirements prescribed by the *Lamot* judgment: the Belgian Supreme Court dictated five preconditions for the transferring company: (i) an absence of *fraus legis*; (ii) all the legal requirements of the emigration country must be obeyed; (iii) the continuing existence of the legal person must be permitted for under the law of the emigration country; (iv) the immigration country must not oppose the continuing existence of the legal person; and finally (v) the structure of the company should be fundamentally compatible with the law of the immigration country: 'essential' changes in the company structure are proscribed.

Although *Lamot* may have been conceived in a spirit conducive to cross-border company seat transfers, it failed to provide detailed instruments to effectuate the procedure of cross-border company transfers in everyday practice.[248] Reconsidering the requirements (ii) and (v), the following questions arise. When and how should the articles of association be adapted to Belgian law? Before or immediately after the seat transfer? (Note that in the *Lamot* case, the amendment of the articles of association was not completed until two and a half years after the transfer took place).[249] What is the precise status of a notary public? Another complication is that under, for example, Dutch law, any amendment of the articles of association requires a 'declaration of no objection' by the Justice Department.[250] One might have a sense of *déjà vu*: the tendency to transfer

[247] See III 1, above.

[248] cf. Wouters (1996/97) 634, summarizing all steps that should be taken consecutively: (i) shareholders' meeting in the country of departure where transfer decision (including the fixed date, etc.) is taken; (ii) amendment of the articles of the association of the company (i.e. adaptation to Belgian law); and (iii) general meeting in Belgium. The meeting to be attended by a Belgian notary public, supervising the transfer as regards for example: the residence of the company's 'real seat' in Belgium, transcription of company capital in Belgian francs, control and approval of articles of association, appointment of (controlling and/or supervisory) managers, publication in national gazette of Belgium and registration of the company at the Chamber of Commerce of the city where the company has its centre of management and control.

[249] Wouters (1996/97) 634.

[250] cf. ss 125 and 235 of the Dutch Company Law Act (contained in the second book of the Dutch Civil Code) prescribing the procedure for amending the articles of association of an NV (public limited company) and of a BV (private limited company). A declaration of no objection is awarded by the Dutch Justice Department only when no (financial) criminal convictions of those in charge of the company's establishment are found. It is, however, awkward that at the same time the 'incorporation' theory is adhered to in the Netherlands. It is noteworthy that this declaration, being one of the formation requirements for both NVs and BVs, turned out to be one of the main incentives for businessmen in the Netherlands to conduct their business by using a 'foreign' company. For the response to this problem see ch 4 II 1, above.

company seats from the Netherlands to Belgium seems to be enhanced by mechanisms of tax law, rather than of company law.[251] Like their English counterparts,[252] the Dutch Treasury authorities feared a loss of revenue resulting from numerous transfers of company headquarters to other countries offering lower tax rates. With the help of the Justice Department they halted the unrestricted freedom of departure, by withholding declarations of no objection from companies wishing to transfer, which after all is required to amend the articles of association, which under the *Lamot* doctrine is a *conditio sine qua non* for a seat transfer.[253]

Flaws in the Lamot *approach*

The *Lamot* judgment is not without inconsistencies: according to article 102 of the Belgian *Vennootschapswet* (Company Act), the thirty-year maximum duration for a company, unless this period is extended in accordance with the law[254] was held not to be retroactive, so that time did not start to run until the transfer had taken place.[255] Why underline the *continuing identity* of the transferred company when the thirty-year period is deemed to have begun at the moment of the transfer, thus implicitly admitting that the company has been re-established as a new company? Why was the amendment of the company's articles of association not carried out until two and a half years had passed? Why then still speak of an *essential* condition?[256] In this respect, one of the major complaints was that *Lamot* created the paradoxical situation of double nationality: under English law, the legal personality was maintained throughout the entire transfer procedure; on the other hand, Belgian company law claimed applicability as well.[257] Last but not least, it is important to meet the formal requirements of the First Company Law Directive on publication and national registration.

---

[251] cf. Bellingwout (1997); Wouters (1995) and (1996/97).

[252] cf. the ECJ *Daily Mail* judgment, ch 2 IV 2, above.

[253] Wouters (1996/97) 634.   [254] See II 1, above.

[255] In other words, the 30 years had not started in 1927 when Lamot Ltd. was established, but in 1932, the year of the company's seat transfer to Belgium.

[256] In this sense Wouters (1996/97) 638.

[257] cf. the intrinsic flaws of the First KPMG Proposal, III 2, above. By analogy, Wouters (1996/97) 640 et seq., suggested providing in the articles of association for jurisdiction to be attributed to Belgian courts (cf. art. 17 of the Brussels Jurisdiction Convention and the ECJ *Powell Duffryn* judgment, above ch 2 IV 2 and ch 6 II 1.) As a consequence of such a prorogation clause, shareholders could no longer claim more favourable 'foreign' company law. He admits, however, that 'outsiders' (i.e. not company organs) would not be bound by such a clause. Neither could it infringe upon the exclusive jurisdiction rule of art. 16(2) of said Convention. A clash of jurisdictions could result, with both the English and the Belgian courts claiming jurisdiction on the basis of their seat theories: cf. art. 2 which can be applied only in conjunction with art. 53 of the Brussels Convention. However, note the calls for a complete reform of this Convention: II 1, above.

Company emigration: the reciprocity of the Lamot *principles*

Meanwhile, it is intriguing to find out whether, from the point of view of reciprocity, Belgian authorities would apply the same criteria to the *emigration* of a company from Belgium to another legal order. Ruling on a transfer of the head office of a Belgian company to the Netherlands, the highest administrative court of Belgium observed that it cannot be concluded from any legal provision that such a company would cease to be a legal person under the law of Belgium. Considering that, *in casu*, the seat transfer to the Netherlands appeared to be of a factual nature, such a 'transfer' could not have been decided on by the competent company organ; consequently, the company could not have lost its Belgian nationality, nor could it have acquired the nationality of another state.[258] However, apart from the question whether the 'transfer' had been correctly performed in accordance with the law, this case was about the transfer of a company from a *siège réel* country to an 'incorporation' country.[259] Moreover, the ascertainment of the proper law of the company (i.e. where the 'real seat' of the company resides) should have been distinguished from the question whether the decision to transfer the seat was valid.[260]

Proposal for a 14th EC Company Law Directive

In 1997 a 'Proposal for a Fourteenth European Parliament and Council Directive on the Transfer of the Registered Office or the De Facto Head Office of a Company from One Member State to Another' was published.[261] Like earlier (draft) directives in the area of company law, this project was based on article 54 of the EC Treaty (now article 44). Acting on the basis of article 189(b) of the EC Treaty (now article 251) the European Parliament and the Council observe the following:

---

[258] R.v.St. 29 June 1987, Arr. R.v.St. 1987, nr. 28.276, commented on by Wouters (1996/97) 641 et seq. Undeniably, parallels exist between this case and, for example, *Segers, Daily Mail*, etc. (cf. Part 1 above): in all these cases the dispute concentrated on issues of company *taxation* rather than *company law* matters: the case of *Vanneste* came before the highest administrative Belgian court, to contest the decision of an administrative transportation authority, pursuant to which transportation permits had been withdrawn for the reason that the company (no longer) had its 'real seat' on Belgian territory.

[259] Note that the *Lamot* case was about a transfer in the opposite direction.

[260] In this sense Wouters (1996/97) 643, quoting Lenaerts. He adds that, though the *Lamot* principles had not been applied correctly, the immigration country will not oppose the transfer: due to the private international law instrument of *renvoi* (remission) the Netherlands, as an 'incorporation' country, will consider this company still to be governed by Belgian law.

[261] Doc. XV/6002/97-EN REV.2 of 20 April 1997. This project was signalled in *European Report* n 2282 of 14 January 1998: Business brief. 'Company Law: UNICE Seeks Clarification on Tax Measures for Migrating Firms'. For detailed comments, see the German *ZGR* 1999 (1–2) which is entirely devoted to this project, and Drury (1999) 362 et seq. (see below).

Whereas, in accordance with the principles of subsidiarity and proportionality, as set out in Article 3b[262] of the Treaty, the objectives of making it possible for a registered office or *de facto* head office to be transferred without affecting the connecting factors established *by albeit diverging national laws cannot be satisfactorily achieved by the Member States acting in isolation; whereas they are not in a position to organize the entire operation in question since it transcends national frontiers whereas these objectives can therefore be achieved only through action at Community level*;

Whereas, under Article 58[263] of the Treaty, companies or firms formed in accordance with the law of a Member State and having their registered office, central administration or principal place of business within the Community must be treated in the same way as natural persons who are nationals of other Member States for the purposes of the rules of the Treaty governing the right of establishment;

Whereas, as Community law stands, such equal treatment is thwarted by the major differences which exist between Member States' national laws, in particular with regard to the *criteria which connect companies with the legal systems under which they fall*;

Whereas Member States' legal systems do not possess *legal structures enabling the legal personality of companies to be retained when they transfer their registered office or* de facto *head office from one Member State to another*;

Whereas the possibility of transferring a company's registered office or *de facto* head office from one Member State to another involves the exercise of the right of establishment, which Community law *should make possible in practice*;

Whereas the fact that Article 220[264] of the Treaty requires Member States to enter into negotiations with each other regarding the retention of the legal personality of companies or firms in the event of a transfer of their seat from one country to another does not prevent this matter from being dealt with by a directive;

Whereas, under Article 54[265] of the Treaty, *Community law must lay down equivalent safeguards for the protection of the interests of members and others affected by the change in the legal system applicable to a company that has transferred its seat* to another Member State;

Whereas Council Directive 68/151/EEC requires among other things *disclosure of the main documents* adopted by a company's governing bodies; whereas this requirement should be *extended to transfers covered by this Directive*, which also relate to other types of company.[266]

The Proposal for a Fourteenth Directive contains 16 provisions, the text of which reads as follows:

Article 1
1. This Directive shall apply to transfers of their registered office or *de facto* head office from one Member State to another by companies formed in accordance with the law of a Member State and having their registered office and central administration within the Community.

---

[262] cf. art. 5 since the Amsterdam Treaty.
[263] cf. art. 48 since the Amsterdam Treaty.
[264] Now art. 293.
[265] Now art. 44.
[266] Emphases added.

Article 2

For the purposes of this Directive,

    a. 'registered office' shall mean the place in which a company is registered, and

    b. *'de facto* head office' shall mean the place at which a company has its central administration and is registered.

Article 3

Member States shall take all measures to allow a company to transfer its registered office or *de facto* head office to another Member State. Such transfer shall not result in the winding up of the company or in the creation of a new legal person but shall involve a change in the law applicable to the company from the date on which it registers its new office in accordance with Article 10.

Article 4

1. The management or administrative body shall draw up a transfer proposal and publicize it in accordance with paragraph 2, without prejudice to any additional forms of publication provided for by the Member State of the future office. The proposal shall cover:

    a. the proposed office of the company;

    b. the proposed statutes of the company including, where appropriate, its new name;

    c. the means by which it is proposed to organize employee participation in cases where employees are represented on the governing bodies of the company prior to the proposed transfer;

    d. the proposed transfer timetable.

2. The transfer proposal shall be published in the manner required by the laws of the Member State under whose jurisdiction the company falls after transfer, in accordance with Council Directive 68/151/EEC,[267] and in particular Articles 2 and 3 thereof.

Article 5

1. The management or administrative body shall draw up a report explaining and justifying the legal and economic aspects of the transfer and indicating the implications of the transfer for members and employees.

2. The company's members, creditors and employee representatives shall be entitled, at least one month before the general meeting called to decide on the transfer, to examine at the company's registered office or *de facto* head office the transfer proposal and the report drawn up pursuant to paragraph 1 and, on request, to obtain copies of those documents free of charge.

Article 6

1. No decision to transfer may be taken for two months after publication of the proposal.

2. A decision to transfer requires a decision adopted by a majority of not less than two-thirds of the votes cast at a general meeting, unless the law applicable to the company requires or allows a larger majority.

---

[267] OJ No L 65, 14.3, 1968, p. 8.

3. However, a Member State may lay down that, where at least half of the company's capital is represented, a simple majority of votes cast at a general meeting is sufficient.

4. Any amendment of the statutes shall be publicized in the manner required by the laws of the Member State under whose jurisdiction the company falls after the transfer, in accordance with Council Directive 68/151/EEC.

Article 7

A Member State may, in respect of the companies falling within its jurisdiction, adopt provisions designed to ensure appropriate protection for minority members who oppose a transfer.

Article 8

1. Creditors and holders of other rights in respect of a company which predate the publication of the transfer proposal may require the company to provide adequate security on their behalf. The exercise of such rights shall be governed by the law applicable to the company before its transfer.

2. A Member State may extend the application of paragraph 1 to those of a company's debts to public bodies which arose to the date of the transfer, determined in accordance with Article 11.

Article 9

In the Member State in which a company has its registered office or *de facto* head office before the transfer, a court, notary or other competent authority shall issue a certificate conclusively attesting to the completion of the pre-transfer acts and formalities.

Article 10

The new registration may not be effected until the certificate referred to in Article 9 has been submitted and evidence produced that the formalities required for registration in the country of the new office have been completed.

Article 11

1. The transfer of a company's registered office or *de facto* head office and the consequent amendment of the statutes shall take effect on the date on which the company is registered, in accordance with Article 10, in the register for its new office.

2. A Member State may refuse to register a company in accordance with Article 10 if its central administration is not situated in that Member State.

3. The deletion of a company's registration from the register for its previous registered office or *de facto* head office may not be effected until evidence has been produced that the company has been registered in the register for its new office.

4. The new registration and the deletion of the old registration shall be publicized in each of the Member States concerned in the manner required by their respective laws, in accordance with Council Directive 68/151/EEC.

Article 12

On publication of a company's new registration, the new office may be relied on as against third parties. However, as long as the deletion of the company's registration from the register for its previous office has not been publicized, third parties may continue to rely on the previous office unless the company proves that such third parties were aware of the new office.

Article 13
A company may not transfer its registered office or *de facto* head office in accordance with this Directive if proceedings for winding up, liquidation, insolvency or suspension of payments or other similar proceedings have been brought against it.

Article 14
1. Member States shall bring into force not later than 1 January 2000[268] the laws, regulations and administrative provisions necessary to comply with this Directive. They shall forthwith inform the Commission thereof. When Member States adopt these provisions, the latter shall contain a reference to this Directive or shall be accompanied by such a reference on the occasion of their official publication. The methods for making such reference shall be laid down by the Member States.
2. Member States shall forthwith communicate to the Commission the text of the essential provisions of domestic law which they adopt in the field governed by this Directive.

Article 15
Each Member State shall designate the competent register for the purposes of Article 9 and shall inform the Commission and the other Member State thereof.

Article 16
This Directive is addressed to the Member States.

Critical observations

General remarks: legal basis

The outcome of consultation amongst member states, business representatives, and legal experts in February 1997[269] was that a legal infrastructure enabling companies to migrate from one member state to another would be highly welcome. As follows from earlier findings, the everlasting controversy between the 'incorporation' theory and the 'real seat' theory frustrates cross-border company mobility in Europe; this explains why any attempt at national level to regulate this subject-matter is doomed to fail.[270] As regards the legal basis[271] for this legislative project, it has been observed that the concept of the Directive—i.e. the creation of instruments to facilitate cross-border transfers, the foundations of the two recognition theories, however, not being touched upon—was necessitated by the subsidiarity principle.[272]

[268] Original text version.
[269] Di Marco (1999) 4. Cf. Neye (1999) 14, with detail on the inquiry, which in Germany involved over 60 organizations.
[270] cf. comments to the *Programmsatz* character of art. 25(3) of the 1995 Italian Private International Law Code: ch 4 III 3, above.
[271] Art. 54(3)(g) of the Treaty (now art. 44(2)(g)), see above.
[272] Di Marco (1999) 6. Priester (1999) 36, who also emphasizes the subsidiarity principle, summarizes this concept as follows: '*Wahrung der Identität, aber Wechsel des anwendbaren Rechts*' (continuity of the company, but alteration of its proper law). Schmidt (1999) 21, 27, though starting with the observation that art. 3 might assign EC member states '*zur*

Scope of the draft directive

When compared to, for example, the draft Tenth Company Law Directive on Cross-Border Mergers of Public Companies, this project has been given a wider scope, in that it also comprises private limited company types.[273] This means *inter alia* that companies from third countries (e.g. Delaware corporations), having their real head office in an 'incorporation' country (e.g. the Netherlands) would not benefit from this piece of EC legislation. As regards the opposite situation, companies having only their registered office on the territory of an EC member state are *de facto* also excluded from primary establishment.[274] As both public and private company types fall within the scope of the Directive, two situations need to be distinguished: (i) the cross-border transfer of a public company from one EC member state to another, whereafter the migrating company adopts a more or less equivalent public company form in accordance with the law of the state of re-establishment; and (ii) the 'cross-over' cross-border transfer of a public company, where a migrating company transforms itself into a *private* company form under the law of the state of re-establishment.[275] From the point of view of governmental supervisory tasks, it has been doubted whether the Directive should also apply to banking and insurance companies.[276]

gesetzlichen "Abschaffung" der Sitztheorie', expresses the belief that the Directive does not impinge upon the 'real seat' theory: 27 Drury (1999) 362, observes that the proposal 'attempts to get the greatest possible *rapprochement* with the least possible change to the two systems'.

[273] This is welcomed by e.g. Boucourechliev (1999) 5: although it may be true that former harmonization efforts concentrated on *public* companies because they have access to public capital (stock exhanges), today the increasing importance of *Mittelstandförderprogramme* (SME stimulation programmes) is beyond doubt. *Private* capital companies should therefore be covered by this Directive as well. Di Marco (1999) 7, on the other hand, observes that *solely* capital companies are covered by this Directive, now that company laws of the member states are adequately harmonized. Neye (1999) 15, criticizes the German text version: the word *Hauptversammlung* should be replaced by *Gesellschafterversammlung*, as the latter notion shows more clearly that the shareholders' meeting of the German private limited company (GmbH) is also covered.

[274] For detail see Wouters (1996/97) 150 et seq. (I 2, above). As regards the definition of 'companies', Rajak (1999) 111 et seq., asserts that particularly for the UK, this means entities registered under the British Companies Act 1985. This Act requires a certificate of incorporation and articles of association, pursuant to which the company is registered in England, Scotland, or Wales. Although subsequent transfers of the registered office are neither explicitly allowed nor prohibited in s 2(1)(b) and (2), there is authority to the effect that even inter-regional transfers (e.g. from Scotland to Wales) are prohibited: cf. P. Davies/L.C.B. Gowers *Principles of Modern Company Law*, 6th edn. 1997 14. Even a purely *domestic* transfer of the registered office (e.g. from London to Liverpool) is subject to numerous formal and material requirements (for the precise details see Davies/Gower (1997)). This also has consequences for a *cross-border* company transfer: see below.

[275] Schmidt (1999) 33, speaks of a *'grenzüberschreitender und typusüberschreitender Formwechsel'*, which should be accomplished *'uno acto'*.

[276] Neye (1999) 15.

Due to considerable divergence between legal concepts in all EC member states, partnerships are exluded from the Directive's scope.[277]

Pursuant to article 1, the draft directive covers cross-border company transfers of the 'registered office or *de facto* head office from one member state to another', on condition that both seats were situated on the territory of the EC and that the company was formed in accordance with the law of a member state.[278]

Article 2 of the draft directive makes no fundamental changes to the well known definitions of the company's 'registered office'[279] and *'de facto* head office'. Taking into account that both recognition theories remain fundamentally unaffected by this legislative project, the image regarding cross-border seat transfers to be covered by the Directive is as follows. (i) All member states involved adhere to the 'incorporation' theory: the transfer of the registered office, either with or without a transfer of the management and control office;[280] (ii) the state of re-establishment applies the 'real seat' theory: both registered office and headquarters of the company must be transferred; and (iii) the mere transfer of the management and control centre is considered to be *exclusively* governed by *internal* law.[281] Many writers take issue with this point.[282] It is highly ironic that to a large

---

[277] Clearly contrasting with ex art. 58 of the EC Treaty. Cf. Rammeloo (Dossier 1999) 80 et seq., concerning freedom of establishment for partnerships in Europe. In this respect, Priester (1999) 37, observes that the inclusion of partnerships would ultimately have jeopardized the success of the entire project. Similarly, Rajak (1999) 115. Nonetheless, the Directive also applies to the German KGaA (partnership limited by shares) 39.

[278] UNICE (1998) 1, speaks of 'community-based companies'. The 'position paper', p. 2, however, advocates a restriction of the scope: it should apply to those company types mentioned in the First Company Law Directive No. 68/151EEC, because other types are governed by widely varying legislation in various member states, which could complicate the application of the new directive.

[279] Drury (1999) 363, observes that the 'proposal's definition of registered office is more subtle than the "official registered address" concept in the (KPMG) *Report*, and it is an improvement on earlier drafts of the Directive'.

[280] cf. Drury (1999) 365: '(t)his will require a considerable change in the conflict of laws rules of the place of incorporation jurisdictions because their innate reaction would be to say that they do not allow a company to transfer its registered office at all, still less to be governed by the law of the new location of the registered office. They must make a considerable compromise in their approach.'

[281] Di Marco (1999) 7.

[282] Timmerman (1999) 156, doubts whether the Directive would also apply to, for example, a company established in the Netherlands planning to transfer its headquarters abroad. Wymeersch (1999) 144, observes that the *'rein faktische Sitzverlegung'* (the informal, *de facto* cross-border transfer) is no longer even *allowed* under the 14th Company Directive regime (which is something quite different): migrating companies should either comply with the requirements in the Directive, or establish a (secondary) branch. A complementary view was expressed by Rajak (1999) 113, who also seems to be convinced that *pursuant to the 14th Company Law Directive* the transfer of *solely the management and control centre* of an English public limited company would entail the company's *'Löschung (. . .) im Britischen Register'* (deregistration in England). He explicitly refers to the *Daily Mail* case (ch 2 IV 2, above).

extent confusion is caused by the fact that so far even recent codifications remain silent on this point: 'incorporation' country legislators hardly felt the need to elaborate rules for the last-mentioned category of cross-border transfers, as this type of transfer causes few problems.[283] An interesting thought is, however, whether companies engaged in these types of transfers could not benefit also from a sophisticated set of flanking protective measures.[284]

Transfer procedure

Draft article 3 is of particular interest, as it obliges member states to 'take all measures to allow a company to transfer'[285] one of its seats to another member state, although a winding up or the creation of a new legal person should not result.[286] Both the state of departure and the state of re-establishment must safeguard the company's survival.[287] In this respect, it may be troublesome to find out whether, for example, an Australian company derived any rights from the 'business rescue regime of administration' (sections 1–27) of the British Insolvency Act.[288] Draft article 3 has been described as

the first line of defence for shareholders who feel that their best interests are not served by the migration proposal, but there is a possible second line of defence in article 7 which provides that a Member State *may* adopt provisions to ensure appropriate protection for minority members who oppose the transfer.[289]

There is no uniformity as regards publication requirements: pursuant to article 4, 'the management or administrative body shall draw up a transfer proposal and publicize it in accordance with paragraph 2, *without*

---

[283] cf. explicitly Timmerman (1999) 152. Cf. further notably ch 4 II 1, above, on the Dutch 1998 CLC Act.

[284] cf. what has been said in another context on preliminary questions put to the ECJ by the Dutch cantonal court of Groningen on 19 October 1999 and by the German BGH on 30 March 2000: see ch 2 IV 2 above.

[285] Drury (1999) 369, provokingly asks whether this 'include(s) an obligation to remove taxation obstacles to migration. If it does, then regulatory privisions like the previous British rules requiring Treasury consent to a departure litigated in the *Daily Mail* case, as well as French rules requiring a migration of a company to be treated as a dissolution with fearsome tax consequences, would be outlawed.'

[286] The British Companies Act contains several disclosure requirements: s 352(1) (shareholders); s 288 (management and secretaries); s 325 (register of directors' interests in shares and other debentures); s 691(1) (official address), cf. Rajak (1999) 119. Furthermore, this provision is interesting when viewed against the background of above assessments of German law: ch 4 III 1.

[287] Di Marco (1999) 7.

[288] This was put forward by Rajak (1999) 119 et seq. He is convinced, that incoming companies may indeed be treated on the same footing as English companies, provided however that both their registered office and headquarters are transferred to Great Britain.

[289] Drury (1999) 364.

prejudice to any additional forms of publication provided for by the Member State of the future office'.[290]

Draft article 5 is striking in that it obliges migrating companies to clarify their strategy: the management or administrative body shall draw up a report 'explaining and justifying the legal and economic aspects of the transfer and indicating the implications of the transfer for members and employees'. Thus, a high degree of transparency is aimed at.[291] Company members, creditors, and *employees* are given *inter alia* the right to advise on the transfer.[292] It has been alleged that this device comes near to that prescribed by section 425 of the English Companies Act, concerning the company's transformation.[293]

Draft article 6 provides:

A decision to transfer requires a decision adopted by a majority of not less than two-thirds of the votes cast at a general meeting, unless the law applicable to the company requires or allows a larger majority. 3. However, a Member State may lay down that, where at least half of the company's capital is represented, a simple majority of votes cast at a general meeting is sufficient.

Considering that cross-border company seat transfers are of major importance, it can be assumed that in many legal orders the implementation of draft article 6(2) will be given preference.[294]

Article 9 prescribes the following: 'In the Member State in which a company has its registered office or *de facto* head office before the transfer, a court, notary or other competent authority shall issue a certificate conclusively attesting to the completion of the pre-transfer acts and formalities'.

Pursuant to draft article 10, '(t)he new registration may not be effected until the certificate referred to in article 9 has been submitted and evidence produced that the formalities required for registration in the country of the

---

[290] Emphasis added. This is more or less in conformity with the Third Directive on co-ordination of company law on mergers of public limited liability companies, and the Sixth Directive on co-ordination of company law on the division of public limited liability companies, see I 2, above. Subs 2 refers to Council Directive 68/151/EEC, OJ No L 65 of 14 March 1968. Electronic publication is likely to be common in the near future, cf. Di Marco (1999) 9. Not surprisingly, the procedure enshrined in the draft for a 14th Company Law Directive closely resembles that of art. 8 of the revised draft Regulation for an SE. Cf. Edwards (1999) 399 et seq. For an overview of recent developments concerning the European *private* company, cf. Drury/Hicks (1999) 429 et seq.

[291] Rajak (1999) 113, advocates extrapolation of the procedure enshrined in the 1985 British Companies Act (originally intended to regulate purely domestic company seat transfers, see above), to cross-border company seat transfers. To that end, s 2(1)(b) and (2) of the British Companies Act must be amended.

[292] For detailed comments, see below.

[293] Rajak (1999) 121, illustrating that British courts demonstrate great discernment in unravelling all possible corporate opportunities for management board members.

[294] In this sense e.g. Rajak (1999) 121 et seq. As regards English law he distinguishes between a management board decision, usually based on a simple majority, and a decision of the shareholders' meeting, requiring a qualified majority.

new office have been completed'. It must not be overlooked that 'real seat' jurisdictions 'can always fall back on the safeguard device in Article 10.2 (11) and refuse to register the transfer if the central administration is not to accompany the registered office'.[295] It is noteworthy that, despite all methodological flaws,[296] the anthropomorphic concept of legal persons still inspires writers to speak of a 'birth certificate' for companies.[297]

What about those companies which entered a 'real seat' country prior to the (future) implementation of the 14th Company Law Directive? This is clearly a matter of transitory law. Subsequent legitimation is likely to be frustrated by the fact that in the past, company managers were confronted with the undesired consequences of personal liability under the law of the country where the company's 'real seat' is located.[298] Solely those company managers who are considered as *'tätige Reue'* (remorseful sinners) should avoid being held personally liable. Their companies should at least not be condemned to dissolution and winding up before being re-established in another legal order.[299]

Protection of shareholders, company creditors, etc.

As regards the protection of those who have legitimate interests in the company's transfer, notably (minority) shareholders, company creditors, debenture holders, employees, national tax and social security authorities, etc. are involved. In this respect, the emphasis appears to be placed on the 'emigration' country, to which draft articles 4–9 are devoted. Draft articles 10 and 11(2) regulate the interests of the 'immigration' country. The complaint that the latter has been treated in a stepmotherly fashion[300] does not make sense: apart from the fact that the number of articles is not relevant, it can safely be assumed that the transfer of an emigrating company requires more intensive supervision in the country of departure than in the country of re-establishment, since business has hitherto been conducted on the territory of the former country. As regards the supervision of an incoming company in the country of re-establishment, it is not certain whether article 10 envisages a 'procedural' test in the sense that all formalities are complied with, or whether more substantial front-loaded control (with the sanction of personal liability of those in charge of the operation) is envisaged by the drafters.[301] An additional back-loaded control is imposed by article 12.

---

[295] Drury (1999) 366.   [296] See ch 4 II 2, above.

[297] Rajak (1999) 123, even speaks of a rebirth after the company's cross-border transfer has been completed.

[298] cf. ch 4 III 1, above.   [299] Schmidt (1999) 34, but without further answers.

[300] Priester (1999) 38.

[301] ibid. 46: front-loaded control in the country on whose territory the company plans to settle is, though not prescribed by the Directive, at least allowed for and desirable (cf. capital requirements and the check by the German *Registergericht*).

Minority shareholders' protection

Shareholders are deemed to deserve protection because they are confronted with different languages, different substantive company laws, and physical 'remoteness' of their company.[302] According to draft article 7, '(a) Member State may, in respect of the companies falling within its jurisdiction, adopt provisions designed to ensure appropriate protection for minority members who oppose a transfer'. In fact, this provision can only be enforced with the help of national company laws. The member states are endowed with considerable discretionary powers.[303] A right of withdrawal is one possible measure.[304] This provision was firmly objected to by UNICE for being 'too vague', as it 'will lead to divergent national regimes'.[305]

Creditor protection

Company creditors should be forewarned about a migrating company: any cross-border transfer requires that the interest of this group be properly protected. Draft article 8 provides that: 'Creditors and holders of other rights in respect of a company which predate the publication of the transfer proposal may require the company to provide adequate security on their behalf. The exercise of such rights shall be governed by the law applicable to the company before its transfer.[306] 2. A Member State may extend the application of paragraph 1 to those of a company's debts to public bodies which arose to the date of the transfer, determined in accordance with Article 11.' Both private and public[307] company creditors should be protected. It has been feared that, as far as creditor protection is concerned, an 'unjustified special and favourable treatment of public bodies among the list of creditors may arise as a result of current wording'.[308]

---

[302] Priester (1999) 38. Cf. the relationship with ECJ *Powell Duffryn*, ch 2 IV 2, above.

[303] Rajak (1999) 122, underscores that pursuant to s 459 of the British Companies Act, the law on minority protection is highly sophisticated in the UK.

[304] Di Marco (1999) 10

[305] UNICE (1998) 2.

[306] Drury (1999) 364, observes the following: 'It is perhaps unfortunate that the sentence in which this security appears also refers to the "holders of other rights", and one could interpret the clause to mean that it is these other rights that are to be, or rather continue to be, governed by the law applicable to the company before the transfer. It might be better to say that "such securities" shall be governed by this law or, in order to provide for the greatest range of possibilities, governed by the law, which governed the debt or other right initially.'

[307] e.g. tax and social security authorities: Di Marco (1999) 10. Drury (1999) 364, observes that 'a Member State can ensure that the company either pays its outstanding taxes before it leaves, or at least gives satisfactory security for their ultimate payment'.

[308] Di Marco (1999) 10. Less worthy of protection, at least in the opinion of UNICE, are those creditors who acquired debts before the transfer but after the publication of the transfer proposal. It should be noted that tax authorities were excluded: Priester (1999) 38.

Insolvency of the transferring company[309]

Creditor protection comprises protection against companies engaged in insolvency procedures. By draft article 13, transfers of *Wirtschaftsflücht-linge* (economic refugees) are explicitly excluded from the scope of this Directive. Any 'rescue attempt' should be undertaken before, not after, the company's transfer.[310] Companies planning migration for no other purpose than to avoid insolvency should also be prevented from completing such a transfer. To that end, the Directive should include a provision such that the law of the member state of origin would remain applicable in any legal proceedings commenced within a given period after the transfer, or requiring a report from the statutory auditor certifying that the ability of the company to continue as a going concern is not under threat.[311]

Employees: co-determination and protection; proper law of employment contracts

According to draft article 4, 'the management or administrative body shall draw up a transfer proposal and publicize it in accordance with paragraph 2, without prejudice to any additional forms of publication provided for by the Member State of the future office. The proposal shall cover: (. . .)

c. the means by which it is proposed to organize *employee participation* in cases where employees are represented on the governing bodies of the company prior to the proposed transfer'. In the past, worker co-determination appeared to be one of the most divisive issues.[312]

Given that attempts to harmonize company law on the 'functioning of the company's organs' have so far failed, this seems to be a rather provocative provision. Employees are bestowed with a crucial position:

1. The management or administrative body shall draw up a report explaining and justifying the legal and economic aspects of the transfer and indicating the implications of the transfer for members and *employees*. 2. The company's members, creditors and *employee representatives* shall be entitled, at least one month before the general meeting called upon to decide on the transfer, to examine at the company's registered office or *de facto* head office the transfer proposal and the report drawn up pursuant to paragraph 1 and, on request, to obtain copies of those documents free of charge.

It is not clear from the wording of this provision how much influence the employee representatives will have. Although the words 'examine (. . .)

---

[309] This subject-matter should be clearly distinguished from that of a foreign company, having completed the cross-border transfer procedure, claiming entitlement to 'rescue administration' under national insolvency laws: see above.

[310] Schmidt (1999) 33. Cf. Di Marco (1999) 7.

[311] UNICE (1998) 2. This reminds us of general concepts such as *fraude à la loi* (see ch 4 II 1 and 3, above).

[312] cf. Neye (1999) 17: '*Also die alte Polarität!*'

the transfer proposal' appear to exclude a right to veto the entire transfer operation, it is possible to imagine that the national laws of EC member states could be enriched with special co-determination procedures.[313]

Furthermore, the draft directive does not elaborate the concept of worker co-determination. At this stage it would be unrealistic to expect a uniform co-determination regime for Europe. The available options regarding the level of co-determination should be co-ordinated with the SE project.[314] Company managers and worker representatives are primarily obliged to reach an agreement which need not be based on any national minimum standard; subsidiarily, a standard should be found which is attractive and acceptable for both camps.[315] As a compromise, Great Britain formulated the 'before–after' model for the SE, on the basis of which negotiations must primarily be held between management board and employees; subsidiarily, the level of co-determination depends on whether any co-determination already existed. If not, a newly established SE should not bring about alterations; however, the SE of companies familiar with co-determination should adopt the co-determination level which is 'advantageous' to all companies which participate in the SE.[316]

So far, the only conclusion which seems to be justified is that the precise level of worker participation, or even 'co-determination', is left to the member states. In this respect, the UNICE position paper takes a preserving position: 'UNICE fears the current wording of the draft proposal implies that worker participation regimes, where they exist, would automatically be maintained when the headquarters of a company is transferred. The bosses' organisation strongly objects to any such possible interpretation of the text and insists that any provisions governing worker participation must reflect the law of the new country in which the company is to be registered.'[317] A more fundamental objection is that 'no

---

[313] e.g. the 1998 Dutch *Wet op de Ondernemingsraden* (co-determination Act), notably s 25 (advisory task of employee representation) and the special inquiry procedure contained in the Dutch Company Act (incorporated in the second book of the Dutch Civil Code), notably ss 344 et seq., concerning court proceedings before the *Ondernemingskamer* (the Enterprise Chamber of the Appeal Court Amsterdam).

[314] cf. Heinze (1999) 55 and 62: with an eye on the SE project, the Commission preferred not to take any position before an agreement is reached by the Council. Lutter (2000) 16, believes that from a German point of view a European private company would be interesting for enterprises with less than 500 employees, not being subject to worker co-determination.

[315] Di Marco (1999) 11, herewith refers to the future outcome of the debate on the Davignon Report. Cf. further Neye (1999) 17. Rajak (1999) 120, supposes that company managers and employee representatives of, for example, Germany and England should meet somewhere in the middle: in England, any incoming German company could appoint an employee director (as a 'symbolic gesture'), whereas an English company entering Germany should comply with German law on co-determination.

[316] Di Marco (1999) 11. Cf. for detailed information, but according to the *ZGR* issue on this subject, not reaching beyond May 1998, Heinze (1999) 62 et seq., and Hoffman (2000).

[317] UNICE (1998) 2.

worker consultation and/or participation provisions whatsoever should find their way into company law proposals'.[318]

Apart from the issue of co-determination, workers may have an interest in the application of draft article 8(1), which reads as follows:

Creditors and holders of other rights in respect of a company which predate the publication of the transfer proposal may require the company to provide adequate security on their behalf. The exercise of such rights shall be governed by the law applicable to the company before its transfer.

Any company transfer which is intended (wrongfully) to dismiss an employee may lead to a court order reviving the departing company's registration, to allow the employee to sue the company in the country of departure.[319]

Drury is concerned that the Commission 'provides no mechanism for employees to oppose the transfer of the head office of their employer, with a possible consequent change in the law governing their contract of employment'.[320] Most cross-border employment relationships are, however, clearly disconnected from the proper law of the company:[321] in order to ascertain the proper law of the employment contract most EC member state courts currently apply article 6 of the 1980 Rome Contracts Convention. This conflict of laws rule is significantly influenced by the policy of protecting the weaker contracting party, the employee.

Tax law

In conformity with the procedure enshrined in the Proposal for a Tenth Directive concerning cross-border mergers of public limited companies,[322] separate treatment of tax law was opted for. The total absence of clear guidelines on taxation,[323] which incited the *Daily Mail* public limited company to consider the (dis)advantages of a seat transfer, is another flaw. Given that company 'departures' are often subject to, for example,

---

[318] ibid., with reference to the Fifth Company Law Directive and the European Company Statute.

[319] cf. Rajak (1999) 118, referring to English case-law: *Creasy v Breachwood Motors Ltd*. [1992] BCC 638 [1993] BCLC 480. From a German law point of view, Heinze (1999) 56 et seq., also insists upon adequate protection of individual employees of transferring companies under the Convention on Jurisdiction and Enforcement of Judgments in Civil and Commercial Matters: see ch 2 IV 2 and ch 6 II 1, above.

[320] Drury (1999) 364 et seq.

[321] It is likely that e.g. members of the management board are more affected by the company transfer than less senior employees.

[322] Submitted by the Commission to the Council on 14 January 1985, COM(84) 727 final, OJ 1985 C 23 11. Cf. Neye (1999) 17.

[323] UNICE (1998) 1. The Unice 'position paper' stresses that 'if the new Directive is not to remain simply a dead letter', it is essential to ensure fiscal neutrality. Drury (1999) 370, observes that '(c)ompartmentalism in the Commission and slow-lane progress in the taxation field combine to prevent a global solution to the problem at this time'.

Liquidationsbesteuerung (company liquidation tax),[324] it is not surprising that this is too high a price for companies planning cross-border seat transfers. This is why any directive concerning cross-border company migration should be accompanied by legal devices granting 'tax neutrality'. Of course, national tax law should be replaced, or at least mutually coordinated by EC law.[325] At the same time, however, the expectation has been expressed that the draft 14th Company Law Directive, although facilitating cross-border company seat transfers, will meet resistance from the British tax authorities.[326] On the other hand, a

simplistic view might be 'if you don't like the provisions of your current tax regime you can simply move your house and pay elsewhere'. While Member States may not like this idea, it is possible that greater freedom to move might encourage competition in the tax field, and voluntarily promote the more level playing field that has been talked about in other contexts, without the need to impose wholesale compulsory harmonization of tax law.[327]

It has also been argued that, although states have a legitimate interest in requiring companies to pay all taxes due in respect of their activities in that state, states no longer have the right to hold companies prisoner in their own regime by imposing on departure an immediate liability for capital gains in respect of assets which have not been disposed of. Once the draft directive is adopted all such obstacles would constitute barriers to the freedom of corporate establishment.[328] How then to 'find a balance between the legitimate right to tax capital gains and the removal of immediate payment in the absence of realisation of the relevant assets'?[329] A solution could be found:

along the lines partially adopted in section 250(3)–(4) Finance Act 1994 where the United Kingdom uses the concept of deferring a deemed disposal until the date of the actual disposal. If a migrating company were legitimately required to settle its outstanding tax liability before departure in respect of everything but capital gains tax on its unrealised assets, and were required to provide a security to the Revenue authorities of the state of departure in respect of the capital gain which until that

---

[324] cf. Hügel (1999) 71 et seq. Neye (1999), quoting arts. 11 and 12 of the German *Körperschaftssteuergestz* (Company Taxes Act). Note that the freedom of 'departure' precedes the freedom of (re-)establishment: ch 2 IV 2, above.

[325] Neye (1999) 16. Cf. Drury (1999) 370: 'Many jurisdictions will fear that the Commission's Proposal will allow large taxpayers to escape from continuing to pay in their original jurisdiction, and this could be the most potent sphere of opposition to the Directive'.

[326] Rajak (1999) 118, again explicitly referring to ECJ *Daily Mail*. Cf. however Clarke (1991) 167: 'by Section 66 and Schedule 7 of the Finance Act 1988, a company incorporated in the United Kingdom is now regarded, with some exceptions, as a resident there for taxation purposes, *even if the central management and control is elsewhere* (emphasis added). The residence of a company incorporated abroad will, however, for tax purposes continue to be determined by reference to the place where its central management and control is exercised.' More information on UK tax law and the *Daily Mail* case in Bentley (1991) 171 et seq. Cf. ch 2 IV 2, above.

[327] Drury (1999) 370.   [328] ibid.   [329] ibid.

time accrued on these assets, this might provide a basis for a compromise solution. The company should be required to pay capital gains tax on the asset when it was eventually realised, accounting to the state of departure for what could be regarded as its share of that tax, proportionate to the period over which the gain accrued.[330]

An abusive transfer should be combated by including a provision in the Directive that approval of cross-border transfers presupposes that these transfers can demonstrate their commercial *bona fides*. This will enable state authorities to reject purely tax-driven transfers (such as that in *Daily Mail*). The possibility of an 'anti-avoidance formula as a ground for objection to the transfer' has been suggested. Accordingly, a clause could be inserted in draft article 10:

(a) member states may refuse to register a company in accordance with paragraph 1 where objective factors show that the proposed transfer was not carried out for valid organisational reasons and the principal purpose or one of the principal purposes of the transfer of the registered office was to avoid mandatory rules of corporate or fiscal law of the State of the company's existing registered office.[331]

Of course, a balance must be found between the interests of the state of departure and those of the state of re-establishment.

National laws on cross-border company transfers reconsidered

EC law and private international law of EC member states: joint efforts

The outline of the Proposal for a Fourteenth Directive on the Transfer of the Registered Office or the *De Facto* Head Office of a Company from One Member State to Another proves that its subject matter cannot be left to the national laws of the EC member states. Neither is it possible to have this matter regulated in a satisfactory manner solely by applying private international law rules.

Modern private international law codes, however, marked the beginning of a new era: some 'incorporation' countries[332] not only show willingness to acknowledge cross-border company transfers, but also heed the multiple interests of company organs, company creditors, employees, etc.[333] However, these codifications are all based on a single-oriented approach: national legislators, although they may be permissive in their attitude towards migrating companies, lack the power to regulate the

---

[330] ibid. [331] ibid., 371.

[332] cf. the Netherlands and Switzerland,ch 4 II 1 and 3 above. English private international law remained uncodified: ch 4 II 2, above.

[333] cf. the differences between the approach pursued by national legislators: from a mere *Programmsatz* (cf., although Italy is not an 'incorporation' country, art. 25(3) of the 1995 Italian Code, ch 4 III 3), to more thorough concepts (cf. the Netherlands and Switzerland, ch 4 II 1 and 3, above).

cross-border effects of such transfers. These can only be regulated at Community level. The draft proposal for a 14th Company Law Directive has been welcomed for being 'more responsive to the demands of real seat states and strongly encourages the move of the central administration to the new state and anticipates that the company will alter its constitution in line with the requirements of the new state, a not unreasonable demand'.[334] On the other hand, the precise reach of this proposal is far from clear at this moment: does it affect only the cross-border transfer of a company's management and control centre? At present, this type of transfer is not even an issue under the private international law of, for example, the Netherlands and England,[335] but there is great uncertainty whether, after its implementation, the scope of the Directive does or does not extend to this category of transfers,[336] or whether *a fortiori*, such transfers are not even allowed any longer.[337]

'Real seat' countries, by contrast, are not concerned about whether any or all imaginable cross-border seat transfers fall within the scope of the proposed Directive: hitherto, the transfer of either the company's management and control centre, or its registered office, or both, has always been highly troublesome under the law of nearly all 'real seat' countries. Regardless of whether companies plan to move in or out of an EC member state, they risk dissolution under the law of the country where they were incorporated. If they survived cross-border migration they would be exposed to another threat, namely joint liability of the company directors.[338] Due to the lack of reciprocity, however, Italy is an exception to the rule: 'domestic' companies departing from Italy remain unaffected, whereas incoming companies are subject to the 'real seat' theory.[339]

Recently, the German scholar Bechtel took the remarkable contrary view that although cross-border company seat transfers should be facilitated (*eklatanter Bedarf der Wirtschaft*), any proposal for a company law directive is redundant, and constitutes an infringement of the subsidiarity principle.[340] But how should the rigid position taken by German courts then be counter-balanced? Only recently, the outcome of a court decision concerning a German GmbH planning to transfer its management and control centre from Germany to Luxembourg was discouraging. In conformity with earlier case-law, the GmbH was deemed to be subject to compulsory dissolution and winding up under German law. No need was felt

---

[334] Drury (1999) 363.

[335] As set out above, the very essence of the 'incorporation' theory is of course that the company's 'real seat' and registered office need not to be situated in the same country (see ch 4 II 1 and 2, above).

[336] If this were the case, migrating companies might, however, benefit from voluntarily submitting themselves to the regime of the Directive.

[337] See above.   [338] See ch 4 III 1, above.

[339] Ch 4 III 3, above.   [340] Bechtel (1998) 348.

even to reiterate preliminary proceedings under the Maastricht Treaty.[341] This consideration met with disapproval, as Bechtel and others observed that the ECJ would by now have changed its position: instead of tolerating the compulsory dissolution of an emigrating company under the law of an EC member state, the Court would have required that the company adjust itself to satisfy the company laws of the immigration country. Bechtel comments that pursuant to the ECJ *Krause* judgment, the ratio for this altered position would no longer lie in non-discrimination but in the prohibition of general restrictions.[342] Vice versa, an incoming company should be able to adjust itself to German company forms, without the risk of being qualified as an OHG (contractual partnership) with joint liability for the 'company' directors.[343]

Proposal for a 14th EC Company Law Directive: timetable

Although it would be premature[344] to judge the merits of this proposed legislation at this stage, some thoughts come to mind. First, awareness is growing that cross-border company mobility is no longer the exclusive domain of national authorities.[345] Secondly, in order to escape from the blind alley,[346] a firm position on the issue of competence was taken: whereas article 293 (previously article 220) of the EC Treaty obliges member states to enter into negotiations with each other regarding the retention of legal personality for companies or firms in the event of a transfer of their seat from one member state to another, this does not prevent the

---

[341] OLG Hamm 30 April 1997, *EuZW* 1998, p. 31. Cf. ch 4 III 1, above. Cf. also OLG Düsseldorf 10 September 1998, JZ 2000 203. This judgment, however, prompted the German BGH to issue preliminary proceedings on 30 March 2000 (see Ch. 2 above).

[342] Bechtel (1998) 348, referring to Case 19/92 *Krause v Land Baden-Württemberg* [1993] ECR I–1663 (incl. further references). Any *Wegzugverbot* (decision of the company management to depart) would violate Maastricht Treaty provisions on the freedom of establishment. Moreover, art. 3(b) of the Treaty would oblige member states to facilitate such interstate company transfers by taking necessary legislative measures. Cf. ch 2 IV 2 and ch 4 III 1, above.

[343] Bechtel (1998) 349, asserting that the incoming company should be classified as a *Vorgesellschaft* (i.e. under the more lenient regime of a pre-incorporation country). Thus, the continuing existence and identity of the company would no longer be jeopardized. Cf. however, Schmidt (1999) 24 et seq., still in favour of the *Rechtsformzwangmodell*. But cf. the preliminary proceedings issued by the German BGH on 30 March 2000 (ch 2 IV 2 above) on whether applying the real seat theory in its strictest consequences to an immigrant Dutch BV (private limited company) is still permitted under the EC Treaty.

[344] cf. however, the alert reaction of the UNICE, in 'European Report' n 2282 of 14 January 1998: Business brief. Company Law: 'UNICE Seeks Clarification on Tax Measures for Migrating Firms'. This is referred to as UNICE (1998).

[345] cf. above findings (ch 6 II) and the italicized phrases (ch 6 III 2), compared to Dutch and German proposals suggesting the analogous application of national substantive company law provisions which were written for domestic conversions of a legal person into another type (ch 4 II 1 and ch 4 III 1, above).

[346] cf. earlier conclusions (ch 3, above). Behrens (1998) 353, observes that at last the ice has been broken: thanks to the new company law directive, the catastrophe of compulsory dissolution and winding up of migrating companies will soon belong to the past.

matter from being dealt with by a directive. The original timetable, however, turned out to be over-optimistic: according to the draft provision of article 14, 'Member States had been expected to bring into force not later than January 2000 the laws, regulations and administrative provisions necessary to comply with this Directive. They shall forthwith inform the Commission thereof'. They must also designate the competent register for the purposes of article 9 and inform the Commission and the other member states (article 15).[347]

3. Cross-border company mobility: conclusions

Although implementation of the 14th Company Law Directive on the Transfer of the Registered Office or the *De Facto* Head Office of a Company from One Member State to Another will take considerable time,[348] a satisfactory level of intra-Community company mobility seems to be within reach. To a large extent this is explained by the complicated multi-party nature of the subject-matter. It is altogether striking that after a period of several decades[349] the Commission's proposal for a Company Law Directive concerning cross-border company mobility is responded to positively.[350] In fact, the indispensable dialogue between EC law and private international law has borne fruit already. A lot of work remains to be done. The prevailing impression is that, at least when compared to efforts undertaken by national legislators and courts, plans to realize cross-border seat transfers were worked out in a far more meticulous manner by the draftsmen who took the responsibility for the KPMG *Report* and, subsequently, the Fourteenth Company Law Directive on the Transfer of the Registered Office or the *De Facto* Head Office of a Company from One Member State to Another. This is not surprising: national private international law legislation, as well as the Belgian *Lamot* judgment, shows yet again that it is not for national legislators or courts to act in isolation: they simply cannot formulate proper conditions to settle all the disputes which could arise from cross-border seat transfers. As regards the status of foreign companies and their transfers, the additional value of recent national

---

[347] cf. UNICE (1998) 1: 'The draft proposal for a Fourteenth Company Law Directive (which still has a long way to go before becoming a formal proposal as it is not even contained in the Commission's work programme for 1998, despite Internal Market Commissioner Mario Monti's hopes to see it grafted onto national statute books by the year 2000) . . .' In the same sense, Rajak (1999) 124.

[348] So far, detailed implementation proposals can only be taken from German and (to a certain extent), Belgian, Dutch, and English writings, cf. in particular *ZGR* (issue 1–2), 1999.

[349] Neye (1999) 13, stresses that thanks to this legislative project, the EC Treaty keeps its promise as regards intra-community company mobility after more than 40 years. At p. 19, he speaks of a '*längst überfälligen Schritt, aber zugleich (. . .) einen Quantensprung* (a long overdue, but giant leap forwards)'.

[350] Di Marco (1999) 12.

codifications lies in paving the way by formulating fundamental principles, rather than offering a detailed masterplan. Even a supranational court cannot be expected to take up the legislator's tasks by providing versatile and detailed instruments in order to effectuate the total procedure of cross-border company transfers. The ancient Savignian private international law concept of ascertaining the closest relationship can no longer be used to regulate international company law relationships. Today, more than ever, it has become almost preposterous to question whether foreign companies or their seat transfers should be 'recognized' *ex post*. Complicated operations, notably multi-party cross-border company relationships, demand an adequate approach, whereby all the interests of the involved parties are balanced against each other *ex ante*. If any conclusion is to be drawn from the foregoing, then it must be that there is no such thing as a fast-track procedure to facilitate cross-border company mobility. Debates as to the implementation of the draft 14th Company Law Directive on cross-border company mobility, however, seem to justify the expectation that intra-community cross-border company mobility is forthcoming.

7

Final Conclusions

I. INTERNATIONAL LAW AND EC LAW: A VACUUM

So far, neither EC law nor private international law has shown itself capable of elaborating the versatile legal instruments needed to tackle the problem of inadequate cross-border company mobility.

Rather than simply trying to ascertain the closest geographical relationship, each of the competing private international law recognition theories reflects the major national economic policies of the legal orders on whose territories companies operate. These national policies either favour stimulating industrialization by attracting foreign investors, or stress the need to control these foreigners by obliging them to opt for a domestic company form. The former policy will lead to the acceptance of the 'incorporation' theory, whereas the latter policy is best safeguarded by the 'real seat' theory.

The interrelationship between private international law and EC law is steadily intensifying. Ascertaining the proper law of the company is no longer a single-track process of trying to find the closest (geographical) relationship with a legal order. Today more than ever, we are becoming conscious of the fact that, apart from the economic impact of recognition theories on economic markets described above, EC law also comprises (overt or hidden) conflict rules. An analysis of both legal disciplines on a complementary basis is therefore required. From a retrospective view, it can be said that occasionally both legal disciplines even carry identical flaws: any analogy which over the years has been construed between natural and legal persons (e.g. the 'birth' and 'death' of a company) by EC law and by private international law specialists may seem attractive, but in practice this approach is artificial and highly problematic.

Primary EC law

Until now neither of the two opposing private international law recognition theories has been imposed upon EC member states by articles 43 and

48 (ex arts. 52 and 58) of the EC Treaty. Recent developments, however, deserve contemplation. The German BHG decided to initiate preliminary proceedings in order to end uncertainty about whether the German *Sitztheorie* (real seat theory) is still in compliance with the EC Treaty. Even if European law as it now stands still permits EC member states to adhere to the real seat theory, this does not mean that the authorities of EC member states are entirely free to apply this theory in its severest consequences. They should at least refrain from sustaining national law provisions that are a disproportionate hindrance to companies planning to cross borders. They should even go beyond this minimum standard, as they are obliged to accommodate their national laws to further cross-border company mobility.

The incorporation theory, being far more appropriate for promoting cross-border company mobility than its counterpart, seems to be compatible with the EC Treaty. However, due to different treatment of genuine and pro-forma foreign companies in the Netherlands, its compatibility with EC law has explicitly been doubted as well. Notwithstanding the fact that preliminary proceedings concerning the compatibility of the Dutch Pro-Forma Foreign Companies Act 1998 Act were cancelled, similar cases are expected to give rise to preliminary proceedings in the near future.

Secondary EC law: the 1968 Draft Treaty on Mutual Recognition of Companies

The Treaty on the European Union (including the Treaties of Maastricht and Amsterdam) does not provide clear guidance on the subject of freedom of establishment for legal persons. Consequently, recourse must be had to secondary EC law. Prior to the piecemeal Company Law Harmonization Programme, there was still a (common?) belief that an overall settlement of the recognition matter was possible. However, the 1968 EC Draft Treaty on the Mutual Recognition of Companies, which was based on article 220 of the EC Treaty, ultimately shared the fate of its Hague Conference counterpart, as it never reached the status of law either. Both legislative projects ended in fiasco which had already been foreshadowed by the frequently criticized compromising and impractical character of the drafts.

The multi-party nature of company relationships and multiple interests

To a large extent, the drawback of European company law is explained by the complexity of the subject-matter involved. Cross-border migration of natural persons is hardly comparable to that of companies: frequently, disputes involving companies are of a compound nature: issues of primary and secondary European law, company law (including conflict of laws), the law on nationality of natural and legal persons, tax law, labour law, social security law, etc., are all entangled. The multi-party nature applies to both internal and external company relationships: company organs (e.g. the shareholders' meeting, the management board, and in civil law-oriented countries, often the supervisory board) and individual share-holders, creditors, debenture holders, employees, all have their own specific interests in the company's prosperity. Besides, the impact of company cross-border mobility on the economy of an EC member state exceeds that of natural persons.

In this respect, the ECJ *Powell Duffryn* judgment is a landmark case, in that it sufficiently demonstrates that the settlement of disputes arising from cross-border operating companies demands an integrated EC law and private (international) law approach. Some progress was made: the value of this judgment lies predominantly in its interdisciplinary reasoning: *inter alia* the search for a uniform interpretation of notions such as 'contract' (article 5), and 'agreement' (article 17) in the Brussels Convention has been realized with the help of substantive law notions. Furthermore, the link between the company law harmonization programme (ex article 54(3)(g) of the EC Treaty) has been established with both substantive company law and private international law notions. But again, the final outcome, achieved at the cost of the authoritative powers of the ECJ, seems to be insufficient to overcome the enduring trench warfare between the 'incorporation' theorists and the 'real seat' theorists.

Since the ECJ case of *Centros*, member states are not allowed to refuse to register a branch set up by a company duly formed in another member state. Such a refusal is contrary to ex articles 52 and 58 of the EC Treaty. However, member states are not precluded from taking other, less restrictive measures to fight or prevent fraud. Examples are the kind of measures promulgated by the Dutch 1998 PFFC Act. Dutch and German writers seem to differ, however, on the extent to which national measures are allowed under the EC Treaty. Any assumption that, following *Centros*, the 'real seat' theory is no longer acknowledged under the EC Treaty is doubtful. The compatibility of the Dutch 1998 PFFC Act with *Centros*, on the other hand, prompted the cantonal court of Groningen (Netherlands) to initiate preliminary proceedings concerning a private limited company which was incorporated in the United Kingdom, whilst conducting business only in the Netherlands.

II. THE COMPARATIVE APPROACH: THE ENVIRONMENTAL CONTEXT OF THE LEGAL ORDERS INVOLVED

Considered from the perspective of a progressively developing Single Market, the law of six legal orders (all except one being EC member states[1]), three of them adhering to the 'incorporation' theory, the others to the 'real seat' theory, has been analysed. A 'vertical' (i.e. country-by-country) treatment of the legal orders involved enables the observer to understand how in a certain legal order and during a certain period the law has evolved. It clearly follows that the unending controversy between the 'incorporation' theory and the 'real seat' theory dates back to the pre-EC law era, and that hardly any EC member states have radically changed their attitude towards foreign companies since that time.

Looking at the historical and socio-economic context of the legal orders explored, one finds that although company law policies are predominantly economically biased, the costs and benefits to society lead to different attitudes towards foreign companies among the sovereign states. Currently, three of the legal orders explored pay homage to the 'incorporation' theory, although for quite different reasons. The Netherlands and Switzerland both preferred the 'incorporation' theory as a tool to further industrial development in the post-war era. England has endorsed the 'incorporation' theory for centuries. Neither English nor foreign businessmen are attracted by the use of any—relatively over-regulated—foreign equivalent of an English private company limited by shares. As a result of their strict substantive company laws, the Netherlands and Switzerland are more frequently concerned by domestic enterprises setting up a proforma foreign private company in order to circumvent stricter domestic company law regimes. This also explains why these legal orders concentrate on fighting the abuse of foreign companies by limiting the more generous 'incorporation' theory.

Germany and France both adhere to the 'real seat' doctrine. The prevailing, underlying policy is that of the classical Savignian approach (i.e. the search for the most significant relationship), thrown together with substantive law-oriented policies: the law of the legal order predominantly affected by the activities of the company is deemed to be that of the state where the company's management and control centre is located. This enables authorities of the affected legal order to control the company effectively, and to safeguard the interests of the company's creditors and other interested actors. Notably in Germany, however, critical voices are raised against an unrestricted application of the *Sitztheorie* in its severest consequences. Compromises between safeguarding those domestic policies and the need to comply with EC law are being sought. Such criticism of the basic concept of the *siège réel* theory is rarely heard in France. Only the concept of a company's 'nationality' appears to be problematic in everyday practice.

---

[1] As regards non-EC Switzerland, integration with the European Union is by no means beyond imagination: see ch 4 II 3, above. Come what may, cross-border contacts between Switzerland and the EU are likely to intensify in the future.

Italy takes an intermediate position. In December 1995, a remodelled Private International Law Code entered into force. Chapter III on *persone giuridiche* (legal persons) consists solely of article 25, which is divided into three subsections. It is remarkable that the *teoria della sede effetiva* governs companies residing on Italian territory, whereas the 'incorporation' theory is applied to companies duly formed in Italy, who are resident abroad. Thus, departing companies are—at least from an Italian legislator's point of view—not submitted to the threat of being dissolved and wound up (cf. German law), though at the expense of irreciprocity.

Rather than trying to bridge the gap between the two opposing recognition concepts, legal orders have thus focused their attention on *national* policies, such as the stimulation of economic growth by attracting foreign investors or imposing the application of national company law to both domestic and foreign investors. They still do so today. But, as will be seen, the progressive stage which the Single Market has reached, places a duty upon these member states to avoid disproportionate measures which hinder companies planning a cross-border transfer from one EC member state to another.

The 'nationality' of natural and legal persons

Ancient relics, such as the concepts of the 'birth' and 'death' of natural and legal persons alike, can be found in 'incorporation', as well as 'real seat' countries: such analogies are inadequate devices for ascertaining the proper law of the company. From a common law, as well as an 'incorporation' point of view, the anthropomorphic concept is troublesome in that it does not cohere well with the (singular or dual) 'domicile' and 'residence' of a company. Neither is there a convincing consistency between the French civil law concept of *nationalité des personnes morales* and the traditional *siège réel*, because the concept of conflict of laws and the law on nationality and alien status are so closely intermingled, they cannot conceal fundamental weaknessess. No doubt this concept serves justified interests: it enables French authorities to expand state sovereignty beyond national borders, as diplomatic protection can be attributed to French *personnes morales* operating on foreign territories. On the other hand motives like these belong to the domain of public, rather than private international law. The unilateral character of the 'nationality' concept causes even more problems: French authorities could never endow a company with, for example, German nationality. Neither is the 'nationality' concept adequate for regulating multinational companies let alone groups of companies. Last but not least, natural and legal persons—both more or less to be considered as 'nationals' of EC member states—cannot be treated on precisely the same footing under the provisions concerning freedom of establishment of the EC Treaty.

Scope of the applicable law

The continuing controversy between the 'incorporation' and 'real seat' theorists hardly affects the scope of the proper law of the company. There is a *communis opinio* that once the proper law of the company is ascertained with the help of one of the theories, the applicable system of law should be applied whenever possible. In this respect, only common law seems to prescribe that each 'issue' should be dealt with by its own proper law: in practice the law under which a company is incorporated usually applies to all formation, organization, dissolution, and winding up matters. This is understandable: (i) submitting separate issues to several (alternating or cumulating) systems of law would disrupt internal coherence; and (ii) both recognition theories are more or less already checked in advance, in the sense that the more permissive 'incorporation' theory allows company managers to choose the *lex societatis*, whereas authorities of 'real seat' countries are no longer affected once they consider a company to have its 'real' seat abroad. In other words, the dispute is about the recognition principle, not about the scope of the applicable law. The 'incorporation' theory and the 'real seat' theory may both frustrate courts that are requested to solve borderline cases (cf. third-party protection related to company representation, tort, or contract law matters, or even local mandatory law provisions).

Cross-border company mobility: seat transfers

The current progressive stage of the Single Market imposes duties upon EC member states to abstain from disproportionately hindering companies planning to migrate from one EC member state to another. The transfer of a company's registered office is highly problematic in both 'incorporation' and 'real seat' countries; the transfer of a company's management and control office, however, raises problems if at least one of the legal orders involved is a 'real seat' country. Several types of problem arise. The expatriation of a company which is duly etablished under the law of a 'real seat' country might end up in the company's compulsory dissolution and winding up. Furthermore, EC member states are reproached for impinging upon EC law by applying the hostile 'real seat' theory towards companies that are duly established in other EC member states, while the more welcoming 'incorporation' theory is applied to companies from third countries on the basis of bilateral treaties. A growing chorus of critics is responding to this phenomenon in Germany. Finally, national conflict of law rules are often just singletrack 'one-liners', not suitable for conducting complicated cross-border company seat transfers. Versatile supranational instruments should facilitate these transfers, taking into account all vital interests, including the continued existence of the company, and internal as well as external company interests.

III. AN INTEGRATED APPROACH: EC LAW AND PRIVATE INTERNATIONAL LAW

Community law and private international law specialists are growing conscious of the need to join forces. At EC law level, it appeared to be a struggle, first to bring the mutually irreconcilable recognition theories (that reappear in articles 43 and 48 of the EC Treaty) into line with the current demands of a Single Market, and secondly, to define the freedom of establishment for legal persons. So far, neither EC law nor private international law have provided suitable instruments to regulate cross-border company relationships in detail, all measures proposed either being dropped[2] or shelved.[3]

There are several reasons why attempts to further Europeanization of company law have ended up in a blind alley for some time. In the first place, companies involve multi-party relationships: the interests of company organs (shareholders, management, and supervisory functionaries), company creditors and debenture holders, employees, national tax and social security authorities often conflict. This has far-reaching consequences for both the applicable law and international jurisdiction: any proliferation of mutually connected court proceedings over several national (European member state) courts forms a serious impediment to a prospering Single Market. It may even give rise to inconsistent court decisions.[4]

Due to this multi-party character, company law is characterized by its interdisciplinary nature: EC law concerning the freedom of establishment, substantive community and national company law, tax law, social security law, worker co-determination, administrative law, private international law: all these demand co-ordinated measures. It is beyond expectation that the solution to all the imaginable issues can be presented in one perfect conflict of law formula. Centralized law-making seems to be the only workable alternative.

The Treaty of Amsterdam

On 1 May 1999 the Treaty of Amsterdam entered into force. Although this Treaty does not explicitly affect freedom of establishment for companies, the fundamental provisions—articles 43, 44, 48, and 293 (ex articles 52, 54,

---

[2] All the attempts to create Treaties on the Mutual Recognition of Foreign Legal Persons undertaken by the Hague Conference on Private International Law and the EC ultimately failed: see ch 2 III 1 and ch 2 IV 1, above.

[3] cf. the 5th EC Law Company Law Directives, on the functioning of company organs, ch 6 I 2, above.

[4] cf. ch 2 IV 2 and ch 6 III 2, above.

58, and 220)—need to be considered against the background of article 65: conflict of law is no longer the exclusive domain of the EC member states. In the long run, awareness will grow that the problem of recognition of foreign companies can only be solved by an integrated approach of EC law and private international law.

Secondary EC law: the company law harmonization programme

Some decades ago, the ambitious Company Law Harmonization Programme was initiated. To date, however, it has not been successful in every respect. Several rhetorical questions were raised: should we not follow the example of the USA, where over fifty types of company compete with each other freely? Should the EC legislator perhaps focus its attention only on corrective measures (e.g. protection of weaker parties or capital protection)? Does it make sense to harmonize the company law of so many countries, including the new member states? What about the subsidiarity principle enshrined in article 10 (previously article 3b) of the EC Treaty, the alleged elusiveness of so many projects undertaken by the Commission, the risk of 'petrification' as a result of over-stressing the need for company law harmonization, etc.? Why not try an alternative route, by shaping *Modellgesetze* such as the American Model Business Corporation Act, or the Uniform Partnership? Why not acknowledge the importance of SMEs (small and medium-sized enterprises) by introducing a Private European Company as a *sui generis* enterprise form?

Specialists in the fields of both EC law and private international law grow conscious of the fact that the complicated matter of the precise status granted to foreign companies and the exercise of rights cannot simply be reduced to one single recognition 'principle', covering all imaginable cross-border company relationship matters. Although several directives were indeed implemented in the national legislation of the EC member states, many others never got beyond the draft stage. For several decades now draft directives, notably those attempting to regulate the heart of the matter (e.g. the Fifth Company Law Directive on the functioning of company organs) carry seeds of disruption. This also largely explains why the draft proposal for a Societas Europea remained so long in a blind alley.

EC law and private international law: different points of departure

The search for conclusive answers to questions concerning the recognition of foreign companies is seriously hampered by the fact that EC law and private international law represent fundamentally different worlds, but cannot be disentangled.

Conflict of law rules, insofar as they have not been harmonized by (Community or international) treaties, belong to the domain of national legislators and courts. Furthermore, EC law and private international law intrinsically serve different goals: whereas the active role of conflict of laws is completed once the proper law of the company is ascertained, EC law perpetually and increasingly influences the substantive (company) law of the member states. A practice-oriented reformulation of these theoretical contemplations leads to the following observations. The 'closest connection' required under an objective proper law test and the genuine and continuous ties between the economy of a member state (including overseas territories) with the EC Market for Community law purposes are by no means to be considered as fully interchangeable concepts.

EC law and private international law: coherence

The mere fact that article 48 (previously article 58) of the EC Treaty is 'conflictually biased' demonstrates that EC law and private international law cannot be disconnected. A satisfactory co-existence must therefore be found one way or another. But defining parameters for such an interdisciplinary approach may also appear complicated. While restricting the search for such parameters to the domain of cross-border company relationships, the objective observer will find parallels between private international law-oriented notions such as the 'freedom of choice', or 'closest relationship' on one hand, and the EC law-based concept of the 'four freedoms' enshrined in article 43 (previously article 52) of the EC Treaty on the other. Insofar as conflict of law rules have to comply with EC law, it has been observed that the ECJ *Dassonville* judgment should be regarded as a touchstone for further debate. In a nutshell, *Dassonville* was about intolerable quantitive restrictions and measures, covering all trading rules enacted by member states which 'are *capable* of hindering, directly or indirectly, actually or potentially, intra-Community trade'. This train of thought is applicable, because conflict of law provisions enacted by member states must be considered capable of (potentially) hindering intra-Community trade as well. In this respect, it has been suggested that party autonomy (i.e. the 'incorporation' theory) best addresses the interests of a Single Market, and should therefore prevail over an objective proper law test (i.e. the 'real seat' theory), which is believed more likely to result in a 'hindrance'. It has to be acknowledged, however, that the *Dassonville* principle, attractive as it may seem at first sight, is not a suitable instrument to regulate all the details of cross-border company relationships. But its value lies in the determination that an objective proper law test to ascertain the *lex societatis* undeniably 'hinders' legal certainty more than a subjective test would do. Of course, it must be acknowledged that it is easier to apply the principle of party autonomy to, for example, international contracts than to companies, the latter being reputed for their multi-party character, involving multiple (company law, tax law, social security law, etc.) interests. This explains why, even given the functional disparities between the disciplines of EC law and private international law, it is over-optimistic to assume that the trench warfare between 'real seat' and 'incorporation' theorists is likely to end all by itself as a result of a steadily increasing party autonomy. Nevertheless, EC law affects private international law methods in that it prohibits the member state of origin from hindering the establishment in another state of one of its nationals or of a company incorporated under its legislation which comes within the definition in article 48 (previously article 58).

The convergence of conflict rules with EC law

This minimum standard has to be taken as a starting point for further debates as to whether, and how, Community law addresses legal persons which operate across borders. National conflict of law rules should be interpreted in conformity with EC law as far as possible. Although the ECJ *Daily Mail* judgment may not have put an end to the controversy between the recognition theories, this does not justify the conclusion that member states have full discretion to model their conflict rules as they wish. On the contrary, it has been argued that now more than ever this circumstance places extra weight on their duty to bring national law into compliance with EC law. It would be a violation of the Treaty to withhold recognition from a company duly established in another EC member state for the sole reason that the legal form of the foreign company is not recognized in the host country. Likewise, unrestricted use of the instrument of *ordre public* could be an infringement of the EC Treaty, (notably article 10). Attempts were made to bridge divergences between European law and private international law, in that article 10 (previously article 5) of the EC Treaty adds an extra dimension to the traditional (obsolete?) Savignian concept of private international law.

It has even been asked whether private international law methodology should be completely Europeanized. Meanwhile, it is highly ironic that, of all the legal orders, those that adhere to the European-law oriented 'incorporation' theory (notably the Dutch 1998 Pro-Forma Foreign Companies Act) will run the highest risk of being reprimanded for having used the instrument of fraud too hastily.

Taking advantage of the EC law vacuum

Both European law and private international law specialists regret that the free movement of companies can be frustrated by a (too) narrow interpretation, or even abuse of EC law for no other purpose than to save the sacrosanct belief in domestic company law institutions. German writers especially inveigh against extreme impediments to foreign companies under German law, as a consequence of which hardly any 'freedom' of establishment for these companies remains.

However, opinions differ on whether such an approach is 'discriminatory' under the EC Treaty. It is commonly accepted that a distinction must be drawn between the recognition matter as such, and the more complicated problem of a company transferring its seat from one EC member state to another. To begin with, the recognition of companies duly established under the law of other EC member states may not *de facto* be totally excluded under the Treaty. Furthermore, any unwillingness to recognize the equivalent of *public* limited companies from other EC member states, all of them being subject to equalized capital requirements, would be a violation of the second EC Company Law Directive. Although there is as yet no EC directive on the worker co-determination which is directly linked to the organization of capital companies, fundamental principles of proportionality may not be disregarded. It would be hard to convince public limited companies from other EC states that they should obey domestic co-determination rules of the host country, if these rules no longer apply to home companies of an equivalent type. In summary, the 'real seat' theory is not dead, but EC member states should not apply this recognition theory in its severest consequences.

Harmony: matching EC law with other areas of law

The ECJ judgment in the case of *Powell Duffryn*,[5] however, demonstrates that occasionally EC law and private international law are on the same wavelength. The Court adequately balanced EC law interests with private international law interests: (i) freedom of establishment of companies under the EC Treaty should not be reduced to mere lip-service; (ii) private international law rules resulting from the (EC) Brussels Convention on Jurisdiction and Recognition and Enforcement of Foreign Judgments in Civil and Commercial Matters should be adjusted to the needs of everyday legal practice; and, last but not least, (iii) how to further transborder business co-operation like that underlying the *Powell Duffryn* judgment, while taking into account the EC company law harmonization programme? The Court's policy to shift away from a proliferation of closely connected disputes under the Brussels Convention, bearing the risk of them ultimately being decided inconsistently, turned out to be fortunate. Streamlining multi-party relationships by concentrating the settlement of disputes before a single court—notably the chosen *forum societatis*—favours equal treatment of all shareholders, whilst the danger of inconsistent court decisions is countered effectively.

The outlook: towards cross-border company mobility?

The puzzling subject of cross-border company mobility cannot be reduced to the oversimplified question of whether a company which has been duly

---

[5] cf. ch 2 IV 2, above.

established in another member state should be 'recognized' elsewhere. Neither is it appropriate to ask when the 'incorporation' theory will take over, simply because it optimizes the freedom of establishment for legal persons from a comparable perspective. Similar conclusions apply *a fortiori* to the legal institution of seat transfers. It is not a matter of all or nothing: the ECJ *Daily Mail* judgment already mirrored the paradoxical situation that, although from now on progress can only be made step by step,[6] everyday practice demands all problems to be tackled simultaneously. Despite some flaws, both the ensuing KPMG *Report* and the attempt to formulate a Proposal for a Fourteenth European Parliament and Council Directive on the Transfer of the Registered Office or the *De Facto* Head Office of a Company from One Member State to Another at least reflect awareness of this need. By now, at least the idea has gained foothold that it would be erroneous to persist in believing that general reconciliatory 'principles' such as those of the 'closest relationship', *Differenzierung*, or *Überlagerung* are suitable instruments to solve the recognition matter; it would be an even greater mistake in judgment to trust in an ongoing progress of issue-by-issue harmonization of company law, eventually resulting in the 'acceptance' of the 'incorporation' theory.

The ancient controversy between the two recognition theories can only be surmounted gradually. We are at the brink of a new era and a glimpse of what may be to come can be gained from both ECJ case-law[7] and the KPMG Proposals, as well as the draft proposal for a Fourteenth Company Law Directive, notwithstanding (or perhaps even thanks to) the fact that both the 'incorporation' theory and the 'real seat' theory remain intact. Real intra-Community mobility for companies can only be achieved if all interested parties are alerted *ex ante*: supervisors (i.e. company organs and other players, as well as authorities of the state of departure and the state of arrival) will have to take care that cross-border transfers are carried out properly. Any form of abuse (e.g. to avoid insolvency procedures) must be countered. Once again, this is demonstrated by the KPMG Proposals and (comments to) the draft proposal for a Fourteenth Company Law Directive.

Perhaps the time has come to realize '(future) legislation or conventions'. At another, more substantive law-oriented level, this might also lead to a re-introduction of the idea of a European Private Company for small and medium-sized enterprises: bottoming up might appear to work out better than down-sizing. But progress seems to be near: there are hopes that the SE project will also be reanimated.

---

[6] cf. Rammeloo (MJ 1999) 105 et seq.

[7] cf. earlier comments on the indirect impact of ECJ *Powell Duffryn* (interdisciplinary thinking): ch 2 IV 2, above; and ECJ *Vlassopoulou* on the freedom of establishment of companies: ch 6 II 1, above.

Perhaps in a time somewhere, I suspect, far in the future, a work of this nature devoted to European Company Law, would not require a chapter on conflicts of law. The laws of the Community will have been harmonised to such an extent, in this field, that the European Company itself will not be just an idea but a reality. Until that time arrives we still require to discover and apply our principles and rules of private international law to company problems within the Community.[8]

[8] Clarke (1991) 161.

Bibliography

Aspects du droit international des sociétés: Etudes suisses de droit international (vol. 92, Schulthess Polygraphischer Verlag, Zürich, 1995)

Audit, B., *Droit international privé* (Economica, Paris, 1997)

Azzolini, C., 'Commenti. Problemi relativi alle persone giuridiche nella riforma del diritto internazionale privato', [1993] Riv.dir.int.priv.proc. 893

Ballarino, T., 'Le società constituite all'estero (art. 2505–2510 Cod. Civ.)', in *Trattato di diritto privato, diretto da Pietro Rescigno*, (Vol. XVII, Impresso e lavoro, Torino, 1985), 401

—— 'Sul progetto di riforma del sistema italiano di diritto internazionale privato', [1990] Riv.dir.int. 525

—— *Diritto internazionale privato* (seconda edizione aggiornata sulla legge 218/1995), (Cedam, Padova, 1996)

Bar, C. von, *Internationales Privatrecht*, C.H. Beck, München (vol. I 1987; vol. II 1991)

Barents, R., *Het Verdrag van Amsterdam*, (Kluwer, Deventer, 1997)

—— *Het Verdrag van Amsterdam in werking* (Kluwer, Deventer, 1999)

Basedow, J., 'Die Umstrukturierung von Unternehmen durch Sitzverlegung oder Fusion über die Grenze im Licht der Niederlassungsfreiheit im Europäischen Binnenmarkt', [1994] ZGR, 1

—— 'Europäisches Internationales Privatrecht', [1996] *NJW* 1921

—— 'Die Harmonisierung des Kollisionsrechts nach dem Vertrag von Amsterdam', [1997] *EuZW* 609

Batiffol, H./P. Lagarde, *Traité de droit international privé* (Librarie générale de droit et de jurisprudence, Paris, 1993)

Bechtel, W., 'Grenzüberschreitende Sitzverlegung de lege lata', [1998] *IPRax*, 348

Behrens, P., 'Identitätswährende Sitzverlegung einer Kapitalgesellschaft von Luxemburg in die Bundesrepublik Deutschland', [1986] *RIW* 590

—— 'Niederlassungsrecht und Internationales Gesellschaftsrecht', [1988] *RabelsZ.* 498

—— 'Die grenzüberschreidende Sitzverlegung von Gesellschaften in der EWG', [1989] *IPRax* 354

—— 'Sind Gesellschaften Niederlassungsberechtigte minderen Rechts?', [1991] *EuZW* 97

—— 'Die Umstrukturierung von Unternehmen durch Sitzverlegung oder Fusion über die Grenze im Licht der Niederlassungsfreiheit im Europäischen Binnenmarkt', [1994] *ZGR* 1

—— 'Krisensymptome in der Gesellschaftsrechtsangleichung', in *FS Mestmäcker* (Nomos, Baden-Baden, 1996), 831

—— 'Gesellschaften sollen Niederlassungsberechtigte gleichen Rechts werden' [1998] *EuZW* 353

—— 'Das Internationale Gesellschaftsrecht nach dem Centros-Urteil des EuGH' [1999] *IPRax* 323

Bellingwout, J.W., 'Europees vennootschapsrecht, vestigingsvrijheid zetelver-plaatsing en IPR. Een reactie' [1989] *AA* 751

—— 'Het euvel van de "puur formeel buitenlandse rechtspersonen". Enige kant-tekeningen bij het advies van de Commissie Vennootschapsrecht d.d. 29 oktober 1992' [1993] WPNR 680

—— 'Company Migration in Motion: The KPMG Report 1993', in Jan Wouters/Hildegard Schneider (eds.), *Current issues of cross-border establishment of companies in the European Union* (Maklu, Antwerpen/Apeldoorn 1995) 75

—— *Zetelverplaatsing van rechtspersonen* (Kluwer, Deventer, 1996)

—— 'Zetelverplaatsing naar België' [1997] NV 202

Bentley, P., Q.C., 'Tax Obstacles to Cross-Border Business', in A. Celia Trenting (managing ed.) *Corporate Law. The European Dimension* (Butterworths, London/Dublin/Edinburgh/Munich, 1991) 195

Blaurock, U., 'Deutsches und Europäisches Gesellschaftsrecht—Bilanz und Perspektiven eines Anpassungsprozesses' [1998] *ZEuP* 460

Bloch, K., 'Die Sitzverlegung von Aktiengesellschaften in das Ausland nach inter-nationalem Recht' [1952] *RSJ* 245

Boele-Woelki, K., 'AA-Katern' [1995] *AA* 2655

Boeschoten, C.D. van, *Internationale zetelverplaatsing van vennootschappen, in: Grensoverschrijdend privaatrecht, Opstellen aangeboden aan Mr. J. van Rijn van Alkemade* (Kluwer, Deventer, 1993) 13

Borges, G., 'Die Sitztheorie in der Centros-Ära: vermeintliche Probleme und unvermeidliche Änderungen' [2000] *RIW* 167

Boschiero, N., 'Die Reform des Italienischen IPR-Systems' [1996] *ZfRvgl.* 143

Boucourechliev, J., 'Die Harmonisierung des Gesellschaftsrechts in der Europäischen Union: Erreichtes und Perspektiven' [1999] *RIW* 1

Bovis, C., *Business law in the European Union* (Sweet & Maxwell, London, 1997)

Braak, S.M. van den, 'Omzetting van een buitenlandse in een Nederlandse ven-nootschap' [1994] WPNR 678

—— 'Het Centros-arrest en het Nederlandse internationaal privaatrecht betref-fende vennootschappen' [2000] WPNR 347

—— /C.R. Huiskes, 'De Delaware constructie onder vuur?' [1992] *NJB* 1165

Broggini, G., 'La riforma del diritto internazionale privato società ed altri enti', in *La riforma del diritto internazionale privato, Comitato regionale notarile Lombardo* (Giuffre, Milano, 1996) 57

Brood, E.A., *De vestigingsplaats van vennootschappen* (Kluwer, Deventer, 1989)

Brödermann, E., 'Europäisches Gemeinschaftsrecht versus IPR: Einflüsse und Konformitätsgebot' [1992] *MDR* 89

Bucher, A. (ed.), *Internationales Privatrecht: Bundesgesetz und Staatsverträge* (Text edition) (4th edn, Helbing & Lichtenhahn, Basel/Frankfurt am Main, 1997)

Bundesgesetz über das Internationale Privatrecht. Darstellung der Stellungnahmen auf Grund des Gesetzesentwurfs der Expertenkommission und des entsprechenden Begleitberichts, 1980

Buxbaum, R.M./K. Hopt, *Legal harmonization and the business enterprise* (de Gruyter, Berlin/New York, 1988)

Capelli, F., 'Trasferimento della sede amministrativa di società nella CEE: diritto di stabilimento e problematice fischali' [1990] Dir.com.degl.sc.int. 50

Carey, W., 'Federalism and Corporate Law: Reflections upon Delaware' [1974] Yale *L.J.* 663
Clarke, M.G., Q.C., 'The Conflicts of Law Dimension', in A. Celia Trenting (managing ed.) *Corporate Law. The European Dimension* (Butterworths, London/ Dublin/Edinburgh/Munich, 1991) 161
Clerici, R./F. Mosconi/F. Pocar, *Legge di riforma del diritto internazionale privato e testi collegati* (Giuffre, Milano, 1995)
Coenen, W.J., 'De "Überlagerungstheorie": een aanzet tot integratie van het vennootschapsrecht' [1993] *NJB* 1272
Cohen Henriquez, E., *Het vennootschapsstatuut* (Tjeenk Willink, Haarlem, 1961)
—— 'Nederlandse ondernemingen in de vorm van buitenlandse rechtspersonen' [1982] *TVVS* 265
Cottier, T./A.R. Kopse (eds.), *Der Beitritt der Schweiz zur Europäischen Union, Brennpunkte und Auswirkungen. l'Adhésion de la Suisse à l'Union Européenne, Enjeux et conséquences* (Schulthess Polygraphischer Verlag, Zürich, 1998)
Current issues of cross-border establishment of companies in the European Union (eds. Jan Wouters/Hildegard Schneider) (Maklu, Antwerpen/Apeldoorn, 1995)
Daniele, L., 'Capacita e diritti delle persone (artt. 20–25), Il corriere Giuridico 1995 (Legislazione), 1239; A. Davi', Le questione generali del diritto internazionale privato nel progetto di riforma' [1990] Riv.dir.int. 556
Davies, P.L., L.C.B., *Gowers Principles of modern company law* (with contr. from D.D. Prentice), (6th edn, Sweet & Maxwell, London, 1997)
Debets, W., *De papieren onderneming* (Vermande, Lelystad, 1987)
Dicey and Morris on the Conflict of Laws (general ed. L. Collins), (12th edn, Sweet & Maxwell, London, 1993)
Dicey and Morris on the Conflict of Laws (general ed. L. Collins), (13th edn, Sweet & Maxwell, London, 2000)
Diephuis, J.H./C.W.A. Timmermans, 'Erkenning van vreemde vennootschappen en rechtspersonen/Het Verdrag van 29 februari 1968 inzake de onderlinge erkenning van vennootschappen en rechtspersonen. Enkele Europeesrechtelijke kanttekeningen, Meded' [1981] NVIR
Dongen, R.C. van, *Identificatie in het rechtspersonenrecht. Rechtsvergelijkende beschouwingen over 'piercing the corporate veil' in het interne en internationaal privaatrecht van Nederland, Duitsland, Zwitserland, New York en Texas* (Kluwer, Deventer, 1995)
—— 'Wet Conflictenrecht Corporaties' 1995 *JutD* (nr. 2), 2
Drobnig, U., 'Gemeinschaftsrecht und Internationales Gesellschaftsrecht. "Daily Mail" und die Folgen', in C. von Bar (ed.), *Europäisches Gemeinschaftsrecht und Internationales Privatrecht* (Heymanns Verlag, Köln, 1990) 185
Drucker, T.C., Companies in private international law [1968] ICLQ 28
Drury, R.R., 'The Regulation and Recognition of Foreign Corporations: Responses to the "Delaware Syndrome"', [1998] *CLJ* 165
—— 'Migrating companies' [1999] ELR 354
—— /A. Hicks, 'The proposal for a European Private Company' [1999] *JBL* 429
Dutoit, B., *Droit international privé Suisse. Commentaire de la loi fédérale* (*etc.*) (Helbing & Lichtenhahn, Basel/Frankfurt am Main, 1997)

Ebenroth, C.T., 'Neuere Entwicklungen im deutschen Internationalen Gesellschaftsrecht' [1988] *JZ* 18

—— /T. Auer, 'Die ausländische Kapitalgesellschaft & Co KG—Ein Beitrag zur Zulässigkeit grenzüberschreitender Typenvermischung' [1990] *DnotZ* 139

—— /B. Bippus, 'Die staatsverträgliche Anerkennung ausländischer Gesellschaften in Abkehr von der Sitztheorie' [1988] *DB* 842

—— /B. Bippus, 'Die Sitztheorie als Theorie effektiver Verknüpfungen der Gesellschaft' [1988] *JZ* 677

—— /D. Einsele, 'Gründungstheorie und Sitztheorie in der Praxis—zwei vergleichbare Theorien?' [1988] *ZvglRWiss* 217

—— /U. Eyles, 'Der Renvoi nach der Novelierung des deutschen IPR' [1989] *IPRax* 1

—— / A. Kaiser, 'Die Reform des Internationalen Gesellschaftsrechts in Italien' [1992] *ZVglRW.* 223

—— /U. Messer, 'Das Gesellschaftsrecht im neuen schweizerischen IPRG' [1989] *ZSR* 51

—— /O. Wilken, 'Entwicklungstendenzen im deutschen Internationalen Gesellschaftsrecht' [1991] *JZ* 1018

Ebke, W.F., 'Die "ausländische Kapitalgesellschaft & Co. KG" und das Europäische Gemeinschaftsrecht' [1987] *ZGR* 245

—— 'Unternehmensrecht und Binnenmarkt—E pluribus unum?' [1998] *RabelsZ.* 195

—— 'Das Schicksal der Sitztheorie nach dem Centros-Urteil des EuGH' [1999] *JZ* 656

—— comment to ECJ C–212/97 *Centros*, [2000] *JZ* 203

Edwards, V., *EC Company Law* (Clarendon Press, Oxford, 1999)

Ehlermann, C.D., 'Differentiation, flexibility, closer co-operation: the new provisions of the Amsterdam Treaty' [1998] *ELJ* 246

Europäisches Gemeinschaftsrecht und Internationales Privatrecht (ed. C. von Bar), (Heymanns Verlag, Köln/Berlin/Bonn/München, 1990)

European Business Law. Legal and economic analyses on integration and harmonisation (eds. Buxbaum *et al.*), (de Gruyter, Berlin/New York, 1991)

The European Private Company? (eds. H.J. de Kluiver/W. Van Gerven), (Maklu, Antwerpen/Apeldoorn, 1995)

Everling, U., 'Das Niederlassungsrecht in der EG als Beschränkungsverbot', in W. Schön (ed.) *Gedächtnisschrift für Brigitte Knobbe-Keuk* (Schmidt, Köln, 1997) 607

Eyles, U., *Das Niederlassungsrecht der Kapitalgesellschaften in der Europäischen Gemeinschaft* (Nomos, Baden-Baden, 1990)

Fallon, M., 'Les conflits des lois et de juridictions dans un espace économique intégré—l'Expérience de la Communauté Européenne' *Receuil des Cours* 253, The Hague 1995

Firsching, F. (cont. by B. von Hoffmann), *Internationales Privatrecht* (C.H. Beck, München, 1995)

Fischer, G., comment to LG Stuttgart 31 June 1989, [1991] *IPRax* 100

Fletcher, I.F., *Conflicts of Laws and European Community Law. With special reference to the Community Conventions on Private International Law* (North Holland Publishing Co., Amsterdam, 1982)

Foote, J.A., 'De la condition légale des sociétés étrangères en Angleterre' [1882] *Clunet* 456

—— *Foreign and domestic law. A concise treatise on private international jurisprudence based on the decisions in the English courts* (London, 4th edn. (Col. Philipsen), 1914)

Francescakis, Ph., comment to ICJ 5 February 1970 (*Barcelona Traction*), [1970] Rev. cr. d.i.p. 609

Franceschelli, V., in *Il nuovo diritto internazionale privato. La legge n. 218/1995 di riforma alle sistema italiano* (Giuffre, Milano, 1995) 42

Fumagalli, L., 'La riforma del diritto internazionale privato nel disegno di legge governativo' [1993] Riv.dir.int.priv.proc. 494

Gaja, G., *La riforma del diritto internazionale privato e processuale—Raccolta in ricordo di Vitta E* (Giuffre, Milano, 1994)

Gaudemet-Tallon, H., comment to ECJ C–214/89, *Powell Duffryn plc v Wolfgang Petereit* [1992] ECR 1755, [1992] Rev. cr. d.i.p. 535

Gavalda, C./G. Parleani, *Droit des affaires de l'Union Européenne* (Litec, Paris, 1998)

Geimer, R., comment to ECJ C–214/89, *Powell Duffryn plc v Wolfgang Petereit* [1992] ECR 1755, [1989] *EWiR*, 886

Ghandchi, J., *Der Geltungsbereich des Art. 159 IPRG* (Schulthess Polygraphischer Verlag, Zürich 1991)

Grasmann, G., *System des Internationalen Gesellschaftsrechts. Außen- und Innenstatut der Gesellschaften im Internationalen Privatrecht* (Verlag neue Wirtschaftsbriefe, Herne/Berlin, 1970)

Grinten, W.C.L. van der, *Handboek voor de Naamloze en de besloten vennootschap* (W.E.J. Tjeenk Willink, Zwolle, 1992)

—— 'Zur Geschichte der Anerkennungsproblematik bei Aktiengesellschaften' [1974] *RabelsZ.* 344

—— 'Die Sitztheorie des Internationalen Gesellschaftsrecht in der Europäischen Gemeinschaft' [1986] *IPRax* 145

—— 'Die ausländische Kapitalgesellschaft & Co. KG' [1986] *IPRax* 351

—— *Staudinger Kommentar zum Bürgerlichen Gesetzbuch mit Einführungsgesetz und Nebengesetzen* (Sellier-de Gruyter, Berlin, 1993)

—— /R. Beckmann, 'Rechtskultur und Internationales Gesellschaftsrecht' [1992] *ZVglRWiss* 351

—— /D. Jasper, 'Identitätswährende Sitzverlegung und Fusion von Kapitalgesellschaften in die Bundesrepublik Deutschland' [1989] *RabelsZ.* 52

—— /T. König, 'Identitätswährende Sitzverlegung in der Europäischen Gemeinschaft' [1991] *IPRax* 380

—— /T. König, 'Das Internationale Gesellschaftsrecht in der Europäischen Gemeinschaft' [1992] *RIW/AWD*, 423

—— /C. Strotmann, 'Ausländische juristische Person aus Nicht-EG-Staat als komplementär einer KG' [1990] *IPRax* 298

Heini, A., 'Zum Neuesten Urteil des Schweizerischen Bundesgerichtes über das Personalstatut ausländischer juristischer Personen' [1992] *IPRax* 405

Heinze, M., 'Arbeitsrechtliche Probleme bei der Grenzüberschreitenden Sitzverlegung in der Europäischen Gemeinschaft' [1999] *ZGR* 54

Hoffmann, J., 'Neue Möglichkeiten zur identitätswährenden Sitzverlegung in Europa?' [2000] *ZHR* 43

Hoffmann, B. von, 'The European Community and Private International Law' in

European Private International Law (ed. B. von Hoffmann), (Ars Aequi, Nijmegen, 1998) 13

Holleaux, D./J. Foyer/G. de Geouffre de la Pradelle, *Droit international privé* (Masson, Paris etc., 1987)

Honsell, H./N. Vogt/K. Schnyder, *Kommentar zum schweizerischen Privatrecht. IPR* (Helbing & Lichtenhahn, Basel/Frankfurt am Main, 1996)

Hopt, K.J., *Company law in the European Union: harmonization or subsidiarity?* (Centro di studi e ricerche di diritto comparato e straniero, Rome, 1998)

—— 'Europäisches Konzernrecht?' [1999] *EuZW* 577

Hügel, H.F., 'Steuerrechtliche Hindernisse bei de internationalen Sitzverlegung' [1999] *ZGR* 71

IPRG-Kommentar (ed. A. Heini/H. Keller/K. Siehr/P. Volken/F. Vischer), (Schulthess Polygraphischer Verlag, Zürich, 1993)

Israel, J., 'Conflicts of law and the EC after Amsterdam. A change for the worse?' [2000] *MJ* 81

Jacob, P., 'Statutaire forumclausules en grensoverschrijdende zetelverplaatsing naar België' [1993] WPNR 897

Jayme, E., 'Internationales Privatrecht und postmoderne Kultur' [1997] *ZfRvgl.* 230

—— /C. Kohler, 'Europäisches Kollisionsrecht 1995. Der Dialog der Quellen' [1995] *IPRax* 343

—— —— 'Europäisches Kollisionsrecht 1996—Anpassung und Transformation der nationalen Rechte' [1996] *IPRax* 377

Karrer, M./K.W. Arnold/M. Pattochi, *Switzerland's Private International Law Statute (etc.)* (Schulthess Polygraphischer Verlag, Zürich, 1994)

Kegel, G./K.Schurig, *Internationales Privatrecht* (C.H. Beck, München, 2000)

Klein, F.E., 'Die gesellschaftsrechtlichen Bestimmungen des IPRG', in *Das neue Bundesgesetz über das Internationale Privatrecht in der praktischen Anwendung* Seminar vom 28. Oktober 1988 an der Universität in Basel, (Schulthess Polygraphischer Verlag, Zürich, 1988) 83

—— 'Die gesellschaftsrechtlichen Bestimmungen des IPRG' [1989] *BJM* 359

Kleman, P., 'Formeel buitenlandse vennootschappen' [1995] NV 186

Kluiver, H.J. de, 'De wet formeel buitenlandse vennootschappen op de tocht?' [1999] WPNR 527

Kneller, M.W., *Die Haftung für die Verwaltung einer Liechtensteinischen Stiftung, unter besonderer Berücksichtigung von Art. 159 IPRG* (Schulthess Polygraphischer Verlag, Zürich, 1995)

Knobbe-Keuk, B., 'Umzug von Gesellschaften in Europa' [1990] *ZHR* 325

Kokkini-Iatridou, D., *Le droit applicable à la détermination de la personne physique ou moral qui contrôle une société anonyme dont une filiale a son activité à l'étranger* Neth. Report to the Eleventh International Congress of Comparative Law, (Kluwer, Deventer, 1982) 125

KPMG Report, *Study of Transfer of the Head Office of a Company from one Member State to Another* KPMG European Business Centre, Luxembourg, (Office for Official Publications of the European Communities, 1993)

Kropholler, J., *Internationales Privatrecht* (J.C.B. Mohr, Tübingen, 1997)

Kronke, H., 'Grenzüberschreitende Personengesellschaftskonzerne—Sachnormen und Internationales Privatrecht' [1989] *ZGR* 473
—— 'Deutsches Gesellschaftsrecht und grenzüberschreitende Strukturänderungen' [1994] *ZGR* 26
Labayle, H., 'Un espace de liberté, de sécurité et de justice' [1997] *RTDE* 105
Lagarde, P./B. von Hoffmann, *L'européanisation du droit privé; die Europäisierung des Internationalen Privatrechts; The Europeanisation of International Private Law* (Heymanns Verlag, Köln, 1996)
Langrish, S., 'The Treaty of Amsterdam: Selected Highlights' [1998] ELR 3
Lenaerts, K., comment to caselaw, [1988] *TVR* 110
—— 'Kroniek van het Internationaal Privaatrecht (1985–1989), 1e deel' (1989/1990) RW 902
Levy, L., *La nationalité des sociétés* (Librarie générale de droit et de jurisprudence, Paris, 1984)
Loussouarn, Y./P. Bourel, *Droit international privé* (Dalloz, Paris, 1996)
Lutter, M., 'Das Europäische Unternehmensrecht im 21. Jahrhundert' [2000] *ZGR* 1
Marco, G. di, 'Der Vorschlag der Kommission für eine 14. Richtlinie. Stand und Perspektiven' [1999] *ZGR* 3
Mayer, P., *Droit international privé* (Editions Montchrestien, 5th edn, Paris, 1994)
—— *Droit international privé* (Editions Montchrestien, 6th edn, Paris, 1998)
Meilicke, W., 'Unvereinbarkeit der Sitztheorie mit der Europäischen Menschenrechtskonvention' [1992] *RIW* 578
—— comment to ECJ C–212/97 *Centros*, [1999] *DB* 627
Meo, F. de, 'Reform des italienischen Internationalen Privatrechts' [1996] *ZfRvgl.* 46
Merkt, H., 'Das Europäische Gesellschaftsrecht und die Idee des "Wettbewerbs der Gesetzgeber"' [1995] *RabelsZ.* 553
Moor, L., *Das Italienische Gesellschaftsrecht: ein Vergleich mit dem schweizerischen IPRG und zu Problemen des schweizerisch-italienischen Rechtsverkehr* (Schulthess Polygraphischer Verlag, Zürich, 1997)
Moser, R., 'Das internationale Obligationen- und Handelsrecht der Schweiz 1954–1963' [1967] *RabelsZ.* 670
—— 'Personalstatut und Außenverhältnis der Aktiengesellschaft' in *Festschrift für Börgi* (Schulthess Polygraphischer Verlag, Zürich, 1981) 283
Münchener Kommentar zum Bürgerlichen Gesetzbuch, Band 10, Einführungsgesetz zum Bürgerlichen Gesetzbuch—Art. 1–38 (ed. H.J. Sonnenberger), (3. Auflage, C.H. Beck, München, 1998)
Neye, H.W., 'Die Vorstellungen der Bundesregierung zum Vorschlag einer 14. Richtlinie' [1999] *ZGR* 13
Nobel, P., 'Zum Internationalen Gesellschaftsrecht im IPR-Gesetz' in I. Schwander (ed.) *Beiträge zum neuen IPR des Sachen-, Schuld- und Gesellschaftsrecht, Festschrift für Rudolf Moser* (Schulthess Polygraphischer Verlag, Zürich, 1987) 179
North, P.M./J.J. Fawcett, *Cheshire and North's Private International Law* (12th edn, Butterworths, London, 1992)
———— *Cheshire and North's Private International Law* (13th edn, Butterworths, London, 1999)

Overbeck, A.E. von, 'Droit des sociétés: l'Article 159 de la Loi Fédérale sur le droit international privé', in I. Meier/K. Siehr (eds.) *Mélanges Heini* (Schulthess Polygraphischer Verlag, Zürich, 1995) 295

Perrin, J-F, *La reconnaissance des sociétés étrangères et ses effets* (Mémoires publiés par la Fac. de droit, Geneva, 1969)

—— 'Les sociétés en droit civil et en droit international privé' [1989] *La Semaine Judiciaire* 553

Pohlmann, J., *Das französische internationale Gesellschaftsrecht* (Duncker & Humblot, Berlin, 1988)

Polak, M.V., 'Relativering van rechtspersoonlijkheid in het internationaal privaatrecht' [1989] *TVVS* 67

——(comment to ECJ C–214/89, *Powell Duffryn plc v Wolfgang Petereit* [1992] ECR 1755, [1993] *CMLR* 419

—— 'Artikelen 71–76 IPR-schets: Corporaties' [1993] WPNR 756

Priester, H.J., 'EU-Sitzverlegung—EU-Verfahrensablauf' [1999] *ZGR* 36

Rabel, E., *The conflict of laws. A comparative study II* (University of Michigan Press, Ann Arbor, 1960) 132

Rahm, R., *Das Internationale Gesellschaftsrechts Italiens. Entwicklung und Reform* (University of Münster, 1990)

Rajak, H., 'Britisches Recht und der Vorschlag einer 14. Richtlinie' [1999] *ZGR* 111

Rammeloo, S.F.G., 'Jurisdiction clauses in transnational company relationships' [1994] *MJ* 426

—— 'Foreign companies in "incorporation" countries: A Dutch perspective', in Jan Wouters/Hildegard Schneider (eds.), *Current issues of cross-border establishment of companies in the European Union* (Maklu, Antwerpen/Apeldoorn, 1995) 47

—— 'Cross-border company mobility and the Proposal for a 14th EC Company Law Directive: "Daily Mail" surmounted?' [1999] *MJ* 105

—— 'Personenvennootschappen en "Europa". Vrijheid van vestiging of vrijheid tot samenwerking. Lood om oud ijzer?' [1999] Dossier 80

'Rechtsfragen der Grenzüberschreitenden Umstrukturierung von Unternehmen im Binnenmarkt' (symposium text, not published), Bonn 1993

Rehbinder, E., 'Sitzverlegung ins Inland und Rechtsfähigkeit ausländischer juristischer Personen' [1985] *IPRax* 324

Reymond, J.A., 'Sociétés étrangères en Suisse. A propos de l'Article 159 LDIP' in F. Dessemontet/P. Piotet (eds.) *Mélanges Pierre Engel* (Payot, Lausanne, 1989) 297

Reymond, P., 'Les personnes morales et les sociétés dans le nouveau droit international privé suisse', in *Le nouveau droit international privé suisse* (ed. F. Dessemontet), (Payot, Lausanne, 1989) 143

Richards, H., 'What is EC corporate law?' in A. Celia Trenting (managing ed.) *Corporate Law. The European Dimension* (Butterworths, London/Dublin/Edinburgh/Munich, 1991) 1

Roelvink, H.L.J., 'Misbruik van buitenlandse rechtspersonen', in P. van Schilfgaarde (ed.) *De nieuwe misbruikwetgeving* (Kluwer, Deventer, 1986)

Roth, W.H., 'Einfluß des Europäischen Gemeinschaftsrechts auf das IPR' [1991] *RabelsZ.* 628

—— 'Die Freiheiten des EG-Vertrages und das nationale Privatrecht' [1994] *ZEuP* 5

—— 'Recognition of foreign companies in *Siège Réel* countries: A German perspective', in Jan Wouters/Hildegard Schneider (eds.), *Current issues of cross-border establishment of companies in the European Union* (Maklu, Antwerpen/Apeldoorn, 1995) 29

—— comment to ECJ C–212/97 *Centros*, [2000] *CMLR* 147

Rijn van Alkemade, J. van, 'Wetsvoorstellen conflictenrecht corporaties en formeel buitenlandse vennootschappen' [1996] WPNR 563

Sack, R., Auswirkungen der Art. 52, 58 EWGV auf das Internationale Gesellschaftsrecht—EuGH, ([1988] *NJW* 2186), [1990] *JuS* 352

Salerno, F., 'European International Civil Procedure', in *European Private International Law* (ed. B. von Hoffmann), (Ars Aequi, Nijmegen, 1998) 115

Samtleben, J., 'Das internationale Privatrecht der Börsentermingeschäfte und der EWG-Vertrag (etc.)' [1981] *RabelsZ.* 218

Samuel, A., 'The New Swiss Private International Law Act' [1988] ICLQ 681

Sanders, P.,/W. Westbroek (bewerkt door F.K. Buijn/M. Storm), *BV en NV* (Kluwer, Deventer, 1998)

Sandrock, O., 'Sitztheorie, Überlagerungstheorie und der EWG-Vertrag: Wasser, Öl und Feuer' [1989] *RIW* 506

—— '*Centros*: ein Etappensieg für die Überlagerungstheorie' [1999] BB 1337.

—— /A. Austmann, 'Das Internationale Gesellschaftsrecht nach der *Daily Mail*-Entscheidung des Europäischen Gerichtshofs: Quo vadis?' [1989] *RIW* 250

Santa Maria, A., *Le società nel diritto internazionale privat*, (A. Giuffre, Milano, 1970)

—— 'Società (dir. internaz.)' in *Enciclopedia del diritto*, (XLII, Varese, 1990) 883–907

—— *EC Commercial Law* (Kluwer Law International, London/The Hague/Boston, 1996)

Schmidt, K., 'Sitzverlegungsrichtlinie, Freizügigkeit und Gesellschaftsrechtspraxis' [1999] *ZGR* 21

Schmidt, S., 'Grenzüberschreitende Sitzverlegung innerhalb der EG' [1992] *DWiR* 448

Schmitthoff, C., 'Tax and company migration' Business Law Brief, 1988 (Dec.) 2

—— 'European Law points. *Daily Mail* loses in the European Court' [1988] *JBL* 454

Schnyder, A.K., *Das neue IPR-Gesetz, Eine Einführung in das Bundesgesetz vom 18. Dezember 1987 über das Internationale Privatrecht (IPRG)*, (Schulthess Polygraphischer Verlag, Zürich, 1990)

Schutte-Veenstra, J.N., comment to ECJ C–212/97 *Centros*, [1999] OR 229

Sedemund, J./F.L. Hausmann, 'Niederlassungsfreiheit contra Sitztheorie—Abschied von Daily Mail?' [1999] *BB* 809

Seipen, C. von der, 'Zur Bestimmung des effektiven Verwaltungssitzes im Internationalen Gesellschaftsrecht' [1986] *IPRax* 91

Shaw,Jo, 'The Treaty of Amsterdam: Challenges of flexibility and legitimacy' [1998] ELJ 63

Siehr, K., 'Entwicklungen im schweizerischen internationalen Privatrecht/Le point sur le droit international privé suisse' [1998] *SJZ* 86

Siemer, R.L.M./G.J. Helmig, 'Een onderzoek naar de omvang van fraude door keuze van een buitenlandse rechtspersoon' [1987] *TVVS* 41

Slagter, W.J., *Zetelverplaatsing* (Kluwer, Deventer, (loose-leaf ed.))

Solinge, G. van, 'Vestigingsvrijheid van vennootschappen' [1991] *TVVS* 169

Sonnenberger, H.J., 'Europarecht und Internationales Privatrecht' [1996] *ZvglRWiss* 3

—— H. Großerichter, 'Konfliktlinien zwischen internationalem Gesellschaftsrecht und Niederlassungsfreiheit. Im Blickpunkt: die Centros-Entscheidung des EuGH als gesetzgeberische Herausforderung' [1999] *RIW/AWD* 721

Steindorff, E., 'Europäisches Gemeinschaftsrecht und deutsches Internationales Privatrecht' [1981] *EuR*. 426

—— '*Centros* und das Recht auf die günstigste Rechtsordnung' [1999] *JZ* 1140

Stille, A.L.G.A., 'Het thans in het Nederlands internationaal rechtspersonenrecht geldende beginsel van de incorporatie leer dient te worden vervangen door dat van de leer van de werkelijke zetel (*siège réel*)' [1998] *S&V* 63

Strikwerda, L., *Inleiding tot het Nederlandse Internationaal Privaatrecht* ch. 3 subdivision R, (Wolters-Noordhof, Groningen, 1997)

—— 'Kroniek van het internationaal privaatrecht' [1998] *NJB* 541

Struycken, A.V.M., 'Doorbraak van aansprakelijkheid in het Internationaal privaatrecht' [1981] WPNR 594

Switzerland's Federal Code on Private International Law (Payot Lausanne 1989)

Timmerman, L., 'Sitzverlegung von Kapitalgesellschaften nach niederländischem Recht und die 14. EU-Richtlinie' [1999] *ZGR* 147

Timmermans, C.W.A., 'Het Verdrag van 29 februari 1968 inzake de onderlinge erkenning van vennootschappen en rechtspersonen, Enkele Europeesrechtelijke kanttekeningen, Preadvies NVIR' (Deventer, 1980)

—— 'Die Europäische Rechtsangleichung im Gesellschaftsrecht' [1984] *RabelsZ*. 1

—— 'Europeesrechtelijke erkenning van pseudo-buitenlandse vennootschappen', in J.H. Christiaanse (ed.) *Tot Vermaak Van Slagter* (Kluwer, Deventer, 1988) 321

—— comment to ECJ C–81/87 *Daily Mail* [1988] ECR 5483, [1991] SEW 69

Ulmer, M.J., 'Die Anerkennung US-amerikanischer Gesellschaften in Deutschland' [1996] *IPRax* 100

Ulmer, P., 'Schutzinstrumente gegen die Gefahren aus der Geschäftstätigkeit inländischer Zweigniederlassungen von Kapitalgesellschaften mit fiktivem Auslandssitz' [1999] *JZ* 662

Uniken Venema, C.A.E., 'Pseudo-buitenlandse vennootschappen in Nederland, een advies van de commissie vennootschapsrecht' [1992] *NV* 266

Vandeginste, S., 'De kwalificatie van een statutaire clausule of overeenkomst' [1992] *TVR* 250

Vaughan Lowe, A., 'Extraterritorial jurisdiction. The British Practice' [1988] *RabelsZ*. 163

Veelken, W., 'Das französische Internationale Gesellschaftsrecht' (J. Pohlmann, Duncker & Humblot, Berlin, 1988) (book comment), [1992] *RabelsZ*. 186

Vischer, F., 'Bemerkungen zur Aktiengesellschaft im Internationalen Privatrecht' [1960] SJR 49.

—— /A. von Planta, *Internationales Privatrecht* (Helbing & Lichtenhahn, Basel, 1982)

Vlas, P., *Rechtspersonen in het internationaal privaatrecht* (Kluwer, Deventer, 1982)

—— 'Methoden ter bestrijding van misbruik van rechtspersonen in Nederland' [1984] WPNR 601

—— 'Rondom de zetel van de rechtspersoon' [1986] *TVVS* 165

—— *Rechtspersonen (praktijkreeks IPR)* (Kluwer, Deventer, 1993)
—— 'Paal en perk aan "puur formeel buitenlandse kapitaalvennootschappen"' [1993] *TVVS* 57
—— 'Doek valt voor EEG-erkenningsverdrag' [1994] *TVVS* 16
—— 'The Fight against Pseudo Foreign Corporations in the Netherlands' in K. Boele-Woelki (ed.) *Comparability and Evaluation, Liber Amicorum D. Kokkini-Iatridou* (T.M.C. Asser Instituut, Dordrecht, 1994) 307
—— 'Twee wetsvoorstellen i.p.r.-rechtspersonenrecht' [1995] *TVVS* 233
—— 'Overzicht Nederlandse rechtspraak (rechtspersonen)' [1996] WPNR 460
—— 'Twee wetten i.r.-rechtspersonenrecht: WCC en WFBV in werking' [1998] *TVVS* 53
—— *Rechtspersonen (praktijkreeks IPR)* (Kluwer, Deventer, 1999)
—— Comment to ECJ C–212/97 (*Centros*), (2000) 48 *NJ* 339
Wagner, R., 'Zum Inkrafttreten des Gesetzes zum Internationalen Privatrecht für außervertragliche Schuldverhältnisse und für Sachen' [1999] *IPRax* 210
Walker, H., 'Provisions on companies in United States Commercial Treaties' [1956] *A.J.Int.L.* 373
Walter, G./M. Jametti Greiner, *Texte zum Internationalen Privat- und Verfahrensrecht* (Stämpfli, Bern, (loose-leaf edn))
Wick, M., *Der Durchgriff und das auf ihn anwendbare Recht gemäß IPRG* (Schulthess Polygraphischer Verlag, Zürich, 1996)
Wezeman, J.B., 'Wet op de formeel buitenlandse vennootschappen' (1995) 14 *JutD* 6
Wiesner, M., 'Überblick über den Stand des Europäischen Unternehmensrecht' [1998] *EuZW* 619
Wilmowsky, P. von, Gesellschafts- und Kapitalmarktsrecht: EG–USA, [1992] *RabelsZ.* 535
—— 'EG-Vertrag und kollisionsrechtliche Wahlfreiheit' [1998] *RabelsZ.* 1
Winter, J.W., 'Voortgang Europese Vennootschap na Davignon' [1998] *TVVS* 14
Wouters, J., 'Over vennootschappen, verwijzingsregels en vrijheid van vestiging' [1991] *TRV* 456
—— 'The EC Court of Justice and Fiscal Barriers to Companies' Cross-Border Establishment' in Jan Wouters/Hildegard Schneider (eds.), *Current issues of cross-border establishment of companies in the European Union* (Maklu, Antwerpen/Apeldoorn 1995) 101
—— *Het Europese vestigingsrecht voor ondernemingen herbekeken. Een onderzoek naar de grondslagen, draagwijdte en begrenzingen van de vrijheid van vestiging van ondernemingen in de Europese Unie* (Leuven, 1996/97)
Wulf, H. de, '*Centros*: vrijheid van vestiging zonder race to the bottom' [1999] OR 318
Wymeersch, E., 'Die Sitzverlegung nach Belgischem Recht' [1999] *ZGR* 126
Yarzagaray, R.E., 'Reactie naar aanleiding van het artikel van mw mr drs S.M. van den Braak, "Omzetting van een buitenlandse in een Nederlandse vennootschap, WPNR 1994, nr. 6153"', 1995 WPNR 617
Zisowski, F., *Grenzüberschreitender Umzug von Kapitalgesellschaften. Eine Untersuchung aus steuerrechtlicher Sicht unter Berücksichtigung gesellschaftsrechtlicher Gesichtspunkte* (Verlag R. Decker, Heidelberg, 1994)
Zimmer, D., 'Mysterium "Centros"', [2000] *ZHR* 23

Index